A Companion to the Works of Max Frisch

Studies in German Literature, Linguistics, and Culture

Camden House Companion Volumes

The Camden House Companions provide well-informed and up-to-date critical commentary on the most significant aspects of major works, periods, or literary figures. The Companions may be read profitably by the reader with a general interest in the subject. For the benefit of student and scholar, quotations are provided in the original language.

A Companion to the Works of Max Frisch

Edited by Olaf Berwald

CAMDEN HOUSE
Rochester, New York

First published 2013
by Camden House

Camden House is an imprint of Boydell & Brewer Inc.
668 Mt. Hope Avenue, Rochester, NY 14620, USA
www.camden-house.com
and of Boydell & Brewer Limited
PO Box 9, Woodbridge, Suffolk IP12 3DF, UK
www.boydellandbrewer.com

ISBN-13: 978-1-57113-418-9
ISBN-10: 1-57113-418-2

Library of Congress Cataloging-in-Publication Data

A companion to the works of Max Frisch / edited by Olaf Berwald.
pages cm. — (Studies in German Literature, Linguistics, and Culture)
Includes bibliographical references and index.
ISBN-13: 978-1-57113-418-9 (hardcover : alk. paper)
ISBN-10: 1-57113-418-2 (hardcover : alk. paper)
1. Frisch, Max, 1911–1991—Criticism and interpretation. I. Berwald, Olaf, editor of compilation.

PT2611.R814Z638 2013
838'.91209—dc23

2013023188

This publication is printed on acid-free paper.
Printed and bound by CPI Group (UK) Ltd, Croydon, CR0 4YY.

Contents

Acknowledgments

I WOULD LIKE TO THANK the contributors whose perceptive essays will stimulate further Frisch research in the twenty-first century. Thanks are also due to the anonymous readers at Camden House. Working with Jim Walker, Camden House's editorial director, has been an immense privilege, and I am deeply grateful to him for his encouragement and intellectual generosity.

O. B.
Kennesaw, Georgia
July 2013

Note on the Abbreviations

THROUGHOUT THIS VOLUME, citations from Frisch are predominantly to the following edition. Abbreviations of individual works are set up in the notes to each chapter as appropriate.

GW = Max Frisch. *Gesammelte Werke in zeitlicher Folge*. Edited by Hans Mayer and Walter Schmitz. 2nd ed. Frankfurt am Main: Suhrkamp, 1986.

Introduction: Max Frisch in the Twenty-First Century

Olaf Berwald

WHY SHOULD WE READ Max Frisch (1911–91) in the twenty-first century? Because his works relentlessly examine an acutely crippling human condition, our addiction to turning ourselves and others into passive recipients of fixed images and projections. But beyond the undiminished relevance of this main thematic thread that runs through all of Frisch's works, his sparse and precise prose style generates a rare level of aesthetic and intellectual pleasure that reintroduces his readers to the intense joy of thinking through what it could mean to be human. The introspective playfulness of this classic writer of late modernism seduces readers to immerse themselves in Socratic skepticism. Frisch's sketchbooks, fictional prose, plays, essays, and speeches offer the reader useful and stimulating antidotes against complacent catchwords and prescriptive solutions that mask the personal crises and social conflicts of today's overmedicated societies. Frisch challenges us to think through who we are by inviting us to imagine who else we might have been.

Nobody has outlined the resilience of curiosity that is at the core of our assessment of Frisch more lucidly than Stefan Zweig. In a letter to his fellow exiled writer Hermann Kesten composed in Petropolis, Brazil, on January 15, 1942, Zweig explains his interest in the French philosopher Montaigne in a way that may also serve as an elucidation of Frisch's continuing relevance to readers in the twenty-first century. Montaigne's radical skepticism and individualism inform Frisch's work, and he quotes the philosopher at the beginning of his novella *Montauk* (1975). The insistent question that drives Zweig's fascination with Montaigne concerns the degree to which individuals protect their right to think clearly in a time increasingly paralyzed by violence and complacency: "wie bleibe ich frei, wie erhalte ich die Klarheit des Hirns in einer herzlosen und fanatisierten Zeit?" (how do I remain free, how can I preserve my clarity of mind amidst an era marked by heartlessness and fanaticism?)[1]

Frisch's narrators and protagonists offer fiercely solitary voices that elude any simplistic political or aesthetic labels and refuse to give easy answers. Frisch also often points out the danger and hypocrisy of remaining a passive member of a social group. Refusing to adopt the didactic impetus that is operative in most of his mentor Bertolt Brecht's works, Frisch favors an inventive method of sustained introspective skepticism. Frisch's writings are driven by a sustained fascination with the human psyche. His works offer variations of trying to understand "ein Geheimnis, das der Mensch ja immerhin ist, ein erregendes Rätsel" (a mystery—which after all is what a human being is [. . .] an exciting puzzle).[2]

For Frisch, radical explorations of the human psyche are at the same time examinations of the ways in which we sustain—or fail to sustain—friendships and other relationships. Trying to understand whether there is such a thing as an autonomous individual and fulfilling relationships, Frisch's texts often abandon linear plot expectations and instead try out shifting constellations of multiple, parallel selves. Frisch's inventive soundings of existential possibilities share affinities with Robert Musil and Luigi Pirandello, as well as with some of his friends and correspondence partners, including Uwe Johnson, Martin Walser, Christa Wolf, and Peter Weiss.

In speeches delivered in his later years Frisch became increasingly outspoken in his criticism of binary Cold War ideologies of "good" versus "evil" that were prevalent in both the Eastern and Western blocs. His fiction, sketchbooks, and dramas explore the human condition, not in order to provide an escape from the systemic cruelty he saw at work across the world, but guided by the conviction that exploring human failures on a personal level is at the same time a multifaceted psychological and political project. Far from offering the reader any plot solutions or successful character developments, Frisch's works invite their audience to ask whether there is such a thing as a coherent individual life, and to what extent personal relationships can be lived in an authentic way. The paradox of a resilient kind of resignation is interwoven into Frisch's texts. Frisch never offers the reader any ideological formula to ease the existential crises that his main characters endure. Many of his protagonists experience their specific roles in life as arbitrary and exchangeable. They create multiple masks to protect themselves from themselves.

The precision and sparse musicality of Frisch prose style corresponds with his refusal to prescribe easy answers that would reduce to a formula the complexities of being alone, forming a relationship, or being a member of a group, nation, or multinational company. Frisch does not believe in dogmatic statements. His narrators and stage characters are parts of an architectonic structure designed to make movements and tensions between preliminary positions audible and visible because, according to Frisch, "das Eigentliche, das Unsagbare, erscheint bestenfalls als Spannung zwischen diesen Aussagen" (the true, the inexpressible experience emerges at best as the tension between these statements; *Tagebuch 1946–1949*, *GW* 2:379; trans. Skelton 25). For Frisch,

Goethe's collection of aphorisms *Maximen und Reflexionen* (Maxims and Reflections, 1833) exemplifies a style of thinking that he strives for and that he calls "wirklich" (real), a conceptual patience that juxtaposes thought and experience, leaving room for contradictions between them. Refusing to subjugate conflicting but equally valid realities, Frisch explicitly learns from Goethe to insist on the flexible nature of understanding, a project that always needs to be grounded in lived experience and that rejects one-dimensional conceptual rigor mortis: "Nichts geht ins Tödliche, weil es die widersprechende Erfahrung nicht überrennt, nicht übermütig unterjocht, sondern die Kraft hat, sie aufzunehmen—die Kraft wirklich zu bleiben, oder genauer: immer aufs neue wirklich zu werden" (There is no fight to the death, because the contradictory experience is not overruled or arrogantly suppressed. The thought has the strength to accept it—the strength to remain real or, more precisely, constantly to renew its reality; *Tagebuch 1946–1949*, *GW* 2:543; trans. Skelton 155). Reading Frisch exposes us to the radical joys and risks of perceptive thinking that moves beyond easy definitions and identifications.

Max Frisch was born in Zurich, Switzerland, on May 15, 1911. In 1930 he began to study German literature at the University of Zurich. When his father, Franz Bruno Frisch, an architect and real estate agent, suddenly died in 1932, Frisch dropped his academic studies and worked as a freelance reporter to support himself and his mother, Karolina Bettina Frisch (née Wildermuth). The first publication of a text by Frisch, the essay "Was bin ich?" (What am I?) appeared in the student magazine *Zürcher Student* in 1932. In 1933, Frisch traveled to Eastern and Southeastern Europe and wrote travel essays for newspapers. One year later, his first novel, *Jürg Reinhart*, was published. With his girlfriend, Käte Rubensohn, Frisch visited Nazi Germany in 1935. Having returned to Switzerland, he began to study architecture at the Eidgenössische Technische Hochschule Zurich in 1936. Frisch's short novel, *Antwort aus der Stille* (An Answer from the Silence) appeared in print one year later and was awarded the Conrad Ferdinand Meyer Prize in 1938. In the same year, Frisch ended his relationship with Käte Rubensohn. From 1939 until the end of the Second World War in 1945, Frisch, like most Swiss men, intermittently served in the army. In 1940, his diaristic prose volume *Blätter aus dem Brotsack* (Pages from the Knapsack) was published. In the same year, during a vacation from his military service, Frisch received his architecture degree. In 1942, he emerged as a successful architect when his proposal to build a public swimming pool in one of Zurich's working class districts was accepted by the city. He immediately founded his own architecture firm and married a fellow architect, Constance von Meyenburg, with whom he would have three children. In 1943 Frisch's novel *J'adore ce qui me brûle oder Die Schwierigen* (I Love that which Burns Me, or, The Difficult Ones) was published. Starting in 1945, Frisch's theater plays premiered at the Schauspielhaus Zurich, including *Nun singen sie wieder* (Now They Are Singing Again, 1945), *Santa Cruz* (1946), *Die Chinesische Mauer* (The Chinese Wall, 1946), *Als der Krieg zu Ende war* (1948), *Graf Öderland* (Count Oederland, 1951), and *Don Juan oder Die Liebe zur Geometrie* (Don Juan, or, The Love of Geometry, 1953).

In 1946 Frisch traveled to Germany and Italy. One year later, Frisch met Bertolt Brecht, whose poetry and intellectual curiosity had a lasting influence on his work. While sharing some of Brecht's political convictions, Frisch rejected the use of art as a merely ideological tool, and argued that Brecht's work is at its best when it does not try to be predominantly didactic. Frisch dismisses "das Nur-Ideologische" as just another way of masking real life, "eine andere Art, nicht wirklich zu sein" (*Tagebuch 1946–1949*, *GW* 2:201). In 1947 Frisch met the writer, translator, and publisher Peter Suhrkamp (1891–1959), a survivor of the Sachsenhausen concentration camp, who became his publisher, mentor, and one of his closest friends. Frisch was an occasional guest at Suhrkamp's house on the island Sylt in the North Sea. When Suhrkamp and his fellow publisher Gottfried Bermann Fischer, who had worked together for the S. Fischer Verlag, ended their collaboration in 1950, Frisch became one of the first authors whose works appeared in the newly founded Suhrkamp Verlag (Frankfurt am Main), along with Hermann Hesse, Bertolt Brecht, Samuel Beckett, and others.

In 1948 Frisch visited Wrocław, Poland, as well as Prague and Berlin. His observations of postwar Berlin are interwoven in his literary sketchbook, *Tagebuch 1946–1949*. One of his most seminal prose works, this volume was published by Suhrkamp in 1950. Having received a Rockefeller stipend in 1951, Frisch spent a year in New York City, Chicago, San Francisco, Los Angeles, and Mexico. In 1953 Frisch's radio plays *Herr Biedermann und die Brandstifter*, a satire on hypocrisy and cowardice embedded in class differences, whose theater version premiered in 1958 (translated under different titles as *The Fire Raisers*, *The Firebugs*, and *The Arsonists*), and *Rip van Winkle* were featured on German radio. In 1954 Frisch's novel *Stiller*, whose protagonist, an unsuccessful artist, attempts to take on a new identity and declares that he does not know his wife and his former life anymore, was published. In the same year, as he was beginning to achieve international success as a writer, Frisch's personal life underwent an irrevocable crisis: he abandoned his wife and his children in Switzerland, and one year later he sold his architecture firm in order to dedicate himself fully to writing. Distancing himself further from his family and his former profession, Frisch traveled again to the United States and Mexico in 1956. In 1957 his bestselling novel *Homo faber* was published. Written in the voice an engineer, Walter Faber, who is dying of cancer and tries to render an account of the last phase of his life, this work is marked by a tragic conflict between Fabers's scientific worldview and the uncontrollable dimensions of nature (German film director Volker Schlöndorff, a friend of Frisch's, based his film *Voyager* (1991) on *Homo faber*). In 1958 Frisch met the Austrian poet Ingeborg Bachmann (1926–73) and appears to have fallen in love with her in short order. As a result of this relationship, in 1959 he divorced Constance Frisch-von Meyenburg and in 1960 moved to Rome, where he lived with Bachmann. In 1961 Frisch's drama *Andorra*, a parable of the beginnings of the Shoah that examines internalized self-hatred of an outsider and the complicity of bystanders, premiered in Switzerland and Germany. Frisch's novel *Mein Name sei Gantenbein* (translated as *A Wilderness of Mirrors*), aesthetically his most ambitious novel and one that offers parallel variations on the impossibility of forming an authentic relationship with a partner, was published in 1964.

In 1965 Frisch ended his relationship with Bachmann and moved from Rome back to Berzona, Switzerland, together with his new partner Marianne Oellers, whom he married one year later. Their marriage lasted until 1979. Frisch's theater play *Biografie: Ein Spiel* (Biography: A Game) premiered in 1966. In the same year he met East German writer Christa Wolf (1929–2011), whose novels and novellas, not unlike Frisch's works, operate on the basis of an explorative ethics and aesthetics, refusing to offer character development and presenting human lives as friable manuscript drafts that lack a definitive edition and can be rendered unrecognizable.

In the meantime Frisch had become a financially independent writer who frequently provided fellow artists with material support. Returning to Europe after several months with friends in New York City, Frisch moved to Berlin in 1972, where he purchased an apartment in which his former partner Marianne Oellers lives to this day. His satirical volume of essayistic prose, *Wilhelm Tell für die Schule* (Wilhelm Tell for Use in Schools), in which he took the official idealization of Tell apart and presented him as a terrorist, inverting conventional Swiss national ideology, was published in 1971, followed by a second sketchbook, *Tagebuch 1966–1971*, in 1972.

Frisch's numerous literary awards include Germany's most prestigious literary prize, the Georg Büchner Award (1958), as well as the Veillon Award (1958), the Man's Freedom Prize of Jerusalem (1965), the Schiller Award (1974), the German Book Trade's Peace Award (1976), the University of Oklahoma's Neustadt Award (1986), the Heinrich Heine Award (1989), as well as honorary degrees from the City University of New York (1982), where he delivered lectures on poetics, and from the Technische Universität Berlin (1987).

Throughout his life, Frisch undertook worldwide travels that inspired his work. Despite his often relentless criticism of American foreign policy and social issues, Frisch maintained a lifelong fascination with the United

States. In addition to his travels and extended stays in the United States, Italy, and Germany, Frisch visited Greece (1957 and 1961), the Middle East (1957), the Soviet Union (1966), Japan (1969), and China (1975).

Frisch's controversial semiautobiographical narrative *Montauk*, about a middle-aged writer by the name of Max Frisch and his significantly younger American lover, based on Frisch's love relationship with the American editorial assistant Alice Locke-Carey, was published in 1975, followed four years later by *Der Mensch erscheint im Holozän* (Man in the Holocene), one of modern literature's most fascinating prose explorations of aging, mental disintegration, and fear of nature. Frisch's play *Triptychon* premiered in Lausanne in 1979. In 1981, Frisch bought a loft in New York City. One year later, his narrative *Blaubart* (Bluebeard) was published. In 1987, Frisch participated in the "Forum for a World free of Nuclear Weapons and the Survival of Mankind" in Moscow, hosted by Mikhail Gorbachev. Two years later, Frisch's intergenerational play about the demilitarization of Switzerland, *Schweiz ohne Armee? Ein Palaver* (Switzerland without an Army? A Conversation), premiered in Lausanne and Zurich. Frisch's lifelong ambivalent relationship with his home country took an irrevocably bitter turn when Frisch learned in 1990 that he had been under surveillance by the Swiss secret service for decades. Having suffered from cancer for several years, Frisch died in his apartment in Zurich on April 4, 1991.

Continuing the transatlantic dialogue that Frisch tried to live, this volume is the result of a fruitful collaboration of Frisch experts from Europe and the United States. The first five chapters offer succinct and engaging discussions of Frisch's theater plays. Walter Schmitz, whom Frisch chose to edit his collected works in the mid-1970s, analyzes Frisch's early dramatic works, *Santa Cruz*, *Nun singen sie wieder*, *Die Chinesische Mauer*, and *Als der Krieg zu Ende war*. Tracing thematic and aesthetic affinities that these Frisch plays from the immediate postwar era share with plays by Hugo von Hofmannsthal, Carl Zuckmayer, and Thornton Wilder, Schmitz shows how Frisch's fundamental skepticism about the idea of humanistic progress and the possibility of individual transformation and a release from existential patterns of repetition, a central thematic undercurrent of his later work, is already interwoven into these early plays of the immediate postwar period.

Focusing on conceptual and stage-design nuances of "Spielraum," alterable stage constructions that highlight variability as a manifestation of a fundamental lack of freedom among Frisch's protagonists, Klaus van den Berg discusses the degree to which Frisch's plays *Graf Öderland* (1951) and *Don Juan oder Die Liebe zur Geometrie* (Don Juan, or, The Love of Geometry, 1953) have advanced postwar theater beyond the dichotomy of Brecht's political didacticism and Beckett's circular philosophical stage arrangements.

Amanda Boyd examines two plays from 1958, the widely played and read *Biedermann und die Brandstifter* and the lesser known *Die große Wut des Philipp Hotz* (The Great Rage of Philip Hotz), discussing their textual evolution and offering stimulating close readings that sharpen our understanding of the plays.

A new interpretive analysis of Frisch's play about the victims, perpetrators, and bystanders of the Shoah, the famous drama *Andorra* (1961), is offered by Caroline Schaumann and Frank Schaumann, who combine their discussion of the play with a concise overview of its conflict-ridden early reception history, a history that prefigured today's debates about the uniqueness of the Shoah and whether it is permissible to discuss it together with other genocides.

John D. Pizer discusses philosophical and psychological threads that run through Frisch's late plays *Biografie: Ein Spiel* (1967) and *Triptychon* (Triptych, 1978), exploring them as dramas that offer soundings of the degree to which an individual's life is an inescapable repetition of behavioral patterns. In addition to providing fresh and lucid readings of these two plays, Pizer alerts the reader to thematic affinities between Frisch on the one hand and Nietzsche and Heidegger on the other regarding the existential question of freedom versus eternal return.

The remaining nine chapters of this Companion provide introductory overviews and fresh interpretations of Frisch's prose works. Margit Unser discusses Frisch's early fictional prose works *Jürg Reinhart* (1934) and *Antwort aus der Stille* (1937), as well as his early journalistic and diaristic texts, providing a measured assessment of the young Frisch's political and aesthetic leanings, finding that they stand in considerable contrast and fruitful tension to the later Frisch's stances as an artist and public intellectual.

Céline Letawe examines the challenge to conventional genre boundaries between fiction and non-fiction presented by Frisch's juxtapositions of several layers of fictionality in his sketchbooks, especially *Tagebuch 1946–1949* (1950) and *Tagebuch 1966–1971* (1972). Letawe's chapter provides concise analyses of key passages from these works and also traces the textual genesis of each of the sketchbooks.

Beatrice Sandberg offers succinct discussions of thematic threads (including the failure of a marriage due to one spouse's inability to let go of fixed images of himself and his partner, self-alienation, and a critique of Switzerland) and narrative technique in Frisch's novel *Stiller* (1954), as well as an overview of its reception history.

In his chapter on Frisch's novel *Homo faber* (1957), Paul A. Youngman focuses on the role of probability and technology, specifically cybernetics, in the novel, juxtaposing Norbert Wiener's cybernetic theories (which are explicitly referred to yet misunderstood by the novel's protagonist Walter Faber) with the novel's presentations of a failed human life.

Olaf Berwald's essay on Frisch's experimental novel *Mein Name sei Gantenbein* (1964) discusses the aesthetics of non-linear plot fragments and psychological aspects of this work, whose protagonist constantly tries on different identities and desires to dissolve and leave behind no traceable history. Drawing from Frisch's unpublished correspondence about *Gantenbein* and tracing its multifaceted reception history, Berwald examines the ways in which the novel insists on an irreconcilable dichotomy between lived experience on the one hand and futile attempts to give one's life a stable narrative frame on the other.

Ruth Vogel-Klein gives a detailed interpretative overview of Frisch's semi-autobiographical narrative *Montauk* (1975). Including discussions of textual genesis and gender aspects in the work, Vogel-Klein's chapter explores the contested and skeptical poetics of autobiography that sustains the aesthetic core of *Montauk*.

Walter Obschlager discusses Frisch's narrative *Der Mensch erscheint im Holozän* (1979), in which an old man's mind slowly disintegrates. Comparing various key passages on the conflict of man and nature from this work as well as from Frisch's early prose and from *Homo faber*, Obschlager outlines affinities between the ways in which Frisch and Freud work through the fragility of the human mind and body, and the porosity of surface layers of culture and order in the face of existential fear.

Daniel de Vin examines Frisch's last narrative, *Blaubart* (1982), in which a man is declared innocent for lack of evidence and despairs because a guilty verdict would at least distract him from his inner emptiness. Presenting a succinct overview of the work's immediate reception among literary critics, and discussing unpublished drafts of *Blaubart* along with the published text, de Vin situates Frisch's late narrative at the extreme periphery of what is translatable into literary art.

Régine Battiston provides new interpretive insights into Frisch's essays and speeches on literature, theater, ethics, and politics. Thematic foci of Battiston's chapter include Frisch's sustained criticism of Switzerland and his own view of his role as a public intellectual.

This volume offers accessible introductions and new interpretive approaches to Frisch's multifaceted and timely works. Requiring courageous readers whose radical curiosity helps them to disregard preconceived certainties, Frisch's texts invite us to understand perceptive individualism and a circumspect sense of world citizenship as mutually enriching dimensions of being alive. Frisch's legacy is a constant reminder to rethink our psychological conditions and social interactions in fresh ways, unafraid of not being able to close the gaps that perforate them. Rather than evading our fears of personal dissociation and global dissolution through various ideologies that offer presumed safety, Frisch invites us to think outside the daily development bath of fixed images (a metaphor from traditional darkroom photography that is at risk of being obscured by the advent of digital photography). Most of Frisch's protagonists feel paralyzed by one-dimensional self-definitions. Attempting to escape into various assumed identities, they often become entangled within the permeable boundaries between their "factual" and imaginary selves. Thinking through the vertiginous mazes that Frisch's characters build for themselves and into which they often disappear is a liberating experience for the reader. Offering an open-ended dialogic experience in a mostly sparse and always precise style, Frisch's works confront us with a hard and fascinating question: What kinds of individuals and partners do we want to be, once we overcome the destructive habit of identifying ourselves and others as mere carriers of predictable behavioral patterns? The following chapters invite the reader to explore the intriguing range of variations on this question that Frisch's works unfold for us.

Notes

[1] Stefan Zweig, *Briefe 1932–1942*, ed. Knut Beck and Jeffrey B. Berlin (Frankfurt am Main: Fischer, 2005), 336.

[2] Max Frisch, *Tagebuch 1946–1949*, in *Gesammelte Werke in zeitlicher Folge (GW)* 2, ed. Hans Mayer and Walter Schmitz, 2nd ed. (Frankfurt am Main: Suhrkamp, 1986): 370. English translation taken from Max Frisch: *Sketchbook 1946–1949*, trans. Geoffrey Skelton (New York, London: Harcourt Brace Jovanovich, 1977), here 17.

1: Max Frisch's Early Plays

Walter Schmitz

MAX FRISCH'S PATH toward authorship did not evolve in a direct and uninterrupted manner. Two traumatic experiences resulted in ruptures and turning points in the early phase of Frisch's development as an author. In 1936, Frisch committed an auto-da-fé, solemnly burning everything he had hitherto written. With this act he intended to reject the writer's profession and turn toward a bourgeois career that provided an income that would enable him to start a family. In his twenty-fifth year, Frisch, a student of German philology, a journalist and writer, realized that life can become a failure, and he decided to build a secure foundation for his life by leaving metaphors behind and studying architecture.

The abrupt break with writing that Frisch staged as a private apocalyptic event corresponds with an acutely endangered new beginning, since the decision to turn away from literature did not turn out to be sustainable. Just six years later, Frisch began to write a more ambitious literary text, not surprisingly a sketchbook that was published in 1940 under the title *Blätter aus dem Brotsack: Geschrieben im Grenzdienst 1939* (Pages from the Knapsack: Written While Serving in the Border Patrol, 1939). The political events at the time, the threatening prospect of Switzerland being occupied by its aggressive neighbor, National Socialist Germany, made it abundantly clear that a merely private existence was confined by boundaries. Not the boundaries of the self but the borders of the home country had to be defended. The work's subtitle, *Geschrieben im Grenzdienst 1939*, is ambiguous because of the wide lexical range of the word "Grenze" (border, limit, boundary): more than the military border was at stake, and "Grenzdienst" can also refer to compulsory service taking place along existential boundaries and limits. Exposure to imminent danger and death forced every individual to conduct new soundings of his or her own existence.

Blätter aus dem Brotsack was followed by *J'adore ce qui me brûle oder Die Schwierigen* (I Love that which Burns Me, or, The Difficult Ones, 1943) a novel that explores the theme of marriage. Frisch was already married at this time. But in this text, marriage serves as a metaphor for life as a project that either fortuitously succeeds or lethally fails. In 1944, before the end of the Second World War, Frisch tried a new genre and emerged as a successful playwright whose early plays all premiered at the Schauspielhaus Zurich.

Shortly before and immediately after the end of the Second World War Frisch wrote the plays that brought him early fame beyond Switzerland. *Nun singen sie wieder: Versuch eines Requiems* (Now They Are Singing Again: Attempt at a Requiem), the first Frisch play that was put on stage, premiered on March 29, 1945. Written in August and September 1944, Frisch's play *Santa Cruz: Eine Romanze*, premiered on March 7, 1946. *Die Chinesische Mauer, eine Farce* (The Chinese Wall, A Farce) premiered on October 10, 1946, followed by *Als der Krieg zu Ende war* (When the War Was Over) on January 8, 1948.

These four plays could hardly be more different from one another. Starting with *Santa Cruz*, which is composed in the style of neo-Romanticism, still an influence on Frisch in the 1930s,[1] the next step in Frisch's development as a playwright, *Nun singen sie wieder: Versuch eines Requiems*, exhibits a form of ritual drama that his contemporaries immediately recognized as highly original. With *Die Chinesische Mauer, eine Farce*, Frisch embraced the revue form without referring to similar experiments with a democratic and even revolutionary theater in the Weimar Republic. *Als der Krieg zu Ende war* represents the end of Frisch's rapid development as a playwright, and can be considered a classically structured political drama. In 1949, when the Federal Republic of Germany was founded, the only established living German-speaking playwright was a Swiss writer: Max Frisch. For a while, Bertolt Brecht was boycotted by some theaters in the Federal Republic. Friedrich Dürrenmatt, Frisch's younger colleague and for several years his friend, would soon catch up to complete the pair of "Swiss dioscuri" who would become celebrated authors of the German postwar stage.

The diagnosis of great diversity and variability among Frisch's early plays has to be qualified to some degree. Their formal variety is accompanied by a lyrical tone that permeates all the plays. Frisch gradually dissolved this stylistic unity by rewriting the plays while they were still being performed, and therefore Frisch scholarship for the most part failed to notice it. Only *Santa Cruz: Eine Romanze* and *Nun singen sie wieder* are offered in their original versions in all Frisch editions. For the 1961 edition, the final act of *Als der Krieg zu Ende war* was cut. *Die Chinesische Mauer* even went through four versions: in 1955 and again in 1965, the play was thoroughly rewritten, and Frisch wrote the Paris version, on which all later editions of the play are based, in 1972. Until 1961 the literary genesis of *Die Chinesische Mauer* ran parallel to Frisch's evolution as a modernist author who was influenced by Brecht's concept of political theater. The lyrical style that Frisch still valued highly in the 1940s was reduced from the 1950s on, and a distant objective tone that is a quality of Brecht's didactic plays now became a stylistic trademark of Frisch's plays, too.

The rehearsal schedule of the Zürcher Schauspielhaus impacted the textual genesis of Frisch's early plays. For Frisch, writing and rehearsing share strong affinities. Having read Frisch's novel *J'adore ce qui me brûle oder Die Schwierigen*, Kurt Hirschfeld, who served as dramaturge at the Schauspielhaus from the 1930s until the early 1960s, encouraged Frisch to try his hand at a play in the 1940s.[2] Frisch was permitted to participate at the rehearsals of plays by Brecht, Sartre, Lorca, Giraudoux, and Claudel.[3] The Schauspielhaus particularly embraced classic modernism and its correlations with humanist ideals of eighteenth-century aesthetics,[4] while it de-emphasized contemporary political theater and avant-garde art. The existentialist treatment of political matters in Frisch's early plays, in which fundamental questions of humanity and barbarism are negotiated, fit well into the programmatic mission of the Schauspielhaus, as it was defined by theater director Oskar Wälterlin and by Kurt Hirschfeld. As Wälterlin outlined in 1945, their programmatic goal was a "disenchanted theater"[5] that tried to elucidate fundamental questions of human existence without allowing itself to be taken hostage by current events. Into this context they integrated a focus on "the other Germany," the cultural nation represented by emigrants even after 1945. From a Swiss point of view, the humanist aesthetics practiced in Frisch's early plays contributed to the rebuilding of a "different Germany."[6] At stake in these efforts was the examination and recovery of cultural traditions that were discredited by the Third Reich's barbarism.

Frisch's early plays were influenced by canonical authors of the early twentieth century. Yet, far from merely imitating these models, Frisch learned from them while developing his own style. For example, *Santa Cruz* clearly exhibits correlations with Hugo von Hofmannsthal's *Christinas Heimreise* (1910), a reference that Frisch explicitly confirmed. Both *Nun singen sie wieder* and *Die Chinesische Mauer* show affinities to the works of Thornton Wilder. This dialogic intertextual element is only seemingly abandoned in Frisch's drama *Als der Krieg zu Ende war*. Its act 3, which Frisch later deleted, can be read as a variation on Carl Zuckmayer's successful play *Des Teufels General* (The Devil's General, 1945; second version 1966). Overall Frisch began to approximate Brecht's art of learning from the masters, his *Kunst zu erben*, but not completely in the sense in which Brecht practiced this art. While Brecht applauded Frisch's use of the Judith theme in *Als der Krieg zu Ende war*, a play that Frisch at first planned to call *Judith*, he regretfully remarked that Frisch's reference to this literary tradition merely operates with allusions without making their meaning explicit. According to Brecht, Frisch was unfortunately content with alluding to, rather than interpreting aspects of, the Judith theme.[7]

Despite its conventional form, Frisch was already experimenting, in his first attempt at a play, with a thematic constellation that had a defining impact not only on his early dramas but also on the development of his work as a whole, the life of human beings on temporal and atemporal levels. On the one hand, there is historical time, time measured by clocks.[8] To their own detriment, most people confuse everything that takes place on this temporal level with reality. They therefore live a life that is not authentic. "True" reality, on the other hand, unfolds in the mind, which remembers and envisions everything in a non-linear way. Existential decisions are made in this internal realm, which does not fit conventional conceptions of time. This leads to the third and decisive order of time, existential time, subjectively experienced historical time, the time of human mortality (*GW* 2:499). Only a life that acknowledges death is actual, fully lived life, "wirkliches Leben." Time and again the characters face the task of integrating these three levels of time into their own lives, and while the protagonists in Frisch's later plays fail to hold these divergent layers of time together, in *Santa Cruz* this integration is still successful.

The play has three main characters: a cavalry captain, Pelegrin the wanderer, and Elvira, "ein herrliches Mädchen" (a lovely girl).[9] For the duration of the time in which the plot unfolds, the time measured by clocks, Elvira is the cavalry captain's wife and the "Herrin" in charge of the castle (*GW* 2:8). The cavalry captain, her husband, is a "man of order" (*GW* 2:11), and he provides for his wife and child. But this order that dominates everyday life leads to an unawareness of real life. The common people live in prehuman passivity, and the aristocrats are locked into their matrimonial "Schloß" ("castle"; also the word for "lock"; *GW* 2:60) by their sense of duty, and sink into the snow. The castle in this theatrical debut of an architect, and also the snow, which freezes all life so that duties weigh on the cavalry captain "like snow" (*GW* 2:18), are poetic keywords that become part of Frisch's metaphorical vocabulary.[10] Frisch's metaphor for a liberating counter-world is the ocean, which represents "the vastness of possibilities" (*GW* 2:43).

In addition to our daily routine there is a possible life that could become real. It is located in our mind, and it is shown on the "Bewusstseinsbühne," a stage inside our mind. In his postscript to the play, "Zu *Santa Cruz*," Frisch explains that his play aims at showing how things appear on the stage of our mind and the unconscious.[11] Therefore the audience sees an additional plot that takes place seventeen years earlier (*GW* 2:7). Chronology is replaced with what Frisch calls "Synchronik."[12] Past events are inserted in dream sequences, and everyone dreams a different story. This is the central problem that is negotiated in the play: that human beings remain secrets to one another even when they want to open themselves in love for the other or when they belong together in marriage. The cavalry captain's existential confusion is triggered by his inability to know what is going on in his sleeping wife's mind (*GW* 2:34, 39).

The play offers the solution of rejecting dreams and accepting reality. Following the poetics of neo-Romanticism around 1900, especially Hofmannsthal, the figure of the child embodies this reality. The final words of Frisch's "Romanze" are: "Ich bin [. . .] das Kind, Viola, die alles von neuem erfährt, die alles noch einmal beginnt" (I am [. . .] the child, Viola, who experiences everything all over again, who starts everything all over again; *GW* 2:75). This turn of events, however, does not provide any solution, let alone redemption, but only an entrance into a circle of repetition. The characters have to consent to the paradoxical structure of life itself. Viola the child is not the cavalry captain's daughter after all but the wanderer's daughter. This constellation shares similarities with Hofmannsthal's *Christinas Heimreise*.

When Pelegrin the wanderer appears at the palace, he is seriously ill. He will only live for one more week, but he will savor every moment. Seventeen years ago Elvira ran away with him. Her fiancé, the cavalry captain, followed her, and caught up with them in Santa Cruz. There he had to decide whether to leave for Hawaii, a place that represents longing for a real life, or to return to the path that would lead to marriage, to the palace, to duty, and to a life routine governed by the dictum "order is always necessary." Pelegrin abandoned Elvira, who was pregnant. The cavalry captain chose duty, marriage, and the child, but the spouses maintain the unfulfilled longing that frequently leads them back to Santa Cruz in their dreams, where they wait to depart for Hawaii. In this way, one life is split into complementary models, and the wanderer lives the cavalry captain's "other life" (*GW* 2:21). Seventeen years later, disrupted and shaken by the encounter with Pelegrin, the cavalry captain leaves his well-organized life in the knapsack he wore in his youth (*GW* 2:41). He departs for a journey to Hawaii and reminisces about the old Santa Cruz. He reaffirms his decision to stay with and marry Elvira by stating that life decisions are predetermined: "Weil keiner ein anderes Leben hätte führen können als jenes, das er führte" (*GW* 2:54). In his postscript to the play, Frisch alludes to Kierkegaard, implying that the ethical insight the play offers is that by experiencing life as a series of repetitions we accept it as something we are destined to suffer—our personal cross, "Santa Cruz."[13] When "the little comedy" of faithfulness that the spouses played for such a long time by denying their dreams comes to an end, Pelegrin's life also ends. The figure that represented longing and self-alienation dies (*GW* 2:77). All characters in this *Romanze* embody attitudes to and expectations for life. They are projections of the ego, as Frisch understood them through the psychological works of Carl Gustav Jung. We encounter them in dreams.[14] It is the task of poetry to give dreams reality on the stage of our mind. This is also demonstrated in the play when Pedro, a poet kidnapped by sailors, tells his captors the story of Pelegrin the wanderer. However, they do not believe him, and tie him up. Even in the realm of the dream, dreams are not held in high regard. But everyone who experiences dreams will comprehend the meaning of true longing for life and of mortality. Even for God, the only hope is to become a reflection in a human eye. Authentic life only belongs to improbable dramatic moments (*GW* 2:43).

While *Santa Cruz* appears to provide an inventory account of Frisch's previous literary works, their themes and motifs, already his next play, *Nun singen sie wieder*, transports this inventory, of whose possession the author had reassured himself in his first play, into the context of current events, a thematic field that was completely new to the poet Frisch. From now on, Frisch would consider it a natural task of the author to analyze contemporary issues or, as he later put it, "die Forderungen des Tages" (the demands of the day).[15] This could not be done in the form of literature as political intervention, so in *Nun singen sie wieder* Frisch instead continued his research on contemporary consciousness. This play also takes place on a mental stage. It is, however, not tied to the imagination of individual characters, as was the case with *Santa Cruz*, but rather shows the suppressed life of a collective during wartime. The play is set somewhere in the Soviet Union during the Second World War. Karl, a German soldier, has twenty-one prisoners of war shot on orders from the SS officer Herbert, with whom Karl had been friends in school. Of the prisoners of war Frisch writes: "Sie haben gesungen: bis zuletzt." (They sang until the very end.)[16] At first Karl wants to resist the order, but then he has it carried out, obeying one last time before he deserts, plagued by guilt. An Orthodox priest who tried to prevent the execution finally gives in and collaborates with the Germans. But instead of rewarding the priest's decision, Herbert has him also shot as an enemy.

Like *Santa Cruz*, this play also highlights the importance of a specific location in the context of the circularity of a life journey and the need for concrete decisions. This becomes clear when Karl deserts after he has tried to plead for the priest's safety (*GW* 2:87). The dead continue to live, they remain present on the "Bewusstseinsbühne" (stage [as in theater stage] of consciousness) of everything that has been suppressed in life. They gather, and whenever a crime is committed, they repeat the song they sang during their execution as a warning for the living who do not listen. At first the dead protagonists cannot comprehend that they are dead. They believe that they are still alive, and it takes them a while to get used to this different world. Beyond the real world of murderous events and a pseudoreality that merely covers up emptiness and nothingness, they learn about the "genuine life" that they could have experienced together (*GW* 2:100, 120, 129). Having joined the group of dead, the priest explains to a newly arrived person that what matters is a simple lifestyle, baking bread, and sharing a meal with others (*GW* 2:116). The allusions to the Bible cannot be overlooked. But God, who could grant redemption, is absent.[17] Woven into this metaphysics without

God is Herbert, a nihilist influenced by Nietzsche. He kills out of rebellion against creation. He wants to force the "Geist" (spirit or mind) to manifest itself in reality (*GW* 2:84), or at least he wants to rip the masks off the hypocrites who only talk about spirit and values (*GW* 2:86).[18] Karl is the son of a teacher who also taught Herbert. Although Karl's father preached respect for the spirit, he also betrayed it when he became a consenting bystander in support of the ruling Nazi criminals. The play suggests that we do not learn from the atrocities of the past, and that the heritage of "Bildung," the humanistic tradition of education and character formation, has lost its value. But *Nun singen sie wieder* ends with a declaration of love. Young Benjamin, an innocent poet without any plans, a man who does not address his writings to anybody (*GW* 2:97), finds Maria, who was Karl's wife before he died. The poet comprehends for the first time what love can be. It, too, might be futile, but it does not despair at its futility, and therefore always remains beautiful (*GW* 2:136).

The secular mysticism in *Nun singen sie wieder* did not go unnoticed in contemporary reviews. The intellectual climate of the immediate postwar period was characterized by discussions of historical guilt, affirmations of myths of innocence, and lamentations about the loss of spiritual values.[19] In everyday life, on the other hand, remembrance of the dead played an important role. Precisely because Frisch's play refuses to take sides and appears to call for reconciliation, it was vehemently criticized, and the author was suspected of being a nihilist.[20] Frisch nevertheless insisted on the aesthetic character of the play, adding that it was not meant to be read as a documentation of the unspeakable horrors of recent history.[21]

The nuclear test on Bikini Atoll in 1946 made it clear to Frisch that while the war had ended, peace had not yet been won. In his *Tagebuch*, Frisch pointed out "daß wir noch einmal die Wahl haben [. . .] es liegt an uns, ob es eine Menschheit gibt oder nicht" (that we must decide [. . .] it is for us to decide whether mankind continues to exist or not).[22] Frisch's next play, *Die Chinesische Mauer*, showcased an avant-garde dramaturgic technique that was not inherited from Brecht but was instead the result of Frisch's reception of Thornton Wilder, whom he admired and who, as a representative of American culture, was immensely successful on the German stage. While the analysis of an idyllic peace in *Nun singen sie wieder* makes use of Wilder's play *Our Town*, in which the dead continue to participate in life, *Die Chinesische Mauer* can be read as Frisch's response to Wilder's world history revue about the recurring patterns that structure human behavior, *The Skin of Our Teeth* (1942), whose German version, with the telling title *Wir sind noch einmal davongekommen*, premiered at the Schauspielhaus Zürich in 1944.

As in Wilder, a moderator presents the play's scenes. In contrast to Brecht's plays, this element is not intended to trigger a defamiliarization of the plot that might point to the fact that it can be altered. On the contrary, the plot is formally presented as the recurrence of the same, even though the possibility and necessity of change is nevertheless the topic. Various subplots are interwoven again on a stage of the mind: one plot is set in a poeticized historical China, its theme a rebellion of the people against the tyrant Hwang Ti, the historical founder of the Chinese empire. In order to achieve absolute peace, he launches countless wars in the name of peace and "the True Order and the Happy Order and the Final Order."[23] After his most recent victory, the building of the Chinese Wall is intended to render his rule definitive and his empire perennial. The goal is to bring history to a standstill. This is illustrated in another variation of the "Bewusstseinsbühne" (theater of mind):[24] a *danse macabre* of rulers and dictators from all time periods, who appear to be dancing inside a musical clock, continuously demonstrating the pattern of tyranny and the (unsuccessful) rebellion of the oppressed.[25] They "populate our brain," preventing us from deciding individually for a new history that would correspond to the new insights and terrifying experiences of the present: that the atom can be split and the end of the world has become a concrete possibility, that time is relative and therefore also changeable,[26] all of which requires humans to embrace a new responsibility for their own future. But instead, time stands still. The moderator is ultimately entangled in the plot. In the later versions of the play (1955, 1965, and 1972) he is a modern intellectual whose inability to keep the recurring masks of the past at bay mirrors the audience's inability to do so. In the first version, however, neo-Romantic questions about dreams and poetry are still prevalent. Here the moderator's name is Min Ko. He is a poet who writes rebellious songs and who, at least at the beginning, believes that he can change the world. But the love between him and the Chinese princess Mee Lan fails miserably. The lovers do not succeed in escaping the realm of violence. Min Ko fights for "the Empire of Truth."[27] With regard to the "wirkliche Leben," he is a relative of the wanderer in *Santa Cruz*, whose words he quotes at times.

Min Ko recognizes that tyrants are as desperate as their subjects. This desperation is grounded in their insight that they are not born emperors at all but instead should perhaps lead a different, simple life. This motif had already been rehearsed in *Nun singen sie wieder*. Only the "truly noble" know about the empire of truth, and the poets decide what is noble.[28] According to Min Ko, even the empire's victims contribute to the system of untruth because the injustice they endure makes them self-righteous and precludes their inner growth, "und das, scheint mir, ist mehr als leiblicher Mord" (and that, it seems to me, is worse than physical murder; ibid.). What is at stake for everyone is self-knowledge, just like it is for the dead in *Nun singen sie wieder*.

In 1955, in preparing the second version of the play, Frisch rewrote the final scene, in which, already in the first version, the poet appears disguised as a fool. In the following version, as well as in the 1972 Paris version, the "Heutige," a contemporary intellectual and poet, is irreversibly confined to the role of the fool since he believes that he can change world history by insight. He is no longer the voice of the people. Now the masks of history, including the Spanish king, Phillip II, who recites verses from Schiller's *Don Carlos*, speak their lines from the plays that made them immortal. The "Heutige" tries to convince the masks of history that their time has passed. While speaking he himself takes over the prescribed role. His speeches are irrelevant but entertaining, and therefore he is promoted to imperial court jester. Meanwhile, a mute man is arrested. He represents the people, who are forced into silence. However, his silence provokes the tyrant, Hwang Ti, to spell out everything that he might be accused of by the people. With this ironic turn Hwang Ti becomes the announcer of truth. But nothing changes. Hwang Ti addresses the audience and declares that he refuses to be deposed or to follow stage directions: "Ich lasse mich nicht stürzen; ich halte mich nicht an Dramaturgie." (I won't let myself be dethroned; I don't believe in dramaturgy.)[29] He rejects the theatrical convention of having the good side win. The tyrant is defeated, but only by his future son-in-law. Princess Mee Lan, on the other hand, who is not needed anymore for maintaining the power structure, is raped and left behind. She courageously declares her love for the fool, who told the truth before without contributing to any change and who has now become mute himself. Character traces of the protagonists in Frisch's later drama *Andorra*, Barblin and the teacher, can already be detected here, analogously to the way in which the teacher from *Nun singen sie wieder* already represented the dilemma of a doctrine and indoctrination that attempt to change the world. The Paris version no longer bears the imprint of Thornton Wilder. Eliminating lyrical passages and neo-Romantic poetics, it approximates Bertolt Brecht's objective style in the way the plot is presented. In the spirit of Brecht's plays, the building of the great wall is negotiated as a business deal between the tyrant and the princess's predestined husband, the "brave" prince. But in the face of the recurrence of failure, the play cannot be a Brechtian didactic play: it does not offer a convincing conclusion. The audience is asked to provide the necessary answer.[30] Frisch's early theater work explores the question of the individual's moral responsibility in a world in which respect for human dignity has become a scarce resource.

Frisch's last play from the immediate postwar era, *Als der Krieg zu Ende war*, poses the questions of individual responsibility, of love and freedom, and of a new language capable of changing history and intensifies their urgency, as is already indicated by the protagonist's name. As Frisch points out in his afterword to the play, its etymology suggests innocence and purity: "Agnes heißt Unschuld, Reinheit."[31] Agnes Anders, the woman who remained innocent during the war, wants to change her life. Her house, which symbolized her former life, has been destroyed in the bombings. All the houses that can still be used are occupied by Russian troops. The Russian officer Stepan and Agnes develop a loving relationship that remains silent because they do not share a common language. It is for this very reason that they understand one another, according to the constitutive paradoxicality of the drama.[32] Thus abandoning fixed images that many Germans had about Russians, Agnes loves Stepan and gets to know him intimately.[33] Although they had belonged to enemy parties, after the war the lovers live together based on their free individual decision.

This mutual understanding is however destroyed when Horst, Agnes's husband, returns from the front. He hides in the basement of the house and supports Agnes's relationship with Stepan as a cover. But when he climbs up the basement stairs as the "owner of the house"—and of the woman—in other words when he re-enters reality, he is identified by Jehuda Karp, a survivor of the Warsaw Ghetto, whose role is written in Yiddish, as a member of the Stroop brigade, the SS group that played a leading role in the brutal liquidation of the ghetto (*GW* 2:274).[34] Stepan turns away. In act 3, which was later deleted, Horst cooperates with the American occupation force. Agnes, who cannot endure this level of hypocrisy, commits suicide in order to maintain her dignity.

The play experiments with a new way of employing tradition. Having practiced imitation and appropriation in *Santa Cruz*, emulation and the pointed use of myth in *Nun singen sie wieder*, and opposition to the "masks of the past" in *Die Chinesische Mauer*, Frisch now adds inversion to the range of his dramaturgic strategies. In a letter to Frisch from July 1948, in which he comments on the manuscript, Bertolt Brecht, to whose work Frisch refers with this technique, recognizes that the protagonist Agnes enriches the Judith theme with a new and paradoxical variation. The rape victim falls in love with the rapist and is not able to live up to her lover's allegedly "higher" moral standards ("höhere Sittlichkeit").[35]

Frisch would not have agreed with the suggestion that the Soviet occupation army embodied a higher degree of morality.[36] In his postscript to the play he consistently relates it to the reflections on the image that he formulated in his *Sketchbook* around the same time. According to Frisch, it is of vital importance to give a voice to individuals who succeed in liberating themselves from the fixed images of themselves that we—and indeed they themselves—constantly fabricate. Frisch highlights the nexus between "die Judenschlächterei" (the butchering of Jews) in Warsaw and "eine Liebe" that, albeit adulterous, Frisch calls "sacred" to the extent to which it overcomes the addiction to trapping someone in a fixed image, "eine Liebe, die, auch wenn man sie als Ehebruch bezeichnen mag, das Gegenteil jener Versündigung darstellt und insofern heilig ist, als sie das Bildnis überwindet" (*GW* 2:279).[37]

The suicide of Agnes Anders also defines the end of Max Frisch's dramatic works from the immediate postwar period, an end that is defined by disorientation. Written after the war, these Frisch plays represent postwar drama in the narrow sense of the term. They confront the historically situated audience with urgent questions: is an authentic life possible after such a catastrophe? Is identity always enclosed in patterns of repetition and remembrance? Neither of these questions is answered in an affirmative way. In contrast to ready-made offers of meaningfulness supplied by convention and tradition, Frisch's series of stage experiments powerfully suggests the powerlessness of literature. It becomes apparent that humanity, love, a common language, and the humanistic heritage of literature do not have any place in history. Love is confronted with its powerlessness, language fails to initiate communication and destroys life with its empty phrases, and literature, which must rely on language, can only give testimony to helplessness and failure. A life that consists of repeated patterns of recycled memories becomes petrified in its fixation on the past. Such fixed images destroy the future and life itself. History as a sequence of external events unfolds in a fateful repetition of the eternally same. An inner transformation of the human being who could make this history his own does not take place. Yet, far from ushering in the end of Max Frisch's literary art, these desperate conclusions firmly establish its working premises.

—*Translated by Olaf Berwald*

Notes

1 Compare Walter Schmitz, *Max Frisch: Das Werk (1931–1961): Studien zu Tradition und Traditionsverarbeitung* (Bern: Lang, 1985).

2 Max Frisch, *Tagebuch 1946–49*, in Max Frisch, *Gesammelte Werke in zeitlicher Folge* (= *GW*) 2, ed. Hans Mayer and Walter Schmitz, 2nd ed. (Frankfurt am Main: Suhrkamp, 1986), 347–750; here 585.

3 Max Frisch, "Anmerkungen zu *Santa Cruz*," in *GW* 2:759.

4 Ursula Amrein: *"Los von Berlin!" Die Literatur- und Theaterpolitik der Schweiz und das "Dritte Reich"* (Zurich: Chronos, 2004), 529.

5 Compare Oskar Wälterlin, *Entzaubertes Theater* (Zurich/New York: Oprecht, 1945). See also Amrein, *"Los von Berlin!,"* 531–32.

6 Amrein, *"Los von Berlin!,"* 533.

7 Bertolt Brecht, letter to Max Frisch, July 1948, in *GW* 4:766–67.

8 Frisch, *Tagebuch 1946–1949*, *GW* 2:499.

9 Frisch, *Santa Cruz: Eine Romanze*. In *GW* 2:5–75; here 8. In the following discussion of *Santa Cruz*, references to the text will be given by page number in parentheses.

10 Compare the list of Frisch's poetic vocabulary in Schmitz, *Max Frisch* (see endnote 1), 129. For a discussion of his existentialist vocabulary, see ibid., 152–55.

[11] Frisch, "Zu *Santa Cruz*," in *GW* 2:76–77; here 76.

[12] Frisch, "Zu *Santa Cruz*," *GW* 2:76.

[13] Frisch, "Zu *Santa Cruz*," *GW* 2:77.

[14] Compare Frisch, *Santa Cruz*, *GW* 2:63: "Das Leben ist ein großer Traum." This sentence evokes a European topos that was translated into literary modernism by Hugo von Hofmannsthal, for example in his play, *Der Turm* (The Tower, premiered 1928), with reference to Calderon's *La vida es sueno.*

[15] Compare Frisch, *Tagebuch 1946–1949*, *GW* 2:443: "Der Brief eines Freundes rührt einmal mehr an die Frage, ob es zur Aufgabe irgendeiner künstlerischen Arbeit gehören kann, sich einzulassen in die Forderung des Tages." (A friend's letter raises once more the question whether it is any part of an artist's job to concern himself with the problems of the day; trans. Skelton 78). The friend's name was Werner Coninx, whose family owned the journal *Tagesspiegel*, a publication that also represents upper-class Zurich society and its intellectual ambitions. Coninx situated art above everyday reality. Quoting Goethe's, as well as Thomas Mann's use of the formula, Frisch chose *Forderungen des Tages* as the title for an anthology that I edited in 1983, see Max Frisch, *Forderungen des Tages: Porträts, Skizzen, Reden 1943–1982*, ed. Walter Schmitz (Frankfurt am Main: Suhrkamp, 1983).

[16] Max Frisch, *Nun singen sie wieder: Versuch eines Requiems*, in *GW* 2:79–136; here 82. In the following discussion of *Nun singen sie wieder*, references to the text will be given by page number in parentheses.

[17] Compare the passage in the New Testament, Matthew 18:3: "Wenn ihr nicht umkehrt und wie die Kinder werdet, könnt ihr nicht in das Himmelreich kommen." (Except ye be converted, and become as little children, ye shall not enter into the kingdom of heaven.) Another ingredient in this context is the symbolism of redemption linked to the Last Supper.

[18] This passage alludes to Georg Büchner's famous criticism of empty rhetoric in his drama *Dantons Tod*, which had a major influence on Frisch. Herbert's world is also "die mimische Übersetzung seiner Worte."

[19] Compare *Nun singen sie wieder*, *GW* 2:103, where a character gives the standard excuse that they were only following orders.

[20] Compare Frisch's sketchbook entry in *Tagebuch 1946–1949*, *GW* 2:518: "Das Wort, womit man zur Zeit am meisten Unfug treiben kann, heißt Nihilismus." For a discussion of the extent to which mainstream Swiss postwar culture launched polemical attacks against everything it deemed a nihilistic threat against its self-image as an "undamaged" country, see Ursula Amrein, "Kulturpolitik und geistige Landesverteidigung. Das Züricher Schauspielhaus," in *50 Jahre danach: Zur Nachgeschichte des Nationalsozialismus*, ed. Siegfried Weigel and Birgit R. Ertel (Zurich: Verlag der Fachvereine, 1996), 281–324; here 313–14.

[21] Max Frisch: Zu *Nun singen sie wieder*," in *GW* 2, 137.

[22] Frisch, *Tagebuch 1946–1949*, *GW* 2:401. English translation taken from *Sketchbook 1946–1949.* Translated by Geoffrey Skelton (New York/London: Harcourt Brace Jovanovich, 1977), 42.

[23] Frisch, *Die Chinesische Mauer: Eine Farce*, in *GW* 2:139–216; here 178.

[24] In a text written for the program of the play, *Wo spielt unser Stück? Brief an die Darstellerin einer Nebenrolle*, Frisch invokes C. G. Jung's position that the psyche is "die mächtigste Tatsache in der Menschenwelt." Frisch writes that the archetypes in our head prevent us from living our actual life. We project our fears on alleged enemies. Whole countries, Frisch continues, are afraid of their negative qualities and therefore project them onto the Jews. Everybody carries a stage in his or her mind (*GW* 2:217–18).

[25] Apart from the twentieth-century dictators, tyrants from further back in history, such as Phillip of Spain and Napoleon, make an appearance, as do Brutus, and the victims, the *inconnue de la Seine*, as well as tragic lovers, including Romeo and Juliet. However, all these characters remain locked into their roles and are incapable of freely choosing the future.

[26] Compare Frisch's reflections on time in *Tagebuch 1946–1949*, *GW* 2:361–62.

[27] Compare the passages from the first version of *Die Chinesische Mauer* that are left out of later versions in the annotations to the play, in *GW* 2:760–65; here 762. Most scholars refer to later versions, often without realizing that by doing so they give an incomplete view of Frisch's work.

[28] Frisch, *Chinesische Mauer* (first version), *GW* 2:763.

[29] Frisch, *Chinesische Mauer*, *GW* 2:175. This segment does not appear in the final version.

[30] Compare Frisch, *Tagebuch 1946–1949*, *GW* 2:467–68.

[31] Max Frisch, "Nachwort zu *Als der Krieg zu Ende war*," in *GW* 2:278–80; here 279.

[32] Compare Frisch, *Tagebuch 1946–1949*, *GW* 2:536: "Das ungeheuere Paradoxon, daß man sich ohne Sprache näherkommt."

[33] Max Frisch, *Als der Krieg zu Ende war*, in *GW* 2:229–76; here 262.

[34] Frisch had recently read the account of the murders committed by the Germans during the destruction of the Warsaw Ghetto in the journal *Die Wandlung*.

[35] Letter from Brecht to Frisch, July 1948, *GW* 2, 766.

[36] Compare Frisch's comment, in "Nachwort zu *Als der Krieg*," *GW* 2:280, about what he calls a misreading of the play as a parable of Cold War conflicts: "Mißverständnis [. . .], das in diesem Stück irgendwie eine Auseinandersetzung zwischen Ost und West erkennen will."

[37] Compare Frisch, *Tagebuch 1946–1949*, *GW* 2:369–71, 374. An outline of this passage is included in Frisch's notes on the "Fall aus der sogenannten Russenzeit," see *GW* 2:530–32, 536–37.

2: *Spielraum* in Max Frisch's *Graf Öderland* and *Don Juan*: Transparency as Mode of Performance

Klaus van den Berg

Frisch conceived his plays *Graf Öderland* (Count Oderland, first version 1951, later versions 1956 and 1961) and *Don Juan oder Die Liebe zur Geometrie* (Don Juan or The Love of Geometry, 1953, later version 1962) during a fascinating period of transformation in international theater in the 1950s. One component of this transformation was the presence of Jean Paul Sartre's existentialism, which painfully examines the roots of the human condition in the twentieth century, on the German stage. Another component was the showcase of the Berliner Ensemble, which staged Brecht's political vision of an alterable world, a showcase that transformed Brecht, in Frisch's own words, into a "Klassiker"[1] whose approach needed to be modified. A third component framing Frisch's work was the success of absurdist writers such as Samuel Beckett, whose most famous works, *Endgame* and *Waiting for Godot*, portray the lack of motivation and the boredom in bureaucratic societies, themes that play a significant role in *Graf Öderland*. Unlike the stage successes of Sartre, Brecht, Beckett, and Ionesco, or even of Frisch's early plays, both *Graf Öderland* and *Don Juan* share the fate of being his first works to be rejected by theater audiences and critics alike, forcing him to rethink his approach within the context of the 1950s. This rejection, as Frisch's written response to the criticism of *Graf Öderland* documents, was an emotional and intellectual blow that caused him to rework both plays within the climate of theatrical experimentation throughout the decade, with the help of well-known directors such as Fritz Kortner. Kortner, a famous Jewish actor in addition to being a powerful director, encouraged Frisch to revise *Graf Öderland* for the 1956 production in Frankfurt.

The history of the revision and reworking of *Graf Öderland* and *Don Juan* reflects Frisch's struggle to find his own dramatic voice amidst this landscape of dramatic and theatrical experimentation. At the center of both plays are men who are trying to preserve a sense of identity in the face of modern alienation either by fighting the power of myth or by shaping a new myth: defying the long line of Don Juan characters from

Tirso de Molina, Mozart, and George Bernard Shaw, Frisch's Don is a modern hero who seeks male identity in isolation from sexuality. In contrast, Graf Öderland, a modern prosecutor, attempts to escape a Beckett-like existence by becoming a murderer rampaging against a soulless society in an act that Ulrich Weisstein has labeled "the apotheosis of the axe."[2] Frisch developed his heroes and his plots as alternatives to those of Brecht, Beckett, or Ionesco: while Brecht sometimes employs historical figures and events as conduits to suggest political change, Beckett typically splits traditional characters into pairs of friends or master-slave configurations that are complements of each other to cast philosophical and abstract themes in theatrical terms. Offering another variation, Ionesco favors physical transformations as in *Rhinoceros* or *Bald Soprano* or even an absence of characters to illustrate the existential situation in the 1950s. In contrast, *Don Juan* and *Graf Öderland* provide alternative visions by balancing absurdist strategies with realistic portrayal, offering an in-depth personal statement about the modern condition.

Some critics have argued that in Frisch's plays the intellectual trumps the theatrical.[3] Conscious of the difficulties inherent in exploring complex characters while providing exciting theater, Frisch responded in theory and practice by developing a unique concept of drama and performance. In "Der Autor und sein Theater," a speech Frisch gave in Frankfurt in 1969, which amounts to one of his most systematic theoretical reflections on theater, he argues for a refined combination of Schiller's theater as a moral institution and of Brecht's political theater. Frisch identifies the strength of theater as creating a transparent and presentable world instead of showing a utopian world.[4] Despite his admiration for Brecht, Frisch remained skeptical about his method, charging that Brecht, in spite of his many innovations, adhered to an old-fashioned mimetic view of the world as presentable on stage—albeit as a world that is alterable. To Frisch this seemed "wie die Übersetzung einer schlichten Kunst-Erfahrung in ein politisches Programm über den Kunst-Akt hinaus" (77; like the translation of a simple aesthetic experience into a political agenda beyond the artistic act).

Graf Öderland and *Don Juan* represent this attempt to refine the Brechtian approach into a genuine idea of play and performance. Frisch focuses less on what is changing in the play than on how the audience's relationship to the world changes. In the same speech, reflecting a similar concern with sociological performance theory, for example Erving Goffman's theory of role-playing, Frisch proposes the idea that the author must take a "Stück-Leben"—what Goffmann calls a "strip of experience"—and rebuild it as a "Theater-Stück," a process that would not yet trigger any political change (79). For Frisch the process of rendering events and characters more transparent in their complexity is the actual productive part of writing, rehearsing, and witnessing a performance. Frisch considers the stage incapable of reproducing reality, thus burdening the artist with the responsibility of replacing "Unabbildbarkeit" (the lack of representability) with "Durchschaubarkeit" (transparency) by offering alternatives to the audience's experience. For Frisch change and transparency are the engines of attempts at representation, and he calls for "Veränderung um der Darstellbarkeit willen" (346; change for the sake of theatrical representation). In this sense, performance becomes productive by creating a transparent world with images. These images, in turn, facilitate *Spielraum*, an imaginative performance space in which the action unfolds through a manipulation of what is presented or withheld in an allegedly transparent view of the world, enabling playful imaginative explorations.[5]

The concern for performance as creation of a transparent world links *Don Juan* and *Count Öderland*. Both plays carry the imprint of having been developed in conjunction with the Schauspielhaus Zürich and as responses to Frisch's interactions and correspondence with Brecht. In *Graf Öderland* performance enters the equation in two ways: on the one hand, the central character, the prosecutor, decides to escape his role of prosecuting the seemingly meaningless murder committed by a cashier and become a ruthless killer in the guise of the mythical figure of Graf Öderland. On the other hand, Frisch originally conceived the play as a performance piece with just four actors playing all the roles. In *Don Juan*, Frisch manipulates the legendary figure of Don Juan by having the central character consciously assume that role, employing it as a mask through which to explore the painful dimension of his longstanding role of seducer. In each of the plays, Frisch casts identity as a play of roles in which the protagonist forms deliberate alliances and constellations.

In his *Tagebuch 1946–1949*, Frisch writes that the production marks a limited *Spielraum* within what he calls "Unzeit," the vast sweep of cosmological time. This night-like time provides the background against which the performance can unfold.[6] Frisch drew on his extensive experience in working with the set designer Teo Otto at the Schauspielhaus Zürich to think of his plays in terms of performance. In a 1964 essay devoted to Otto's scenography, Frisch describes the insights he had gained from working with Otto for shaping the action of plays. Frisch detects in Otto's work something he was keen on achieving in his plays: the interlacing of "Schaumaße," the imaginative space of the audience, and the "Realmaße," the real space of the stage.[7] Frisch praises Otto's work for its precise control of this real space—which it did not by completing a picture or trying to overpower the actor with a finished picture but by offering openings that empowered the actor to unfold the scene. Frisch particularly emphasizes Otto's concept of ellipsis (in the case of scenography, this meant the omitting of walls that would complete a space in realistic terms), which imbues the space with paradigmatic power. Frisch's invention of a space in which to act is quite original because he defines space as comprised of fragments—mythical, realistic, absurd spaces—and their variations. Jürgen Petersen calls the result of this composition with regard to *Graf Öderland* a "phantastischer Raum" (phantasmagoric space).[8] Consequently, the writer, much like the scenographer, must create action that gains its power by unfolding, or as Walter Benjamin would have it, by creating a "Schwelle," not merely a threshold but a surge connecting audience and *Spielraum*. Above all, Frisch's efforts to experiment with different versions of *Graf Öderland* must be seen as an attempt to control this process of unfolding in a larger sense: to carve out *Spielraum* for the international reception of his work.

Graf Öderland's Performance

Martin, a prosecutor, a familiar figure in Frisch's work, has a crisis: faced with prosecuting a cashier who has killed his landlord without an apparent motive, he senses a deep bond with the murderer. Instead of performing his prosecutorial duties, he decides to leave his safe and well-to-do world and re-invent himself as the mythical figure of Graf Öderland. In the snow-covered woods at a charcoal-burner's cabin, he becomes a murderer and self-declared rebel who starts to kill people with his signature weapon, the axe. As the play progresses, the prosecutor becomes not only a wanted man but a dangerous precedent for others to take up the axe. While he dreams of escaping to a beautiful island near Greece, Graf Öderland attracts followers who live with him, quite contrary to the dream, in a sewage canal. Finally, the prosecutor and his followers occupy a seat of government and offer its officials a deal: putting him in possession of the seat of government in exchange for no bloodshed. In the end, Frisch shifts the scene back to the prosecutor's study in scene 1, where he contemplates whether he dreamt the action, while gunfire can be heard in the background. Now the prosecutor is offered a deal: to avoid execution as a murderer he is asked to take over the government and restore order—the violator of order is to restore order. The murderer's fate unfolds parallel to the main action: first imprisoned as killer, he later receives clemency before being arrested again, ironically, for a murder he did not commit. He is shot when he tries to escape. Ultimately, Frisch leaves the audience with a troubling question: the Count (and by extension the audience) is asked to provide reasons for the murderous acts the Count committed.

Frisch examined the Oderlandic condition of the soul ("das Öderländische") over the fifteen years of the play's gestation between 1946 and 1961.[9] The initial ideas of what Jürgen Petersen has labeled the "Öderland Komplex" appear in several short stories published in Frisch's *Tagebuch 1946–1949*.[10] The piece titled "Aus der Zeitung" (From the Newspaper) offers the theme of a cashier killing his family without a reason; "Am See" (At the Lake) examines the desire to break out of the monotony of modern life. In the earlier story "Skizze" (Sketch) Frisch presents the plot thread of a lawyer who tries just such a break from society.[11] This version still lacked the framing devices of the opening and final scene at the prosecutor's office and the scenes in the sewage system and at the residence, which were ultimately added to what is now known as the play's first version, which premiered at the Schauspielhaus Zürich in 1951 and failed miserably with audience and critics. The idea of a man without any goal or redemption, a man "am Leben verhindert," was first published in his *Tagebuch 1946–1949* as a scenario of seven scenes.[12] In this first draft, with which Frisch believed he had created an image of a soulless society,[13] he stages the state of emergency in a postwar Europe that has lost its soul.[14]

The Oderlandic condition rests on a paradox that Frisch articulates as follows: the prosecutor, who suffers from a soulless society, wants to live, and kills everyone who would prevent him from doing so. His is an existence based on the loss of memory of civilization and ethical values. In a letter to Gustaf Gründgens (1899–1963), one of Germany's most influential actors and directors of the twentieth century, who has been criticized for his close collaboration with the Nazi regime and who served as artistic director of the Hamburg Schauspielhaus from 1955 until 1963, Frisch called Graf Öderland the "Prototyp des modernen Neurotikers": someone who is only able to see external solutions and whose violence turns ultimately against himself.[15] Much like his contemporary Samuel Beckett, who also zeroed in on the devastation of a soulless society, Frisch struggled to find a theatrical concept and a form of action for his social and political diagnosis.

The three versions of the play offer variations on the prosecutor's ultimate fate and, as critics have charged, expose Frisch's struggle to find a satisfying formal structure for the play. The number of scenes differs considerably: the original scenario from Frisch's *Tagebuch* contains only seven scenes; the "first version" contains ten scenes; the second (never published) version has eleven; while the final version contains twelve (the encounter with the charcoal burners only appears in the last version, where it is scene 5). There are also significant shifts in the play's emotional effect and political stance. Frisch summarized these changes in a letter to then-Suhrkamp editor Siegfried Unseld (cited in *GW* 3:840), and in a report about the play's gestation (*GW* 3:92–94). The first version may be considered a private play in which the prosecutor seeks his suicide because he is unable to solve the paradox of how to escape from the constraints of an overly regulated society through violence; the second version may be considered a political drama that, under the influence of director Fritz Kortner, comes closer to a Brechtian didactic drama in that it not only includes a scene in which the prosecutor betrays his fellow rebels but also turns the prosecutor into a Hitleresque figure. The final version presents an open ending in which the prosecutor, withdrawing to his private study, the setting of the play's beginning, refuses to decide between surrendering to justice or accepting the offer of being restored to power.[16]

Frisch explained his willingness to repeatedly change the play by declaring his concern for achieving plausibility through theatricality. In his "Werkbericht" for the play, Frisch specifically asks how a figure such as Graf Öderland may inspire a suspenseful theater. Frisch outlines three possibilities, reflecting the ending of each version. First, following the outlines of Greek tragedy, the prosecutor might gain insight into his course of action and acting. Of course, the trick here is to let the protagonist achieve emotional greatness and offer his audience insight—which is what the scenario for the first version attempts. Frisch's second model for creating theatrical suspense is the Brechtian model of making the audience recognize the society they inhabit, as well as its leader. The third possibility, which Frisch put into practice in the final version, operates with complex ambiguity and constructs a dichotomy between the enjoyment the audience experiences in watching the prosecutor leaving his familiar life, almost an emotional connection to the spectacle of his deeds and the exposure of his freedom as emptiness unmoored from moral and ethical principles and devoid of a political vision ("Werkbericht," in *GÖ* 90–91). As Frisch points out, instead of a feeling of remorse, the prosecutor of the final version dreads the curse of repetition of violence and is unable to enjoy his existence as rebel. This ending seemed to offer formal symmetry and a sense of awakening that Frisch felt it was important to achieve. Frisch stands here in the tradition of the expressionistic drama as conceived by Strindberg and later adapted by German playwrights such as Georg Kaiser and the early Bertolt Brecht. In his so-called post-inferno plays, Strindberg conceived patterns of action in which a central character undertakes a journey that begins and ends in the same external place. Strindberg aligns external and psychological action in plays such as *To Damascus* and *A Dream Play*, in which the travel to and from a place mirrors the psychological journey into and out of layers of the unconscious. For example, in Strindberg's *A Dream Play*, the central character, Indra's daughter, descends from heaven to earth, experiencing the misery of the world in a series of scenes; the scenes that mark her starting and end points are frames for a scene at the play's center, the lowest emotional point of descent.

Examining the play from a literary perspective, its genealogy and slow gestation through multiple versions, it appears as a search for form through the adaptation of various modes of performance: the open ending of the play's final version represents in the true sense Brecht's dictum, from *The Good Woman*, "curtain closed and all questions unresolved," throwing the onus of decision-making onto the audience. The ending also resembles Beckett's model of concluding with great uneasiness and darkness: when the prosecutor is asked to explain the meaning of his deeds, he is unable to do so. This scene resembles the failure of meaning at the end of *Waiting for Godot*. The final version's concluding scene, when we find the prosecutor back in his study as in scene 1, suggests the possibility that everything that has happened throughout the play took place in a bad dream, a central trope borrowed from Strindberg and the expressionists. These affinities point to a rich intellectual heritage and need to be discussed in the context of the play's performance aspects, rather than solely focusing on textual analysis.

Graf Öderland revolves around the interlacing of two plot strands that are developed in the alternating and merging roles of the prosecutor and murderer. From the initial stages of conception this was the core of the action, and its two levels of reality as well as its two levels of behavior reveal the layers of action and decision-making. During the play there are only a few instances when their lives intersect. In the courtroom, the prosecutor begins to feel a bond with the murderer since they both suffer from the same malady, a complete discomfort with the boredom and soullessness of society. Later, in scene 8, at the time he is being released from prison, the murderer states that he has heard of the Graf Öderland myth, offering the potential for further interaction between them, which, however, Frisch fails to provide. The murderer lives in a realistic world that punishes him for committing a crime. When he is released in an act of clemency he continues to be perceived as a criminal.[17] The prosecutor, on the other hand, moves into a fantasy world in which he not only lives out his life but also becomes a paradigm for others. As Frisch notes, it is actually the murderer who articulates the motivation for the action in scene 8: he sees the divide between those who have to work for money and those who let money work for them (*GÖ* 59).

The separation of mythical and realistic levels of action allows Frisch a complementary strategy of unfolding a perspective on society similar to the one he admired so much in the scenographic work of Teo Otto: in many ways the prosecutor's and the murderer's plot are the equivalent of the "Schaumaß" and "Realmaß" categories Frisch discusses in his 1964 essay on Otto mentioned earlier. The configuration of these two spaces, or the worlds that these characters cross, opens a "Spielraum" that offers the audience a transparent look at the mythical, legal, and criminal sides of behavior: the experience of the prosecutor in his fantasy world from which he may awake if he so chooses, and the real world of punishment that condemns the murderer.

Frisch's original performance idea of having a few actors play multiple roles underscores the fundamental existential problem in the play of being captured in a soulless society. It was Frisch's intention to have four actors play twelve roles. The final version, however, has almost twice as many roles. The additional roles either have to be cut, or the actors have to play more roles. In this scenario, one actress would perform the central female roles (the prosecutor's wife in the first scene, and the women that accompany him on his journey)—while one actor would perform the key supporting roles (Dr. Hahn, the murderer's attorney, the secretary of the interior, and the detective), and a third actor would perform the smaller roles. Finally, the main actor would portray both the prosecutor and the murderer. In this constellation the play not only becomes a star vehicle for a male actor but also would correspond with Frisch's initial idea that prosecutor and murderer understand each other as operating in a force field of "Interferenzen" transmitting between them.[18] Most productions, while indeed attracting star actors to the role of the prosecutor, such as Gustav Knuth for the original production or Bernhard Minetti for the final version, avoid Frisch's theatrical solution, foregoing the possibility of having one actor probe both the abstract, mythical level represented by the prosecutor and the level of reality represented by the murderer. In the performance mode that Frisch envisioned, theater itself, the playing of roles, the wearing of masks, the problem with identity or surface and depth, would unveil the soulless civilization.

Frisch complements the stylistic levels on which the prosecutor and the murderer operate with characteristic imagery. In Frisch's universe, images not only express sense perception, thus linking the stage and reality, but also serve a narrative function. Manfred Jurgensen has identified night and snow as constant cosmological images in Frisch's work.[19] They align each character with a distinct reality, symbolizing the power of Frisch's play in cosmological terms, particularly for performances that rely on theatrical metaphor, double casting, and minimal stage design. Frisch casts the opening scene at nighttime, showing the prosecutor in his study in anguish over his duty to prosecute the murderer. In Frisch's work, according to Jurgensen, the night stands for "cosmic nothingness" and meaninglessness, the general condition of our lives, which the light can only break through occasionally (15). This sense of persistent night is particularly reinforced in scene 5 of the final version, in which the prosecutor aka Graf Öderland spends the night celebrating violence with the charcoal burners, expressing the sentiment: "Lang ist die Nacht, kurz ist das Leben." (*GÖ* 41; Long is the night, short is life.)[20] Although Frisch does not use the word "night" in his stage directions for the scene in the sewage system, the implication of darkness is obvious. Completing the frame for the action is the final scene in the prosecutor's study, which again takes place at nighttime.

Frisch associates the murderer with the other central image in his work: snow.[21] In scene two of *Graf Öderland*, Frisch creates a scenographic context of the murderer's existence: a synthesis of prison cell in the foreground and a snow landscape in the background. In a sense Frisch doubles and reinforces the sense of a soulless society by imprisoning the murderer in a legal sense while also surrounding him with an image of the sterile society he tried to escape.

The roles of the actors and the imagery converge in the final scene at the prosecutor's study. Similar to Strindberg's post-inferno plays or the drama of expressionism, the action has come full circle, arriving at the moment where awakening is possible. The scene is the same as in scene 1, but Frisch rebuilds it into a grandiose tableau. The prosecutor still wears the boots he wore down in the sewage system, which lends credibility to the thought that the foregoing action was not just a dream or fairy tale. Similar to the staging of Strindberg's *Dream Play*, in which walls often move to make room for another site, the back wall of the prosecutor's study opens, revealing the gold-clad and red-carpeted residence (*GÖ* 89). By unfolding the performance space, Frisch asks his protagonist who has finished his rampage against both bourgeois society and the audience representing that society: can he, can they accept the deal? Can they imagine social and political action?

Don Juan or Resisting Performance

While *Graf Öderland* offers performance as a form of role-playing using the potential vehicle of doubling and as an exploration of violence by multiple characters, Frisch reverses the problem in *Don Juan*, completed a few years after *Graf Öderland* in 1953. Instead of dramatizing the effects of a soulless contemporary society, Frisch enlists the Don Juan legend as a template for a different performance: a reversal of the centuries-old performance model of Don Juan as a paradigm of male sexuality, a paradigm that seemed to be etched in stone, Don Juan being rumored to have seduced no less than 1,003 women in Spain alone. Don Juan may be considered the other side of a Janus-faced individual, a counterpart to Graf Öderland, since the former combats an established myth about his identity rather than performing a new one. For Frisch's Don Juan, the central issue becomes not only how to destroy one's existing identity but above all how to create an identity in the face of the legend.

Eduard Stäuble has called *Don Juan* Frisch's "glänzendstes Theaterstück" (most brilliant play), the product of a "vitaler Theatermensch."[22] Among the play's multiple strengths Stäuble lists its effective theatrical situations, its vital comedy, its surprising construction of the action, its great pacing, its brilliant inventions in manipulating the Don Juan story, its great dialogue, and how it glides perfectly between stylistic levels of grotesque, idyll, and elegy. Still, Stäuble stops short of a whole-hearted endorsement, recommending the play's enjoyment as a drama with philosophical and psychological merits. Critics and the original audience apparently failed to see these qualities, and the play was Frisch's second successive stage failure. Stäuble blames the critics for emphasizing what they saw as the "immoral" qualities of the play relating to the Don Juan story while failing to uncover genuine Frisch-like qualities in his dramatizing of the topic of self-realization (158).

Frisch situates his Don Juan figure in between the legend that has emerged since the seventeenth-century version of Spanish writer Tirso de Molina, entitled *El burlador de Sevilla y convidado de piedra* (The Trickster of Seville and the Stone Guest; around 1630), and a modern tragicomic individual. In most versions of Don Juan, including the arguably best-known version, Mozart's *Don Giovanni*, the hero quickly seduces a large number of women and subsequently seeks refuge from once-loved, now-deserted women, and from husbands or fathers wanting revenge for their dishonored wives or daughters. It is a game of exercising masculine power.

In an ironic inversion, Frisch transformed this dynamic of sexual exhilaration and flight from responsibility into a dynamic in which the women seek Don Juan and he becomes a lover against his will. As Frisch pointed out, his *Don Juan* is not a carefree rogue but a man in search of his identity.[23] Here Don Juan's journey to hell becomes a theatrical coup d'état: Don Juan consciously plans to—and then does—destroy his image with the help of a woman, no less, creating a new life for himself. Unlike most plays based on the Don Juan legend, which generally conclude when the honor of the women is restored and Don Juan has been removed like a cancer, Frisch sketches this new form of existence in act 5: Don Juan lives a bourgeois life with a wife who is expecting a child from him. The play's general idea and its comic premise is to turn the Don Juan legend on its head. Instead of portraying Don Juan enjoying his prowess in his sexual marathon, Frisch's Don Juan rejects the idea of seduction as a form of pleasure and conquest. On the contrary, he prides himself on his quest to master geometry, thus the subtitle of the play "Die Liebe zur Geometrie." Mathematical expertise serves as a form of masculine rationality and intellect and as the road to male perfection or in Michael Butler's words "the "flight into abstraction."[24] Despite the radical departure, Frisch, as Ulrich Weisstein has pointed out, stands in the long tradition of Don Juan representations by accepting the idea that Juan possesses "magnetic power" in attracting women.[25] However, as much as the traditional Don Juan relishes in the presence of women, Frisch's reincarnation is more or less disturbed by their presence if not to say bored by the constant repetition of love affairs. Thus, Frisch pits two forces of male identity, sexuality and intellectuality, against each other, the one established through the historical paradigm of the Don Juan legend and the other offered by Frisch as an escape route from the historical cliché.

In an essay on *Don Juan*, Frisch pointed out that theater is the perfect medium for his hero since theater, by its nature, marks the difference between Don Juan's role—in Frisch's words, the mask he wears—and his being.[26] The force of role-playing that is inscribed into the medium challenges the actor how to integrate his or her being into the role to expand his or her own insight into the character. Although Frisch expresses a somewhat dim view of theater, claiming that, always wearing a mask, "der Mensch nicht ist, sondern sich selber sucht" (rather than simply being, man is always searching for himself), he finds great potential in dramas such as *Don Juan* precisely because the human fails to reveal itself in this type of melodramatic play (171).

In replaying the Don Juan legend, Frisch explores Don Juan's relationships with a few women, revising the game of constant seduction and conquest, as well as the call for revenge. Frisch divides the action into two parts that reach their climaxes in the third and fifth acts respectively: act 3 brings to a close the more traditional side of the plot with Don Juan's escape; act 5 concludes with the startling news that Don Juan's wife is expecting a baby. The plot strategy is to keep the focus strictly on Don Juan's quest for identity, defining his relationship to women through it. This strategy leads to the play's first part being employed to stage Don Juan's struggle with his masks and its second part offering a dramatic resolution by destroying the traditional Don Juan image.

What might be called the Donna Anna plot runs its ironic, dark course from act 1 through the end of act 3. In the first act, Frisch stages a masked ball where Seville celebrates the impending wedding between Don Juan and Donna Anna. The scene is set at night outside the castle. Don Juan and Donna Anna are equally afraid of meeting each other. To cap the uneasy situation, the bride disappears at the end of the act. The second act shifts to the wedding day the next morning. Frisch reveals Donna Anna with grass in her wet hair stating that she made love to someone in the black water of the night. Don Juan appears as handsome as ever, but according to Donna Anna's mother, Donna Elvira, he looks like he is approaching his execution (*DJ* 116). At the wedding, Don Juan says "no" and reveals that it was he whom Donna Anna had made love to the night before. Reprising the dichotomy of night and day from *Graf Öderland*, Frisch casts the nocturnal lovemaking as representing the dichotomy of true existence versus rigidity and petrification: the daylight operates like a mask made up of social conventions, which hide true feelings and sexual attraction that might play out in the night.

The end of act 2 and the beginning of act 3 present a sharp contrast between the Don Juan legend and Frisch's version. The audience witnesses the wide gap between Don Juan's sexual affairs and his expressed disclaimers of any sexual interest. Following his refusal to marry Donna Anna, Juan immediately spends the night with Donna Elvira, and, in the subsequent act, with the bride of his friend Rodrigo. Don Juan blames the women for pursuing him (*DJ* 128) and voices his preference for the precise science of geometry over the ambivalent moods of love, "voll Bedürfnis nach männlicher Geometrie" (filled with the need for masculine geometry; 131).[27] The act concludes with Don Juan killing Donna Anna's father against his own intentions, while Donna Anna and Roderigo commit suicide as a consequence of Don Juan's actions. In this way, Frisch explores the shifts between comic aspects of the play, Don Juan's refusal and rejection of love relationships, and the tragic consequences of his behavior.

In the final two acts Frisch focuses on two different women. He has introduced both of them, in a nod to the Brechtian tradition, in several interludes that broke up the narrative of the main plot. Labeled intermezzos in the stage directions, they feature Celestina, a pimp, who treats sexuality as a business, and Miranda, a whore, who has fallen in love. The women become a conscious prop in the destruction of the male image. The initial step of this operation takes place in act 4 when Don Juan invites thirteen ex-lovers to a feast at a festive table. The occasion is designed to stage his journey to hell, which in other versions is a real event that provides the moral vision of the play. In Frisch's play it is a theatrical ploy: Don Juan makes an offer to the bishop, who is responsible for upholding morality in society: he (Don Juan) will stage his journey to hell as a morality play for the church in exchange for a nice pension, a room in a cloister, and a truce with the women he has wronged. He has engaged Celestina as supporting cast for the piece, playing Donna Elvira's husband. It is one of the many ironies in the play that a female pimp participates in the moral act of punishing Don Juan's misdeeds.

The fourth act offers a turning point that sets the stage for the conclusion. A lady clad all in black visits Don Juan. She introduces herself as someone whom he loved before and who has become a widow. The lady is Miranda, who first appeared as the whore in the interludes, and who has now been reincarnated as the Countess of Ronda. The dark lady offers Don Juan a deal: she will marry him and give him free access to her castle with the assurance of solitude under the condition that he will fully accept the relationship and that he give credence to women as human beings rather than sexual objects: "Du hast uns stets als Weib genommen, nie als Frau" (*DJ* 145; You always took us as sexual objects, never as women).[28] From her perspective, this would be his salvation and the only path by which he can master geometry (145). In act 5 we meet Don Juan once again: he has accepted the lady's deal. Now, however, he complains to the bishop about how creation has divided man and woman into two types of existence, cursed forever with mutual desire (164).

From a theatrical perspective *Don Juan* reveals two distinct styles. The first part, consisting of the first three acts, follows the melodramatic tradition from which Frisch has borrowed the grand theatrical or cinematic scale of outdoor settings, love affairs, festivities, and duels, although with ironic twists. In the second part, the final two acts, Frisch foregrounds his familiar theme of the individual's separation and alienation from society (140). Furthermore, Frisch clearly differentiates the two parts by making Don Juan appear passive, making love against his will (if one takes his statements about the women's ravenous sexual appetite at face value), within the framework of the melodramatic first part of the play. In contrast, he assumes an active role in the second part by staging the destruction of Juan's legendary image and getting married in what Rolf Kieser has called "the domestication of a myth."[29]

In *Don Juan* Frisch also follows the strategy he outlined in the Teo Otto essay with regard to Otto's scenographic approach, that is, carving out a larger *Spielraum* for his protagonist. As long as Don Juan appears in the role of the miscast seducer, he may be described as an inversion of Henri Bergson's rigid machine.[30] This concept is, of course, also inherent in the traditional reading of the Don Juan legend where the hero, almost like a machine, must seduce every woman in reach. Conversely, in the first acts of Frisch's comedy, the title character follows each encounter with a woman by reflexively escaping into his "love" for geometry. However, Frisch himself diminishes the significance of this effect by stating that Don Juan is sexually attractive because of his intellect, calling him "eine geistige Figur."[31] What renders the play comical is not only the idea of rejecting the act of seduction in light of the legend, but also the reflex of escape. Visually, Frisch echoes the idea of rigidity by having actors wear masks throughout the first three acts. This behavioral pattern changes with the dramatic actions of act 4: the countess's offer of companionship, Juan's intentional conceit of destroying his image, and finally, in the ultimate insult to the Don Juan legend, his decision to transform himself into a domesticated father.

In his essay on *Don Juan*, Frisch admits that the ending might have a sense of absurdity and rigidity. To change the register of comic effects Frisch manipulates the legend's traditional structure to bend the idea of rigidity into the realm of the absurd with a surprising twist: he applies the idea of boredom—often used as theme and plot pattern in absurdist drama—to Don Juan becoming numb from seducing women and trying to escape from that numbness. Frisch supplies his hero with a consciousness that Frisch labels, in the spirit of cultural critic Walter Benjamin, as melancholy: Don Juan's insight that he has failed to achieve the impossible manifests itself as boredom (175). While Graf Öderland faces existential numbness by committing violence over and over again, Don Juan's boredom is reinforced by his repeated love affairs (174).

The Effectiveness of *Spielraum* and Image

In his *Tagebuch* Frisch expounded the idea of a theatrical *Spielraum* as a limited space against the vast backdrop of cosmological time. Performance is inserted into this space and creates an image space for the unfolding of action inside this time frame.[32] Frisch's idea of an imaginative space of unfolding must be seen also as a search for a different model than Brecht's parable, in an effort to avoid the didacticism of Brecht's plays and Beckett's strategies of portraying modern alienation. Although Frisch, following Brecht's technique, conceived very successful plays in the form of the parable, such as *Biedermann und die Brandstifter*, he harbored great reservations about the genre. Frisch thought that the parable, particularly the way Brecht employed it, interpreted the material from an ideological perspective but failed to make it transparent.

Ultimately, Frisch measured the success of playwriting and performance by the author's ability to transform an idea into "die Bildkraft seiner [the author's] Intellektualität," or the transformation of ideas into images.[33] In *Graf Öderland* and *Don Juan*, Frisch explored how the male characters relate to pre-existing images of male identity and how they desperately create new ones in the face of a reality that bores and alienates them. Theatricality becomes the strategy for shaping a new social role—an escape that allows for the probing of a new reality. Frisch effectively expands the stories of Don Juan and Graf Öderland into an image space. The act of unfolding space means to engage these narrative patterns as the basis for his *Spielraum*: a structure that may be altered or revised. Analogous to Otto's design idea of unfolding a scenography with deliberate withholding and release of properties, Frisch develops male figures that offer two variations of coping with contemporary identity. Like Janus-faced twins, the two plays might be considered to present variations of and different solutions to male identity.

Notes

[1] Max Frisch, "Brecht der Klassiker." Unless otherwise stated, Frisch's essays are cited from *Max Frisch: Gesammelte Werke in zeitlicher Folge* (= *GW*) 5, ed. Hans Mayer, 2nd ed. (Frankfurt am Main: Suhrkamp, 1986), here 343. The German texts of *Graf Öderland* (*GÖ*) and *Don Juan* (*DJ*) are cited from volume 3 of the same edition (*GW* 3).

[2] Ulrich Weisstein, *Max Frisch* (New York: Twayne, 1967), 126.

[3] Siegfried Melchinger, *Theater der Gegenwart* (Frankfurt am Main: Fischer, 1956). Cited in Eduard Stäuble, *Max Frisch: Gesamtdarstellung seines Werkes* (St. Gallen: Erker, 1967), 99.

[4] Max Frisch, "Der Autor und das Theater," *GW* 5:339. Subsequent references to this source will be by page number in parentheses.

[5] Max Frisch, "Teo Otto," *GW* 5:335–38; here 338.

[6] Max Frisch, *Tagebuch 1946–1949* (Frankfurt am Main: Suhrkamp, 1950), 13.

[7] Max Frisch, "Teo Otto," *GW* 5:335–38; here 337.

[8] Jürgen Petersen, *Max Frisch*, 3rd ed. (Stuttgart: Metzler, 2002), 67.

[9] Max Frisch, "Zu Graf Öderland," *GW* 5:90.

[10] Jürgen Petersen, *Max Frisch* (Stuttgart: Metzler, 2002), 64–67.

[11] Frisch, *Tagebuch*, 57–87.

[12] Max Frisch, "Werkbericht," *GW* 5:92.

[13] Max Frisch, "Das Öderländische," *Jetzt ist Sehenszeit: Briefe, Notate, Dokumente 1943–1963*, ed. Julian Schütt (Frankfurt: Suhrkamp, 1998), 89.

[14] Christoph Kuhn describes the murders committed by Count Oderland as an "Amoklauf gegen die bürgerliche Ordnung," see Kuhn, "Max Frisch—eine Theaterbiographie," in *Max Frisch*, ed. Arthur Zimmermann (Bern: Zytglogge, 1981), 23.

[15] Max Frisch, "An Gustaf Gründgens," Schütt, *Jetzt ist Sehenszeit*, 102.

[16] The *Graf Öderland* scenario was published in Frisch's *Tagebuch 1946–49* (*GW* 2:406–43); the first version appeared in 1951 as *Graf Öderland: Ein Spiel in zehn Bildern* (Frankfurt am Main: Suhrkamp, 1951). The second version was never published. The authorized third and final version appeared in *GW* 3:5–89.

[17] Frisch, "Das Öderländische," 89.

[18] Frisch, "Das Öderländische," 89.

[19] Manfred Jurgensen, *Max Frisch: Die Dramen* (Bern: Lukianos, 1968).

[20] English translations from *Count Oederland: A Crime Story in Twelve Scenes*, trans. Michael Bullock (translation of the play's final 1961 version). In *Three Plays: The Fire Raisers; Count Oederland; Andorra* (London: Methuen, 1962), 89–164; here 123.

[21] As Manfred Jurgensen has pointed out, throughout his work, Frisch constructed a series of nuanced meanings of snow, see Jurgensen, *Max Frisch: Die Dramen*, 19.

[22] Eduard Stäuble, *Max Frisch: Gesamtdarstellung seines Werkes* (St. Gallen: Erker, 1967), 157.

[23] Frisch, "Nachträgliches zu *Don Juan*," *GW* 5:168–75; here 168.

[24] Michael Butler, *The Plays of Max Frisch* (London: MacMillan, 1985), 47.

[25] Weisstein, *Max Frisch*, 141.

[26] Max Frisch, "Nachträgliches zu *Don Juan*," *GW* 5:171.

[27] Unless otherwise noted, English translations are from *Don Juan, or The Love of Geometry*, trans. Michael Bullock. In *Four Plays: The Great Wall of China; Don Juan, or The Love of Geometry; Philipp Hotz's Fury; Biography: A Game* (London: Methuen, 1969), 85–160; here 119.

[28] Translation by Olaf Berwald.

[29] Rolf Kieser, "Wedding Bells for Don Juan: Frisch's Domestication of a Myth," in *Perspectives on Max Frisch*, ed. Gerhard Probst and Jay F. Bodine (Lexington: University Press of Kentucky, 1982), 119.

[30] The French philosopher Henri Bergson (1859–1941), challenging the Kantian separation of time and space, developed the idea of duration, a model of the

continuous flow of time and the simultaneous presence of data in the consciousness that allows humans to experience freedom. Bergson rejected mechanistic causality and rigidity, seeing them as the prime enemies of the duration of consciousness. His theory of comedy was a direct application of his philosophy of duration. Bergson claimed that characters lose individuality or become less human when they fall into a rigid pattern of behavior. In his close analysis of Molière's plays, he demonstrated how characters become laughable when they regress into repetitions of words or actions, or when the body becomes rigid and mechanistic (such as when we laugh at a man slipping on a banana peel—or similar types of actions when the body loses flexibility as exemplified in Charlie Chaplin or Buster Keaton movies). One of the performance issues in Frisch's play is that his Don Juan feels the need to escape being type cast—having to seduce every woman in his path. In the action of the play, Frisch toys with the inversion of this behavior in Don Juan's attempts to escape role expectations becoming, in turn, a rigid reflex in its own way. This rigidity, and what Bergson calls the machinelike quality of behavior, plays out on the level of language and action when, for example, in act 2, Donna Elvira's father, Don Gonzalo, challenges Don Juan to a duel. Each time Don Juan refuses to fight, Don Gonzalo responds, four times in all, with the phrase "nur über meine Leiche" (*GW* 3:120). Don Juan's attempt to avoid being forced into a traditional role, that is, his repeated refusal to fight, may be interpreted as a new form of rigidity, and thus seen as highly comical.

[31] Frisch, "Nachträgliches zu *Don Juan*," *GW* 5:168.

[32] Cited in Stäuble, *Max Frisch: Gesamtdarstellung seines Werkes*, 26.

[33] Max Frisch, "Vom Umgang mit dem Einfall," *GW* 3:355–57; here 357.

3: Max Frisch's *Biedermann und die Brandstifter* and *Die große Wut des Philipp Hotz*

Amanda Charitina Boyd

Biedermann und die Brandstifter (1958; translated under various titles: *The Fire Raisers*, *The Firebugs*, and *The Arsonists*) has attained international renown and is considered Max Frisch's most famous play. Yet many are aware neither of its complex evolution through various literary genres, nor of its relationship with *Die große Wut des Philipp Hotz* (The Great Rage of Philipp Hotz, 1958), its sister drama originally written to accompany *Biedermann*, but now only rarely performed.[1] This chapter seeks to provide an overview of the literary life of both plays by introducing their primary themes, possible scholarly interpretations, and, when possible, the authorial intent behind their inception.[2]

Biedermann und die Brandstifter

The Inception and Evolution of *Biedermann*

The versatile writer Max Frisch proved successful as an author of prose as well as drama and clearly enjoyed manipulating genre boundaries in his works. *Biedermann und die Brandstifter* provides us with such an example. Over the course of its development, the story took form in four different genres: short prose sketch, radio play, stage play, and television film.[3]

Frisch penned the first incarnation of the Biedermann story, entitled "Burleske," in a 1948 *Tagebuch* entry.[4] This six-page fable sketches out the work that would eventually become known as *Biedermann und die Brandstifter*. In it Frisch offers only a very general outline of the action, introduces no specific characters, and addresses the reader directly as the protagonist using the second-person familiar form "du." The most valuable aspect of this document is that Frisch simultaneously interprets the action as he lays out the plot, granting the reader a glimpse into his authorial intent:

> Eines Morgens kommt ein Mann, ein Unbekannter, und du kannst nicht umhin, du gibst ihm eine Suppe und ein Brot dazu. Denn das

> Unrecht, das er seiner Erzählung nach erfahren hat, ist unleugbar, und du möchtest nicht, daß es an dir gerächt werde. Und daß es eines Tages gerächt wird, daran gebe es keinen Zweifel, sagt der Mann. [. . .] Du bist einverstanden mit ihm, denn wärest du es nicht, müßtest du sozusagen zugeben, daß du selber Unrecht tust [. . .] Du willst das Gefühl, ein guter und anständiger Mensch zu sein [. . .][5]
>
> [One morning a man comes to your house, a stranger, and you cannot help yourself, you give him a bowl of soup and some bread. For the injustice he has suffered, according to his own account, cannot be denied, and you don't wish him to take it out on you. And there is no doubt, the man says, that he will one day have his revenge. [. . .] You agree with him, for if you did not, you would have to admit, more or less, that you are being unjust yourself [. . .] You wish to have the feeling of being a good and upright person.]

The fable contains all the plot elements that are vital to Frisch's Biedermann tale, from the arsonist's first appearance at the businessman's house to the demise of the latter, while also offering the protagonist's rationale for his seemingly irrational desire to assist dangerous arsonists who will inevitably burn down his house, killing him and destroying everything he holds dear.

The "Burleske" entry in *Tagebuch 1946–1949* directly follows a brief commentary on the Communist takeover in Czechoslovakia and has therefore led some to interpret the text, and its latter incarnations, within this context.[6] But Walter Schmitz warns that while "Burleske" follows Frisch's comments on the invasion of Czechoslovakia, the sketch is not meant to be read as a coded representation of Communist military interventions.[7] This allows for more open interpretations of the sketch.[8] The underlying premise of *Biedermann und die Brandstifter* is that a society can just as well be at risk from the inaction of its citizens as the actions of criminals. And while this message can be applied to the Czech political situation in the 1950s, it is much more obviously a commentary on the rise of the Third Reich and not only the German, but more specifically, the Swiss complacency during that period.[9] As Judith Ricker-Abderhalden states, "a great part of the power and durability of *Biedermann* is its universal applicability as a cautionary parable."[10] Indeed, the plot can easily be interpreted within the context of certain historical events, but Hans Bänziger notes that it cannot be exhausted by relating it to specific historical events.[11]

Although we do know that "Burleske" provided the foundation for the radio play *Herr Biedermann und die Brandstifter*, Frisch's next incarnation of the material, there is some conflicting information concerning the latter's evolution. In 1949, Frisch was commissioned to write a radio play for Radio Zürich and subsequently sent the producers an outline for the proposed work, *Die Brandstifter*, in early 1950, but completion of the radio play was delayed due to work on numerous other projects.[12] During this time, Frisch received a generous offer from the Bayerischer Rundfunk for the radio play. According to Frisch, he was experiencing financial difficulties as a freelance writer and desperately needed the 3,000 DM advance they offered him.[13] As a result, Frisch sent his manuscript to both the Bayerischer Rundfunk and Radio Zürich, and the Germans were the first to broadcast it, on March 26, 1953. Radio Zürich received a revised version less than two weeks later, on April 7.[14] What remains unclear are the circumstances that led Frisch to reach for the "Burleske" material for his radio play. Frisch writes that when he was approached by the Bayerischer Rundfunk, he claimed to have no appropriate material and the representative from the Rundfunk suggested he look in his first diary, which had just been published in 1950.[15]

In this version of the work, the reader is presented with the basic characters and plot common to the storyline, but with a few slight variations. The most important new feature of this version is Frisch's use of the *Verfasser* (author), a character who not only comments on the action, but also interacts directly with Biedermann, a role that would later be replaced by the chorus.[16] The character of the "Verfasser" allows Frisch to include the plot interpretation present in the play's source material, "Burleske," while softening what could be perceived as an accusatory tone that was aimed directly at the listener or reader. Later, as he transformed the material into a stage play, Frisch replaced the modern-day interpretive voice with a Greek chorus.

In the fall of 1957, the Schauspielhaus Zürich requested a play from Frisch, but the author claimed to lack appropriate material. Once again, it was suggested that Frisch revisit his Biedermann tale, in this case, the radio play.[17] *Biedermann und die Brandstifter: Ein Lehrstück ohne Lehre* debuted at the Schauspielhaus on March 29, 1958. This one-act play, set in the home of Gottlieb and Babette Biedermann, sheds a damning light on the mentality of its protagonist, Gottlieb Biedermann, a character conceived by Frisch to represent a typical middle-class man. A successful manufacturer of hair tonic, Biedermann enjoys the comforts of a bourgeois life: fine wine, good cigars, elegant meals, a nice home, a loving wife, and even a servant to cook and clean. Yet it is clear from Biedermann's conversations with the arsonist Schmitz and with his wife in scenes 1 and 2 that he has not earned the comfort he enjoys. Biedermann has fired his former employee Knechtling, the actual inventor of the hair tonic formula that has made Biedermann's fortune. In scene 3, a policeman informs Biedermann that Knechtling has killed himself. While Knechtling's suicide does not unsettle Biedermann, his sense of security is shaken by a string of arson attacks that threaten to destroy his town of Seldwyla, and, more important, his quiet life.[18] Concerned that he will be perceived as an *Unmensch*, Biedermann grants two homeless men shelter and consciously ignores innumerable clues that identify these guests as the arsonists plaguing the town. In the end, Biedermann not only allows them to house barrels of gasoline in his attic, but actually supplies the men with the matches to ignite the fire. The play's dark humor was intended to incite the audience to critical thinking, and in anticipation of this, Frisch composed a short farce, *Die große Wut des Philipp Hotz* (1958), to be performed after *Biedermann* "um den Zuschauer nicht zu entlassen mit Detonationen" (so that the audience does not go home with detonations in their ears).[19] In response to Bänziger's comment, "Der Zuschauer wird in das Geschehen miteinbezogen, nicht als lernend-kritischer Betrachter, sondern als Komplize" (the audience member is drawn into the action not as a critical, learning observer but instead as an accomplice), I posit that Frisch manages to draw the audience in in both ways.[20] In presenting his audience with a parable open to several possible interpretations, the author motivates them to do just that, interpret. But while doing so, he also implicates the audience in a complicit role. The second play also served a more mundane function, namely, to extend the length of the theater event, because the one-act *Biedermann* was too short for an evening at the theater.[21]

On September 9, 1958, *Biedermann und die Brandstifter* had its German premiere in Frankfurt am Main, and Frisch wrote the *Nachspiel* to *Biedermann* specifically for this event.[22] Frisch worked on the piece for two months and originally gave it the title "Herr Biedermann kommt in den Himmel."[23] One must ask why Frisch felt compelled to offer his German audience such a radically different conclusion to the play. The *Nachspiel* forecloses any open interpretation of the play. In this second act of the *Biedermann* play, Frisch condemns Gottlieb and Babette to an eternity in hell and reveals both Schmitz and Eisenring to be devils, thus explaining their attraction to fire.[24] Now a postwar interpretation vis-à-vis the Nazi regime seems all but unavoidable. Biedermann not only assumes that he is in heaven, an aspect that further emphasizes his inability to learn from his actions, but goes so far as to demand reparations for his lost possessions, while the devils threaten to go on strike because "eine Reihe von Persönlichkeiten" were granted a pardon and admitted into heaven.[25] Frisch explained his compulsion to write a second act in an unpublished text quoted by Schmitz:

> Obschon Gottlieb Biedermann sich in seinen Reden selbst entlarvt [. . .] fanden die Biedermänner von Zürich es nicht zum Lachen, sondern spendeten ernsten Beifall: So kommt es, ja, so kommt es, wenn man Kommunisten in sein Haus läßt! Um diese bequeme Mißdeutung zu stoppen, schrieb ich für die deutschen Bühnen ein

> Nachspiel: Herr Biedermann als deutscher Bourgeois, der aus Angst mit den Nazi fraternisiert.[26]
>
> [Although Gottlieb Biedermann displays his hypocrisy in his speeches [. . .] the Biedermänner in the audience in Zurich didn't find it laughable, but instead applauded with serious faces: That is what happens, yes, that is what happens when you let communists into your house! In order to preclude this convenient misinterpretation I wrote an additional act for German theaters: Herr Biedermann as a German bourgeois who fraternizes with the Nazis out of fear.]

Despite these comments, Frisch banned the performance of the act from 1973 to 1978, claiming that it was superfluous and even damaging to the overall interpretation of the play.[27] Karasek posits that the *Nachspiel* not only fails to add anything to the play but takes away from its stringent composition.[28] In his unpublished comments reproduced in Schmitz's *Materialien* volume, Frisch goes on to say, "Kurz darauf zog ich dieses Nachspiel zurück, da es die Parabel auf die Vergangenheit bezieht und auf ein bestimmtes Land, also die Parabel als solche aufhebt: die Parabel für die Inkongruenz von Phraseologie und Praxis" (Shortly thereafter I withdrew this *Nachspiel* because it ties the parable to the past and to a specific country and therefore obliterates the parable: the parable for the incongruity of what we say and what we do).[29] Be that as it may, the inclusion of the *Nachspiel* does allow for a more comprehensive analysis of *Biedermann und die Brandstifter* vis-à-vis the *Jedermann* tradition.

Biedermann and *Jedermann*

Frisch's use of the name Biedermann is symbolic on several levels. First, the name is comprised of *bieder*, meaning "worthy," "respectable," or "honest," and "-mann" (man). With this common surname, Frisch evokes an everyman, that is, a common citizen or *Bürger*. The term is pejorative. In the nineteenth century, the figures behind the humorous Munich weekly *Fliegende Blätter*, Ludwig Eichrodt and Adolf Kussmaul, created the character Gottlieb Biedermann or Biedermaier (subsequently Biedermeier) to parody the middle class. The term later came to denote, though not uncontroversially, an entire period of German literature from ca. 1815 to 1848. Given Frisch's social criticisms, it is clear that his choice of the name is not a coincidence. Frisch wrote, "Es handelt sich [. . .] um ein Spiel, ein Bei-Spiel—um einen Gottlieb Biedermann, der sich sehr unwahrscheinlich verhält" (It's about a game, an exemplary game—about a Gottlieb Biedermann, who behaves very improbably).[30]

More important, both the title and content of Frisch's drama allude to the *Jedermannspiel* tradition, perhaps most prominently represented by the anonymous fifteenth-century English morality play "Everyman."

Although its plot elements may differ, Herbert Knust breaks the *Jedermannspiel* down into three quintessential elements: (1) a protagonist confronted with his own mortality, (2) a physical confrontation with death, and (3) the protagonist being judged in the afterlife.[31]

The main text of *Biedermann und die Brandstifter* only reveals the first element, presenting Gottlieb Biedermann as a middle-class factory owner, who, having created a successful business and acquired financial stability, now recognizes the limits to his own power. The town is plagued by arsonists, and Biedermann, fearing the loss of his life's possessions, calls upon the authorities to administer swift and merciless retribution: "Aufhängen sollte man sie!" (91; They should be hanged!)[32] His disquiet concerning the situation is evident. As a self-made man who has attained a considerable amount of wealth, Biedermann now enjoys an affluent lifestyle. When the reader first meets him, he is not working, but rather enjoying the comforts of his home, an environment he does not want infiltrated by his work.[33] Frisch paints a picture of the protagonist seated in his handsomely furnished living room, reading the paper and enjoying fine cigars and wine served to him by his maid. Biedermann is the master of his house and clearly controls what occurs within its walls; however, he is powerless over his external environment. Biedermann's outrage over recent criminal events in the city is a direct reaction to this feeling of impotence and foreshadows the impending confrontation with his own mortality.

In order to identify the other *Jedermannspiel* elements, we must look beyond the canonical text to the less commonly read *Nachspiel*. Conceived as a final scene of the play, the *Nachspiel* depicts Gottlieb and Babette Biedermann in hell, though they do not realize it at first. After reaching the conclusion that they are indeed dead, Biedermann assumes that they must be in heaven; after all, according to Biedermann, he was a compassionate man who led a relatively exemplary life (*N* 326). The vital *Jedermannspiel* motif, a face-to-face confrontation with death, occurs when Sepp Schmitz is revealed to be Beelzebub. The final component to the *Jedermannspiel* comprises the closing pages of the scene as Biedermann and Babette struggle to influence their final judgment while their deeds and misdeeds are calculated. Similar to many other examples of the *Jedermannspiel* and characteristic of Frisch's criticism of the bourgeoisie, this play emphasizes its middle-class characters' attachment to the material goods they accumulated during their lives and the desire to keep them after death. For instance, in the opening lines of the *Nachspiel*, Biedermann asks his wife why she did not try to escape from the house before the stairs caught fire, but rather returned to the bedroom; her response is that she wished to retrieve her jewelry (*N* 323). In their attempts to garner favor with the rulers of this realm, the couple portray themselves as victims who have lost all their worldly possessions, including their treasured home:

> Babette: Mein Mann und ich sind Opfer.
> Biedermann: Unsere Villa ist eine Ruine. [. . .] Was unsereiner durchgemacht hat, das kann er sich ja nicht vorstellen. [. . .]
> Wir haben alles verloren. [. . .]
> Babette: Mein ganzer Schmuck ist geschmolzen! (*N* 326)
>
> [Babette: My husband and I are victims.
> Biedermann: Our villa is in ruins. [. . .] He simply can't imagine what we've been through. [. . .] We've lost everything. [. . .]
> Babette: All my jewelry was melted!][34]

On realizing that they are in hell and not heaven, these vain attempts become even more forceful as Biedermann seeks to impose worldly law on this otherworldly realm:

> Babette: Wir hatten ein Eigenheim.
> [. . .]
> Biedermann: Wir fordern Wiedergutmachung! [. . .] Wir haben Anspruch auf alles, was verbrannt ist. Wir waren versichert. (*N* 330)
>
> [Babette: We had a home of our own.
> [. . .]
> Biedermann: We demand restitution! [. . .] We have a claim to everything that was burnt. We were insured. (*FR* 74)]

The closing lines of the play reiterate the its main theme, namely, that Biedermann has learned nothing. Breaking tradition with the *Jedermannspiel*, whose protagonist usually undergoes a change of heart and subsequent transformation, Frisch leaves his Biedermann in hell wondering if he will be saved.[35]

Characterization in *Biedermann*

As the title *Biedermann und die Brandstifter* reflects, the main figures in the play are Biedermann and the arsonists Sepp Schmitz and Wilhelm Eisenring. Characterization in the play revolves around a theme central to Frisch's oeuvre, as Gerhard Probst has framed it, "the search for identity as the questioning of the existence of a self-contained character or personality, its dependence on the reciprocity of interpersonal image-making, and the impossibility of escaping from the roles we assign to each other."[36]

Representing "everyman," the character of Gottlieb Biedermann induces the audience to introspection. The complexity of Biedermann's character is manifest in his conflicted language. Jurgensen states that "in *Biedermann* [. . .] Frisch relies [. . .] more heavily on the spoken word than on [. . .] theatrical demonstration. [. . .] The grotesque humor of

Biedermann derives almost entirely from linguistic misunderstandings or a particular kind of hypocrisy that expresses itself in language."[37] The protagonist clearly struggles with feelings of insecurity as exhibited in his concern with being labeled an *Unmensch.* Repeatedly Biedermann claims that he is not without compassion for his fellow man, but his inability to reconcile his self-centered beliefs and the image of himself that he is eager to convey to the outside world gradually leads to his demise.

Although the interaction between Biedermann and the arsonists lies at the forefront of the play's action, another subplot is delicately interwoven into the play—the complex relationship between Biedermann and his former employee Knechtling. As his name implies, Knechtling has become a servant to Biedermann, and when he takes some initiative and pursues ownership rights to the hair tonic formula he invented, Biedermann feels threatened. Knechtling is fired, all attempts made by him and his family to communicate with Biedermann are shunned, and, as a result, Knechtling commits suicide. Upon revisiting the opening lines of the play, we find Biedermann trying to convince his servant Anna, and perhaps himself, that he is not inhumane: "ich bin kein Unmensch, Anna, das wissen Sie ganz genau!" (*B* 92; I'm not a monster, Anna, you know that!; *FR* 5, translation modified!) We soon learn during an exchange with Schmitz that the word *Unmensch* carries special meaning for Biedermann. Knechtling, wishing to converse with Biedermann regarding his dismissal, has been turned away from Biedermann's door, resulting in the following exchange:

> Biedermann: Sie müssen jetzt nicht denken, Herr Schmitz, daß ich ein Unmensch sei—
> [. . .]
> Schmitz: Wenn Sie ein Unmensch wären, Herr Biedermann, dann würden Sie mir heute nacht kein Obdach geben, das ist mal klar. (*B* 11)
>
> [Biedermann: You mustn't start thinking now that I'm inhuman, Herr Schmitz.
> [. . .]
> Schmitz: If you were inhuman, Herr Biedermann, you wouldn't be giving me shelter tonight, that's obvious. (*FR* 100)]

Until this exchange, it seemed that Biedermann still possessed the resolve to get rid of the intruders, but at this moment, he passes the point of no return—Biedermann cannot bear to risk being called an *Unmensch* and, therefore, feels obligated to offer Schmitz a bed in his house and whatever else he may request.

Obviously, there is a discrepancy between the true Biedermann and the man he wishes others to see in him. This incongruity runs throughout the play, and can be seen not only in his actions, but also in his language.

Biedermann is very vocal concerning his political views and the fate of the arsonists ("Aufhängen soll man sie!"), but as the critic Marianne Biedermann has argued, he is merely echoing the view of the public, or *Jedermann*, printed in the newspaper.[38] Similarly, he knows from these news reports that the arsonists plaguing the city present themselves as peddlers looking for refuge in attics. Because Schmitz denies being a peddler and, furthermore, an arsonist, Biedermann tries to convince his wife, and indeed himself, that this is true. As Marianne Biedermann states, "Sein Verhalten verändert sich je nach der augenblicklichen Lage, ausschließlich geleitet von dem Bestreben, der jeweiligen Verhaltensnorm zu entsprechen" (His behavior always adapts to the specific situation and is driven solely by his aspiration to adhere to the norms of society).[39]

Schmitz, too, is a complex figure. Although Jurgensen states that "the fire raisers are clearly meant to be types, identifiable only through their model behavior," there is much more significance to these characters.[40] Bänziger refers to Schmitz and Eisenring as coming from another world,[41] and, in fact, they do. First, within the play proper, they are both circus performers—nomadic outcasts. And, second, if one takes the *Nachspiel* into account, they are devils from hell. In the Romantic sense, these figures live on the fringes of society and are, therefore, more capable of offering a critical interpretation of society, as Schmitz surely does. Despite the fact that he is an orphan and has spent his adult life in the circus, he is very well versed in high society and demonstrates his knowledge of wine, cigars, and food—lending an interesting dichotomy to this complex character. And after Biedermann asks Anna to remove all signs of their wealth at the dining table in preparation for dinner with the two circus performers, Schmitz questions the absence of a candelabra and a tablecloth. Yet as a circus performer, Sepp is trained in deception. He witnessed Biedermann's "performance" in the tavern the previous evening and chose to stalk him like prey, most likely because Biedermann was so outspoken about how he would deal with the arsonists who are terrorizing the town. In a cat-and-mouse game, Sepp has chosen his prey, and sets out on the hunt to fool, trap, and kill Biedermann. So, while it is true that, in comparison to Biedermann, who hides his intentions by being subservient to the intruders and by claiming solidarity with the poor, Schmitz and Eisenring never disguise their plans as arsonists, as Jurgensen attests, the character of Schmitz is not an open book.[42] He can neither be viewed as a "type" nor as a one-dimensional character, but rather plays an integral role in spurring the audience on to critical social analysis and self-reflection.

"Ein Lehrstück ohne Lehre"

Over the course of his career, Frisch made many skeptical statements concerning the role of art, specifically drama, in society. One memorable quote reads: "Unser Spiel, verstanden als Antwort auf die Unabbildbarkeit der Welt, ändert diese Welt noch nicht, aber unser Verhältnis zu ihr: es entsteht immerhin ein Vergnügen sogar an tragischen Gegenständen, und dieses Vergnügen bedarf keiner Rechtfertigung daraus, daß unser Spiel didaktisch sei." (Taken as a response to our inability to represent the world, our play does not change this world yet, but it does change the way we relate to it. At least this way we extract some pleasure even from tragic themes, and this enjoyment does not need to be justified by stating that our play has a didactic purpose.)[43] Karasek writes: "Kein anderer Autor des Gegenwartstheater verbindet in seinem Werk wie in seinen theoretischen Äußerungen die Einsichten in die Unbelehrbarkeit der Menschen durch Kunst mit der unüberhörbaren moralischen und gesellschaftlichen Verpflichtung, es immer wieder zu versuchen." (No other contemporary playwright combines in his work as well as in his theoretical statements insights into the impossibility of teaching humans anything through art with the unmistakable moral and social obligation to try it over and over again.)[44] *Biedermann und die Brandstifter* is perhaps Frisch's strongest testament to this assertion, demonstrated not only in content, but also highlighted in the subtitle Frisch assigned to this work: *Ein Lehrstück ohne Lehre.* The dramatic subgenre of the *Lehrstück* or didactic play is an obvious reference to Bertolt Brecht, who, next to Frisch's Swiss compatriot Friedrich Dürrenmatt, had the greatest influence on the author's theory and practice of theater.[45] In fact, many scholars argue that Frisch was a successor of Brecht, the most noticeable difference being that Frisch was less politically outspoken in his literary works.[46] That said, it remains a fact that two Frisch dramas directly treat the Second World War, its roots, and its legacy, *Nun singen sie wieder* (1945) and *Als der Krieg zu Ende war* (1949), and that Frisch was working within the area of *Vergangenheitsbewältigung*, with *Biedermann* and *Andorra* (1961) long before German authors.[47]

Despite the tendency of scholars to link Frisch to Brecht, this does not mean that Frisch considered Brecht to be a role model. In his *Tagebücher*, Frisch merely states that he benefited from and was creatively influenced by his discussions and interactions with Brecht.[48] Frisch had his first encounter with Brecht in 1947 and addressed his frustration with the dramatist in a *Tagebuch* entry from 1948. Whenever Brecht checkmated him with his dialectic method, Frisch found their conversation not fruitful at all: "Meinerseits habe ich dort, wo Brecht mit seiner Dialektik mattsetzt, am wenigsten von unserem Gespräch; man ist geschlagen aber nicht überzeugt." (I myself get least from our conversations when Brecht checkmates me with his argument: one feels beaten, but not convinced.)[49]

While Frisch employed genres and techniques commonly attributed to Brecht, for instance, the parable, the *Lehrstück*, and alienation techniques, his artistic intent was quite different. Stromšík states that while for Brecht, the purpose of art is to help us move forward, Frisch pursues the goal of inviting us to get to know ourselves better: "Für Brecht ist die Kunst das, was die Menschen vorwärtsbringt, für Frisch das, was den Menschen zu sich selbst bringt."[50] In this sense, Brecht and his ideologies became an object of critical engagement (or "Auseinandersetzung") for Frisch, fueling his creative fire, and this should be taken into account when examining Brechtian elements in *Biedermann und die Brandstifter*.

Biedermann is not only Frisch's most successful play; according to Gerhard Probst its success should be "attributed to its being a most fortuitous blend of the theater of the absurd with the Brechtian didactic play."[51] Of all of Frisch's plays, *Biedermann* is the most Brechtian. From the outset, the audience knows, or at least strongly suspects, that Schmitz and Eisenring are arsonists and that the play will end in Biedermann's demise. In the tradition of Brecht, the focus is not on the action itself, but rather on how the events come to pass. In the case of *Biedermann und die Brandstifter*, the audience's focus is on Gottlieb Biedermann and the search for an explanation why he would allow his own downfall. Unlike *Andorra*, another play exhibiting strong Brechtian influence, the power of *Biedermann* is found in its language rather than its visual imagery—an aspect that can partly be attributed to its roots in the radio-play genre.

In *Biedermann und die Brandstifter* Frisch employs many Brechtian elements, including alienation techniques common to Brecht's epic theater. One aspect of the work that has been credited to Brechtian influence is Frisch's innovative use of the classical Greek chorus, which in this case is composed of city firefighters. The author, concerned about the reception of the chorus, stated, "Der Chor ist nicht parodistisch gemeint, nur komisch" (The chorus is not meant to be parodistic, only comic).[52] And while the chorus is often a source of humor, more importantly, it plays a vital role as the primary didactic voice in what was meant to be a didactic work. Manfred Jurgensen states, "No doubt, despite its subtitle, Frisch's *Biedermann* hopes to incite in his audience a willingness to political action. [. . .] [*Biedermann* is] an appeal for greater political consciousness, for a more articulate identification of social values."[53]

Frisch's chorus bears both similarities and striking differences to its ancient model. Similar to the classical chorus, Frisch's chorus responds to and comments on the play's action and warns the players of impending danger (*B* 89). In addition, the chorus addresses the probable outcome of events should the citizens refuse to take action (*B* 89). And, indeed, the members of the chorus have a responsibility to do so. As the city's firefighters, they are paid by the citizens to perform a service.[54] When questioned about Brechtian influences in *Biedermann*, Frisch cited the alienating function of the chorus.[55] However, while employing the chorus as a voice of a "morally sound" city in the tradition of Brecht, he also denounces it (that is, the fire department) as an institution that is indirectly complicit in the action.[56]

Finally, the form of the play, a parable, is the most prominent reference to Brecht. According to Karasek, Frisch's parable plays offer the most original advancement of Brecht's style in contemporary theater: "Frischs Parabeln sind die lebendigste Weiterentwicklung des Brechtschen Theaters, die das Gegenwartsdrama aufzuweisen hat."[57] Yet, once again, Frisch manipulated the genre to serve his own ideological and artistic goals. This is a *Lehrstück ohne Lehre*, thus the emphasis is on the lack of change, because nothing is learned. Bänziger accurately states that Frisch has turned Brecht on his head.[58] The chorus exclaims in its first stanza introducing the closing scene of the drama:

> Sinnlos ist viel, und nichts
> Sinnloser als diese Geschichte:
> Die nämlich, einmal entfacht,
> Tötete viele, ach, aber nicht alle
> Und änderte gar nichts. (*B* 155–56)
>
> [There is much that is senseless and nothing
> More so than this story:
> Which once it was started
> Killed many, ah, but not all
> And changed nothing. (*FR* 62; translation modified)]

Should the audience have missed Frisch's intended message up till now, these lines spoken by the chorus reiterate it, highlighting the overarching theme of stagnation witnessed throughout the play.[59]

While Gottlieb Biedermann is given innumerable opportunities to learn from his situation and amend his behavior, he never takes the initiative. The chorus addresses this predicament:

> Feuergefährlich ist viel,
> Aber nicht alles, was feuert, ist Schicksal,
> Unabwendbares.
>
> [Many things may start a fire,
> But not every fire that starts
> Is the work of inexorable
> Fate.]

A condemnation follows:

> Anderes nämlich, Schicksal genannt,
> Daß du nicht fragest, wie's kommt,
> Städtevernichtendes auch, Ungeheueres,
> Ist Unfug.

Menschlicher,
Allzumenschlicher,
Tilgend das sterbliche Bürgergeschlecht. (*B* 89–90)

[Other things, called fate to prevent you
From asking how they happened,
Monstruous events,
Even the total destruction of a city,
Are mischief.
Human,
All too human,
Mischief that wipes out
Our mortal fellow citizens. (*FR* 3–4)]

Already before the action begins, the inability (or unwillingness) to change is addressed by the chorus. Although this need not be the fate of Biedermann, it does become a self-fulfilling prophecy and one that Frisch wishes his audience to consider. As Marianne Biedermann summarizes, rather than attempting to spread any dogmatic teachings, Frisch's plays try to trigger a reflective process in the audience.[60] And although he did want *Biedermann und die Brandstifter* to resonate with the audience, he also did not wish to end the theatrical evening on such an explosive note.

Die große Wut des Philipp Hotz

As previously mentioned, *Biedermann und die Brandstifter* was too short to fill a complete evening at the theater: therefore, in 1957–58, Frisch wrote a second, even shorter, and farcical work, *Die große Wut des Philipp Hotz*, which premiered, together with the *Biedermann* play, at the Schauspielhaus Zürich on March 29, 1958.[61] For the German premiere of *Biedermann* at the Städtische Bühnen Frankfurt on September 28, 1958, Frisch replaced *Die große Wut* with the *Nachspiel*. Both plays served very specific purposes. Whereas the *Nachspiel* still emphasizes that Biedermann and his wife have not learned anything from their experience, *Die große Wut des Philipp Hotz* was intended to defuse with its lighthearted humor the tension created by *Biedermann*.[62] And, indeed, the calamity and absurdity of the *Philipp Hotz* plot surely succeeded in doing just that.

Similar to *Biedermann*, this play is also set in the home of a middle-class couple, but the atmosphere is quite different. Philipp Hotz, who holds a PhD in the humanities, and his wife Dorli have been married for seven years and their marriage has had its share of challenges. A year before, Dorli informed Philipp that she had an affair with his friend Wilfrid, and the couple is now in the midst of divorce proceedings. Not known as a man of great convictions, Philipp is determined to show Dorli that he truly is a man of his word. This time he will follow through—he will destroy his material goods and join the Foreign Legion, as he has often threatened to do. When we meet the couple in their apartment, Philipp has put this plan into motion. Hired hands arrive to help Philipp demolish everything that is not *Frauengut*, while Dorli remains locked in a wardrobe. Soon Wilfrid arrives. He has returned from a three-year stay abroad and, through conversations between the characters, the audience discovers details of the complex relationship between Philipp and Dorli. Given Max Frisch's demonstrated history of producing works laden with political, social, and historical commentary and criticism, it is difficult to view *Philipp Hotz* as a satire of marital relations; the informed reader searches for deeper meaning and finds it in the play's characterization, plot, and use of language.

One cannot help but ask if events in Frisch's personal life inspired the play. He married Constance von Meyenburg, a fellow architect, in 1942 and the two divorced in 1954, only three years before he started writing *Philipp Hotz*. But the protagonist bears only one striking similarity to Frisch—he is a writer, a point of some contention and humor for his alleged friend Wilfrid. Shortly after arriving in the apartment, Wilfrid asks Philipp whether he is still a writer, after which, having received an affirmative answer, he laughs and slaps Philipp on the shoulder (*PH* 170). This is but one indication that Philipp is not respected by his friends, and there are other indications that his family does not respect him either.

The discussions on stage divulge that Hotz is viewed by the other characters as a feeble man of few convictions. The mention of "great rage" in the title of the play satirizes this aspect of Philipp's character, a fact that becomes more apparent as the plot progresses. Throughout, Philipp attempts to encourage himself by saying, "Nur jetzt nicht die Wut verlieren!" (Don't lose your rage now!) when one would expect to hear "jetzt nicht den Mut verlieren" (Don't lose your courage now). But since his character lacks courage, Philipp uses anger in its place, an anger that stems from years of being mocked by others. No one believes that Philipp will follow through with his threats, not his friend Wilfrid, not his wife Dorli, and not Dorli's lawyer. Hotz is viewed by all as impotent. He does not even possess the power to destroy his apartment, but rather hires two men to help him. And one could interpret the facts that the couple is childless, and that something drove Dorli to an extramarital affair, as indications that his impotence carries into the bedroom as well.

When *Philipp Hotz* premiered along with *Biedermann* on March 29, 1958 in the Schauspielhaus Zürich, reviewers interpreted the combination of the two plays as a parodistic reference to classical Greek theater, where a satyr play followed a tragedy.[63] But Frisch may have had other intentions as well. Upon closer inspection, we see that the two plays bear similarities. Both are set in bourgeois households and highlight a life padded by material comforts, but infiltrated by outsiders. In addition, the downfall of the protagonist in each play is caused by his own tragic flaw. Hotz, the powerless intellectual Frisch so often portrays in his works, is trying to present himself as someone he is not. He wishes to prove everyone wrong by becoming a man of action and making good on his threats. But he fails in every respect, because his attempts are ineffective or lack sincerity. Hotz locks Dorli in a closet as he prepares for his departure. Even then, his captive audience escapes from her prison and continues with her normal life, embracing her lover Wilfrid while Philipp is offstage, shopping for groceries, and preparing their evening meal, as if nothing had changed. Hotz is incapable of instructing the men he has hired to destroy the apartment on how to proceed with the task at hand. Rather than having them destroy the chairs, he has the workers shorten their legs, thus enabling Wilfrid to use one of the chairs later in the scene. We also learn that Hotz has presented himself as an adulterer in the divorce proceedings in order to benefit Dorli (*PH* 180). He has not committed adultery, but has instead given false testimony to the court. His interactions with Wilfrid, Dorli's lover, also lack conviction. As the action plays out, he is incapable of expressing anger toward this homewrecker; instead, he engages him in small talk. And, finally, when he does set off for the Foreign Legion, he does so with trepidation (*PH* 184).

Despite the fact that *Philipp Hotz* is a farce, which incites the audience to laughter, Frisch leaves his audience with the same message conveyed by *Biedermann und die Brandstifter*: the unwillingness of man to address and effectively act upon his own fate. In the final lines of the play, Philipp returns to the apartment and to his routine life with Dorli, informing her that the Foreign Legion turned him down because of his myopia and asking her whether any mail has arrived for him: "Ist Post für mich gekommen?" (*PH* 197).

Notes

1 An internet search of recent performances in German-speaking countries indicated that while *Biedermann und die Brandstifter* is performed often, the same cannot be said of *Die große Wut des Philipp Hotz*. Two exceptions must be noted: the Düsseldorfer Schauspielhaus did recently perform both plays together, and the Schaffhauser Openair Theater performed *Philipp Hotz* in 2009.

2 Unless otherwise noted, all quotes from *Biedermann und die Brandstifter* and *Die große Wut des Philipp Hotz* are cited from Max Frisch, *Stücke 2* (Frankfurt am Main: Suhrkamp, 1962). References to *Biedermann und die Brandstifter* will be indicated with the abbreviation *B* and page number in parentheses; those to *Die große Wut des Philipp Hotz* will be indicated with the abbreviation *PH* and page number in parentheses.

3 Although Frisch's short prose sketch "Burleske" (1948) is the primary source for the Biedermann plot, Walter Schmitz notes that many of the characters

originate from "Der Harlekin" (1949), an outline for a film project that can also be found in Frisch's *Tagebuch 1946–1949.* Schmitz, "Biedermanns Wandlungen: Von der 'Burleske' zum 'Lehrstück ohne Lehre,'" in *Materialien zu Max Frisch Biedermann und die Brandstifter* (Frankfurt am Main: Suhrkamp, 1979), 143. As for the German-language television film incarnations of the material, a total of three were produced, including a Norddeutscher Rundfunk production in 1958, a Swiss Fernsehen (Zurich) production in 1963, and a Radio Bremen production in 1967 (Schmitz, *Materialien*, 14). Due to the confines of this article, I have chosen not to treat the film renditions. For information on the various productions see Schmitz, *Materialien*, 155–56 and Ingo Springmann, *Biedermann und die Brandstifter* (Stuttgart: Reclam, 1975), 37–42, 44–45.

[4] Max Frisch, "Burleske," *Tagebuch 1946–1949*, in *Gesammelte Werke* (*GW*) 2, ed. Hans Mayer and Walter Schmitz (Frankfurt am Main: Suhrkamp, 1986), 556–61. English translations are taken from *Sketchbook 1946–1949*, trans. Geoffrey Skelton (New York/London: Harcourt Brace Jovanovich, 1977), 167–72.

[5] *Tagebuch 1946–1949*, *GW* 2:556; trans. Skelton, 167. Translation modified.

[6] See *Tagebuch 1946–1949*, *GW* 2:555–56. For interpretations that follow this line, see Hellmuth Karasek, *Max Frisch* (Velber: Friedrich, 1974), 68, Hans Jürg Lüthi, "Max Frisch," in *Bürgerlichkeit und Unbürgerlichkeit in der Literatur der Deutschen Schweiz*, ed. Werner Kohlschmidt (Bern: Francke Verlag, 1978), 177, and Jürgen H. Petersen, *Max Frisch* (Stuttgart: Metzler, 2002), 68, just to name a few. See also Frisch's own comments on this interpretation in Schmitz, *Materialien*, 153.

[7] Schmitz, *Materialien*, 138.

[8] Schmitz, *Materialien*, 138.

[9] Clearly, Frisch's next dramatic work, *Andorra*, specifically addressed this latter theme.

[10] Judith Ricker-Abderhalden, "Max Frisch: *Biedermann und die Brandstifter: Ein Lehrstück ohne Lehre (1952–1958)*," in *The Literary Encyclopedia* 30 (March 2005), unpaginated.

[11] Hans Bänziger, *Frisch und Dürrenmatt* (Bern: Francke, 1967), 93.

[12] See Springmann, *Biedermann und die Brandstifter*, 25–26.

[13] Max Frisch, "Herr Biedermann und die Brandstifter, Hörspiel (1952)—M. F. zur Entstehungsgeschichte," in *Herr Biedermann und die Brandstifter, Rip van Winkle: Zwei Hörspiele* (Frankfurt am Main: Suhrkamp, 1960), 112.

[14] Schmitz, *Materialien*, 142. Radio Zürich did not broadcast the play until three months later. Springmann, *Biedermann und die Brandstifter*, 27.

[15] Springmann, *Biedermann und die Brandstifter*, 27.

[16] According to Judith Ricker-Abderhalden, in adapting the sketch for radio, "Frisch dropped the direct, highly didactic voice of an omniscient narrator speaking to a *you* with whom the reader was to identify. Instead, the radio play adds a moderator, who fills in details about the town and its situation, and who introduces characters."

[17] Frisch found it very ironic that, for the second time, another party had led him to the Biedermann material for inspiration. Frisch, "Herr Biedermann und die Brandstifter, Hörspiel," 112.

[18] The name Seldwyla is a direct reference to the works of Frisch's countryman Gottfried Keller. It implies staidness and self-satisfaction.

[19] The phrase is from Frisch's introduction to the play in the "Programmheft zu *Biedermann und die Brandstifter*" quoted in Springmann, *Biedermann und die Brandstifter*, 36. It should also be noted that Frisch was pursuing a collaborative project with Friedrich Dürrenmatt, who wanted to write a play about Johannes Knechtling, the actual inventor of Biedermann's hair tonic, to follow *Biedermann und die Brandstifter*. Karasek, *Max Frisch*, 68.

[20] See Bänziger, *Frisch und Dürrenmatt*, 94.

[21] Karasek, *Max Frisch*, 76.

[22] See Frisch, *Stücke 2*, 322.

[23] Schmitz, *Materialien*, 153. However, critics commonly called the piece "Biedermann in der Hölle," see Springmann, *Biedermann und die Brandstifter*, 74–78.

[24] Springmann offers detailed information on Frisch's textual references to the Bible, Goethe's *Faust*, Sartre's *No Exit*, and historical events of the Third Reich, see Springmann, *Biedermann und die Brandstifter*, 12–13.

[25] Frisch is likely referring to Nazi criminals who were not prosecuted after the war. Frisch, *Nachspiel*, *Stücke 2* (Frankfurt am Main: Suhrkamp, 1962), appendix 323–44; here 333. Further references to the *Nachspiel* will be by the abbreviation *N* and page number in parentheses. (The *Nachspiel* was also published in the first book edition released by Suhrkamp in 1958.)

[26] Frisch quoted in Schmitz, *Materialien*, 153.

[27] Schmitz, *Materialien*, 154.

[28] Karasek, *Max Frisch*, 76.

[29] Frisch, quoted in Schmitz, *Materialien*, 153.

[30] Max Frisch, "Herr Biedermann und die Brandstifter," in Schmitz, *Materialien*, 65.

[31] Knust, "Moderne Variationen des Jedermann-Spiels," in *Materialen zu Max Frisch Biedermann und die Brandstifter*, ed. Walter Schmitz (Frankfurt am Main: Suhrkamp, 1979), 223–26.

[32] Biedermann's repeated exclamation marks a noteworthy linguistic characteristic of the play, repetition. Springmann states, "Die Häufung der Doppelung im Drama zeigt an, daß es sich um besonders affektgeladenes Reden handelt." (The predominance of doubling in the drama shows that this is a case of especially affect-laden speech; Springmann, *Biedermann und die Brandstifter*, 5).

[33] When the servant, Anna, announces a visitor, Biedermann states that he does not wish to see him; that instead, "er soll morgen ins Geschäft kommen" (*B* 91; he should come to [see me at] the firm tomorrow).

[34] Translation taken from *The Fire Raisers: A Morality without a Moral with an Afterpiece*, trans. Michael Bullock (London: Methuen, 1962), 70. Further references to this translation will be indicated by the abbreviation *FR* and page number in parentheses.

[35] Knust, "Moderne Variationen des Jedermann-Spiels," 235.

[36] Gerhard Probst, "Introduction," in *Perspectives on Max Frisch*, ed. Gerhard Probst and Jay F. Bodine (Lexington: University Press of Kentucky, 1982), 1.

[37] Manfred Jurgensen, "The Drama of Frisch," in *Perspectives on Max Frisch*, ed. Probst and Bodine, 20.

[38] Marianne Biedermann, *Das politische Theater von Max Frisch* (Lampertheim: Schäuble, 1974), 14.

[39] Marianne Biedermann, "Politisches Theater oder radikale Verinnerlichung?" In *Text und Kritik* 47/48. Special volume *Max Frisch* (1976): 46.

[40] Jurgensen, "The Drama of Frisch," 21.

[41] Bänziger, *Frisch und Dürrenmatt*, 93.

[42] Jurgensen, "The Drama of Frisch," 21.

[43] Frisch, "Der Autor und das Theater," *GW* 10:346–47.

[44] Karasek, *Max Frisch*, 12.

[45] Frisch himself said little about his dramatic influences, but in his writings as a whole he mentions Brecht more than any other writer; see Petersen, *Max Frisch*, 10–11. In addition, Frisch credits Dürrenmatt's *Besuch der alten Dame* as an inspiration for *Biedermann und die Brandstifter*. See Petersen 18–19.

[46] See Marianne Biedermann, *Das politische Theater von Max Frisch* and Helmut Heissenbüttel, "Max Frisch oder die Kunst des Schreibens in dieser Zeit," in *Über Max Frisch*, ed. Thomas Beckermann (Frankfurt am Main: Suhrkamp, 1971), 54–68. Marianne Biedermann also presents the counterargument to Frisch as a successor to Brecht.

[47] Biedermann, *Das politische Theater von Max Frisch*, 1.

[48] Jiří Stromšík, "Biedermann und die Brandstifter. Schwierigkeiten beim Schreiben eines Lehrstücks," in *Max Frisch: Aspekte des Bühnenwerks*, ed. Gerhard P. Knapp (Bern: Lang, 1979), 288.

[49] Frisch, "Brecht," *Tagebuch 1946–1949*, *GW* 2:593. Transl. Skelton 200.

[50] Stromšík, "Biedermann und die Brandstifter. Schwierigkeiten," 294.

[51] Probst, "Introduction," in *Perspectives on Max Frisch*, 2.

[52] Frisch, "Nachbemerkungen zu Biedermann und Hotz," in Schmitz, *Materialien*, 66.

[53] Jurgensen, "The Drama of Frisch," 22.

[54] For a more detailed analysis of the chorus, see Biedermann, *Das politische Theater von Max Frisch*, 148–53.

[55] Frisch quoted in Petersen, *Max Frisch*, 11.

[56] Stromšík, "Biedermann und die Brandstifter. Schwierigkeiten," 293.

[57] Karasek, *Max Frisch*, 12.

[58] Bänziger, *Frisch und Dürrenmatt*, 93.

[59] According to Malcolm Pender, the stagnation is meant to reflect Swiss middle-class society and its "resistance to change." See Pender, *Max Frisch: His Work and Its Swiss Background* (Stuttgart: Heinz, 1979), 42.

[60] Biedermann, *Das politische Theater von Max Frisch*, 56.

[61] The following edition of the play is quoted in this chapter, with the abbreviation *PH*. Max Frisch, *Die große Wut des Philipp Hotz*, *Stücke* 2 (Frankfurt am Main: Suhrkamp, 1962).

[62] Petersen, *Max Frisch*, 69.

[63] Karasek, *Max Frisch*, 77.

4: Max Frisch's *Andorra*: Balancing Act between Pattern and Particular

Caroline Schaumann and Frank Schaumann

THE THEME OF *Andorra: Ein Stück in zwölf Bildern* (Andorra: A Play in Twelve Scenes, 1961), both as a geographical topos and as an allegory of isolation and narrowness, absorbed Max Frisch since the early stages of his career. In Frisch's *Tagebuch 1946–1949*, one finds a first reference to the small state: "Andorra ist ein kleines Land, sogar ein sehr kleines Land, und schon darum ist das Volk, das darin lebt, ein sonderbares Volk, ebenso mißtrauisch wie ehrgeizig, mißtrauisch gegen alles, was aus den eigenen Tälern kommt" (Andorra is a small country, very small indeed, and just for this very reason the people living there are odd people, as distrustful as they are ambitious, suspicious of everything even when it comes out of their own valleys).[1] A few entries later, under the heading "The Andorran Jew," Frisch converges the thematic complex in one person who will eventually evolve into the main character of the play, a young man who was believed to be a Jew and onto whom everyone projected a ready-made image, "das fertige Bildnis, das ihn überall erwartet" (372; the fixed image that meets him everywhere: 19).

This description of an imagined Jew—his conflicts and his reputation in Andorran society are further elaborated on in Frisch's *Tagebuch 1946–1949*—already contains the nucleus of the later play. In an interview with Horst Bienek, Frisch elaborated on the creative process leading from the diary entry to the stage work:

> Erst nach Jahren, nachdem ich die erwähnte Tagebuchskizze mehrere Mal vorgelesen hatte, entdeckte ich, dass das ein großer Stoff ist, so groß, daß er mir Angst machte, Lust und Angst zugleich—vor allem aber, nachdem ich mich inzwischen aus meinen bisherigen Versuchen kennengelernt hatte, sah ich, daß dieser Stoff *mein* Stoff ist. Gerade darum zögerte ich lang, wissend, daß man nicht jedes Jahr seinen Stoff findet. Ich habe das Stück fünfmal geschrieben, bevor ich es aus der Hand gab.[2]

> [Only years later after I had read the sketch to others several times, I discovered that this is great material, so great that it triggered fear

> in me, desire and fear at the same time. But what is more important, having learned about myself from my previous projects, I saw that this material was genuinely *mine*. That is why I hesitated for so long, since one does not find one's own material every year. I wrote the play five times before sharing it with anyone.]

Here Frisch hints at the deeply personal nature of the material, a connection that at first sight might appear surprising but to which we will return later in this essay, in the context of Yahya Elsaghe's interpretation of the play. In "The Andorran Jew," Frisch also says what particularly fascinates him about this material: "Du sollst dir kein Bildnis machen, heißt es, von Gott. Es dürfte auch in diesem Sinne gelten: Gott als das Lebendige in jedem Menschen, das, was nicht erfaßbar ist. Es ist eine Versündigung, die wir, so wie sie an uns begangen wird, fast ohne Unterlaß wieder begehen-Ausgenommen wenn wir lieben" (374; Thou shalt not, it is said, make unto thee any graven image of God. The same commandment should apply when God is taken to mean the living part of every human being, the part that cannot be grasped. It is a sin that, however much it is committed against us, we almost continually commit ourselves: 21). The Mosaic commandment invoked here—"You shall not make unto you any graven image, or any likeness of any thing that is in heaven above, or that is in the earth beneath, or that is in the water under the earth" (Exodus 20:2)—in Frisch's case, however, does not primarily refer to images of God, whose magnificence shall not be measured by man's image or analogy. Instead, Frisch converts the ban on fixed images of God to one on fixed images of humans: to make a graven image thus implies constraining humans, leaving them vulnerable to prejudice, and depriving them of their very essence, which is the fate of the Andorran Jew, Andri, in the play.

Back to the starting point and title of the play, the small country of Andorra. The actual, real-life principality of Andorra is a co-protectorate of the Spanish Bishop of Urgell and the French president. It is situated in and surrounded by the eastern Pyrenees and bordered by Spain and France. Due to its isolated location and its protectorate status linking it to two countries, Andorra remained somewhat independent from European history and did not take part in the two world wars. Its estimated 85,000 citizens profit from a thriving year-round tourist industry, and to a smaller degree from the agricultural, timber, and tobacco trade. Boasting relative prosperity (Andorra has one of the world's lowest unemployment rates) and seclusion (Andorra is not part of the European Union but enjoys special relations with it), Andorra is sometimes called the Switzerland between Spain and France.

If Andorra's wealth, mountainous terrain, independence, and small size strongly suggest a link to a similar country, Switzerland, Frisch decisively rejects such comparison, asserting in the preface to his play that the Andorra he put on stage "is the name of a model" and has nothing to do with the country of the same name: "Das Andorra dieses Stücks hat nichts zu tun mit dem wirklichen Kleinstaat dieses Namens, gemeint ist auch nicht ein anderer wirklicher Kleinstaat; Andorra ist der Name für ein Modell" (The Andorra of this play has nothing to do with the actual small state of this name, nor does it stand for another actual small state; Andorra is the name of a model).[3] Yet Frisch manages to bury a specific allusion to Switzerland in his negation, indirectly urging the reader to pursue precisely such a comparison. He furthermore underscores such a connection by giving his characters Rhaeto-Romanic names and by imbuing them with stereotypical Swiss characteristics such as self-satisfaction and a sense of entitlement. Wolfgang Frühwald and Walter Schmitz have noted the differences in language between the Swiss-like dialect of the Andorrans and the High German of the Señora and the physician.[4] Just as Switzerland tends to be upheld as the ultimate model of freedom and neutrality, the physician in *Andorra* emphasizes that their country embodies justice (513). With similar suggestiveness, Frisch insists in the notes to his play that the uniforms used should not be immediately reminiscent of "the uniform of the past": "Bei der Uniform der Schwarzen ist jeder Anklang an die Uniform der Vergangenheit zu vermeiden,"[5] yet the allusions to *the* past and its uniform have to be understood as references to Nazi Germany.

If one disregards such allusions and, following Frisch's assertions, reads *Andorra* purely as a portrayal of the formation and consequence of prejudice, the *Stück in zwölf Bildern*, mirroring the twelve gospels, unfolds gradually and excruciatingly to culminate in an inescapable final catastrophe. Frisch discloses patterns of behavior that begin with preconception and compliance and end with complicity in murder. According to Frisch, the example of Andorra can be applied to any society breeding violence. Characteristically, Frisch refers to most Andorrans by their occupation and paradigmatic role within society, rather than by their proper names: there is the teacher, the soldier, the physician, the innkeeper, the carpenter, the assistant, the priest, the mother, and the "someone" ("der Jemand"). Pars pro toto, these characters exemplify various types of Andorran society. Only two young individuals stand out, not having yet acquired a fixed role in Andorran society: Barblin, the teacher's daughter, and Andri, an allegedly Jewish foundling who also lives in the teacher's house. Connected by their similar-sounding names, Andri and Barblin are the only characters who voice personal wishes, show emotions, and point to conflicts lurking behind Andorra's white façade. The play opens with Barblin whitewashing the walls of her parents' house for St. Georg's Day, while Peider, the soldier, looks on, leeringly commenting on her actions. In this way, Barblin's desire for a "schneeweißes Andorra" (464), a community where everyone has her place and her task and is valued and respected by her compatriots, is promptly undermined by the soldier's indecent, crude remarks.

Andri has fallen in love with Barblin, who reciprocates his affection. But when he asks his foster-father for Barblin's hand, the teacher rejects the request, for reasons revealed only later, when we find out that Andri is in fact his biological son, conceived in an affair with the Señora, a citizen from the neighboring "black" country. Can, the teacher, does not find the courage to tell Andri the truth about his origins until it is too late. Instead, Andri wills himself into accepting his outsider status as Jew until the invading "black" soldiers drag him away, with malicious Andorrans aiding and abetting the "Judenschau" (Jew Inspection). Barblin is denounced as a "Judenhure," her hair shorn. Their father, Can, hangs himself after witnessing his children's demise. The play concludes with Barblin in a traumatized haze, her continued frantic whitewashing now exposing the Andorrans' thinly veiled lack of integrity. Rather than correcting the lie that ultimately costs him his life, Andri accepts his fate, expresses his solidarity with the unknown victims and willingly joins them (534).

He thus identifies with the role that the Andorrans bestow upon him and accepts their imputation to him of stereotypically anti-Semitic character traits, even though the Andorrans rather than Andri display such traits. They pronounce him greedy because he pockets a tip rather than wasting it in the jukebox, but it is the master carpenter who demands the exorbitant amount of fifty pounds for Andri's apprenticeship. The Andorrans call Andri dishonest because he does not confess to producing a faulty chair, but it is the other apprentice who lies by pretending he produced Andri's chair, which is flawless. They label him cowardly because he evades the soldier who seduced Barblin, but all the Andorrans behave cowardly at the "Jew Inspection." Finally, they brand him as homeless, but it is his father who keeps Andri's origins secret from him. As Frühwald and Schmitz point out, Frisch in baroque tradition puts on stage the seven deadly sins: wrath (the physician), greed (the carpenter), lust (the soldier), envy (the intern), gluttony (the teacher), sloth (the priest), and pride (Andri).[6] Accepting his status as foreigner who needs to be sacrificed, Andri is executed, the fascist "black" soldiers leave the country, and Andorran order is restored just as the physician had predicted: "Nur keine Aufregung. Wenn die Judenschau vorbei ist, bleibt alles wie bisher. Kein Andorraner hat etwas zu fürchten, das haben wir schwarz auf weiß. Ich bleibe Amtsarzt und der Wirt bleibt Wirt, Andorra bleibt andorranisch" (543; Keep calm, everyone. Once the Jew Inspection is over, everything will be as before. No Andorran has anything to fear; we've got that in black and white. I shall remain the medical officer, the innkeeper will remain the innkeeper, Andorra will remain Andorra: 73).

If, however, one reads Frisch against the grain of his own statements, *Andorra* emerges as the first literary work addressing the role of Switzerland in the Second World War. Considering the by now familiar recent discussions—from Switzerland's inflexible immigration policies to its bureaucratic harassment of and often cruel refusal to accept political refugees, as well as the scandals about Nazi gold in Swiss banks—Frisch's play appears exceedingly timely. In the early 1960s, however, Frisch was one of a small number who argued for the Swiss to come to terms with the past, criticizing the tendency to shift all blame to Germany:

> Wer von unbewältigter Vergangenheit hört, denkt an Deutschland; der Begriff ist in Deutschland formuliert worden. Sprechen wir von der unbewältigten Vergangenheit der Schweiz, so wirkt es peinlich, Gewissensqual aus zweiter Hand [. . .] Wir sind, indem wir uns terminologisch der deutschen Selbsterforschung anschließen, vergleichsweise immer die Unschuldigen, und was in der Schweiz geschehen oder unterlassen worden ist, scheint nicht der Rede wert.[7]

> [Everyone who hears about the failure to come to terms with the past thinks of Germany. The concept was coined in Germany. When we talk about the failure of coming to terms with the Swiss past it seems embarrassing, second-hand guilt. [. . .] By conceptually relating to the Germans' self-analysis, we always assume the role of a relatively innocent people, and what happened and what we failed to do in Switzerland does not seem to be worth mentioning.]

In the vehemence of his political demands, Frisch almost seems to question the general and unspecific parable form of his own *Andorra*, which facilitates the discussion of responsibility in an abstract rather than a specific context: "Wir befassen uns nicht mit Schuld. Wenn Schuld, dann Allerweltsschuld oder Schuld einer Person, aber nicht Landesschuld" (we do not concern ourselves with guilt. If we do, it is a general guilt or the specific guilt of a person but not national guilt).[8] And, in a way, Frisch does not seem to have minded a more specific interpretation of the play. In an interview with Ernst Wendt, he admits that one of his intentions was to attack Swiss hypocrisy in the context of German historical guilt: "Andorra hat das schweizerische Publikum getroffen—und dies nicht unbeabsichtigt; eine Attacke gegen das pharisäerhafte Verhalten gegenüber der deutschen Schuld."[9] Yet it seems that for the most part, Frisch's play was readily interpreted in a generic context, as a welcome inquiry into forms of compliance, too general to provoke any particular country but lauded for its appeal to humanism and ethics.

Yahya Elsaghe goes one step further by suggesting that Frisch not only investigated the (questionable) stance of his own country but also his own role during the Nazi era.[10] Considering the teacher's peculiar, monosyllabic name "Can" (a name that is not listed at the beginning but only emerges in the dialogues of the play) and his unique function in the play, Elsaghe points to affinities between the teacher and Frisch himself that he substantiates with further biographic parallels. Can demonstrates to the Andorrans their shortcomings just as Frisch holds a mirror up to his audience. While Can engages in a relationship with a woman who belongs to "the blacks" and raises their child as an adopted son, claiming that he saved a Jewish child, in Frisch's *Homo Faber* the main protagonist wrestles with the aftermath of a past love affair between himself and Hanna Landsberg, a "half-Jewish" woman from Munich. As Elsaghe elaborates, Frisch later disclosed the parallels between Landsberg's and Faber's relationship and the events of his own life by admitting to his own relationship with Käte Rubensohn, a German-Jewish woman, in the 1930s, an affair hampered by the racial politics of its time.[11]

In *Andorra*, Frisch may well have reflected on his own actions during Nazi rule, reckoning with omissions and failings that still grasped him decades after the actual events. Was Frisch referring to such self-examination when he called Andorra "his material"? Was this a reason why he conceived the play as a prototypical rather than a specific scenario?

While leaving questions like these open, Frisch masterfully refined the structure and style of his play to allude to and expand on his literary role models, Georg Büchner and Bertolt Brecht. In this way, Frisch does not offer a continually progressing plot but illustrates in twelve "images" paradigmatic situations that attest to the bigotry and smugness of the Andorrans. In terms of its typecast characters, language, and composition, *Andorra* is reminiscent of Büchner's *Woyzeck*, in which Marie betrays Woyzeck with the bestial "Tambourmajor" (drum major)—which can be seen as a parallel to Barblin's episode with the soldier because Frisch purposefully leaves open the question of whether she willingly gets involved with the soldier or is forced to do so. Likewise, the scene of "the physician" and Woyzeck has its equivalent in *Andorra* in that both doctors treat the protagonists Woyzeck and Andri in a condescending and humiliating way.

The Brechtian didactic play is another literary model that obviously influenced Frisch; he had seen three Brecht plays staged at the Zurich Schauspielhaus during the war, *Mutter Courage und ihre Kinder* (Mother Courage and Her Children, 1941), *Der gute Mensch von Sezuan* (The Good Woman of Setzuan, 1943), and *Das Leben des Galilei* (The Life of Galileo, 1943). After Brecht returned from American exile and settled in Herrliberg near Zurich in 1948, Frisch had the opportunity to meet in person the poet whose intellect and theatrical sense he deeply admired. A lively exchange of ideas followed. In August 1948, Brecht gave Frisch a manuscript entitled "Kleines Organon für das Theater" (A Short Organum for the Theater). Frisch discusses in his first sketchbook

Brecht's main idea of the "Verfremdungseffekt," defamiliarizing the audience from what is conventionally accepted as normal and stimulating the audience's rational thought.[12]

Developing these ideas in *Andorra*, Frisch depicts patterns of behavior, human responses, and political reactions for their exemplary function and general significance, and simultaneously demonstrates the consequences and lessons that can be drawn from the actions on stage. Comparable to the function of a chorus in Classical drama, this is achieved through commentary, evaluation, and thus alienation, that is, interruption of the plot in a way that encourages reflection and insight on the part of the viewer. Yet in contrast to Brecht's plays, Frisch's actors do not step out of their roles but evaluate their former actions in a fictional trial staged in the present. Thus, Frisch ingeniously turns the entire plot into a flashback while foreshadowing what is to come in these interludes depicting the trial. Frisch uses eight performances in the "Vordergrund" (foreground) in front of a "Zeugenschranke" (witness gate), where all the characters, with the exception of Andri, Barblin, and the mother, give testimony, and for the most part claim they are innocent. They did not know that Andri was not Jewish; they did not want anything bad to happen to him; they meant well. The innkeeper, the carpenters, and the doctor claim their innocence with the identical phrase, "Ich bin nicht schuld." The soldier states that he only followed orders, and the anonymous "Jemand" mentions that he does not recall the events in detail and says that it is time to move on and forget the past.[13]

As witnesses in a trial that presumably concerns Andri's murder, the characters are encouraged to reflect about past actions and omissions. Yet collectively, they fall back on universal negation, exempting themselves from specific liability. Even though all the protagonists seem well off in the present (the soldier is now in civilian clothes and the intern presumably owns a motorcycle) and have had the time and distance to re-evaluate their behavior, they miss that chance, caught up as they are in defense and denial. In contrast to their outer appearance, their attitudes have not changed much from the past. Here Frisch anticipates psychological studies such as Alexander and Margarete Mitscherlichs' *Die Unfähigkeit zu trauern* (The Inability to Mourn, 1967) analyzing the defense mechanisms prevalent in postwar Germany. The sweeping pattern of justification was also bound to remind viewers of a widely known contemporary parallel, the Eichmann trial, which took place in November 1961, the same month *Andorra* premiered. Like the various Andorrans, Eichmann proclaimed his innocence in front of the court in Jerusalem (as did the defendants in the Nuremberg trials). Eichmann, too, claimed that he did not want to inflict pain, that he was a friend of Jews, but that the political leadership and his superiors forced him to supervise the deportations and killing process. A similar argumentative thread was also used by the accused in the Frankfurt Auschwitz trials (1963–68) where none of the perpetrators—many of them in higher positions of authority—admitted responsibility for the crimes of which they were accused, or showed signs of remorse or empathy.

Focusing on the bystanders rather than the perpetrators themselves, Frisch allows for more differentiation, if only slightly. In a key dialogue right before intermission, also taking place at the "Vordergrund," importantly not in front of the witness gate but in front of his own house, Can, the teacher, faces the accusations of the Señora. Rather than defending himself, Can falls silent, signaling a process of introspection and reflection. Neither Can nor the Señora survive to insist on the truth (thus they are not present at the fictional trial). In an interview with Hans Riess, Frisch takes over Can's role, holding up a mirror to the members of the audience to expose their guilty reflection:

> Die Schuldigen sitzen ja im Parkett. Sie, die sagen, daß sie es nicht gewollt haben. Sie, die schuldig wurden, sich aber nicht mitschuldig fühlen. Sie sollen erschrecken, sie sollen, wenn sie das Stück gesehen haben, nachts wachliegen. Die Mitschuldigen sind überall.[14]
>
> [The guilty ones are in the audience. Those who claim that they did not want it to happen. Those who became guilty but did not feel any guilt. I want them to be terrified, I want them to lie awake at night. The guilty ones are everywhere.]

The priest is the only person in *Andorra* who takes the witness stand and declares personal responsibility and does not invoke a higher level of authority. Importantly, the priest kneels while giving testimony. He confesses that he is guilty of having contributed to Andri's death by having forced him into a fixed image (509). The priest is also the only character who goes through a process of development and insight at the witness stand. Returning to the Biblical passage that Frisch quotes in his *Tagebuch* entry "The Andorran Jew," "you shall make no graven image," the priest also hints at the love that could have saved Andri. As a product of the image that others made, Andri is deprived of the freedom to choose his actions and affect his fate. In his novels *Stiller* (1954), *Homo Faber* (1957), and *Mein Name sei Gantenbein* (1964), Frisch depicts how such prejudice and limitation, whether by society, marriage, family, or profession, leads to a loss of identity that can only be offset when the protagonist leaves the role assigned to him and takes on a new identity. That such a change, in turn, can also result in a dead end is one of the paradoxes that Frisch never solved.

Yet, returning to *Andorra* and its aniconism, the question remains whether for Frisch, Andri's fate is merely the result of a prejudice. Friedrich Torberg rightly points out that in this case, the protagonist could also be a member of any other marginalized group,[15] especially if one consistently applies the model character of Frisch's play without considering the political and historical background. Such a perspective, however, subsumes the Holocaust under a general category of discrimination and persecution while losing sight of its unprecedented hatred and racism, and seems related to East and West German attempts to level victims of political persecution, the Holocaust, and the war in general. Yet a victim is never just a victim, and specifics such as race and gender matter. This becomes particularly noticeable when one considers that in Frisch's play, Andri turns out *not* to be Jewish. Clearly, the prejudices exist only in the Andorrans' heads, but one could counter that they remain unquestioned and undefeated. In his essay "*Andorra* mit anderen Augen" (*Andorra* with Different Eyes), Karl August Horst argues that the play's stance against racism is undermined by the complexity of the main character's identity construction.[16]

For the viewer, the assumption may stand that a Jew cannot be a good carpenter. Certainly this is not the conclusion that Frisch intended with his play. Still, the wavering between the general and the particular hinders a clear interpretation: while the play intends to make a universal statement about prejudice, the only characterizations of Jews that are mentioned are stereotypes, which are thus arguably reproduced. Since even Frisch would hardly have claimed that anti-Semitism can simply be explained as a historical prejudice, or that persecution is merely based on misunderstanding, the author faces a dilemma: if the play is indeed a parable, the parallels to National Socialism and its aftermath are too obvious to be ignored and point to the deeply problematic strategy of using the Holocaust as one example of many. If, however, one presumes that Frisch is addressing the history of anti-Semitism in particular, his play cannot do justice to the scope of the endeavor. In his incisive analysis of the play, Peter Pütz points to this impasse:

> Die einen lehnten sich aufatmend in ihren Theatersesseln zurück und sahen ein düsteres Kapitel deutscher Geschichte—zumindest literarisch—bewältigt. Andere zeigten sich empört; denn sie vermißten in dem Stück eine angemessene Darstellung und Verarbeitung des unsagbaren Grauens, fragten aber in den seltensten Fällen, ob dieses als historische Realität auch nur annähernd literarisch darzustellen und zu verarbeiten ist. Andere wiederum sahen die Behandlung des Judenmordes verquickt und—wie sie meinten—verunreinigt mit Frischs angeblich persönlicher Identitätsproblematik [. . .].[17]

> [There were those who leaned back in their chairs, relieved that one had come to terms with a dark chapter of German history, at least in literary form. Others were infuriated because in their view the play failed to represent and work through the unspeakable terror. But in

> most cases they did not ask whether it could be presented and processed as a historical reality at all. For others the play's treatment of the murder of Jews was mixed and, as they claimed, contaminated with Frisch's allegedly personal theme of the problematic status of identity [. . .]]

In a similar vein, the unresolved tension between pattern and particular affects Frisch's approach to Jewish religion and culture. While the play centers on the murder of a so-called Jew, its message is embedded in familiar Christian symbolism, imagery, and commandments. Frisch thus to a certain extent Christianizes the Holocaust, a strategy that has recently come under criticism with respect to public memorial sites.

Decades before public debates such as the German "Historikerstreit" (Historians' Debate) about the unprecedentedness of the Nazi regime, the international reception of *Andorra* anticipated arguments and controversies of the discourse to come. The response to its premiere in Zurich on November 2, 1961 was mixed, but three German productions, in Düsseldorf, Frankfurt, and Munich, simultaneously premiered on January 20, 1962, all with resounding success. Initial reviewers raged about the audiences' emotional responses oscillating between "Beifall" and "Beklemmung,"[18] "Bewunderung und Betroffenheit" (acclamation and trepidation, admiration and dismay),[19] and *Andorra* quickly became one of the most popular plays of the postwar era in West Germany. The sharply divergent reception in Switzerland and Germany is entirely conceivable when considering the different audiences in the two countries, which included viewers who recognized how Frisch's play stained the to-date immaculate reputation of Switzerland on the one hand, and a society welcoming a moralistic yet unspecific piece of *Vergangenheitsbewältigung* (coming to terms with the past) on the other. In his remarkable production at the Berlin Schiller Theater that premiered on March 23, 1962 and was touted by some as the strongest performance of *Andorra*,[20] Fritz Kortner attempted to go beyond general patterns by lending the characters an individual shape and sharpening their psychological impact: Andri turns bitter and abrasive, Can's failure becomes obvious. Yet the not-so-subtle differences in the reception of the play in different countries continued: in Austria, Erik Wickenburg interpreted the play's theme in the context of his country's national character and advanced state of assimilation, refusing to see its usefulness.[21] In a similar vein, Hans Weigel voiced reservations after *Andorra*'s performance at the Vienna Volkstheater: "Max Frisch hat das angestrebte Gleichnis nicht verwirklicht. [. . .] Wer gegen Vorurteile und ihre grausigen Konsequenzen ist, braucht *Andorra* nicht. Wer zu gewinnen, zu bessern, zu überzeugen wäre, wird mit *Andorra* nichts anfangen können" (Max Frisch did not achieve the parable he aimed for. [. . .] Anyone who opposes prejudices and their ghastly consequences does not need *Andorra*. Anyone who needs to be won over, reformed, and convinced will not know what to do with *Andorra*).[22]

In the GDR, critics considered *Andorra* less a confrontation with prejudice and anti-Semitism than an obvious critique of the West German state under Adenauer and its chauvinistic tendencies. In the East German *Berliner Zeitung*, Fritz Rödel fumed about the play's alleged allusions to the Adenauer era's refusal to investigate crimes of the Nazi past.[23] In Britain, there were also critical remarks after the performance at the London National Theatre in January 1964, questioning the relevance of the play for a British audience.[24]

In Israel, inevitably, reviewers were particularly sensitive to the odd contrast between Frisch's general claim and the play's particular Jewish references. Reviewing the performance in Haifa in March 1962, Jedioth Hajom praised the play but disagreed with its premise that there are no genuine differences between Jews and non-Jews.[25]

Such objections question the central premise of the play: that humans are basically the same and differences among them only culturally constructed. While an admirable utopian construct, this idea misses the point that only the acceptance of differences leads to a truly multicultural society. Possibly this quandary also hindered the play's reception in the United States, where *Andorra* was met with downright incomprehension. Neither critics nor viewers could warm to the fate of a Jew who turns out not to be a Jew. Even the large-scale Broadway production, George Tabori's translation, nor Horst Buchholz in the role of Andri could change this perception. The reviews were largely negative, such as that of Walter Kerr, writing in the *New York Herald Tribune*, who termed the play a mixture of parable and editorial. After only one week of performances in February 1963, *Andorra* disappeared from the program of the New York Biltmore Theater. While Frisch shrugged off this defeat with the words "Ich habe einen Kontinent verloren" (I have lost a continent).[26] Sabina Lietzmann analyzes the reasons for such failure, noting that most American critics termed the play heavy-handed, ponderous, and monotonous. To Lietzmann, this reception was a defense mechanism of an optimistic people that believed in progress: "Die Massenverführung einer ganzen Gemeinde, eines ganzen Volkes gilt in dem Lande der heftigsten Konsumverführung als ausgeschlossen" (In the country that is most acutely seduced by consumption, mass seduction of a whole community or a whole people is deemed impossible).[27]

The question remains how we can reassess *Andorra* today, almost fifty years after its premiere. One can see from the often skeptical tone of the reviews that Andri's internalization of his assumed Jewishness as an otherness he does not want to accept is a highly problematic setup leading to numerous misunderstandings and misconceptions. On the one hand, Frisch positions Andri as a representative of most any minority, negating Jewish specificity, on the other, he assigns to Andri—and stigmatizes—so-called Jewish attributes. Even if Frisch wants to have his play understood as a general parable of prejudice, the references and parallels to the events and concerns of the time cannot be overlooked and remain relevant for contemporary viewers and readers. A play in twelve images cannot offer a fundamental confrontation with anti-Semitism. But it can show the mechanisms leading to the formation of racism, hate, and persecution. Primarily, *Andorra* is a period play addressing postwar themes in Switzerland and Germany: the sealing off of "foreign influences," the marginalization of those who think differently, and the complacent self-satisfaction with window-dressing measures of change in a new state that despite all declarations to the contrary uncannily resembles the old one.[28]

Half a century later, at a time when the popularity of university courses, art exhibits, survivor testimonials, and major movie productions on the Holocaust testify to a continuous interest in the event and its representation, Frisch's play is worth revisiting precisely because it brings up the taboos, misconceptions, obstacles, and intricacies involved in confronting Germany's Nazi past. Frisch's engagement with Nazi Germany runs counter to familiar expectations that the audience might have of a Holocaust play. Rather than representing the Holocaust as an evil without comparison, and thus necessarily removed from contemporary life, Frisch draws attention to the fact that the mere plea to "never forget" may not suffice as a lesson of the Holocaust. Significantly, such an approach has also been adopted in the often-provocative art of the post-Holocaust generations,[29] making *Andorra* an important if problematic contribution to the still-growing body of art confronting the Holocaust.

Notes

[1] Max Frisch, *Tagebuch 1946–49*, in *Gesammelte Werke* (=*GW*) 2, ed. Hans Mayer and Walter Schmitz, 2nd ed. (Frankfurt am Main: Suhrkamp, 1986), 352. Translations from *Sketchbook 1946–1949*, trans. Geoffrey Skelton (New York/ London: Harcourt Brace Jovanovich, 1977), 6. Further references to this source will be to these editions, by parenthetical page numbers in the text.

[2] Max Frisch, "Interview with Horst Bienek," *Der Tagesspiegel*, September 16, 1962.

[3] Max Frisch, *Andorra: Stück in zwölf Bildern*, *GW* 4:461–560; here 462. English translations from *Andorra: A Play in Twelve Scenes*, trans. Michael Bullock (New York: Hill and Wang, 1962), 6. Further references to the play will be to these editions, by parenthetical page numbers in the text.

[4] See Wolfgang Frühwald and Walter Schmitz, *Max Frisch: Andorra/Wilhelm Tell: Materialien, Kommentare* (Munich: Hanser, 1977), 56–62.

[5] Max Frisch, "Anmerkungen zu Andorra (1961)," in *GW* 4:561.

[6] See Frühwald and Schmitz, *Max Frisch: Andorra/Wilhelm Tell*, 55.

[7] Max Frisch, "Unbewältigte schweizerische Vergangenheit," *GW* 5:370–73; here 370.

[8] Frisch, "Unbewältigte schweizerische Vergangenheit," *GW* 5:372.

[9] "Max Frisch, befragt von Ernst Wendt," in *jetzt: max frisch*, ed. Luis Bolliger, Walter Obschlager, and Julian Schütt (Frankfurt am Main: Suhrkamp, 2001), 160.

[10] Yahya Elsaghe, "Der Antisemitismus und seine Fortschreibung in Max Frischs *Andorra. Stück in zwölf Bildern*," in "Juden: Bilder," ed. Heinz Ludwig Arnold, special issue, *Edition Text+Kritik* 180 (2008): 6–17.

[11] Max Frisch, *Montauk*, *GW* 6:617–784, 727–28. Also quoted in Elsaghe, "Der Antisemitismus und seine Fortschreibung," 10.

[12] Frisch, *Tagebuch 1946–1949*, *GW* 2:600.

[13] The trial interludes appear on pages 477, 481, 487, 503, 529, and 542.

[14] Max Frisch, "Interview with Hans Riess," in *Materialien zu Max Frischs "Andorra,"* ed. Ernst Wendt and Walter Schmitz (Frankfurt am Main: Suhrkamp, 1978), 63. Translation OB.

[15] Friedrich Torberg quoting the program of the debut performance in Zurich in 1961, "Ein fruchtbares Mißverständnis," *Forum* 7 (1961): 455. Reprinted in *Erläuterungen und Dokumente: Max Frisch, "Andorra,"* ed. Hans Bänziger (Stuttgart: Reclam, 1985), 51.

[16] Karl August Horst, "*Andorra* mit anderen Augen," *Merkur* 16 (1962): 396–99. Reprinted in *Materialien zu Max Frischs "Andorra,"* 108–12; here 110.

[17] Peter Pütz, "Max Frischs *Andorra*—ein Modell der Mißverständnisse," *Text & Kritik* 47/48 (1976): 37–43; here 37.

[18] Albert Schulze-Vellinghausen, Günther Rühle, and Wolfgang Drews, "Dreimal Andorra," *Frankfurter Allgemeine Zeitung*, January 22, 1962. Reprinted in *Materialien zu Max Frischs "Andorra,"* 201–3; here 203.

[19] Schulze-Vellinghausen, et al., "Dreimal Andorra," 203.

[20] See Joachim Kaiser, "Verdammte in Andorra," *Das Schönste* 7 (July 1962) in *Materialien zu Max Frischs "Andorra,"* 219–21.

[21] Erick G. Wickenburg, "*Andorra* hat es in Österreich schwer," *Die Welt*, April 14, 1962, 19. Reprinted in *Erläuterungen und Dokumente: Max Frisch's "Andorra,"* 53.

[22] Hans Weigel, "Warnung vor *Andorra*," *Illustrierte Kronenzeitung* (Vienna), March 31, 1962. Reprinted in *Materialien zu Max Frischs "Andorra,"* 225–29; here 227.

[23] Fritz Rödel, ". . . sie wollen's nicht wissen," *Berliner Zeitung*, February 14, 1963 in *Erläuterungen und Dokumente: Max Frisch's "Andorra,"* 61–62.

[24] G. Bode, "*Andorra*," in *Christ und Welt* (London) 7, February 14, 1964, 22. Reprinted in *Erläuterungen und Dokumente: Max Frisch's "Andorra,"* 57.

[25] Anonymous, "*Andorra* von Max Frisch im Haifaer Stadttheater," *Jedioth Hajom* (March 1962), trans. Barbara Seiftert. Reprinted in *Materialien zu Max Frischs "Andorra,"* 253–57; here 255.

[26] After only one week of performances in February 1963, *Andorra* disappeared from the program of the New York Biltmore Theater. See Sabina Lietzmann, "Warum Frischs *Andorra* in New York unterging," *Frankfurter Allgemeine Zeitung*, February 26, 1963. Reprinted in *Materialien zu Max Frischs "Andorra,"* 244–48; here 245.

[27] Lietzmann, "Warum Frischs *Andorra* in New York unterging," 247.

[28] Hans Rudolf Hilty's excellent essay "Tabu *Andorra*?" arrives at a similar conclusion, see *Materialien zu Max Frischs "Andorra,"* 113–21; here 119.

[29] See, for instance, the section "American 'Third Generation' Post-Holocaust Art," in Caroline Schaumann, *Memory Matters: Generational Responses to Germany's Nazi Past in Recent Women's Literature* (Berlin: De Gruyter, 2008), 238–42.

5: Eternal Recurrence in Life and Death in Max Frisch's Late Plays

John D. Pizer

THIS ESSAY WILL EXAMINE Frisch's two last plays, *Biografie: Ein Spiel* (Biography: A Game, 1967) and *Triptychon: Drei szenische Bilder* (Triptych: Three Scenic Panels, 1978).[1] *Biografie* was first performed on February 1, 1968 at the Schauspielhaus Zürich under the direction of Leopold Lindtberg. *Triptychon* was initially staged in French at the Centre dramatique de Lausanne on October 10, 1979 and was directed by Michel Soutter. Its German premiere took place on February 1, 1981 at the Akademietheater Vienna. The director on this occasion was Erwin Axer.[2] While these two dramatic works have been extensively analyzed by Frisch scholars, the common thematic, philosophical, and even structural elements binding them have been the object of only cursory attention. Although it has been recognized that they continued to develop the author's central paradigms of permutation and repetition, thus linking them to another late work, the novel *Mein Name sei Gantenbein* (1964, Let My Name Be Gantenbein, translated as *A Wilderness of Mirrors*, 1965),[3] the two plays also strikingly invoke the principle of eternal recurrence in the realms of both life and death. While *Biografie* provides its chief protagonist the chance to alter the development of his life by changing key moments in his existence but constantly confronts this protagonist with dilemmas that cause him to repeat his life in almost all its particulars, the third "panel" of *Triptychon* shows a man apparently permitted to alter the last moments of his relationship to a deceased lover. However, the irreversible condition of her death forces the essential iteration of these last moments of the life they shared. Essentially, then, *Biografie* and *Triptychon* enact what the philosopher Friedrich Nietzsche, who exercised an important influence on Frisch, referred to as the "eternal recurrence of the same," though without the philosopher's positive spin that we should live our lives in such a manner that eternal recurrence would be an ideal one would embrace. On the other hand, we will also see, particularly in *Triptychon*, that Frisch seems to embrace mortality as a positive condition; like the philosopher Martin Heidegger, Frisch shows us that precisely our finitude allows us to positively shape and define our existence, although we do not tend to realize this as we pursue quotidian goals.[4] In *Triptychon*, the insight of how death defines life is a fleeting one, and is forgotten, in the play's last panel, by the protagonist who formulated it in the first one.

The leading figure of *Biografie* is Hannes Kürmann. He is a professor as well as the Director of the Institute for Behavioral Studies, a somewhat ironic circumstance given his own assigned role in the play as the paradigmatic example of how humans would fail to fundamentally change their behavior even if literally given a second chance at life, the chance to alter events and choices that had been detrimental to one's existence as well as that of friends and family. This irony extends to the chief protagonist's name as well. As Wulf Koepke has noted, "Kürmann" signifies "literally the man who makes the choices (*Kür*)" but is nevertheless "destined to repeat his first existence" despite being given the possibility to reshape it.[5] Throughout the play, Kürmann is given the opportunity to restage various key episodes of his life. These restagings are supervised by a "Spielleiter," literally a play director, who constantly consults the book of Kürmann's life in order to establish the parameters of possible permutations. He is assisted in this endeavor by two "assistants," one male and one female, who take on the roles of various men and women with whom Kürmann interacted earlier in time. In the later version of the play cited in this essay, the only character listed in play besides Kürmann, the play director, and the female and male assistants ("Assistentin," "Assistent"), is Antoinette Stein, with whom Kürmann has lived in a long-term but unhappy relationship.[6] In most cases, the possible permutations presented to Kürmann by the play director prompt him to decide against the life-altering changes after being exposed to the direction the permutations would bring about in his life.

An example of an alternative road not taken by Kürmann in his new life with almost open-ended possibilities is an episode from his childhood, a confrontation with an obnoxious ten-year-old schoolboy nicknamed Rotz ("Snot"). As a way of avoiding his initial fateful encounter with Antoinette leading to their unfortunate relationship, Kürmann allows himself to be transported back to his school days, when he had a snowball fight with Rotz, whose real name was Rotzler but who acquired the odious diminution Rotz through his failure to ever use a handkerchief. As the scene transitions from the apartment where Kürmann met Antoinette, the neon light at the director's podium is unscrewed and a spotlight is switched on; Frisch employs a variety of lighting arrangements to signal the introduction of newly-to-be re-enacted episodes from his protagonist's life.[7] Into this spotlight the assistant strides wearing a snow-covered wool cap to signify his transformation into Rotz's character. Throughout this briefly restaged episode Rotz provokes Kürmann with taunting refrains. The appeal to Kürmann of creating a permutation of his childhood is not simply that it would allow him to avoid having ever seen Antoinette, though the dialogue immediately preceding the snowball fight re-enactment indicates that his aversion toward her plays a role even in this regard. More significantly, with respect to the actual childhood event, eliminating the fight, or at least altering its outcome, would allow the erasure of a powerful feeling of guilt still burdening the adult Kürmann; one of the snowballs he threw during what we can describe as the professor's actual historical life hit his rival's left eye with such force that it was knocked out. Nevertheless, when the play director makes it clear to Kürmann that re-experiencing his existence without the tragic snowball toss would mean having once again to live through his school years and puberty, he allows this chance for a redeemed new life to pass by. Rotz's freshly iterated taunts, reminding Kürmann of childhood pain, also play a role in this decision. However, immediately following Kürmann's tacit rejection of this opportunity, he also fails to go back in time to his semester as a student in Berkeley, California to rescue his relationship with his one true love, the mulatto American, Helen. After he must bear her curses once again, this time uttered by the female assistant playing the role of his beloved, he tells her, in English, "My mother is dying, I have to go." After she responds by accusing him of being a liar and exclaiming "Fuck you!," Kürmann again lets the redemptive chance to turn back the clock of his existence pass by (46–52).

As we will soon see, Kürmann does not entirely reject all the occasions he is afforded, under the supervision of the play director, to make amendments to the book—or, to use the precise term employed by the play director, the "Dossier"—of his life. He chooses a career-altering permutation that allows Frisch to imbue *Biografie* with a political dimension. Opportunities for changes are also not unconditional; not only must Kürmann be willing to repeat his entire life from the moment of a chosen alteration, but his insights into the past cannot alter the nature of his own intelligence (44–45), nor can permutations necessitate changes to the personalities of the other figures involved in the episodes from his life that he wishes to alter. He sometimes has compelling, unselfish reasons for not changing the historical status quo. For example, he decides not to cancel his unhappy marriage to a woman named Brigitte, a cancellation which would have prevented her suicide, because doing so would have annulled the birth of his child (55–58). Nevertheless, Kürmann's general tendency to leave the particulars of his past intact, to allow potential life-altering permutations to slip by when he briefly relives his encounters with key figures from that past, constitutes itself an interesting permutation of Nietzsche's principle of eternal recurrence. As Robert Holub has noted in his pithy summary of this concept, Nietzsche developed it in a range of works. In *Die fröhliche Wissenschaft* (*The Gay Science*, 1882), he first introduces the idea by way of a rhetorical question. He asks how his reader would respond should a demon tell him or her that he or she is fated to infinitely repeat the course of his or her life in every particular detail, down to the most infinitesimal experienced moment. Nietzsche maintains that either despair or a completely affirmative embrace are the possible, albeit antithetical, responses to such a fate. In *Also sprach Zarathustra* (*Thus spoke Zarathustra*, 1883–84), the eponymous prophet posits that all things, including the spider and the moonlight drawn on as eternally iterated details in *Die fröhliche Wissenschaft*, must have existed previously, that life itself is an eternal repetition of all that has already taken place. As Holub argues, a positive response to the demon's query (or to Zarathustra's parable of an infinite backwards-leading road) "can potentially lead to a radically different self-understanding, for one would have to be well disposed toward oneself" to choose this path, a choice indicative of absolute self-confirmation.[8] Kürmann's decision to allow seminal past events to remain unaltered when he does begin to relive them illustrates a response considerably more ambiguous than the radically antithetical possibilities of affirmation or despairing rejection in reaction to the promise—or threat—of eternal recurrence articulated by Nietzsche. Kürmann's predilection for stasis is partly visceral—he recoils at Rotz's taunts and at Helen's curses, and one reason he breaks off the chance to reshape his past is so that he does not have to endure it once again. However, this lukewarm decision essentially to allow his history to remain in the trajectory that brought him to his current life circumstances is clearly also grounded in a *fear* of possible permutations. Based on his biographical decisions, one might reasonably assume that Kürmann, confronted with the potential or threat of eternal recurrence, would respond: "I'll choose this Zarathustrian path, for I fear the possible consequences of deviating from it."

At the outset of her chapter on repetition ("Wiederholung") in a book on time and the experience of time in Frisch's oeuvre, Erna Dahms takes note of Frisch's reference to the experience of "'ewigen Wiederholung' oder der Wiederholbarkeit verblaßter Erlebnisse" ("eternal recurrence" or repeatability of faded experiences) and sees in Frisch's discussion of this experience a clear reference to Nietzsche's "eternal recurrence" paradigm.[9] Dahms's elucidation of repetition and its experience in Frisch draws on a wide range of this author's works. His use of the "Wiederholung" motif allows for the integration of past and present in temporal experience, and a frequent enactment of missed opportunities from earlier in life burdens the current existence of his protagonists. Sometimes the past is repeated in the form of dreams, illuminating the present with an inner truth. With respect to *Biografie*, Dahms finds that every story gains its meaning through the backward glance ("im Rückblick") and describes both Kürmann and the eponymous protagonist of *Homo faber* (1957) as victims of a portentous coincidence.[10] Certainly, Kürmann's unfortunate snowball toss and the multiply re-enacted—and permutated—initial encounter with Antoinette at the conclusion of a party in his apartment, as well as his re-experience of these events under the supervision of the play director, represent Frisch's effort to show the potency of apparently fateful chance occurrence, and of the past in general, for life, as well as for the consciousness of life, in the present. Like the common enactment of the dream topos in Frisch's work, *Biografie* shows that the past is not only repeatable in one's existence, but largely (especially given Kürmann's general inclination toward stasis) immutable.

Nevertheless, Kürmann does choose to make one change in his past life, with profound, life-altering consequences. He is judged by the Marxist ideologue Wladimir Krolewsky, an academic colleague, to be a fundamentally bourgeois intellectual with vaguely leftist sympathies, based on their original encounter. In discussing this historical meeting with the assistant acting the role of the Communist professor, Kürmann claims that he need not repeat himself concerning his fundamental reservations about joining any political party ("ich brauche mich nicht zu wiederholen") and shortly thereafter adds, concerning their antagonistic first encounter, "auch Sie brauchen sich nicht zu wiederholen, Krolewsky, ich habe es nicht vergessen!" (68) Indeed, Kürmann's memory of their confrontation is still so vivid that no iteration of past dialogue is necessary. This circumstance cues the audience that instead of the typical unaltered iteration of a past experience, a genuine permutation will take place. For this time Kürmann surprises his colleague by announcing that he is entering the Communist Party. This event indeed changes his life, as it thwarts his academic advancement. However, as Michael Butler notes, Kürmann does not act here out of conviction based on a sincere change of political heart. Instead, he joins the Communist Party mainly to cancel the soiree celebrating his acquisition of a university chair. This was the celebration at which he first made Antoinette's acquaintance, and its annulment would also annul their fateful initial encounter. As Butler states: "This scene of intellectual bad faith is immediately followed by the first indication of Kürmann's deteriorating physical condition—a timely warning of the finite nature of all games."[11] Additionally, there is a political dimension to Frisch's characterization of Kürmann in this regard; his fundamental passivity and indecisiveness with respect to genuine commitment and engagement constitutes an indictment of the bourgeois intellectual.[12]

With respect to the career advancement thwarted by Kürmann's decision to alter his past by becoming a Marxist, the admiration one might feel for this character, in spite of his bad faith, for taking a step involving clear self-sacrifice is further mitigated by an important element in that portentous first encounter with Antoinette he so desperately wants to nullify. Because he failed to insist on Antoinette's departure the morning after their initial night together, instead of opting to go with her on an automobile excursion, he misses a morning conference at his university called to select its new rector. He was intent on attending this meeting in order to prevent the selection of the archconservative Hornacher, who, as Kürmann well knew—and as the play director reminds him—would undertake any measure to remove him, the vaguely leftist sympathizer, from his institute. In the original version ("Fassung") of his biography, Kürmann was not a Communist, so Hornacher could not have successfully intrigued against him (104–5). Had he not given in to the temptation to spend the selection day with Antoinette, indeed, had he not met Antoinette, Kürmann could have prevented Hornacher from becoming rector and could have continued his career climb even as a closet Communist, for Krolewsky himself insists on Kürmann's extreme tact with respect to his new political affiliation as well as their social relationship. Instead, given the permutation in his biography, Hornacher unleashes a spy who discovers Kürmann's secret and is therefore able to bring about his dismissal. This circumstance further mitigates any respect one might feel for Kürmann for deviating—in the apparent direction of political commitment—from Zarathustra's path, because this political commitment in his permutated life would have had no consequences for him if he had *not* met Antoinette and *would* therefore have acted to prevent Hornacher's selection.

Kürmann's other significant permutation involves a practical matter concerning his health. He had been a somewhat heavy drinker in his original life as a busy professor. However, the Kürmann who is unemployed as the result of his altered political stance has no whisky in his house. Having heeded his doctor's warnings about troubling symptoms apparently connected to his liver, he feels better than he had in his original life, as the play director notes (120). Nevertheless, these symptoms, described by Butler as a portent of failing health metaphorically tied to his insincere embrace of Marxism, turn out to signal incurable stomach cancer, though his doctor, played by the assistant, tries to hide this circumstance from him late in the play, when Kürmann is shown in a hospital-like tableau recovering from an operation performed two weeks prior. He is visited there by Antoinette, who helps him pass the time by assisting in lessons of basic Italian (158–72). Thus, it is apparent that all undertakings designed to free him of his attachment to Antoinette fail. He is desperate enough even to consider the option of shooting her with a revolver, but cannot initially bring himself to do so. Indeed, when the play director wonders why Kürmann had not chosen a daring but obviously less drastic option, such as emigration, and notes that the only thing he has altered in his entire relationship with Antoinette is a slap in the face and his abstinence from alcohol, Kürmann confesses that he actually loves Antoinette (148). Perhaps the play director's goading is what prompts him, finally, to shoot her. He must fire at her five times, as the first four shots seem to take place as a waking dream and she is not even aware of them. As Dahms notes, dreams in Frisch's work are designed to show the multiplicity of possibilities capable of being acted out by an individual, and, in *Gantenbein* and *Biografie*, a testing out of different variations.[13] Nevertheless, in this permutation late in *Biografie*, it would seem the four failed—indeed unperceived—shots reflect Kürmann's consistent passivity and hesitancy, his inability to move from dream/fantasy to reality. Only when he surmises that Antoinette herself thinks he is dreaming does the final, fifth, shot cause her to collapse. However, reflecting on the consequences of his deed, Kürmann revokes this permutation (148–52). The play director soon thereafter sarcastically summarizes the total number of changes to his life actually enacted by Kürmann as the result of his unusual freedom: abstinence from alcohol and the revocation of his faculty status (155). As Koepke notes, the play seems therefore to illustrate the existentialist dictum "nothing that has been done can be undone,"[14] for Kürmann seems incapable of changing the events and contours of his past. Eternal recurrence appears not a choice to be affirmatively embraced or despairingly rejected, as in Nietzsche's *Die fröhliche Wissenschaft*. Rather, it seems to be a path inevitably chosen, as in *Zarathustra*.

What, then, are we to make of the play's conclusion, which seems to turn *Biografie*'s ambience of fated iteration on its head? Up to this point, all possible permutations revolved around Kürmann's decisions, which were only limited by restrictions imposed by the play director as rules of the game. Antoinette is portrayed as an alluring, compelling figure; not only did she inspire Kürmann to act against his better judgment in allowing their initial encounter to turn into a relationship that endures despite his repeated opportunities to intervene in his past and nullify it, but her extramarital dalliances, while deeply vexing to Kürmann, fail to disturb the basic trajectory of their life together. Even the play director, who opens the work re-enacting Kürmann's initial encounter with her (7–17), refers to Antoinette as a "liebevolle junge Dame" in conversation with the professor (63). At the conclusion to *Biografie*, when their introduction after the celebratory soiree has ended is re-enacted a final time, their conversation seems to portend a Nietzschean return of the same, particularly when she begins to repeat her comment concerning her fascination with musical clocks of the sort she sees in Kürmann's apartment: "Figuren, die immer die gleichen Gesten machen, sobald es klimpert" (9, 17, 174, with a slight variation on 20). Her enthusiasm for the endlessly repeated gestures and tones of these clocks signifies her willingness, even pleasure, at playing the "game" of eternal recurrence, and Kürmann's cranking of the clock until its waltz comes to an end after these comments (20, 174) shows his entrapment in the game. However, immediately after Kürmann cranks the clock in *Biografie*'s penultimate scene, Antoinette announces she is leaving, picks up her jacket, strides to the door with Kürmann, and literally walks out of his life. Finally, then, Kürmann is free, free to live out a "Biografie ohne Antoinette," but only for the seven years after their initial encounter that remain in his life (174–75). Kürmann cannot alter the parameters of his mortality.

Has the resolute Antoinette accomplished what the irresolute Kürmann could not, the reversal of history and the overcoming of eternal recurrence? The play's final words referring to Kürmann's remaining seven-year lifespan indicate that any such accomplishment is conditioned by mortality, a Heideggerian motif that will be taken up in *Triptychon*. Nevertheless, the life-affirming aspect of mortality, echoing Heidegger's existential thought and (albeit briefly) brought to expression in Frisch's last full theatrical piece, is not in evidence in *Biografie*. As Heinz Gockel has noted, Antoinette's bold departure might awaken the appearance that Kürmann's inalterable destiny has been revoked, but the fact that the play ends right here and that no Antoinette-free permutations in the protagonist's life (or, one could add, Kürmann-free permutations in Antoinette's life) are even hinted at indicates his life would still be governed by the course of destiny. Furthermore, Kürmann's fundamental perplexity remains unchanged. This helplessness is caused by his profound misconception (abetted by the play director) that a change in circumstances or events in his life could bring about its fundamental/foundational ("grundsätzlich") alteration. He can only change his attitude toward his destiny, not the destiny itself. While Gockel accurately posits Kürmann's dilemma as imposing upon him either an ethical acceptance or an aesthetic choice-postponing play with this decisive life question along the lines of Kierkegaard,[15] one might also posit his possible responses as either a life-affirming "yes" to the demon's query on eternal recurrence in *Die fröhliche Wissenschaft* or a despairing rejection, which would amount to a futile refusal to accept his fate, trapping him in a continuous state of perplexity and helplessness. Given Kürmann's character traits and attitudes as displayed throughout the course of Frisch's play, one could assert that he remains in the trap by tacitly accepting eternal recurrence *without* an affirmative perspective.

Despite its iconoclastic play with the existential paradigms of iteration and permutation, *Biografie* is informed by a clear cohesion, revolving as it does around the life, or life choices, of a central protagonist. This is not the case with *Triptychon*. The discrete, quasi-autonomous character of each of the "three scenic panels" named in the play's subtitle is established by the title itself, for a "triptych" is not only a tripartite work of art constituted by three paintings, but each painting itself is a stand-alone object. The three panels only establish a unified structure by virtue of being held together with hinges, which allow them to be folded together. In most, but not all, triptychs, the middle panel is the largest, so that it is winged by two other tableaux, which are therefore structurally and thematically somewhat subordinate to it, though again, these side panels can be considered discrete works of art. Frisch himself underscored the independent character of each dramatic panel, noting that they were not three stages ("Stationen") of a dramatic plot, but rather constituted three scenic aspects of one theme.[16] The overarching theme of *Triptychon*, the topic uniting all three panels, is death. The first panel revolves around the funeral and wake of Matthis Proll, whose latent presence is evoked by a silent actor who sits in a white rocking chair. This mute figure is the object of constant comments and entreaties by his widow. Broadly speaking, this panel evokes the impact of death and the dead upon the living, for the deceased, and the nature of mortality, are the focus of much of the dialogue. The second, and by far the largest, tableau—the equivalent of the central panel in a triptych altarpiece—takes place in the realm of the dead. All the characters are deceased, represented on stage at the age at which they died, so that Matthis Proll—whose empty rocking chair stands in the foreground of the stage in this panel—appears older than his late father, with whom he converses at various moments. All interactions among the deceased are framed by their deeds and relationships in life, so the variation on the theme here is how life *in death* is shaped by prior earthly existence.

The third panel is dominated by the dialogue of Roger and Francine, a young couple who met at Proll's funeral in the first panel, and, offstage, subsequently developed a relationship. Though neither figure appears in the second panel, Francine is deceased in the third. As Butler notes, Roger in this concluding tableau is "presented as a latter-day Orpheus who tries to rescue Francine" from the domain of the dead.[17] Roger is intent on bringing his twentieth-century Eurydice back to the realm of the living by staging a permutated version of their final encounter as two living beings, a late-evening dialogue on a Paris bench, which had been followed by Francine's departure for a train station and concomitant permanent exit from his life. Despite the talkative Roger's best efforts, this encounter evolves as it had in the past; Francine can only repeat her original lines, as Roger continuously observes, and the activities that had provided the backdrop for (and sometimes interrupted) their conversation occur exactly as they had in history. Given Francine's status, and the circumstance that posthumous facticity rather than the proclivities and existential limits of a living being like *Biografie*'s Kürmann conditions the motif of repetition, one can speak of the third panel's variation on the earlier play's core thematic as the enactment of eternal recurrence in death. Though this third panel will therefore be the focus of attention, the triptych-like interlocking of the drama as a whole necessitates an examination of the other two panels as well, particularly the second one, where patterns established in life are fundamentally iterated in the realm of the dead. However, the first panel is also of structural interest for the final tableau, for if "Das erste Bild" demonstrates how the dead—and mortality in general—shape the discourse of the living, "Das dritte Bild" inverts this topos by showing how the living futilely attempt to impact, indeed alter the life course of, the dead.

The irrevocability of chance statements and deeds that take place in a relationship once one of the partners is deceased is a powerful motif in the first panel. It is a relatively realistic scene; the only fantastic element is the presence of a silent Proll, a presence simply symbolic of the powerful force he still exerts in his wife's memory, and thus he is not truly a revenant like Francine in the third panel or the living dead in the drama's centerpiece. Sophie Proll had sat next to her mortally ill husband the night before he died, but he had dismissed her, claiming that he wished to be alone. She found him dead the next morning.[18] This circumstance seems to pain her more than other, logically more troubling episodes in their relationship, such as his affairs. He was a materialist who did not wish for a pastor to be present at his funeral, but was perhaps not so extreme in this regard as Roger, who emphasizes the absence of human consciousness without a biological foundation, regards perspectives on death that go beyond its aspect as a biological fact as mystifications, and stresses the finality of life's events: "Ich meine: die einzelnen Ereignisse unsres Lebens, jedes an seinem Platz in der Zeit, verändern sich nicht." (The various events in our lives, each one in its own place and time—there they stand, unalterable.)[19] Clearly, there is no play director of the sort found in *Biografie* to contradict this materialist perspective, but it becomes ironic when one considers Roger's attempt to alter the course of an event in his life—his final encounter with Francine—in *Triptychon*'s last panel. The living Francine of the first panel is rather put off by Roger's rationalist ("vernünftig") thinking (15), and it is striking that Frisch shows no real affinity between the two figures, making the revelation that they had become lovers offstage a bit of a mystery. However, they are both intellectuals and are clearly engaged in their conversation concerning the relationship between biology and theology, a conversation inspired by the funeral for Matthis Proll.

In the case of Roger and Francine, then, the impact of the dead upon the living is constituted by the kindling of their relationship. For Sophie, her husband's death creates the material manifestation of a circumstance already latent in their life together and evident through her half-scolding, half-despairing monologues with the deceased; the end of a marriage, the disappearance of a relationship. This is made evident in the first panel's only truly supernatural moment; at the conclusion, Matthis leaves his rocking chair and departs the stage; the final line has the shocked Sophie ask: "Matthis, wo bist du?" (Matthis, where are you?)[20] With respect to the other guests, the funeral engenders another variation on Frisch's repetition motif; from the pastor who cites Christian dogma concerning resurrection to funeral attendees discussing finance and politics to the awkward condolences proffered to Sophie to dietary advice, there are only iterations of the same clichés one hears all the time, the infinitely repetitive qualities of which are enhanced by an utter lack of metaphoric nuance and refinement. The conversations of these guests constitute Nietzsche's eternal recurrence of the same at its most banal level.

In one of her tirades against the deceased Matthis in the first panel, Sophie expresses irritation at the presence of his "Mannequin," a lover of her husband who, contrary to the widow's expressed prohibition, attended the funeral (21). In the expansive second panel, with its large cast of characters, this model, Katrin Schimanski, becomes the central character ("Zentralgestalt"), as Ulrich Ramer has observed, for around her figure threads are spun that create a nexus among the other figures who make an appearance there, some of whom—including Matthis Proll—are her former lovers. Katrin reflects the inescapable certitudes of the infinite beyond, and it is she who expresses the insight that the dead are condemned to eternally repeat themselves, to say the same things again and again without the capacity to change things, or even to cause pain to others.[21]

Hans Jürg Lüthi has articulated an interesting intersection in *Biografie* between what he describes as the theme of repetition and the dramaturgy of permutation. This is a cogent way of describing the dialectic between variations in the course of life permitted by the play director, in other words, *his* dramaturgy of permutation, and the fundamental iterations Kürmann's persona and external limitations on reshaping his past force upon him, elements that constitute the theme of repetition. Lüthi contrasts the dramaturgy of permutation in *Biografie* with what he terms the dramaturgy of necessity ("Notwendigkeit") in *Andorra*, which shapes the fated historical determinism in that play's developing narrative.[22] In the second panel of *Triptychon*, it is the irrevocable quality of death imbuing the netherworld existence of the characters that enacts a dramaturgy of necessity and the eternal recurrence, or repetition, of the same of which Katrin complains. These take the form, in Katrin's case, of brief life encounters between herself and former lovers that are reenacted without variation in the realm of the dead. However, this panel also offers striking permutations in life relationships created by what we might call death circumstances. Thus, the panel opens with a dialogue between an old man ("Alter") and a physically younger gas-station attendant (31). Gradually, it is revealed that the old man is Matthis Proll and the younger individual is his father, who had died at a younger age than his son. Repetition and permutation mark their dialogue in the netherworld; as in life, the father criticizes the son's fishing techniques, but the son is permitted to vent his displeasure at the gas-station attendant for leaving his wife (Matthis Proll's mother) in debt when he died (36–37), a resentment Matthis obviously could not have expressed at that time in his life. Matthis also tells his father about his participation in the Spanish Civil War, a political act that took place after the father's death. Thus, as in *Biografie*, there is an interplay between permutation/variation and repetition/recurrence. However, while in *Biografie* this dialectic is determined and circumscribed by conditions in life supervised by the play director, in Frisch's later play it is conditioned by the permanent facticity of death. Given the immutability and irreversibility of the realm of death brought to the stage in the second panel, there is no need for a "Spielleiter" to manage the contours of this dialectic.

Nevertheless, a figure who appears in the second and third panels of *Triptychon* plays a key role somewhat dramaturgically related to that of *Biografie*'s play director: the "Clochard." The French term signifies a tramp or vagabond, and the Clochard had indeed ended his life in destitution and vagrancy, having been unable to endure the success he finally gained as an actor. He remains an outcast in the netherworld, ignored there by the characters whom he addresses. However, he also functions, as Cornelia Steffahn has noted, as a commentator who sometimes steps out of the dramatic action and explains what is taking place. As a marginalized observer who also interprets for the audience, he is reminiscent of the Shakespearean fool.[23] While the play director of Frisch's earlier work is the central empowered figure, and in this sense diametrically opposite to the Clochard, his role is also invested with an explanatory function for the audience, and he—as a director—stands outside the narrative action of the plays within the play. While, as Beda Allemann has noted, *Biografie*'s director serves his clients without commenting on their behavior or establishing a connection with the audience behind their back,[24] his instructions and commands constitute for the audience the equivalent explanatory function, as when he tells Kürmann that having become a Communist based on the acceptance of this one significant permutation, he is no longer tenable as a professor; this sets up the appearance of the assistant as Hornacher in the professor's apartment, a meeting that leads to Kürmann's dismissal (116–18). While the pastor from the first panel of *Triptychon* reappears in the second panel and poses diverse questions to the deceased, questions designed to provide the audience information on the earthly existence of these now departed souls, it is the Clochard who is most effective at evoking the banality and repetitiveness of eternity. For example, after the pastor—who, because of his role as a sort of mediator between the reader and the dead in the second panel,[25] actually converses with the Clochard—lets him know that a pilot who dies in a plane crash has found his child, the vagabond observes this reunion. He describes verbally the game of toss and catch between parent and child, stripping it of its potential visual charm by stressing its repetitive character, with permutations that do not relieve this monotonous quality: "Jetzt wirft das

Kind, jetzt fängt der Papa, jetzt wirft der Papa, jetzt fängt das Kind—nein, es fängt nicht, aber der Papa holt den Ball und wirft noch einmal, jetzt fängt das Kind." (Now the child throws, now Daddy catches, now Daddy throws, now the child catches—no, he misses, but Daddy fetches the ball and throws again, now the child catches.)[26] Earlier, he had explained what the dead do and do not do; they do not curse, beg, piss, copulate, etc., but they do wander in the eternity of their pasts "und lecken an ihren dummen Geschichten, bis sie aufgeleckt sind" (and lick their stupid life stories till they're licked right away).[27] This explanation is central to revealing to the reader or audience member what he or she is witnessing the characters do as they re-enact scenes from their lives, or experience slightly permutated relationships, as in the encounter between Matthis Proll and his father discussed above. In the netherworld as the Clochard describes it and as we perceive it, there is an eternal return of the banal same, a same that becomes more desiccated with each repetition.

The best examples of how the dead continuously lick at the wounds of their old "dumb" histories are provided by minor figures such as a criminal who continually seeks to forge a bond with the man he killed; as they were strangers in life, the victim can barely perceive even the existence of his murderer, and no one knows the killer in the netherworld. A man who courts a woman with roses is unable to speak with her, as they had not spoken in life. A flute player keeps repeating the same melody and always breaks off when he makes the same mistake. A man named Klas is condemned to experience eternally his frustration at his former lover Katrin's slovenliness. Only the dead who reconcile themselves to the inalterability of their posthumous existence find a certain peace of mind, as is the case with Matthis Proll and Katrin. As Gertrud Pickar argues: "In this world after death, the only relief appears to be the realization of the inescapability of the situation, and the acceptance of its inalterability. Unlike Sartre, where the figures continue to resist and struggle and thereby maintain their claim to existence, here the only hope is the gradual acknowledgement of the inevitability of eternal repetition."[28] When Nietzsche suggested the embrace of the eternal return of the same was the human individual's most life-affirming act, he was, of course, referring to the world of the living. In the netherworld, Frisch seems to suggest, resignation rather than affirmation is the only insightful response to the paradigm of eternal recurrence.

If the first panel portrays how the dead impact the existence and discourse of the living, while the second panel shows how the events of their own lives set the eternal pattern for the intercourse, or isolation, of the dead, the third panel's central plot strand illustrates the attempt of the living to influence the—obviously past—life on earth of the dead. Of course, this effort is completely futile, for, as Roger proclaims: "Das ist es, was ich treibe: Ich rede mit einer Toten" (This is what I'm doing:

talking to a dead woman), but "Man soll nicht mit den Toten reden!" (One shouldn't talk with the dead.)[29] This latter remark is made after a Parisian policeman comes upon them and Francine repeats a comment Roger remembered her uttering at their last meeting as a living couple to the same gendarme: "NOUS ATTENDONS LE MATIN, MONSIEUR" (93, 105; caps in the original). During their conversation, Francine, talking about their past together, proclaims: "Wir sind nicht tot gewesen, Roger, das nicht!—wie jetzt." (We weren't dead, Roger, never dead—as we are now.)[30] She seems to imply here that Roger himself is dead. Indeed, Pickar claims (contrary, as she acknowledges, to a majority of critics) that Roger's suicide at the conclusion of the play is "a repetition of an earlier event," that "both Francine and Roger are among the dead, caught up in the web of their painful and unresolved relationship and forced to utter again the words of their past, to suffer anew the agony of their heartache."[31] However, this perspective seems implausible for a couple of reasons. For one thing, as Katrin noted in the second panel in a previously cited remark, iterated conversations and events in the underworld do *not* cause the dead pain, and only Roger betrays real emotional anguish in the last panel. Second, Roger, contrary to the dead, and contrary to Francine in the third panel, is desperately trying to avoid a simple repetition of his last conversation with his lover when she was alive. He attempts the sort of illocutionary manipulation the dead are simply incapable of undertaking in the play. Throughout their encounter in the third panel, Roger consistently tries to have Francine say something that would break her silence in their final encounter as living lovers, and expresses exasperation when she does break her silence by simply repeating her lines from that last meeting. When she concludes this final encounter as a dead woman with a slew of sentences, interrupted by pauses, uttered during their breakup, Roger realizes that all such restaging of this agonizing last mutual event in their lives would involve an eternal recurrence of the same. Reacting with the despair of those horrified at the proposition of Nietzsche's demon in *Die fröhliche Wissenschaft*, a despair only the living can experience, he shoots himself (114–15). Because Francine simply repeats everything she said when she was alive in her terminal encounter with Roger in this third panel, one must assume that her reference to their both being dead now was also uttered when they were alive, and underscores their emotional state after their love has come to an end.

After Roger places the revolver at his temple and (apparently) pulls the trigger, there is no sound, but only sudden darkness, followed by daylight. The park bench occupied by Roger and Francine is now empty, and the only sound is of traffic. As at the outset of this panel, one hears the drone of traffic at regularized intervals (87, 115). This represents the play's final iteration; existence goes on as before, in routine impersonal patterns. The same returns with one exception; human individuals are absent. *Triptychon* thus concludes with an almost apocalyptic bleakness. Koepke has indeed argued that the play is imbued by "pervasive pessimism," exuding an atmosphere of hopelessness and futility. He opines that, though Frisch revised *Triptychon* a number of times, "It has not become more acceptable." This play constitutes in Koepke's view the literary equivalent of the "grim morality play" tableaux evident in the church art from which the work draws its name, "a monument to the burden of the dead past."[32] Certainly, the desolate ambience manifest in the drama's final image is not relieved by any note of optimism; the silent suicide and subsequent absence of visible humanity seems to negate even the validity of existentialist struggle evident in some of Sartre's dramas, which constituted a key influence on Frisch's late theater.

Nevertheless, when we consider that *Triptychon* is more a literary play than a performance piece, we need not regard its last scene as its last word. Indeed, Roger's comments quite early in the first panel posit a constructive view of mortality, certainly reflective of the existentialist philosophy central to Frisch's worldview and possibly influenced, in this instance, by Heideggerian ontology.[33] In his discussion with Francine on the biological and spiritual dimensions of human consciousness, Roger claims that even if the concept of eternal life is untenable, death's mystification consists in the circumstance that it establishes the truth of our lives by imbuing them with finality. When Francine asks him to explain this perspective, Roger responds: "Es gilt, was wir leben. Ich meine: die einzelnen Ereignisse unsres Lebens, jedes an seinem Platz in der Zeit, verändern sich nicht. Das ist ihre Ewigkeit" (It is what we have lived that counts. The various events in our lives, each one in its own place and time—there they stand, unalterable. And in that sense eternal.)[34] To be sure, Roger's view here accords with Frisch's general tendency to represent how life's miscarriages have consequences that extend into eternity, a theme, Lüthi notes, that occupied the author since his youth and received its final expression in *Triptychon*.[35] The eternal recurrences of the netherworld evident in the second panel and in the deceased Francine's iterative utterances in the third panel exist in a virtually ekphrastic relationship to Roger's comments here. However, Roger's argument that death imbues our life with its truth because of its finality, so that "Wir leben endgültig" (we live definitively),[36] also echoes Heidegger's famous and highly influential analysis of death as the constituent quality for individuated human existence (*Dasein*) in *Sein und Zeit* (*Being and Time*, 1927). Roger's assertion that mortality imposes a conclusive, definitive quality to the character of our lives is closely related to Heidegger's view in *Sein und Zeit* that death's permanency is what provides *Dasein* its existential possibilities and enables its meaningfulness. A genuine awareness that we live in a manner necessarily imbued by finality affords *Dasein* both its authenticity and its responsibility, according to Heidegger.

Of course, Roger's view as enunciated early in the first panel is only theoretical, and his life after meeting Francine is as marked by miscalculation and failure as that of the other characters in *Triptychon*. Francine's question to Roger in the first panel, immediately after he explained his views on how life acquires permanency through death, whether he had ever lost someone he had loved as no other (15) was answered, as Roger indicates in the third panel, in a buffet line, where he was told he had never loved anyone. This accusation in Roger's memory was enunciated in both the formal "Sie" and the informal "du" modes of second-person address, and confirmed by his behavior toward women, including Francine (101–3). He remarks that Ernst Bloch has died, and that the future belongs to fear, implying that Bloch's death extinguishes "the principle of hope" proclaimed in the title of Bloch's most famous book, so that only fear remains and the individual is subject to a bleak fate for which he or she is not responsible. Roger then wonders if it is true that he had extorted Francine with his threats of suicide. He is so incapable of accepting existential responsibility for his actions, indeed for the shaping and defining of the individual events of his life, and for living with a sense of the finality that comes from inevitable death—in other words, for living according to the parameters of the worldview he had enunciated in the first panel—that he wishes Francine to take responsibility for defining his past deeds. He wants Francine to decide whether he had indeed tormented her for three years with threats to take his own life, and whether his drunken attempt to scale a building represented extortion ("Erpressung") by revealing such a suicidal intention (92–93). Having failed to live as though life's deeds take on permanent consequences through mortality, he futilely attempts to obviate these consequences by revising his disastrous relationship with Francine after she has already died.

However, Roger's failure to live according to his existentialist perspective does not lessen its ontological validity. Despite the brevity of its articulation, Roger's postulate that mortality fundamentally defines life moves toward Heidegger's "understanding of human finitude as a supreme possibility of existence that both intimates freedom and reveals selfhood," a pithy summary of Heidegger's treatment of death in *Sein und Zeit* by Sean Ireton, who finds a precedence for this view in Nietzsche, among others.[37] While Heidegger, as Ireton notes, came to refute Nietzsche's paradigm of the eternal recurrence of the same because he found that it was rooted in Western metaphysics,[38] both Heidegger's ontological principle concerning the awareness of death as a grounding for life and Nietzsche's life-affirming formulations on the eternal recurrence of the same provide related modes of guidance for those seeking to live in an aware, self-reflexive, individuated, forward-looking manner. Frisch may have sought to convey such thinking in his late plays.[39] However, *Biografie*'s Kürmann and *Triptychon*'s Roger reveal that fallen humanity is unlikely to follow the dictates of lofty but iconoclastic philosophical ideals—metaphysical, existential, or otherwise. As Ireton claims in his summary of Heidegger's position on human finitude in *Sein und Zeit*, "generally we live and die according to the habits of everyday *Dasein*, but he goes to great lengths to point us toward a more authentic style of existence, which of course presupposes an authentic comprehension of death."[40] Caught up in what Heidegger famously referred to as the thrownness (*Geworfenheit*) of such everyday *Dasein*,[41] even perspicacious intellectuals such as Kürmann and Roger can neither break from, alter, nor affirmatively embrace the cycle of eternal return. Thus, Kürmann can only repeat his life without affirming it, and Roger's "authentic comprehension of death" is ultimately of no avail to him, for, in the last panel, he vainly tries to overcome the conclusiveness of mortality and shows that he has forgotten his own, earlier, insight.

Notes

[1] Late in life, Frisch published a brief dramatic sketch entitled *Jonas und sein Veteran* (Jonas and His Veteran, 1989). It has been cogently argued that this work represents only conditionally an exception to his lack of poetic activity in his declining years, for it is essentially a polemic in dialogue form, lacking an aesthetic dimension, against Switzerland's continued maintenance of an extensive and expensive military. See Jürgen H. Petersen, *Max Frisch*, 3rd ed. (Stuttgart: J. B. Metzler, 2002), 181–82.

[2] See Michael Butler, *The Plays of Max Frisch* (London: Macmillan, 1985), 144–45, which lists the world premieres of all of Frisch's plays (obviously not including *Jonas und sein Veteran*). *Triptychon* is the only play listed by Butler not to have received its initial staging at the Schauspielhaus Zürich. Frisch's unusual decision to have the play first performed in French reflects his early reticence about this work. See Butler, 131.

[3] See, for example, Sigrid Mayer, "*Biografie: Ein Spiel*: Stiller und/oder Gantenbein auf der Bühne?" in *Max Frisch: Aspekte des Bühnenwerks*, ed. Gerhard P. Knapp (Bern: Lang, 1979), 371–400; Cornelia Steffahn, *Altern, Sterben und Tod im Spätwerk von Max Frisch* (Hamburg: Dr. Kovač, 2000), 5–6; and Karin and Lutz Tantow, *Max Frisch: Ein Klassiker der Moderne* (Munich: Heyne, 1994), 145–46.

[4] The influence of Nietzsche and Heidegger on different aspects of Frisch's late work has been noted by Walter Schmitz, *Max Frisch: Das Spätwerk (1962–1982); Eine Einführung* (Tübingen: Francke, 1985), 15 and 166n85.

[5] Wulf Koepke, *Understanding Max Frisch* (Columbia: University of South Carolina Press, 1991), 84–85.

[6] Max Frisch, *Biografie: Ein Spiel; Neue Fassung 1984* (Frankfurt am Main: Suhrkamp, 1985), 6. Hereafter cited in the text. English translations taken from *Biography: A Game*, trans. Birgit Schreyer Duarte (London/New York/Calcutta: Seagull, 2010). In earlier variants, such as the one printed in the 1976 edition

of Frisch's collected works, the "Spielleiter" is referred to as the "Registrator" (recorder), and the various roles assumed by the male and female assistants in the later edition are listed among the cast of characters. See Frisch, *Gesammelte Werke* (*GW*) 5, ed. Hans Mayer and Walter Schmitz (Frankfurt am Main: Suhrkamp, 1986), 482. The switch to the designation "play director" from "recorder," and the consistent reference to this director's "assistants" rather than the naming of the characters they perform enhance the revised drama's "play within a play" architectonics.

[7] On Frisch's use of lighting alternatives to indicate stages in the course of enacting variations in Kürmann's biography, see Butler, *The Plays of Max Frisch*, 117–18.

[8] Robert C. Holub, *Friedrich Nietzsche* (New York: Twayne, 1995), 62–63.

[9] Erna M. Dahms, *Zeit und Zeiterlebnis in den Werken Max Frischs: Bedeutung und technische Darstellung* (Berlin: Walter de Gruyter, 1976), 60 and 60n96.

[10] Dahms, *Zeit und Zeiterlebnis*, 60–76.

[11] Butler, *The Plays of Max Frisch*, 121.

[12] On this point, see Marianne Biedermann, *Das politische Theater von Max Frisch* (Lampertheim: Schäuble, 1974), 128–32.

[13] Dahms, *Zeit und Zeiterlebnis*, 167.

[14] Koepke, *Understanding Max Frisch*, 84.

[15] Heinz Gockel, *Max Frisch: Drama und Dramaturgie* (Munich: R. Oldenbourg, 1989), 106–8. In the earlier version of the play cited by Gockel, this destiny is clearly posited by the "Registrator" to be an irrevocably imminent death, death in seven years (Frisch, *Gesammelte Werke*, 5.2:573 and 578), while the "Spielleiter" in the later version holds out the hope for a possible cure of Kürmann's illness in a few years (171).

[16] Frisch, cited in Schmitz, *Max Frisch: Das Spätwerk*, 126. Schmitz also provides in this opening page of his discussion of *Triptychon* a concise analysis of how Frisch's play employs the architectonics of a traditional Christian triptych altarpiece.

[17] Butler, *The Plays of Max Frisch*, 138.

[18] Frisch, *Triptychon: Drei Szenische Bilder* (Frankfurt am Main: Suhrkamp, 1978), 19. Hereafter cited in the text.

[19] *Triptychon*, 15. English translation taken from *Triptych: Three Scenic Panels*, trans. Geoffrey Skelton (New York/London: Harcourt Brace Jovanovich, 1981), 6.

[20] *Triptychon*, 28. Trans. Skelton, 13.

[21] Ulrich Ramer, *Max Frisch: Rollen-Spiele* (Frankfurt am Main: R. G. Fischer, 1993), 302–3.

[22] Hans Jürg Lüthi, *Max Frisch* (Munich: A. Francke, 1981), 96.

[23] Steffahn, *Altern, Sterben und Tod*, 126.

[24] Beda Allemann, "Die Struktur der Komödie bei Max Frisch," in *Max Frisch*, ed. Walter Schmitz (Frankfurt am Main: Suhrkamp, 1987), 328. Citing the edition of the play printed in the fifth volume of the *Gesammelte Werke*, Allemann

refers to this figure as the "Registrator." This is also the case with Walter Höllerer, who finds that this figure is related to the "Kommentator" of Brecht's epic theater. See Frisch, *Dramaturgisches: Ein Briefwechsel mit Walter Höllerer* (Berlin: Literarisches Colloquium, 1976), 21.

[25] See Ramer, *Max Frisch: Rollen-Spiele*, 303–4.

[26] *Triptychon*, 81. Trans. Skelton, 51.

[27] *Triptychon*, 43. Trans. Skelton, 26.

[28] Gertrud Bauer Pickar, "Hades Revisited: Max Frisch's *Triptychon*," *German Quarterly* 59 (1986): 61. Like other critics interested in the issue of prior dramatic works that influenced the composition of *Triptychon*, Pickar cites not only Sartre's *Huis clos* (*No Exit*, 1944), but also Thornton Wilder's *Our Town* (1938). See, in addition to 61, esp. 52–53, 55, 59, 62, and 62n1.

[29] *Triptychon*, 99, 105. Trans. Skelton, 63, 66. Translation modified.

[30] *Triptychon*, 107. Trans. Skelton, 67.

[31] Pickar, "Hades Revisited," 58.

[32] Koepke, *Understanding Max Frisch*, 107–8.

[33] See Schmitz, *Max Frisch: Das Spätwerk*, 15 and 41.

[34] *Triptychon*, 15. Trans. Skelton, 6.

[35] Lüthi, *Max Frisch*, 103.

[36] *Triptychon*, 15. Trans. Skelton, 6.

[37] Sean Ireton, *An Ontological Study of Death: From Hegel to Heidegger* (Pittsburgh: Duquesne University Press, 2007), 229.

[38] Ireton, *An Ontological Study of Death*, 235–36. In his two-volume work on Nietzsche, Heidegger argues that the eternal return of the same is metaphysical by virtue of its rendering existent being, "das Seiende," infinite, indeed transforming becoming into a stabilized being as the manifestation of the highest will to power. See Heidegger, *Nietzsche: Erster Band*, in *Gesamtausgabe*, vol. 6.1 (Frankfurt am Main: Klostermann, 1996), 225–423, esp. 418.

[39] For a reading of Frisch's late works that contrasts his own interpretation of this mature fiction, a self-interpretation enunciated in interviews and correspondence, as showing the need for individuals to assume agency in their lives and revise their thinking, with the deep, pervasive ambience of pessimism, stagnation, and inescapable repetition that in fact imbues his prose and drama after *Gantenbein*, see Marga I. Weigel, "'Gebärde eines Gesteuerten'? Zum Spätwerk Max Frischs," *Seminar* 24 (1988): 58–70. Frisch himself commented on his consternation that *Biografie* comes across as a "Schicksalslauf," that audiences mostly interpreted the play as a confirmation of the fated character of existence, of the belief that we cannot change anything about our biographies. See Frisch, *Dramaturgisches*, 28.

[40] Ireton, *An Ontological Study of Death*, 270.

[41] On Heidegger's reflections regarding how everyday being blocks an authentic engagement with being-unto-death and superficially renders less burdensome the individual's perception of his "Geworfenheit in den Tod" (Thrownness into death), see Heidegger, *Sein und Zeit*, 6th ed. (Tübingen: Neomarius, 1949), 255–60.

6: Max Frisch's Early Fiction

Margit Unser

Max Frisch was sixteen when he sent his first play, *Stahl* (Steel), to Max Reinhardt at the Deutsches Theater in Berlin, but when the rejection slip came back from Berlin, the play was consigned to flames. So it was not in 1937, but as early as 1927 that he first voluntarily destroyed some of his own writings. The play had been typed on a rented typewriter, for which Frisch had to use his pocket money. That is perhaps why he was writing in a hurry. However, the rejection from Berlin did not give rise to any sense of resignation or self-doubt; on the contrary, Frisch immediately began writing a new play.[1]

We do not know what exactly he destroyed in 1937 when he went into a forest to consign all his unpublished early manuscripts to the flames. Frisch said that his diaries were among the irretrievably lost texts.[2] They probably also included the play *Der Schüler im Himmel* (Schoolboy in Heaven),[3] which he wrote in March 1927 for a school performance, and also presumably the three-act play entitled *13. Trupp* (Troop 13),[4] which was announced for a family evening of the Free Military Preparatory Training organization (F.M.V.) in 1928. Was the manuscript of *Flucht* (Escape), which he had sent to his friend Werner Coninx to look at in 1935,[5] among the works destroyed? Or was *Stern des Friedens: Ein Märchen für Zeitgenossen*, which he mentions in a letter to his professor Walter Muschg, written on February 1, 1936 among them?[6] Or perhaps he destroyed the "Doppelgänger" story, on which he stopped working after a damning verdict from Werner Coninx?[7] We do not know. On the other hand, Frisch's journalistic writings and his first two works of prose dating from the 1930s have, luckily, been preserved for researchers to study.

A Freelance Journalist

After a first text, *Mimische Partitur?* (Mimical Score?), which Frisch sent to the *Neue Zürcher Zeitung* unsolicited and which, to his great astonishment and pleasure, was published on May 27, 1931, we know of no other writings during the next twelve months.

In March 1932, Frisch's father died, leaving the family facing a mountain of debt. The young Max felt obliged to cut short his German studies in order to keep his own and his mother's heads above water. During this personal crisis, Max Frisch became interested in a subject that he would approach from all angles throughout his life as a writer: the suffering of the self. In April 1932, his article *Was bin ich?* (What Am I?) appeared in the student magazine *Zürcher Student*, in which the young student questioned the meaning of life. This article can be read as a key text not only for the 1930s but for all his future work. In it, the young student raises the existentialist question and thus, almost certainly still unconsciously, discovered one of the themes that was to be of burning interest to him: the quest for the purpose, the position, the role of every single individual. This self-questioning was to find expression in his first two novels, and would ultimately lead to the conclusion that it is necessary to conduct a radical search for one's role in life.[8]

In order to support his mother financially, Max Frisch began work as a freelance journalist, initially for the *Neue Zürcher Zeitung* and later for other German-language newspapers. In an interview in 1974, he describes this as a mistake, because, as he puts it, he practiced journalism not for its own sake but rather as a lesser kind of literature.[9] Against that background, his level of productivity is astonishing. Between 1931 and 1954, the year in which his novel *Stiller* was published, he wrote 189 articles for the *Neue Zürcher Zeitung* alone. They generally appeared in the literary section. He began his autobiographical writing very early on; for one thing, this was his way of working through his relationships with the opposite sex. For example, his parting from the eighteen-year-old actress Else Schebesta, with whom Frisch was unhappily in love, was given literary expression in an early feature article.[10]

One has the feeling that, in the first few months after the death of his father, Frisch embarked on a search that plunged him into the deepest self-doubt. It was not only a search for a material livelihood, but also, and probably even more intensely, a search for clarity; clarity about his own well-being, about his spiritual torments, about finding his own way in life. In the summer of 1932, he joined a student labor colony building a forest road. In an article that appeared in the *Neue Zürcher Zeitung* on September 29, 1932, Frisch describes this work as a pilgrimage to "Selbsterlösung," a liberation from oneself, hoping "to be able to shake off one's whole ego," "sein ganzes Ich abschütteln zu können."

In 1933, Max Frisch felt compelled to travel abroad. One may speculate about what it was that gave rise to this desire. In any case, the World Ice Hockey Championships in Prague provided him with a good opportunity to escape the self-destructive doubts that tortured his everyday life at home. To be able to afford the visit, he offered his services as a journalist to both the *Neue Zürcher Zeitung* and the *Tages-Anzeiger*.

However, the trip was only an excuse to spend nine months after the World Championships traveling in the Balkans.[11] His travels, which involved many long, solitary walks, took him from Prague to Hungary, then through Serbia, Bosnia, and Dalmatia to the Black Sea, to what is now called Istanbul, and through central Greece. Many of his impressions of this journey and the happy summer days he spent in the *Pension Solitudo* in Ragusa (now Dubrovnik) on the Dalmatian coast are reflected in his first novel. Just a few months after he returned, *Jürg Reinhart: Eine sommerliche Schicksalsfahrt* (Jürg Reinhart: A Fateful Summer Trip) was published, a poetic invocation of this, his first encounter with the sea.

Jürg Reinhart: Eine sommerliche Schicksalsfahrt

His first novel gives an insight into how the young Frisch worked. In Zurich, the subjectively colored reports that he brought back from his Balkan journey were "patched together" into a novel.[12] Rendered more literary and distanced, yet clearly peppered with autobiographical reflections, the novel tells the story of a young man who sets off to discover the world and achieve something.[13]

Jürg Reinhart spends some carefree summer months in Ragusa, staying in a small hotel by the sea. The sea plays an important symbolic role in the novel. He earns his living by writing newspaper articles that are published in his home country. He often goes out sailing, with this thoughts circling round three women: a Dutch baroness, the maid Hilde, and the invalid Inge, daughter of the hotel landlady. While he tries to evade the amorous attentions of the baroness, his clumsy attempts to come closer to Hilde fail. Inge, however, becomes a real friend, with whom he can share his ideas about love and sexuality.

At this time Max Frisch had little experience with women. He had fallen in love a few times, but he was otherwise very reserved in his relations with women. It is therefore all the more surprising how openly he was able to write in his novel about relationships with the opposite sex. At the same time, there is more to this first work than the purely autobiographical subject matter.

> Nun muss ich mich irgendwo und irgendwie bewähren, damit ich diese Angst loswerde und meine Selbstachtung nicht durch die Frau suche, wo ich sie [. . .] niemals finden werde. So wenig wie ich sie im verdienten Geld fand. Man wird nicht Mann durch die Frau. [. . .] auch ein keuscher Mann ist ein Mann. Und erst, wenn ich mir dies bewiesen habe, nämlich durch eine männliche Tat [. . .] (123–24)

> [Now I have to prove myself somewhere and somehow in order to overcome this fear and not to seek self-respect through woman, where I will never find it. Just like I never found it in the money I

> earned. You don't become a man through woman. [. . .] a chaste man is also a man. And only when I have proved that to myself by committing a manly deed [. . .]]

Here again we see the thread that runs throughout Max Frisch's life and work: the search for the meaning of life, for the truest form of existence, for self-determination in living.

Even in this inaugural work, we can see the first hints of the concept that Frisch would explore throughout his later works, the idea that fixed images are to be avoided, in this case others' fixed images of who and what an individual should be or become:

> [. . .] wenn ich ringsum von fertigen Menschen gestossen werde, wenn ich sozusagen von Hand zu Hand gereicht werde und mich jedermann formen kann nach seinem Bilde, so zerbröckelt man schliesslich. Jetzt bin ich wieder allein [. . .] ich glaube, man muss sein Ich austragen [. . .] (121)

> [[. . .] when I am pushed around by ready-made people who encircle me, when I am so to speak passed on from hand to hand and everyone can shape me according to his image, that is a way to finally crumble. Now I am alone again [. . .] I believe that one has to allow one's self to slowly grow inside oneself.]

This passage shows Frisch battling against his lifelong fear of being pigeonholed or reduced to a mere imitation.

This novel also tackles another weighty problem: Jürg Reinhart must face the question of whether assisting his sick friend Inge to die can be ethically justified. When he returns to Ragusa from a long journey, Inge is dying. An injection could bring her suffering to an end. Only one person has the strength to perform this act: Jürg. Max Frisch sometimes engages in philosophical speculation about a controversial topic here. It is surprising to see, so early in his oeuvre, the stylistic patterns and the themes to which he would return in his later work, for example, the dialogue with the kingdom of the dead in *Triptychon* or the familiar motif of an indeterminate guilt that is beyond the jurisdiction of any court in *Blaubart.*[14]

Frisch used his debut novel as building material for a sequel. In 1943, *Jürg Reinhart*, in a revised version and shortened by two-thirds, reappeared as the first part of Frisch's third novel *J'adore ce qui me brûle oder Die Schwierigen* (I Love What Burns me, or The Difficult Ones). In the new version, Jürg Reinhart is a failure in life and finishes by committing suicide. Once again the problematic theme of relationships between the sexes becomes a central thread: the women whom Jürg Reinhart is now able to attract without any difficulty, but ultimately loses, plunge him into an abyss of jealousy he has never experienced before.

The prose written by the young Frisch in the mid-1930s was inspired and shaped by the prevalent Swiss writing style of the time. The "Zeitgeist" of the time was dominated by popular, conservative "Heimatliteratur" (literature rooted in the homeland).[15] Daniel Foppa comes to the conclusion that Frisch's reviews in the *Neue Zürcher Zeitung* display vitalistic and anti-intellectual traits of the "Heimatdichtung" (regionalist, rural literature) movement.[16] Could this verdict be mitigated by the knowledge that the articles in question were commissioned pieces of work and that Frisch's assessments and opinions coincided with those of Eduard Korrodi, editor of the *NZZ* literary section from 1928 to 1950, not least because the young author was dependent on his approval? Probably not, because, as Alexander Stephan argues, the picture of Frisch as an apolitical, bourgeois writer is supported by his comments on contemporary authors in his early essays.[17] All the reviews, critiques, and essays that he wrote in 1933 and 1934 about books by Richard Billinger, Max René Hesse, Hans Carossa, and Hermann Burte are written in the language of the intellectual and literary trends of the mid-1930s.

Frisch was never anti-Semitic, but he was also not always antifascist. He was locked into isolationist thinking, dominated, as was the case for the majority of the Swiss population at the time, by a complacent, self-satisfied image of Switzerland and by its self-confidence as a nation. Trapped in the cultural and political climate of intellectual defense of the nation, he was in no position to foresee the scale of the catastrophes that German National Socialism would bring. The fact that Frisch's writings at this time were largely apolitical, or to the extent that they were political at all, stolidly pro-Swiss and isolationist, was probably the only reason he was able to get his apolitical first novels published by the Deutsche Verlags-Anstalt, which was already subject to censorship by the National Socialists at that time. This is why, in a brochure produced by the publishers with the heading "Important new publications by the Deutsche Verlags-Anstalt (DVA) in 1934," *Jürg Reinhart* finds itself alongside titles such as *Die Erhebung wider die moderne Welt, Kämpfe um Volk und Reich, Weltwende, Solange die Erde steht* and *Offenbarung in deutscher Landschaft* (Uprising against the Modern World, Fighting for the People and the Reich, World Change, As Long as the Earth Remains, and Revelation in a German Landscape).[18] In contrast to these books, which were pervaded by conservative-nationalistic ideas and a profoundly religious-romantic view of the world, the protagonist in Frisch's first work is swimming against the tide, wanting to create his own experiences as an individual and test the limits of the possible. Frisch never supported the ideology of the German National Socialists.

A later brochure contained only excerpts from press reviews of Frisch's *Jürg Reinhart.* The sources of these laudatory reviews ranged from the *Thurgauer Zeitung* and the *Luzerner Neueste Nachrichten* to the *Dresdener Neueste Nachrichten*. Even Robert Faesi, a Swiss German scholar and writer, and Eduard Korrodi eulogized the novel. While Faesi applauded its rendering of human experience and its stylistic merits,[19] Korrodi called Frisch a "magician" and praised his mellifluous and lively narrative style, his "durchhaltende Anmut, dieses Fluidum und die Erregtheit seines Erzählens" (sustained gracefulness, the aura and passionate energy of his writing).[20]

As a Swiss author with a German publishing house, Frisch was exposed to two dangers in the 1930s. On the one hand, in Swiss literary circles he could be stigmatized as a new writer who was currying favor with the Germans, and, on the other, as a Swiss writer, he could be isolated on the German bookselling market, which was already being forced into conformity ("gleichgeschaltet").[21] It should be noted in this context that publishing and literary exchanges between Switzerland and Germany remained active and open during the 1930s and 1940s. Frisch made efforts to ensure that he was also being read in Switzerland by having his work pre-published in the *Neue Zürcher Zeitung*. Yet he did not want to jeopardize his position with his German publishers. When his *Kleines Tagebuch einer deutschen Reise* (Little Journal from a Journey through Germany) was published in the *NZZ* in the spring of 1935, he began to worry that the DVA would not print his work anymore because of his criticisms. In his anxiety he turned to the Swiss writer Maria Waser and asked whether she agreed "dass es sich nicht lohnen würde, um ein paar fruchtloser Zeitungssätze willen sich selber zu schaden, gibt es doch noch genug bedeutendere Gelegenheiten, wo einer seinen wahren Mut beweisen muss" (that it would not be worthwhile to damage oneself because of a few useless sentences in a newspaper. There are still plenty more meaningful opportunities where one must prove one's genuine courage).[22]

Even today, little research has been done on Frisch's literary debut. Scholars have preferred to study the novel's autobiographical references in those of its thematic threads that also define his later work. There has been hardly any consideration of the problematic aspects of his first work, even with regard to the time and place in which it was published.[23] Only Yahya Elsaghe has written an article discussing the racist and anti-Semitic stereotypes in the Istanbul chapter of *Jürg Reinhart*.[24]

Most readers of Frisch's work are not familiar with his first two novels, so they are also unaware of what Lukas Schmid has diagnosed as his "Entwicklung von einem patriotisch-konservativen Jungautor in den 1930er-Jahren [. . .] hin zu einem der prominentesten Kritiker des Staates seit den 1950er-Jahren" (transformation from a patriotic conservative young author in the 1930s [. . .] to one of the most prominent critics of the state since the 1950s).[25] Schmid may well be correct when he suggests that it is no accident that Frisch's early work has been overlooked, but is instead a result of a selective and idealized perception of the Swiss author. Readers preferred, and still prefer, to see him as the critical left-wing intellectual who was so highly regarded from the 1960s onwards.

Frisch himself, of course, has not played an entirely innocent part in the way things have turned out. From early on, he took an active part in shaping criticism of his first work. In a letter to Walter Muschg, written in February 1936, he says: "[. . .] heute muss ich selber seine [Jürg Reinhart's] allzu individuelle Fragestellung ablehnen; ich begreife sie aber als eine Stufe, die sich nur überwinden, nicht überspringen liess" ([. . .] today I have to reject his all too individual problem, but I see it as a stage that had to be overcome by working through it rather than skipping it).[26] Then, much later, in 1975, when it was time to make the selection for the edition of his collected works, he gave the following explanation to the editor Hans Mayer as to why he could not permit a number of texts, including *Antwort aus der Stille*, to be included:

> Es geht tatsächlich nicht darum, dass ich in dieser Gesamtausgabe verleugne, was mir von der Denkart her oder wegen der Schwäche des Textes missfällt; es gibt schon einige Stellen in der verbleibenden Auswahl, die mich beschämen. Zu den wenigen Texten, die ich noch ausgeschlossen haben möchte, ist zu sagen, dass sie einfach zu unergiebig sind; wir unterschlagen nichts wesentliches, indem wir sie auslassen.[27]
>
> [It is really not my intention in this edition of my collected works to distance myself from anything that I dislike because of its mode of thought or its weakness. There are already some passages in the selected texts that cause me shame. All one can say about the few texts that I still want to be excluded is that they are simply unproductive. We do not deprive the reader of anything essential by leaving them out.]

Hugo Loetscher, on the other hand, states in an essay published in 2003:

> Ich möchte die Anfänge nicht missen. Nicht aus Lust am Dekuvrieren. Nicht einfach, um einen andern Frisch zu zeigen als den, der uns gängigerweise einfällt. [. . .] Um den Weg ganz abzustecken: die Entwicklung vom patriotisch gesinnten Jungautor bürgerlichen Credos zum kritischen Zeitgenossen einer Gelddemokratie.[28]
>
> [I don't want to miss the beginnings. Not driven by a desire to expose him. Not simply in order to show a different Frisch than the one we usually have in mind. [. . .] In order to to mark out the entire route: his development from a patriotically minded young author with bourgeois beliefs to a critical observer of a capitalist democracy.]

The Journal

In addition to the novel and play, in the mid-1930s Frisch also discovered another genre: the literary journal or diary. When he traveled to Germany for the first time in spring 1935, then under National Socialism, he summarized his impressions in his *Kleines Tagebuch einer deutschen Reise.*[29] He made fun of German novels that "in Blut und Scholle wühlen" and which, with their "Mistgeruch" were not even selling in Germany any more. The first stop on this tour was Stuttgart, home of the Deutsche Verlags-Anstalt, which published Frisch's first two novels. Robert Faesi apparently established the contact between them.[30] All in all, his remarks about Nazi Germany, which he encountered in the form of daggers and hoisted flags, ranged from ironic to sarcastic. Here Frisch's radical individualism is shown to be decidedly different from the "nationalistic collective" thinking of the brown dictatorship. He is critical of the anti-Semitism with which he is confronted at the "rassekundlichen" exhibition *Wunder des Lebens* (Wonder of Life) that he visited in Berlin:

> Was diese Ausstellung über die Juden bringt, die sie als auserwähltes Volk verspottet, lässt es uns äusserst schwer werden, über diesem dritten Reich das ewige Deutschland nicht zu vergessen; und man möchte wohl wünschen, dass das heutige Reich nach jenem notwendigen Zurückdämmen die Rassenfrage nicht länger auf die Spitze treibe.[31]
>
> [This exhibition about the Jews who are made fun of as a chosen people makes it extremely difficult for us not to forget the eternal Germany while focusing on this third Reich, and one wishes that after that necessary protection, today's Reich would stop pursuing the question of race in such an extreme manner.]

While this statement may express Frisch's critical or even hostile attitude towards the Nazi holders of power, the second half of the sentence is nevertheless disturbing with its highly objectionable use of words ("notwendigen Zurückdämmen"). It is also surprising, in the context of this journal, that Frisch's girlfriend at the time, Käte Rubensohn, who accompanied him on this trip and as a Jew was subjected to various kinds of harassment, is not mentioned at all. On the other hand, Frisch did demonstrate considerable courage when, at a procession celebrating the wedding of Hermann Göring in Berlin, he stood in the middle of the crowd "Hände in den Hosentaschen, nicht ohne Bangnis, da alle ringsum ihre Arme strecken [. . .]" (hands in my pockets, not without fear while all the people around me were stretching out their arms).[32] Even in this report, there are glimpses of another stylistic device used by Max Frisch: critical questioning. In contrast to his earlier travel articles, the *Kleines Tagebuch einer deutschen Reise* is distinguished "durch einen deutlich höheren Reflexionsgrad."[33]

In September 1935, the *Neue Zürcher Zeitung* published Frisch's *Tagebuch eines Soldaten* (Journal of a Soldier)[34] in three parts, which in its tone is very similar to the later *Blätter aus dem Brotsack* (Pages from the Knapsack). Frisch's *Tagebuch eines Soldaten* is written in the voice of a soldier who is unenthusiastic yet dutiful. This text can be regarded as Frisch's first experiment with the diary or journal as literary genre.

Antwort aus der Stille: Eine Erzählung aus den Bergen

> Sie, als Leser, können unser Buch zur Seite legen, mit seinem eigenen Herz kann man das nicht. Und für unsereinen ist es doch alleweil ein Stück vom eigenen Herz, was wir da anbieten, für 3 Franken 85.[35]

> [You, the reader, can put our book aside but one cannot do that with one's own heart. And for someone like me it is always a piece cut from one's own heart that we offer, for 3.85 Swiss Francs.]

This is the beginning of a radio address that Max Frisch was asked to give in 1937 in order to introduce his second novel, *Antwort aus der Stille*. He continues:

> Unser Leben [. . .] ein grosser Alltag, der nicht mehr wert ist, dass man ihn lebt und man fängt an und fragt sich, für was man eigentlich da ist: Brot verdienen und Heiraten und Kinder haben und weiss alleweil weniger, ob das alles überhaupt einen Sinn hat, so ein Leben. Mit solchen Gedanken kommt der junge Mensch, dessen Geschichte ich erzählt habe, in unsere Berge, verzweifelt und entschlossen, dass er ein Leben ohne Sinn nicht ertragen will. Er will seinen letzten Versuch unternehmen, um seine jugendliche Hoffnung einzulösen, einzulösen durch eine grosse und aussergewöhnliche Tat, die seinen ganzen unbefriedigenden Ehrgeiz stillen könnte. (ibid.)

> [Our life [. . .] one continuous routine that is not worth anymore to be lived, and you start and you wonder what you are really here for: Making a living, getting married, having children, and you become more and more skeptical whether all this, such a life makes any sense. With these thoughts the young man whose story I have told arrives at our mountains, in despair and determined not to endure a life without any meaning. He wants to make his final attempt to make good on his youthful hope, to make good on it with a great and unusual deed that could fulfill all his frustrating ambition.]

These words suggest that Max Frisch was going through a profound existential crisis when he wrote his emotionally charged story. How else should we interpret the words: "Das also ist mein Leben, denkt er immer wieder und findet, dass es kein Leben sei, sondern nur ein Dasein" (So that's my life, he keeps thinking and it seems to him that it's no life at all, simply an existence),[36] which he puts into the mouth of his protagonist? In his afterword to the new edition published by Suhrkamp in 2009, Peter von Matt emphasizes the parallels between the lives of heroes in novels and those of the people writing about them (150–51).

Antwort aus der Stille is the story of someone breaking free from petty bourgeois constraints and self-imposed compulsions: the teacher Balz Leuthold leaves his fiancée to go on a dangerous mountain hike, in order to discover what he is really looking for, namely "ein wirkliches Leben, ein Leben ohne Gewöhnung, ein Leben voll Erlebnis, ein Leben, wie es unsere Sehnsucht kennt, ein neues und anderes, ein lebenswertes Leben—!" (96; a real life, a life not stuck in a rut but open to experience, a life we know from our longings, a new, a different life, a life worth living—!: 66).

The painful process in which Max Frisch was engaged in the mid-1930s was intended to give his life a "radical turn," as Peter von Matt points out in his afterword to the novel (151). In the early summer of 1934, he had met Käte Rubensohn at the University of Zurich, with whom he embarked on his first serious love affair. At that time, both were attending a proseminar given by Robert Faesi. At the end of term, however, Frisch gave up his German studies, explaining that it did not teach him anything about the craft of writing, "dass ich dort nichts lerne fürs Handwerk."[37] He continued to find earning a living as a journalist unsatisfactory. In order to shake himself free of this existence, midway between compulsion and freedom, and because he was beginning to make wedding plans with Rubensohn, Frisch began to study architecture at the Swiss Federal Institute of Technology (ETH) in Zurich in the winter semester of 1936/37, financed by his friend Werner Coninx. As he reached this decision, he also for the first time seriously entertained the thought that life could become a failure, "dass das Leben misslingen kann."[38] Peter von Matt provides convincing evidence that this was a key idea that would play a crucial role both in *Antwort aus der Stille* and in Frisch's later life: the fundamental existential question, the fear of failure, the search for meaning and the essential in life.[39] So, just as Max Frisch, after a sincere and thorough analysis of his situation, prepared to strike a blow for freedom, so too did his protagonist. It is not entirely clear where the boundaries of biographical interpretation should lie in this particular case.

But what about the two main female characters, the fiancée Barbara and the emancipated Irene? There was an episode in Max Frisch's life that may have found its way into *Antwort aus der Stille*: a visit by a female friend of his actual fiancée, Käte, gave rise to jealousy and bitter disappointment when the friend made unambiguous advances towards Frisch, to which he responded.[40] Can the reader therefore detect traces of Käte and her friend in Barbara and Irene? In his afterword, Peter von Matt refers to double layers of experience, the immediate experience of the young author who is still searching, and the later one of the established author who has settled into a bourgeois lifestyle. According to von Matt, the protagonist of the novel, who, after his near-accident, becomes reconciled with a well-ordered life, shares strong affinities with Frisch's early break with literature and switch to architecture and his decision to start a family with Meyenburg.[41] Nevertheless, Frisch continued to write for a year after commencing his studies. He received official support and encouragement when in April 1936, the City of Zurich's Literature Commission awarded him one thousand Swiss Francs in recognition of his literary work. In return it requested a sample of his current project after it had gone to press.[42] Frisch sought to inoculate his story against attempts to classify it as a homeland and mountaineering novel, a popular genre at the time. For his protagonist, the flight into nature does not bring the solution to his problems he was hoping for. The dichotomy between the artist and the bourgeois citizen that is described in the novel is resolved only momentarily.

Frisch also sent this story to Hermann Hesse, in the hope that Hesse would help him either by offering him encouragement or by warning him of inherent dangers, "indem er uns vielleicht in einer Richtung bestärkt oder in einer andern vor den Gefahren unsrer Anlage warnt."[43] However, no guidance was forthcoming.

Conclusion

Frisch's early works are locked in the spirit of their time, conveying its specific tone, its style, and occasionally a naïve pathos. Some reviews of the new edition of *Antwort aus der Stille* have therefore raised the question of how much importance should be attached to Frisch's early work and whether it is even appropriate to bring out a new edition at all. It is easy to find conclusive answers. With *Jürg Reinhart*, the world opened up for Max Frisch for the first time; his encounter with the sea led to an "existential oceanography," as he discovered an inner as well as an outer marine cartography that was to guide the writer throughout his life.[44] As Hugo Loetscher mentions in connection with Frisch's late novel *Der Mensch erscheint im Holozän* (Man in the Holocene, 1979), there are strong correlations between Frisch's early and late work.[45] Frisch's first two prose works are of crucial importance because they indicate the substantial development he underwent as a writer. These early texts provide us with insights into how Max Frisch evolved from a proponent of an intellectual defense of the Swiss nation to an alert and engaged citizen of the world.

Notes

[1] Max Frisch, radio interview, produced for Swiss Radio DRS, 1950. Max Frisch Archive, Zurich.

[2] Max Frisch, *Tagebuch 1946–1949* (Frankfurt am Main: Suhrkamp, 1985), 246.

[3] Published in *Mundus vult Schundus*, the school magazine of the Kantonales Realgymnasium Rämibühl Zurich, March 25, 1927. Max Frisch Archive.

[4] Mentioned in Eduard Rübel, *Eduard Einstein: Erinnerungen ehemaliger Klassenkameraden am Zürcher Gymnasium* (Bern: Haupt, 1986), 93.

[5] Letter from Werner Coninx to Max Frisch, August 28, 1935. Max Frisch Archive.

[6] Max Frisch Archive.

[7] Source cannot be disclosed to protect confidentiality.

[8] Max Frisch, "Was bin ich?," *Zürcher Student* X/1, April 1932, 9–10. Max Frisch Archive.

[9] Heinz Ludwig Arnold, *Was bin ich? Über Max Frisch* (Göttingen: Wallstein, 2002), 10.

[10] "Ein Mensch geht weg," *Neue Zürcher Zeitung*, June 26, 1932.

[11] The publication *"Im übrigen bin ich immer völlig allein": Briefwechsel mit der Mutter 1933*, edited by Walter Obschlager (Frankfurt am Main: Suhrkamp, 2000), contains his correspondence with his mother and the travel articles and sports reports that were mainly published in the *Neue Zürcher Zeitung*.

[12] Arnold, *Was bin ich?*, 21.

[13] Max Frisch, *Jürg Reinhart: Eine sommerliche Schicksalsfahrt* (Stuttgart/Berlin: DVA, 1934), 61.

[14] Volker Hage, *Max Frisch* (Reinbek: Rowohlt, 1988), 25.

[15] Emil Zopfi, *Dichter am Berg: Alpine Literatur aus der Schweiz* (Zurich: AS Verlag, 2009), 233.

[16] Daniel Foppa, *Max Frisch und die NZZ* (Zurich: Verlag Neue Zürcher Zeitung, 2003), 84.

[17] Alexander Stephan, *Max Frisch* (Munich: Beck, 1983), 18.

[18] Brochure published by Deutsche Verlags-Anstalt in 1934. Max Frisch Archive.

[19] Robert Faesi, "Ein junger Schweizer," in literary supplement to *Basler Nachrichten*, December 9, 1934.

[20] Brochure published by Deutsche Verlags-Anstalt, 1934, quoting Eduard Korrodi's review originally published in *Neue Zürcher Zeitung*, October 14, 1934. Max Frisch Archive.

[21] Julian Schütt, "Durchschlagende Wirkung. Frischs Werdegang zwischen nationaler Integration und ästhetischer/politischer Differenzierung 1932–1950," in

Was bleibt? Ex-Territorialisierung in der deutschsprachigen Prosa seit 1945, ed. Bart Philipsen, Clemens Ruthner, and Daniel de Vin (Tübingen/Basel: Francke, 2000), 121–32.

22 Letter from Max Frisch to Maria Waser, May 13, 1935. Max Frisch Archive.

23 For a useful recent study of the novel, see Lukas Schmid, *"Indessen wäre er, der Drecktürke, ein Gentleman. . ." Zur Eigen- und Fremddarstellung in Max Frischs Jürg Reinhart* (Bern: Universität Bern, 2009), 12.

24 See section on *Jürg Reinhart* in Yahya Elsaghe, "Der Antisemitismus und seine Fortschreibung in Max Frischs *Andorra. Stück in zwölf Bildern.*" *Text+Kritik* 180, *Juden Bilder* (September 2008): 14.

25 Lukas Schmid, *Zur Eigen- und Fremddarstellung in Max Frischs Jürg Reinhart*, 2.

26 Letter from Max Frisch to Walter Muschg, February 1, 1936. Max Frisch Archive.

27 Letter from Max Frisch to Hans Mayer, July 17, 1975. Max Frisch Archive.

28 Hugo Loetscher, "Max Frisch—erschwerte Verehrung," in *Lesen statt Klettern: Aufsätze zur literarischen Schweiz*, ed. Hugo Loetscher (Zurich: Diogenes, 2003), 234–62; here 241–42.

29 Only published in *Neue Zürcher Zeitung*, Part 1 on April 30, 1935, Part 2 on May 7, 1935, and Part 3 on May 20, 1935.

30 *Neue Zürcher Zeitung*, April 30, 1935.

31 *Neue Zürcher Zeitung*, May 7, 1935.

32 Max Frisch, acceptance speech on being awarded an honorary doctorate from the Technical University of Berlin on June 29, 1987. Max Frisch Archive.

33 Foppa, "Max Frisch und die *NZZ*," 59.

34 *Neue Zürcher Zeitung*, Part 1 on September 16, 1935, Part 2 on September 18, 1935, and Part 3 on September 22, 1935.

35 Max Frisch, short speech on Swiss national radio, 1937 (audio cassette). Max Frisch Archive.

36 Max Frisch, *Antwort aus der Stille: Eine Erzählung aus den Bergen* (Frankfurt am Main: Suhrkamp, 2009), 15. Translation taken from *An Answer from the Silence: A Story from the Mountains*, trans. Mike Mitchell (Calcutta/London/New York: Seagull, 2011), 6. Further references to this work will be to these editions, indicated by page numbers in parentheses.

37 Arnold, *Was bin ich?*, 10.

38 Frisch, *Tagebuch 1946–1949*, 245.

39 Frisch, *Antwort aus der Stille*, 153.

40 Source cannot be disclosed.

41 Frisch, *Antwort aus der Stille*, 157–59.

42 Letter from the Literature Commission of the City of Zurich, April 27, 1936. Max Frisch Archive. Compare Frisch's short speech on Swiss national radio, 1937 (audio cassette). Max Frisch Archive.

[43] Letter from Max Frisch to Hermann Hesse, October 21, 1937. Max Frisch Archive.

[44] Beatrice von Matt, *Ozeanisches im Binnenland: Die Suche der Schweizer Literatur nach dem Unendlichen* (Zurich: Nagel & Kimche, 2008), 13.

[45] Loetscher, "Max Frisch—erschwerte Verehrung," 261.

7: From Life to Literature: Max Frisch's *Tagebücher*

Céline Letawe

MAX FRISCH'S TAGEBÜCHER mainly consist of *Tagebuch 1946–1949* (1950) and *Tagebuch 1966–1971* (1972). The first volume received close attention only after the second was published and rapidly became a bestseller in 1972, with extremely positive reviews by Rudolf Hartung[1] and Marcel Reich-Ranicki[2] in *Die Zeit* and by Hans Mayer in *Der Spiegel*.[3] Thus, it is not surprising that the first volume to be translated into English, in 1974, was the *Tagebuch 1966–1971* (under the English title *Sketchbook 1966–1971*), followed a few years later, in 1977, by the *Tagebuch 1946–1949* (*Sketchbook 1946–1949*), more than twenty-five years after its first publication in German.

Yet *Tagebuch 1946–1949* was not the first Tagebuch[4] written by Max Frisch. Indeed, besides the *Tagebuch with Marion*—the first part of the *Tagebuch 1946–1949*, covering the years 1946 and 1947, which had already been published in 1947—Frisch had written *Blätter aus dem Brotsack* (Pages from the Knapsack) in 1939, which was his first longer prose work after the novels *Jürg Reinhart* (1934) and *Antwort aus der Stille* (An Answer from the Silence, 1937).[5] *Blätter aus dem Brotsack* was also the first work that Max Frisch wrote after he had burned his unpublished manuscripts in 1937 and had decided never to write again (*Tb* 1, 588). As Frisch explained later in an interview with Rolf Kieser, in this very particular situation he naturally chose the diary form because he did not have enough time for longer literary forms.[6] However, one should not be misled by the fact that Frisch himself often presented the Tagebuch form as a makeshift one that he could use en passant, during his service in the Swiss army or, as he did later with the *Tagebuch 1946–1949*, next to his work as both playwright and architect: the books themselves are the result of an artful construction, as Daniel de Vin convincingly argues in his 1977 study, *Max Frischs Tagebücher*. The entries, even though they might first have been written down en passant, were afterwards sorted, modified and structured—detailed examples will be provided later.

In the 1972 discussion "Sind Tagebücher zeitgemäss?" with Walter Höllerer, Elias Canetti, Lars Gustafsson, Uwe Johnson, and Barbara

König, Max Frisch confessed that he had always kept a journal. But in the same discussion, he makes a distinction between the "sogenannte wirkliche Tagebuch" (so-called genuine diary) and the "literarisches Tagebuch" (literary sketchbook),[7] which, ten years earlier, in a conversation with Horst Bienek, he also calls "Tagebuch als literarische Form" (777; sketchbook as a literary form).[8] The most substantial difference, according to Frisch, is that the literary Tagebuch is written in the knowledge that it will be published, unlike what would normally be called the diary in English. Of course, there are other possible criteria on which one could base a definition of the literary Tagebuch, such as the fictionality of some of the contents or the fact that the author is a novelist, but they are not less problematic than Frisch's own criterion. So we will adopt Frisch's criterion here, while adding that a literary Tagebuch need not necessarily be *written* with publication in mind, but if it is not, it must be edited and reworked for publication. In either case, the focus is on the artistic form of the entries, as Klaus Günther Just pointed out in his 1966 article "Das Tagebuch als literarische Form."[9]

As Frisch explained to Walter Höllerer, he was always writing one of those two kinds of Tagebuch, but found it impossible to write both at the same time: "Es ist mir so ergangen, daß, wenn ich ein öffentliches Tagebuch schreibe, daß ich dann kein privates daneben führen kann" (781). Such a private diary is the unpublished so-called Berlin Journal that Frisch wrote from February 1973 to April 1980. In a 1980 letter to his German friend and fellow writer Uwe Johnson, Frisch self-critically commented about its content: "Ich weiss nicht mehr, was darin steht, viel Krudes, so vermute ich, viel Selbstgerechtigkeiten."[10] (I don't know any more what is in it, much crudity I suppose, much self-righteousness.) This kind of "Tagebuch" is not the subject of this chapter, which examines the sketchbook as a literary form. First I will discuss the specificities of *Tagebuch 1946–1949* and *Tagebuch 1966–1971* as opposed to *Blätter aus dem Brotsack*. Then I will turn my attention to the literary aspects of the *Tagebücher*, concentrating mostly on the last work phase of *Tagebuch 1966–1971* in order to show how Frisch proceeded to turn life into literature, partly under the influence of one of his readers: Uwe Johnson. At the end of 1970 Johnson edited the *Tagebuch* entries from 1966 until 1970,[11] sending Frisch eighteen pages of very precise commentaries which were published in 1999 along with the correspondence between the two writers (*F/J*, 241–404).[12] Frisch's letter from January 1971 conveys a clear sense of satisfaction about Johnson's remarks and editorial skills: "Sie sind der beste Lektor, den ich bisher gehabt habe." (*F/J*, 20; You're the best reader that I've ever had.) According to Fahlke, Johnson's editorial input was particularly relevant in the development of the *Sketchbook 1966–1971* into a more literary form (*F/J*, 412).

Specific Aspects of *Tagebuch 1946–1949* and *Tagebuch 1966–1971*

Blätter aus dem Brotsack, *Tagebuch 1946–1949*, and *Tagebuch 1966–1971* all have in common that they are literary "Tagebücher." But the two *Sketchbooks* are very different from *Blätter aus dem Brotsack*, in which Frisch deals with his experience as a gunner in the Swiss army in a way that creates the illusion that it is an authentic diary.[13]

The specificities of the two *Tagebücher* were not understood at once. Indeed, there were three tendencies in the first phase of their reception: they were regarded as either autobiographical documents (misled by the German title *Tagebuch*, many readers expected private diaries and read the books in the hope of gathering information about their author), or as autopoetological documents (especially the first *Tagebuch* was seen this way), or as collections of ideas for future works. The numerous literary sketches included in *Tagebuch 1946–1949*, some of which Frisch later developed into plays and novels, caused Hans Mayer to highlight that it contained many ideas that Frisch later developed into other works.[14] In my view, all three types of reception essentially misunderstand Frisch's project, a claim I will try to buttress here.

The most fundamental way in which the two *Tagebücher* differ from *Blätter aus dem Brotsack* is that they are more explicitly directed to the reader than it is, and, as such, they contrast strongly with the self-receptive diary. It is significant that *Tagebuch 1946–1949* begins with an address to the reader, asking him or her to pay attention to the sequence of the sketches and stories in the book and to follow its "zusammensetzende Folge," thereby trying to steer the reception of the book in a particular direction (*Tb* 1, 349). As he explains later in the book, Frisch explicitly considers his reader "a partner" whom he "has to think up." According to Frisch, the invention of a reader constitutes an integral part of a writer's work: "Seinen Leser, glaube ich, muss man sich denken; das ist schon ein Teil unsrer Arbeit, die Erfindung eines Lesers" (*Tb* 1, 502). In *Tagebuch 1966–1971*, Frisch even tries to engage in a kind of dialogue with the reader. He himself calls this effort an attempt at a dialogue.[15] He opens the book with a questionnaire. Altogether nine questionnaires are integrated into the text, each containing twenty-five or twenty-six unanswered questions about life, marriage, women, hope, humor, money, home, property, and death. In the version of the second *Tagebuch* that he included in the 1975 version of the *Gesammelte Werke*, there are two more questionnaires—one about friendship and one about fatherhood. Twenty years after he quoted Ibsen's famous statement, "I am here to ask questions, not to answer them" in *Tagebuch 1946–1949* (*GW* 2:87), Frisch seems to apply this principle himself. He states that he even inserted questionnaires in order to "invite or force" the reader to actively participate.[16] However, this statement needs to be somewhat relativized: as de Vin points out, these questionnaires are first and foremost "Selbstbefragung," questions that Frisch above all asks of himself.[17] A look at the literary genesis of the questionnaire about financial matters later in this essay will show this very clearly. At this stage of the analysis, suffice it to note that unmarried women without children, for example, will not feel concerned by such questions as "How many of your children do not owe their existence to deliberate intention?," "Do you still find marriage a problem?" or "Did you choose the woman who shares your life?" (*Tb* 2, 3, 43, 112).

Another salient characteristic that I would like to emphasize is the very obvious fragmentary form of the *Tagebücher*. It is no surprise that Marcel Reich-Ranicki called Max Frisch "Der Klassiker der Skizze" in his 1972 review.[18] I believe this feature to be particularly relevant for the English-speaking readership because of the choice of the word "sketchbook" (German "Skizzenbuch") rather than "diary" or "journal" (both of which the translator uses in the books themselves to translate the word "Tagebuch") for the titles of the English translations of the *Tagebücher*, whereas in French, Italian, Dutch, and Danish a word was chosen that contains the root "day" as in the original "Tagebuch" ("Journal," "Diario," "Dagboek," and "Dagbogsblade").[19] The word "sketchbook" does not stress the time-oriented structure as the original does but rather underlines the work's fragmentary style. Such a change of focus in the title may influence the reader in a considerable way.

Already in his first *Tagebuch* the Swiss writer makes interesting observations on the tendency to sketchiness among his contemporaries:

> Mindestens ließe sich denken, daß ein spätes Geschlecht, wie wir es vermutlich sind, besonders der Skizze bedarf, damit es nicht in übernommenen Vollendungen, die keine eigene Geburt mehr bedeuten, erstarrt und erstirbt. [. . .] Die Skizze hat eine Richtung, aber kein Ende; die Skizze als Ausdruck eines Weltbildes, das sich nicht mehr schließt oder noch nicht schließt [. . .] Die Haltung der meisten Zeitgenossen aber, glaube ich, ist die Frage, ihre Form, solange eine ganze Antwort fehlt, kann nur vorläufig sein; für sie ist vielleicht das einzige Gesicht, das sich mit Anstand tragen läßt, wirklich das Fragment. (*Tb* 1, 447–51)
>
> [It is conceivable at least that a late generation, such as we presumably are, has particular need of the sketch, in order not to be strangled to death by inherited conceptions which preclude new births. [. . .] The sketch has direction, but no ending; the sketch as reflection of a view of life that is no longer conclusive [. . .] But the attitude of most of my contemporaries is, I believe, one of questioning, and as long as a complete answer is missing, the formal framework

can be only temporary. Perhaps the only form they can decently use is indeed the fragmentary one. (*Sb* 1, 82–84)]

The fragmentary form that is a feature of the Tagebuch in general (a new entry usually corresponding to a new day), is even more developed and apparent in Frisch's *Tagebücher*. It is particularly clear on the level of macrostructure, as both *Tagebücher* contain texts of different status, a combination whose heterogeneity is reinforced by the different typefaces used in *Tagebuch 1966–1971*: typescript, antiqua, grotesque, and italic. This disillusioning element, which shows the reader that he is not reading an authentic diary but a literary construction, was a technique used in the project from its early stages, as is clear from the paper Frisch used for his typescript. The texts were written on yellow, white, green and red pages according to the status the author wanted to give them: yellow/typescript for autobiographical notes; white/antiqua for the dialogues, interrogations, and questionnaires, plus the fictional sketches and the reflections on personal experiences; green/grotesque for quotations; and red/italic for the "Notizen zu einem Handbuch für Mitglieder" (Notes for a Handbook for Members). But the structure is more complex than it seems at first glance. Writing in 1973, Horst Steinmetz does not see any coherent semantic classification, and he concludes that Frisch simply wants to create confusion, blurring the boundaries between reality and fiction.[20] Steinmetz sees in this "Scheinverschiedenheit" (illusory difference) the "Bestätigung einer substantiellen Einheitlichkeit" (confirmation of a substantial unity).[21] But there *are* differences, which are even essential to the understanding of the *Tagebuch 1966–1971* if we want to take seriously Frisch's "wish to confront what is fictional [. . .] with [. . .] *de facto* reality."[22] However, as Jürgen H. Petersen points out, the important question is not "ob der berichtete Vorgang selbst persönlich erlebt wurde, faktisch stattgefunden hat oder dem Arsenal von Fiktionen entstammt" (whether the reported happening was experienced personally, whether it actually happened, or whether it issues from the arsenal of fiction), but rather "wie der Rezipient den Text einordnet" (how the recipient classifies the text).[23] Through his use of different typefaces, Max Frisch wants to influence the way the readers perceive the different texts. Texts about personal experiences, for instance, are set in typescript or antiqua depending on the treatment they are given or the way the readers should read them—typescript giving the impression that one is reading an extract from a personal diary, written spontaneously and directly, antiqua on the other hand expressing a certain distance gained through time and reflection. So the lettering is very clearly a construction with which Frisch is consciously trying to steer the reception of his *Tagebuch*.

The fragmentary nature of the *Tagebücher* is also readily visible on the level of microstructure, that is: within the different parts. These are often divided into numerous small paragraphs that are sometimes separated by blank line spaces. As Heinz F. Schafroth points out, in several instances there are "mehr Leerstellen als Text" (more empty spaces than text).[24] In some cases the different paragraphs are not directly related to each other, so that the reader has the impression that the blank spaces correspond to mental leaps; in other cases the different paragraphs form a fragmented whole, the blank spaces embodying the parts that were omitted. The fictional stories for example are characterized by the principle of omission referred to by Meike Heinrich-Korpys as "Auslassung" (leaving out) or "explizite Aussparung" (explicit omission).[25] Omissions on the content level are sometimes made even more explicit by the use of suspension marks emphasizing the blank spaces, a conspicuous visual element. Added to this, the different parts of the story of Marion, the puppet artist, are scattered throughout the 1946 and 1947 sections of the *Tagebuch 1946–1949*, aptly illustrating what Frisch calls the "Auflösung überlieferter Einheiten" (*Tb* 1, 448; breaking down of traditional unities) in his reflections on the tendency to sketchiness. This fragmentation is less striking in the English translation, since three parts of the Marion story were deleted, whereas in the original German version the story is divided into six parts.[26] As Kieser notes about the German text, "there is never a clear-cut beginning nor is there any conclusion offering a satisfactory 'solution.'"[27] It should finally be mentioned that *Tagebuch 1946–1949* contains many very short paragraphs that resemble aphorisms.

Both *Tagebücher* include many fictional stories that are explicitly announced as such: "Marion und die Marionetten" (Marion and the Marionettes) and its continuation in various passages, "Der andorranische Jude" (The Andorran Jew), "Graf Öderland" (Count Oederland), "Burleske" (Burlesque), and "Skizze" (Sketch) in *Tagebuch 1946–1949*, and "Bodega Gorgot" and its continuation "Der Goldschmied" (The Goldsmith), "Skizze," "Ehen nach dem Tod" (Marriage after Death), "Der Traum des Apothekers von Locarno" (The Locarno Pharmacist's Dream), "Skizze eines Unglücks" (Outline of an Accident), "Glück" (Luck), "Statik" (Statics), and "Rip van Winkle" in *Tagebuch 1966–1971*. To this list can be added "Der Harlekin, Entwurf zu einem Film" in *Tagebuch 1946–1949* and the two-part "Kabusch" in *Tagebuch 1966–1971*, three stories that were not retained in the English translation. All these stories can be regarded as "invented examples" through which Frisch tries to express experiences, as he explains in the following extract from *Tagebuch 1946–1949*:

> [. . .] jedes Erlebnis bleibt im Grunde unsäglich, solange wir hoffen, es ausdrücken zu können mit dem wirklichen Beispiel, das uns betroffen hat. Ausdrücken kann mich nur das Beispiel, das mir so ferne ist wie dem Zuhörer: nämlich das erfundene. Vermitteln kann

> wesentlich nur das Erdichtete, das Verwandelte, das Umgestaltete, das Gestaltete [. . .] (*Tb* 1, 703)
>
> [[. . .] every experience basically defies description as long as we try to express it through the actual example that has impressed us. I can express what I want to say only by means of an example that is as remote from me as it is from the listener, that is to say, an invented one. Essentially only fiction—things altered, transformed, shaped [. . .] (*Sb* 1, 259)]

Frisch responds to his need to distance himself from what actually happened by providing changes in content and form. This is a process that may necessitate several steps, as we will see later. But let us first take a closer look at one of the fictional stories.

In her monograph *Tagebuch und Fiktionalität*, Meike Heinrich-Korpys analyzes the sketch "Statik" (Statics) the second text of the *Tagebuch 1966–1971*, in which Frisch introduces the theme of old age, in order to show how he signals the fictional status of this kind of text (165–76). Here are some extracts from the text that she analyzes:

> Als er, lange schon mit dem Hut in der Hand, endlich an die Reihe kommt und sich in den Schalter beugt, um zu wiederholen, dass er Anzeige erstatten müsse gegen sich selbst, blickt der Beamte ihn gar nicht an [. . .] Sein Fach: Statik für Architekten [. . .] Er zeigt immer Lichtbilder: Risse im Beton. [. . .] Es ist jetzt nur noch die Frage, wann sie es merken, daß er nichts von Statik versteht, eine Frage der Zeit. [. . .] Die sichtbare Tatsache, daß die Bauten seiner Schüler [. . .] allesamt nicht einstürzten, ändert nichts an seiner Selbsterkenntnis:—er verstehe nichts von Statik, habe nie verstanden, was er gelehrt habe— (*Tb* 2, 364–74)
>
> [When, after a long wait, with hat in hand, he at last reaches the desk and bends down to repeat that he has come to make a charge against himself, the official does not even look at him [. . .] His subject: statics for architects [. . .] He always shows them slides: cracks in concrete. [. . .] The question is now simply when they will notice that he knows nothing about statistics [*sic*]—a question of time. [. . .] The visible fact that his pupil's [*sic*] buildings [. . .] have none of them collapsed so far does nothing do alter his inner feeling: that he understands nothing of statistics [*sic*], had never understood the things he taught. . . (*Sb*, 308–17)]

Heinrich-Korpys points out numerous conventional signals given by Frisch to alert the reader to the fictional status of the text: the personal narrative mode (a term coined by Stanzel with contrasting perspectives), the abstract vagueness of time, place, and persons, the presentation of figures as types, and the formal structure of the text with its blank spaces stressed by the use of suspension marks.[28] According to Heinrich-Korpys, these signals show the reader that the text does not present a historically verifiable individual case but rather a decipherable illustration of an existential crisis.[29] "Statik" is not the only sketch in which Frisch uses such signals. We find a combination of them in the other stories mentioned above. As we will see, these stories and their obvious markers of fictionality are part of Frisch's conscious search for a more literary form.

Uwe Johnson and the Literary Genesis of Frisch's *Tagebuch 1966–1971*: *Tagebuch* as Literary Form

A look at the 1970 typescript of *Tagebuch 1966–1971* shows that Frisch did not intend to write so many fictional stories at the onset of his project: there we only find "Bodega Gorgot" and "Der Goldschmied" "Skizze," and "Skizze eines Unglücks." Frisch's change of mind could be explained by the way Uwe Johnson reacted to the texts "Bodega Gorgot" on the seventy-fourth page of the typescript and its continuation a bit later in "Der Goldschmied." Johnson's reaction was extremely positive: "Die Geschichte kann gar nicht lang genug sein." (*F/J*, 278; The story cannot be long enough.) It was even a "relief" for Johnson to see that the new *Tagebuch* contained such stories, as the first one did: "Hier war ich recht erleichtert, dass Sie nur aus List abgestritten haben, auch dies neue Tagebuch enthalte einen geheimen Projektkatalog, indirekte Copyrights sozusagen." (*F/J*, 277; Here I was quite relieved that it was a ruse when you denied that this new sketchbook contained a secret catalog of projects, indirect copyrights so to speak.) This might be the reason why Frisch moved the text "Bodega Gorgot" towards the beginning of the book, so that the reader could rapidly see that the book contained this kind of story. In this respect, a closer look at the 1970 version of "Statik," the 1972 version of which was briefly discussed above, is particularly enlightening:

> Prof. J., unser Lehrer für Statik an der Eidgenössischen Technischen Hochschule in Zürich, war die Gewissenhaftigkeit in Person. [. . .] Was er sagte, schrieb er immer auch noch mit Kreide an die Tafel, um ganz sicher zu gehen, dass kein Missverständnis unsere künftigen Bauten einstürzen lässt. [. . .] Eines Tages, lange nach meinem Diplom, kam er ins Irrenhaus: was er gelehrt habe, sei falsch, er habe die Statik nicht verstanden. Ich sah ihn noch einmal auf der Strasse, geführt von seiner Frau, er erkannte den ehemaligen Schüler, aber sein Gesicht war eingestürzt, sein Blick voll Entsetzen. Er ist längst verstorben. Die statischen Formeln, die er gelehrt hat, gelten nachwievor. (*F/J*, 356–57)

> [Prof. J., our teacher of statics at the ETH in Zurich, was conscientiousness personified. [. . .] Everything he said he also wrote on the blackboard with chalk in order to be absolutely certain that no misunderstanding might cause our future buildings to collapse. [. . .] One day, long after I had finished my degree, he was admitted to a psychiatric hospital: According to him, everything he had taught was wrong, he did not understand statics. I saw him once again on the street, his wife was guiding him, he recognized his former student, but his face had collapsed, his gaze filled with terror. He died long ago. The equations in statics that he taught are still valid.]

The text is written in the first person, and at the very beginning it locates the events in Frisch's reality, as most readers know that he studied architecture in Zurich in the late 1930s. Frisch had already taken some distance from the autobiographical facts (if only a temporal distance, as the story happened more than thirty years before), but for Uwe Johnson, it was clearly not enough: he rejected the text with the three letters "d.s.p."—*deleatur, se possible* (*F/J*, 356). Frisch apparently did not want to delete this topic totally, so he decided to change the text, making a ten-page story out of it, which was partly quoted and discussed above. The development is clear: the autobiographical facts are hidden, the first person pronouns deleted, the first-person perspective of the diary modified into a personal narrative mode, the protagonist is not located in the real world anymore. He remains anonymous until the end, and the text is presented in a fragmented form that is emphasized, as we have seen, by the blank spaces and the suspension marks. In this way the initial text develops into an overtly fictional story.

Moving Away from the Personal Diary

Frisch revealed more about himself and his personal life in the 1970 typescript of the *Tagebuch 1966–1971* than he eventually did in the published version. For instance, in "Berzona"—a text typed on yellow paper, that is to say presented as an autobiographical note—he originally planned to describe his new house and his guests' reaction to it. The text, which is included in Frisch's and Johnson's correspondence, begins this way:

> Kaum ein Gast, der nicht früher oder später sagt: Hier, jaja, hier lässt sich arbeiten! Diese Luft, diese Ruhe usw. Wenn ein Gast es nicht sagt, dann sage ich's! Warum wir an dieser Stelle der Erde wohnen. Wir sind, glaube ich, sehr artig zu den Gästen; wir brauchen sie. Es werden Blumen für sie gepflanzt und gepflegt, die Terrasse gerodet, ich hacke Holz fürs Kamin usw., und natürlich nützt alles nichts—eines Tages werden sie sagen: Ich habe mich gewundert, dass Ihr dort habt leben können. . . . (*F/J*, 253)

> [Hardly any guest who doesn't sooner or later say: This is indeed a great place to work! This air, this quiet, etc. Whenever a guest fails to say it, I do! Why we live on this place on earth. We are, I believe, quite polite to the guests; we need them. For them flowers are planted and taken care of, the patio is cleared, I chop wood for the fireplace, etc., and of course all this is of no avail—one day they will say: I was amazed that you were able to live there. . .]

In his commentary Johnson advised Frisch to delete the text, explaining that passages should be eliminated "wenn sie mir auf eine rein subjektive, geradezu private Qualität beschränkt scheinen; nicht nur unverständlich für Aussenstehende, auch kaum bestimmt für sie" (*F/J*, 253; whenever I have the feeling that they [the passages] are confined to a merely subjective, even private quality; not only impenetrable for outsiders but hardly even meant for them). Johnson further justified his criticism of some passages written on yellow paper later on, when commenting on a text in which Frisch meant to talk about his wealth: "Die Ehrlichkeit, mit der Sie auch Ihr Privatleben nicht unterschlagen wollen, könnte beim Leser als Indiskretion funktionieren." (*F/J*, 276; The honesty with which you want to reveal your private life could be read as an indiscretion.) Here it must be said that the two writers had very different opinions on whether private elements should be included in literature or not. Frisch's comments, in the text "Vom Schreiben in Ich-Form," which is included in *Tagebuch 1966–1971*, on "indiscretion" show that the Swiss writer worked with a particular definition of the concept:

> [. . .] Was man gemeinhin als Indiskretion bezeichnet: Mitteilungen aus dem privaten Bezirk des Schreibers, die den Leser nichts angehen. Und was die eigentliche Indiskretion ist: wenn einer mitteilt, was den Leser etwas angeht und was der Leser selber weiß, aber seinerseits nie ausspricht— (*Tb* 2, 286–87).

> [[. . .] What is commonly considered indiscretion: information from the writer's private world that is no concern of the reader. And true indiscretion? When one informs the reader of something that does concern him, something the reader himself knows but never admits. . . (*Sb* 2, 238–39)]

Thus, to Frisch, "information from the writer's private world that is no concern of the reader" was not necessarily synonymous with indiscretion. He explained this again in the 1972 discussion published by Walter Höllerer as "Sind Tagebücher zeitgemäß?": "Wenn ich mich preisgebe, das ist nicht indiskret, sondern wenn ich den Leser preisgebe oder andere Leute." (782; It is not indiscrete to reveal something about myself but to reveal something about the reader or about other people.) For Johnson, on the other hand, the private does not belong to a Tagebuch meant to be published. In asking Frisch to delete more than ten texts written on yellow paper[30] because they appeared to him to be too subjective or too private, Johnson ultimately reminded Frisch that the book the latter was writing was not meant to be a diary, but a literary Tagebuch.

However, Johnson did not criticize all the texts on yellow paper—he even praised some of them: "Kürze, Beziehung zu den umgebenden Texten, Stoik: unübertrefflich." (*F/J*, 252; Brevity, correlations with the surrounding texts, stoicism: unsurpassable.) One of these texts, an ironic description of life in a Swiss spa for well-to-do patients, is titled "Vulpera-Tarasp" and is quoted here to illustrate what exactly Johnson was praising:

> Alle mit dem numerierten Glas in der Hand, SANKT BONIFACIUS, hilf uns, daß wir nicht altern, SANKT LUCIUS, vergib uns unsere Jahre. [. . .] dann Frühstück, Diät je nach Fall. Im Lauf des Tages eine Massage, Blick auf die Waage, nachmittags Spaziergang auf säuberlichen Wegen durch Wald, Ozon, bis es wieder Zeit ist für die Trinkhalle, SANKT BONIFACIUS, sieh unsere Askese, SANKT LUCIUS, lass uns nicht verkalken. [. . .] Krank sieht eigentlich niemand aus: Gesundheit scheint käuflich zu sein. Alle von der Sonne gebräunt. Im Bridge-Salon ist man allein. Alle Herren in dunklen Anzügen, Damen mit Juwelen; wartend vor dem Lift studieren sie den Diät-Zettel für morgen. (*F/J*, 293–94, *Tb* 2, 78–79)

> [Everyone with numbered drinking glass in hand. Saint Boniface, help us not to grow old; Saint Lucius, forgive us our years. [. . .] then breakfast according to individual diet. In the course of the day, massage, weight check, afternoon walk on tidy paths through the woods, ozone, until it is again time for the pump room. Saint Boniface, observe our ascetic habits; Saint Lucius, save us from calcifying. [. . .] Nobody looks at all ill; health, it seems, can be bought. Everyone sun-tanned. There is nobody else in the bridge room. All the men in dark suits, ladies with jewels. Waiting for the elevator, they study the diet sheets for tomorrow. (*Sb* 2, 67–68)]

Commenting on this text, Johnson explained what he was generally expecting from the passages written on yellow paper: "die genaue Beobachtung, und die genaue Auswahl des Beobachteten für die Mitteilung. Der persönliche Gestus stellt sich dar durch die Methode, nicht wie sonst oft durch die Erwähnung der Person." (*F/J*, 293; precise observation, and meticulous selection of that which is observed for the text. The personal style manifests itself through the method, not as usual by referring to one's own person). Johnson praised this in other texts as well, as for example "Zürich": "Auch wer Ihre Stimme nicht kennt, muss sie hier erkennen." (*Tb* 2, 38; *F/J*, 252; Even those who don't know your voice have to recognize it here.)

A detailed analysis[31] shows that Johnson's criticism and praise led Frisch to make many modifications so as to produce more general texts, deleting much autobiographical information,[32] allowing Kieser to conclude in 1972 that "the *Tagebuch*—obviously a splendid opportunity for a potential exhibitionist to drag personal matters out into the open—is conspicuously free of any 'revealing stories' from Frisch's private life."[33]

Beyond the Sketchbook

Sometimes Johnson also criticized texts in which he found a reflective dimension to be missing. This is the case when, in a text written on yellow paper, Frisch refers to world affairs in an extremely concise way, as in the text "27. 4. 1969," which contains only the sentence "General de Gaulle dankt ab." (*F/J*, 343; General de Gaulle resigns.) Johnson writes: "Die blosse Mitteilung von de Gaulles Rücktritt genügt nicht. Es ist deutlich, dass die Nachricht Sie angeht; nicht deutlich, wieso" (*F/J*, 343; Merely reporting de Gaulle's resignation is not enough. It is clear that the news matters to you. It is not clear why.) Frisch decided to delete the text. Commenting on another passage, Johnson writes: "Ja, wenn das nun mit Ihren Anmerkungen, Reflexionen, Empfindungen versetzt wäre—!" (*F/J*, 393; Now if this were interwoven with your comments, reflections, feelings—!) Johnson criticizes Frisch because these texts sometimes resemble newspaper articles (*F/J*, 381)—again, according to him, something personal was missing: "Hier mit einem Mal fehlt ein persönliches Wort." (*F/J*, 289; All of a sudden a personal tone is missing here.) Johnson wants Frisch to describe world affairs from his personal perspective, as he occasionally does in passages about Prague and Moscow. Johnson applauds those segments: "Ein typisches Beispiel für Ihre ausserordentliche Fähigkeit, Zeuge zu sein, als Zeuge zurückzukommen" (*F/J*, 250; An example of your extraordinary gift to be a witness, to return as a witness.)

Johnson also considered that a reflective dimension was missing in some texts that are marked as quotations by the fact that Frisch wrote them on green paper.[34] This is for example the case of a two-page quotation from Georg Lukács: "Zitate dieser Länge hätten in einem Tagebuch nur alle Berechtigung, wenn dessen Verfasser sich mit ihnen auseinandersetzte oder auch nur seinen Senf dazutäte. Es ist ja kein Merk-Buch." (*F/J*, 311–12; Quotations of this length would only be appropriate in a sketchbook if its author discussed them or at least added some mustard to them. After all, this book is not a memory aid.) When Frisch quotes Apollinaire in his typescript as having said, "Der wahre Ruhm hat die Dichtung verlassen, um sich der Wissenschaft, der Philosophie, der Akrobatik, der Philanthropie, der Soziologie usw. zuzuwenden [. . .]" (*F/J*, 328; True fame has abandoned poetry in order to turn to science, philosophy, acrobatics, philanthropy, sociology, etc.),

Johnson again expresses disapproval: "Dies hat, wegen Ihrer fehlenden Teilnahme, leider wieder etwas Merkbuch-Charakter." (*F/J*, 328; Unfortunately this has again somewhat the character of a memory aid because you are uninvolved.) Here Johnson reminds Frisch that the art form he has developed should not become a mere notebook. Adopting a more personal perspective, Frisch eventually deleted the quotation but used its beginning in a segment on Charlie Chaplin in which the quotation becomes a sentence that he himself cites in a conversation about the role of literature in society.[35]

Considering Johnson's aversion to mere quotations, it could seem surprising that he was not disturbed by Frisch's lengthy quotation from the "Zürcher Manifest" (Zurich Manifesto, *Tb* 2, 170–73; *Sb* 2, 128–29). But here something else was at stake. As Johnson remarked: "Ein solches Zitat, im Gegensatz zu dem von Lukács, kommt ganz selbstverständlich daher: weil Sie an ihm beteiligt waren." (*F/J*, 313; This kind of quotation, in contrast to the one from Lukács, sounds quite natural because you were actively involved.) Frisch indeed helped to put this manifesto together and—as is specified in brackets—he signed it.[36] In the next work phase, in order to further emphasize his involvement in the events, Frisch followed up this quotation with the text "Protokoll" (For the Record), which makes clear from the outset that Frisch was personally concerned about the youth protests: "Meine jüngste Tochter ist dabei gewesen" (*Tb* 2, 157; My youngest daughter was there; *Sb* 2, 129). Moreover, he placed newspaper quotes concerning the same subject immediately after each of these two pieces, so that the two quoted texts acquired a reflective dimension through the more personal text, "Protokoll," that separates them. Here we have a good example of what Daniel de Vin calls "das Aufbauprinzip der Einrahmung," a framing structure typical of the *Tagebücher*, which he discerns in groups of three levels that form a larger unit.[37]

In sum, it seems that Johnson wanted Frisch to avoid egocentricity on the one hand and the absence of reflection on the other, constantly reminding him that the Tagebuch is a literary form. It should neither become a personal diary with too-private information about its writer, nor should it look like a notebook only kept for storing interesting quotations. Johnson wanted Frisch to find a balance between subjectivity and objectivity, between autobiography and exemplarity, which is remarkably achieved in the published version of the *Tagebuch 1966–1971*.

Confronting Fiction with Reality

Frisch did not always agree with Johnson's suggestions. For instance, Johnson tried to delete repetitions when Frisch sometimes intended them to mean something. The note "Statistics" for example, revealing the theme of old age as a central theme of the work, was considered redundant by Johnson because it also appears later within the fiction "Vereinigung Freitod" (Voluntary Death Association), where it is condensed by Frisch "zu einem konkreten Problem von Lebenserwartung" (to a concrete problem of life expectancy; *F/J*, 247). Frisch kept both texts:

> Die durchschnittliche Lebensdauer betrug um Christi Geburt nur 22, zur Zeit von Martin Luther schon 35,5, um 1900 noch 49,2 und heute 68,7 Lebensjahre. Die Lebensverlängerung bedeutet zugleich eine Umschichtung der Altersklassen. Um 1900 stellten die Jugendlichen (bis zum zwanzigsten Lebensjahr) noch 46% der Bevölkerung, 1925 nur noch 36%, 1950 noch 31%, und für 1975 rechnet man mit 28% jugendlichen Menschen. Entsprechend steigen die Altersklassen (nach dem sechzigsten Jahr); um 1900 waren es noch 7% der Bevölkerung, um 1975 werden es 20% sein. [. . .] Zuerst verlese ich die Statistik, gefaßt auf Einwände gegen Statistik überhaupt: die Säuglingssterblichkeit zur Zeit um Christi Geburt. . . . Nach einigem Palaver, das der Vorsitzende leider zuläßt, einigt man sich, daß eine gewisse (ich habe gesagt: eine katastrophale) Überalterung unsrer Gesellschaft nicht ohne weiteres in Zahlen auszudrücken, aber Tatsache ist. (*Tb* 2, 9 and 82)

> [The average life expectancy of a human being at the time of Christ's birth was 22.0 years; around 1600 it was 33.5 years; in 1900, still only 49.2 years; while today it is 68.7 years. The longer life expectancy affects the distribution of age groups. In 1900 young people up to the age of twenty comprised 46 percent of the population; in 1925, only 36 percent, and in 1950, 31 percent. According to calculations the proportion of young people in the year 1975 will be 28 percent of the whole. The proportion of old people (over sixty) increases correspondingly: in 1900 they comprised 7 percent of the population. In 1975 the figure will be 20 percent. [. . .] first I read out the statistics, expecting objections to statistics on principle: infant mortality at the time of Christ's birth. . . . After a lot of palaver, which the chairman unfortunately permits, agreement is reached that a certain (I had said a catastrophic) degree of aging is discernible in our civilization, though it can't be expressed only in figures. (*Sb* 2, 5 and 70)]

Frisch might have kept this text against Johnson's advice because it allowed him to show how he came to the idea of the "Vereinigung Freitod." This fiction developed out of a real social problem and needed to remain linked to it. With the repetition of the theme in "Statistik" and "Vereinigung Freitod" Frisch ultimately forges a link between fiction and concrete reality, he brings them into confrontation with each other, as he explains in his 1972 interview with Kieser.

A second example should help to make this clear. Montaigne's motto "C'est ainsi que je fons et eschape à moi" (Thus do I dissolve and take leave of myself) was also quoted twice in the manuscript, and again this seemed to disturb Johnson: "Ist die Wiederholung des Montaigne-Mottos als Zitat tatsächlich unabdingbar?" (Is the repetition of the Montaigne motto as a quotation really indispensable?; *F/J*, 302) Notwithstanding Johnson's query, Frisch kept the repetition and even used the quote a third time, in an autobiographical passage about himself realizing that he was getting old, a text that appears quite early in the *Tagebuch*, near the beginning of the 1967 part:

> [. . .] Beim Anschnallen der Skier schon ein kurioses Gefühl; nicht Sorge, denn die Abfahrt ist nicht schwierig, der Schnee wie gewünscht. Es geht denn auch ohne Sturz, trotzdem bleibt das kuriose Gefühl. Was ist anders als früher? Vielleicht macht es die Brille; also halte ich auf der Strecke an und putze sie. Es bleibt das kuriose Gefühl, bis ich am Ziel bin und die Skier losschnalle, dabei entdecke: ich fuhr die ganze Strecke mit der Pfeife im Mund. Das war vor einem Jahr. Um über das Altern zu schreiben, genügte es für Michel de Montaigne, daß er einen Zahn verlor; er schrieb: "So löse ich mich auf und komme mir abhanden." (*Tb* 2, 64)

> [[. . .] A curious feeling even as I strap on my skis: not anxiety, for the descent is not difficult, the snow just as it should be. And everything goes all right, no tumbles—yet still that curious feeling. What is different from before? Maybe it's the spectacles: so I stop along the track and polish them. The curious feeling remains until I reach my goal and unstrap the skis, when I realize I had done the whole stretch with my pipe in my mouth. That was a year ago. To start writing about approaching age it was enough for Michel de Montaigne to have lost a tooth. He wrote [. . .] "Thus do I dissolve and take leave of myself." (*Sb* 2, 55)]

It is significant that with a remark seemingly made en passant—"That was a year ago"—Max Frisch situates this episode at the beginning of 1966, that is, when he actually began writing his second *Tagebuch*. Interestingly, in this way he presents aging as the trigger for writing his *Tagebuch*.[38] The fact that the Montaigne quote appears in an autobiographical context before being repeated twice in the "Notizen zu einem Handbuch für Mitglieder" is important too: Frisch shows very early that the theme of the fictive handbook, which is also a major theme of the *Tagebuch*, is linked to his personal experience. This rapprochement of fictionality and autobiography recurs throughout the *Tagebuch* and is one of its main features. Following Meike Heinrich-Korpys, we can also note that this rapprochement provides "ein Signal, das die Subjektivität der persönlichen

Eintragungen relativiert" (a signal that relativizes the subjectivity of the personal entries), indicating that what is at stake are not pieces of information about an individual's biography but rather "ein allgemeines Erlebnismuster" (a general pattern of experience; 193).

In this respect, it is particularly interesting to look at the literary genesis of the questionnaire about money that is one of the nine questionnaires included in the second *Tagebuch*. The starting point for this text, we know from the Frisch-Johnson correspondence, was a fictional interview titled "Spiegel-Interview über Geld" that Frisch had written for his typescript but which had been criticized by Johnson (*F/J*, 350–56). In this "interview" the answers were Frisch's own, as becomes clear from the abbreviation "F." and the content. When the issue of art patronage is raised, for example, the answer recognizably concerns Frisch's own experience, since he was able to study architecture with the support of an affluent benefactor, and later became a benefactor himself (*F/J*, 352, 354). After Johnson had criticized this fictional interview, Frisch decided to use some of its content in a questionnaire, altering the form by leaving out the answers, but re-integrating much of their content in the new questions. Questions six and seventeen, for instance, are clearly derived from the questions referred to above and, ultimately, from Frisch's experience, but they are phrased in a more general way and presented as hypothetical situations:

> Gesetzt den Fall, Sie sind ein großer Mäzen, d.h. Sie verteilen an Leute, die Sie persönlich schätzen, teilweise die beträchtlichen Zinsen aus der Arbeit anderer Leute: verstehen Sie die öffentliche Hochachtung, die Sie als Mäzen genießen, und Ihre eigene Unbefangenheit dabei? (*Tb* 2, 240)
>
> [Assume you are a great benefactor, that is to say, you pass on to people whom you personally admire a share of the considerable interest you earn from the work of others: can you understand the public esteem in which you are held as benefactor, and your own easy conscience? (*Sb* 2, 208)]

This example clearly shows that the questionnaires primarily serve as "Selbstbefragung," even though they do engage the reader as well.

In this case the development of the text, and the link to Frisch's personal experience, are not obvious to the reader of the published *Tagebuch*, but, as we have seen before, Frisch often deliberately renders the link visible. And this is not a particularity of *Tagebuch 1966–1971*: it is also the case in *Tagebuch 1946–1949*, and indeed from the very first pages onwards. Indeed, the book begins with an autobiographical situation in "Zurich, Café de la Terrasse," where an "I" persona describes the young puppeteer he saw performing on the sidewalk the day before, and the arrival of a policeman telling him that he could not perform there. This situation is developed into fiction in the next text, "Marion und die Marionetten," with the first reference to the policeman as "jenem Polizisten," emphasizing the link between both texts. Eventually we come back to the autobiographical situation in "Café de la Terrasse," where the first-person narrator's age coincides with Frisch's age at the time, another example of the framing structure discussed by Daniel de Vin. A similar development catches the reader's eye when a newspaper article about a man who has spent most of his life working as a reliable cashier and suddenly kills his family is followed by Frisch's reflection on his own personal situation, asking himself why he does not turn his back on his conventional life, before the same topic is treated in a more obvious way in the fictional sketch "Graf Öderland," the nucleus of Frisch's play of the same name. In these cases the confrontation of fiction and reality is made particularly visible.

Conclusion

Usually the spontaneous reaction of someone reading a book that contains both autobiographical and fictional texts is to ask him- or herself which parts of it really happened. As we have seen, this is a question the reader will ask when reading Max Frisch's *Tagebücher*, but it is not a particularly relevant one. Indeed, the Swiss author consciously juxtaposes and blends diverse textual genres, even marking them through his use of different typefaces in *Tagebuch 1966–1971*, in order to bring reality and fiction into confrontation, ultimately conveying that what is important is not what happened historically but the literary expression of human experience. Taking his personal experiences as points of departure, Frisch eventually manages to depict more general patterns of experience through literary construction, on the one hand by fictionalizing them in form and content, and on the other by confronting these texts with other fictional texts. This is at the heart of the *Tagebücher* and also what makes them two of the most remarkable literary works of the twentieth century.

Notes

[1] Rudolf Hartung, "Versuch, ein Meisterwerk zu beschreiben. Über Max Frischs neues Tagebuch," *Die Zeit*, May 5, 1972. The following editions and translations of Frisch's "Tagebücher" are cited in this chapter: *Tagebuch 1946–1949*, in *Gesammelte Werke in zeitlicher Folge* (*GW*) 2, ed. Hans Mayer and Walter Schmitz, 2nd ed. (Frankfurt am Main: Suhrkamp, 1986); *Tagebuch 1966–1971*, in *GW* 6. These works will be referred to in the text as *Tb* 1 and *Tb* 2. English translations: *Sketchbook 1946–1949*, trans. Geoffrey Skelton (New York/London: Harcourt Brace Jovanovich, 1977); *Sketchbook 1966–1971*, trans. Geoffrey Skelton (New

York: Harcourt Brace Jovanovich, 1974). The translations will be referenced in the text as *Sb* 1 and *Sb* 2.

[2] Marcel Reich-Ranicki, "Der Klassiker der Skizze. Zu Max Frischs 'Tagebuch 1966–1971,'" *Die Zeit*, May 5, 1972.

[3] Hans Mayer, "Die Schuld der Schuldlosen. Max Frischs 'Tagebuch 1966–1971,'" *Der Spiegel*, June 12, 1972, 124.

[4] In order to avoid any misunderstandings I will sometimes use the German word *Tagebuch* in the English text. I will reflect on the possible English translations of the word later in this essay.

[5] Frisch had already published diaristic writings, mostly travel notes, before *Blätter aus dem Brotsack*: for example *Ungarische Skizzen* (1933, *GW* 1:39–45); *Glück in Griechenland* (1933, *GW* 1:57–65); and *Kleines Tagebuch einer deutschen Reise* (1935, *GW* 1:84–97). He continued to publish travel notes during his entire career; see *Spanien im ersten Eindruck* (1951, *GW* 3:179–95), *Orchideen und Aasgeier* (1951, *GW* 3:196–221), *Begegnung mit Negern* (1954, *GW* 3:243–59), and *Notizen von einer kurzen Reise nach China* (1975, *GW* 6:757–84).

[6] Rolf Kieser, *Max Frisch: Das literarische Tagebuch* (Frauenfeld: Huber, 1975), 18.

[7] Max Frisch quoted in Walter Höllerer, "Sind Tagebücher zeitgemäss? Gespräch mit Elias Canetti, Max Frisch, Lars Gustafsson, Uwe Johnson und Barbara König 1972," *Sinn und Form* (6/1997): 780 and 777.

[8] Horst Bienek, *Werkstattgespräche mit Schriftstellern* (Munich: Hanser, 1962), 24.

[9] Klaus Günther Just, "Das Tagebuch als literarische Form," in *Übergänge, Probleme und Gestalten der Literatur* (Bern: Francke, 1966), 38.

[10] Max Frisch to Uwe Johnson, 26 October 1980. In *Max Frisch/Uwe Johnson: Der Briefwechsel, 1964–1983*, ed. Eberhard Fahlke (1999; Frankfurt am Main: Suhrkamp, 2001), 27. Subsequent references to this source in the text as *F/J*, and page number.

[11] Johnson only commented orally on the entries from 1971.

[12] Note that the 163-page span given for the eighteen pages of commentary is due to the fact that the *Frisch/Johnson* volume also includes the text passages on which Frisch and Johnson comment.

[13] Daniel de Vin, *Max Frischs Tagebücher: Studie über "Blätter aus dem Brotsack" (1940), "Tagebuch 1946–1949" (1950) und "Tagebuch 1966–1971" (1972) im Rahmen des bisherigen Gesamtwerks (1932–1975)* (Cologne: Böhlau, 1977), 255. De Vin shows the "Literarisierung der ursprünglichen Notizen" (literarizing of the original notes) and demonstrates that the authenticity is only an illusion (254).

[14] Hans Mayer, "Die Schuld der Schuldlosen. Max Frischs 'Tagebuch 1966–1971,'" *Der Spiegel*, June 12, 1972, 124.

[15] Quoted in Höllerer, "Sind Tagebücher zeitgemäss?," 781.

[16] Quoted in Höllerer, "Sind Tagebücher zeitgemäss?," 781.

[17] De Vin, *Max Frischs Tagebücher*, 210.

[18] Marcel Reich-Ranicki, "Der Klassiker der Skizze. Zu Max Frischs 'Tagebuch 1966–1971,'" *Die Zeit*, May 5, 1972.

[19] The correspondence between Max Frisch and his American translator Geoffrey Skelton shows that the Swiss writer had originally opted for the title "Journal." In a letter of February 1973, Frisch writes to his translator: "Ich vergass Helen Wolff zu schreiben, dass wir uns über den Titel geeinigt haben: JOURNAL 1966–1971" (Max Frisch Archive). But a few months later, this title had been replaced by "Sketchbook," apparently favored by the American publisher Helen Wolff. Indeed, in a letter of August 1973, Geoffrey Skelton writes to Max Frisch: "Soeben hörte ich von Helen Wolff in New York, dass das TAGEBUCH jetzt in die Produktion geht und dass es mit Ihrem Einverständnis den Titel SKETCHBOOK trägt. Warum auch nicht? Der Unterschied ist gering, und wenn dieser Titel dem Verleger besser gefällt [. . .]" (Max Frisch Archive). I thank Dr. Margit Unser for her assistance and the permission to quote from unpublished letters.

[20] Horst Steinmetz, *Max Frisch: Tagebuch, Drama, Roman* (Göttingen: Vandenhoeck & Ruprecht, 1973), 86.

[21] Steinmetz, *Max Frisch*, 87.

[22] Rolf Kieser, "An Interview with Max Frisch. Conducted by Rolf Kieser," *Contemporary Literature* 13/1 (1972): 7.

[23] Jürgen H. Petersen, *Max Frisch* (Stuttgart/Weimar: Metzler, 2002), 93. Petersen distinguishes three kinds of texts: "Faktum" (fact), set in grotesque font, "Fiktion" (fiction), set in italics, and "Persönliches" (personal notes), set in typescript, and calls the texts set in antiqua "einen die drei Bereiche vermittelnden, ihren Gegensatz aufhebenden 'literarischen' Text" (a "literary" text that mediates between the three areas and sublates their oppositions), but as he himself notices, "manche Textpassagen sind (damit) nicht zureichend zu fassen" (some passages in the text cannot be adequately grasped with this model), see Petersen 87.

[24] Heinz F. Schafroth, "Bruchstücke einer großen Fiktion. Über Max Frischs Tagebücher," *Text + Kritik* 47/48 (October 1975): 63.

[25] Meike Heinrich-Korpys, *Tagebuch und Fiktionalität: Signalstrukturen des literarischen Tagebuchs am Beispiel der Tagebücher von Max Frisch* (St. Ingbert: Röhrig, 2003), 175.

[26] See the translator's note in *Sketchbook 1946–1949*: "All divergences from the original text [. . .] have been made either at the author's instigation or with his consent." The American publisher Helen Wolff seems to have influenced Frisch's decision to delete some passages for the English translation. We know this from a letter Frisch wrote to his translator in February 1974: "Lieber Herr Skelton, ich habe Ihnen das TAGEBUCH 46–49 geschickt, die gekürzte Version als Vorlage für die Übersetzung. Im Oktober besuchte mich Helen Wolff, machte einige Vorschläge [. . .]" (Max Frisch Archive). I thank Dr. Margit Unser for her assistance and the permission to quote from unpublished letters. Five texts were completely left out of *Sketchbook 1946–1949*: "Nachtrag zu Marion" (219), "Marion und das Gespenst" (24), "Kalendergeschichte" (113), "Marion und der Engel" (160), and "Der Harlekin, Entwurf zu einem Film" (648–93). Three texts were

also left out of *Sketchbook 1966–1971*: “8.2.1968” (*GW* 6:103), “Kabusch” (*GW* 6:258–60), and “Kabusch II” (*GW* 6:263–71).

27 Rolf Kieser, “Man as His Own Novel: Max Frisch and the Literary Diary,” *Germanic Review* 47, no. 2 (March 1972): 114.

28 See Franz Karl Stanzel, *Theorie des Erzählens* (Götttingen: Vandenhoeck & Ruprecht, 1979).

29 Heinrich-Korpys, *Tagebuch und Fiktionalität*, 169.

30 See Johnson’s reactions to various passages, *Frisch/Johnson* 246, 253, 276–77, 288, 294, 314, 336, 343, 357, 367.

31 See Céline Letawe, *Max Frisch–Uwe Johnson: Eine literarische Wechselbeziehung* (St. Ingbert: Röhrig, 2009).

32 This is the case with the “Berzona” text quoted earlier. Here is the published version of the beginning of that text:

> Das Dorf, wenige Kilometer von der Grenze entfernt, hat 82 Einwohner, die Italienisch sprechen; kein Ristorante, nicht einmal eine Bar, da es nicht an der Talstraße liegt, sondern abseits. Jeder Gast aus den Städten sagt sofort: Diese Luft! dann etwas bänglich: Und diese Stille! Das Gelände ist steil: Terrassen mit den üblichen Trockenmauern, Kastanien, ein Feigenbaum, der Mühe hat, Dschungel mit Brombeeren, zwei große Nußbäume, Disteln usw. [. . .] (*Tb* 2, 11).

33 Rolf Kieser, “Man as His Own Novel,” 116.

34 See Johnson’s reactions to various passages, *F/J*, 303, 311–12, 328, 341, 348, 367, 402–4.

35 “‘Der Ruhm habe die Dichtung verlassen, er gebühre den Wissenschaftlern und den Akrobaten; es ist Apollinaire, der das gesagt hat’, sagt jemand.” (*Tb* 2, 105–6).

36 The manifesto is available online at http://68.abstractidea.ch/img/zh_manifest_82kb.jpg (accessed March 8, 2013).

37 Daniel de Vin, *Max Frischs Tagebücher*, 148. John Russell also refers to the “three-part plan” as something that “seems to come naturally to Max Frisch.” John Russell, *Reciprocities in the Nonfiction Novel* (Athens, GA: University of Georgia Press, 2000), 178.

38 Frisch initially planned to start his *Tagebuch* with the question whether it was still worth beginning such a book at his age: “Frage beim Schneiden der Fingernägel: wie lang (in Metern oder Zentimetern) werden die noch wachsen?—ob ein Tagebuch anzufangen sich noch lohnt.” (Question while cutting fingernails: how long (in meters or centimeters) are they still going to grow? Whether it will still be worth it to start a sketchbook; *F/J*, 246). Johnson’s reaction to the short text—“die Frage eines Mannes von fünfundfünfzig Jahren nach der erwartbaren Länge seiner Fingernägel [erscheint] vordringlich kokett” (a man asking at the age of fifty-five how long his fingernails can be expected to grow appears quite cocquettish)—caused Frisch to replace it with the questionnaire.

8: “Writing in order to be a stranger to oneself”: Max Frisch’s *Stiller*

Beatrice Sandberg

Frisch’s novel *Stiller* (1954) begins with an exclamation: “Ich bin nicht Stiller!” (I’m not Stiller!)[1] The novel’s protagonist, Anatol Stiller, a Swiss sculptor who has taken on a new identity and moved to the United States and then to Mexico, returns to his home country and is arrested upon his arrival after an altercation with a Swiss border guard who questions the validity of his identification papers. The novel consists of two parts, a journal that Stiller writes in a series of notebooks while in pre-trial confinement, and an account in which the district attorney, who had become a friend of Stiller’s, outlines Stiller’s life after his release. Throughout Stiller’s notebooks, the prisoner claims that his name is not Stiller, but James White, a position that he continues to insist on even when his wife confronts him. Like many of Frisch’s works, the novel negotiates conflicts between subjective and external reality and questions the stability of selfhood. The notebooks display a clear structure. Segments on Stiller’s wife Julika and on the district attorney Rolf and his wife Sibylle alternate with reflections, dialogues, and stories that Stiller/White invents for his prison guard in order to entertain him while at the same time revealing a lot of himself.

There is a stark contrast in both style and content between Stiller’s notebooks and the fictional editor’s account. While the notebooks contain detailed descriptions and subjective assessments, Rolf’s editorial appendix condenses time frames and focuses on his conversations with Stiller and on existential and religious questions of self-acceptance. According to Rolf, Stiller’s self-alienation reaches religious depths: in his diagnosis, Stiller’s inability to love or accept himself is a symptom of his refusal to accept God. Rolf maintains that for Stiller, self-acceptance will only be possible if he overcomes his hubris of self-sufficiency and self-redemption. Only at the very end does Rolf notice a change in Stiller. Stiller stops seeing the world exclusively as projections of himself: “Er selbst fing an, in der Welt zu sein” (*S* 752; He himself was beginning to be in the world; *INS* 336). Until this point, Stiller’s passionate efforts to achieve a mode of existence free of prejudice and of prefabricated images missed the target because his preconceived notions got in the way. The ironic tragedy of his failure to take full ownership of his life plays itself out in a self-perpetuating vicious cycle of guilt and longing for compassion, entitlement and slight, excessive demands and resignation. Having abandoned the project of acting out an invented identity, the only option available to Stiller appears to be a solitary life. How much of this can be read as insightfulness on Stiller's part and how much of it is mere resignation remains an open question.

The *Stiller* materials preserved at the Max Frisch Archive in Zurich document that Frisch had not decided on the first sentence until he corrected the galley proofs.[2] While earlier versions of the novel start with the remand prisoner James L. White's curt request for whiskey, underscoring his American lifestyle, the new first sentence abruptly focuses on White's/Stiller's refusal to be confined to one identity upon his arrival in or return to Switzerland. Right from the beginning, the reader faces the question of what kind of narrator is at work. The narrative voice is not merely marked by a subjective position, which characterizes any journal writer.[3] Since the narrator refuses to identify himself, the reader has to consider him an unreliable narrator. White's/Stiller's double perspective also impacts the people he observes, especially Julika. He insists that the woman who visits him is not his wife. This ingenious focusing on the core problem of an unstable identity with all its consequences notwithstanding, Frisch emphasized, in a conversation with the literary scholar Walter Schmitz, the editor of Frisch's collected works published by Suhrkamp, that the novel never explicitly uses the word "identity."[4]

Frisch wrote the first draft of the novel, a manuscript of 600 pages, during his stay in the United States in 1951–52, which was sponsored by a Rockefeller Foundation scholarship. He was, however, not content with this first version. In the summer of 1953, Frisch reconceptualized plotlines and the narrative perspective: The protagonist's defense attorney asks him to write down his experiences. Now the heterogeneous elements of the manuscript could be woven together, and Frisch's writing process accelerated. Parts of the first draft consist of travel notes about the United States, some of which had been published as accounts of his travels, impressions of New York City and of desert landscapes,[5] as well as a story that is based on Washington Irving's short story "Rip van Winkle" (1819), and a story about the discovery of the Carlsberg Caverns in New Mexico by James Larkin White (1882–1946), whose name is used for Stiller's alter ego. Since his notes fail to live up to the defense attorney's expectations, Stiller finally seizes the opportunity to write only for himself, which results in the mixture of stories and precise accounts of conversations and dreams.

Frisch's American Experience

Frisch's first stay in the United States had a sustained impact on him, and it provided him with material that he integrated and rearranged in the novel. In a letter from New York to Helga Roloff from June 1951, Frisch describes his life in a black neighborhood in Berkeley, which in the novel he varied slightly to Oakland, where he was able to live in a small house owned by a married student couple. He absorbed community events in his neighborhood: "Gesang von der nahen, kleinen Negerkirche, Geburtstagsparty im Nachbarsgarten" (songs from the small nearby black church, a birthday party in the neighbors' garden).[6]

In *Stiller* the birthday is changed to a colorful wedding party (*S* 187–89). The letter continues with a postscript in which Frisch points out that he does not have to pay any rent but is obligated to feed the cat even though he cannot tolerate cats: "Die Katze muss fortan im Freien essen, gegenseitiger Hass, dann kommt sie eines Tages mit einer blutenden Wunde an der Wange [. . .] Sie zwingt mich zu Mitleid und schlechtem Gewissen [. . .]" (The cat has to eat outside the house, mutual hatred, then one day she comes with a bleeding wound at her cheek [. . .] She forces me to be compassionate and to have a guilty conscience [. . .]).[7] In *Stiller* the related scene with a cat is exaggerated for Stiller's/White's audience, the prison guard Knobel. The cat episode is symbolically linked to Stiller's maltreatment of Julika, who is physically ill and also suffers psychologically, and his feeling of failure. Knobel remains unaware of these correlations because he is only interested in the plot (*S* 415). It is tempting to read turbulences in Frisch's own life, as manifest in his separation from his family after he completed *Stiller*, into the novel. But in contrast to Frisch, Stiller's attempt to return to and to prevail in Switzerland with an identity that he crafted in America fails. For several protagonists in the novel, however, experiencing America triggers personal liberation and self-realization. Sibylle, the prosecutor's wife and Stiller's former lover, also decides to spend two years in the United States and uses her stay to rethink and scrutinize the viability of her marriage. Sibylle succeeds in resolving the conflict. She learns from experience, as does Rolf, who uses the time of their separation as an opportunity to change his attitude. Sibylle is ready to return home, since both agree to give their marriage another chance.

Thematic Clusters

In a notebook entry written in December 1950, Frisch reminds himself that he still has the energy to experience a new beginning, "im Frühling möchte ich nach Amerika, die Erde ist noch sehr gross, im Frühling bin ich vierzigjährig."[8] The same notebook contains the first notes for *Stiller*. This archival finding documents that Frisch began to work on the novel before his stay in the United States and not, as scholars previously assumed, during his time in America. Frisch starts his Stiller sketch in his notebook as follows: "Plötzlich [. . .] ein überwältigendes Gefühl von Impotenz" (All of a sudden [. . .] an overwhelming feeling of impotence).[9] Feelings of boredom, fear, and impotence are omnipresent for Stiller and constitute a central motif of his suffering. Fear of impotence, in part in a broad sense, re-emerges in a passage from Frisch's unpublished notebooks, dated March 1951, in a more detailed way:

> Roman: Stiller:—Angst vor der Impotenz—Es zugeben: das Gefühl, dass alles stimmt, plötzlich sieht er auch den Zusammenhang der Zufälle: für ihn. [. . .] Impotenz gegenüber dem Leben: Grund in der schöpferischen Fantasie? [. . .] Zweifel: Kunst als blosser Ersatz; aus Lebensschwäche [. . .] Seine Einsicht, die alle frühere Deutung verschiebt [. . .] Wiederholung, kurz, die schon erzählten Situationen: mit Umdeutung.[10]

> [Novel: Stiller: Fear of impotence. To admit it, the feeling that all this actually is true, suddenly he also sees how all the coincidences fit together: for him. [. . .] Impotence with regard to life caused by creative imagination? [. . .] Doubts: art as a mere substitute because one is to weak to be alive [. . .] His insight that displaces all previous interpretation [. . .] repetition, in sum the already narrated situations. Reinterpreted.]

Impotence is not only understood in a narrowly sexual sense but more comprehensively as a weakness that permeates his life, possibly as a consequence of artistic creativity. Here Frisch refers to the classical conflict between artist and bourgeois and to the oppositional forces of art and life, themes he encountered in the works of Thomas Mann.[11] Fear of impotence is linked to an existential *Angst* that emerges throughout the novel in various manifestations as Stiller's core problem (*S* 617). Impotence is also a recurrent element in Stiller's criticism of Switzerland (*S* 594). Ironically and paradoxically, Stiller's criticisms of Switzerland fall back on himself, highlighting his artistic mediocrity, his lack of scope, and his self-righteousness. In contrast to an ailing Switzerland, from which Stiller takes flight only to end up in one of its prisons upon his return, America presents itself to him as a paradise of opportunities that endows him with a kind of rebirth—if not with the new identity he yearns for and that is denied him by the Swiss authorities and the people who knew him.[12] In every regard, Stiller's behavior turns out to be a flight from himself, an attempt at escape whose futility he admits early on (*S* 412).

The Impossibility of Narrating One's Own Life

A notebook entry by Frisch from March 1952 includes the nucleus of an early version of the novel: "Warum ist es schwer, zu sein, wie man ist? Einer zu sein, nicht alle; das fällt ihnen schwer." (Why is it so difficult to be the way one is? To be one, not everyone. This is difficult for them.)[13] This passage shares a strong affinity with the Kierkegaard epigraph that Frisch chose for *Stiller*, "darum ist es so schwer, sich selbst zu wählen" (therefore it is so hard to choose oneself). The passage also refers to the central topic in Hermann Hesse's work, the difficulty of self-realization.[14] Frisch's first notes towards the novel culminate in the exclamation: "was ich will!—dass du mich frei machst, Du kannst es!—Was mich fesselt: dass wir nicht lebten" (what I want!—that you set me free, you are capable of doing it!—What constrains me: that we did not live).[15]

In his lectures on poetics that he delivered at the City College of New York in November 1981 (published in 2008 as *Schwarzes Quadrat*), Frisch discusses the genesis of *Stiller* and describes its core problem as follows: "Man kann alles erzählen, nur nicht sein wirkliches Leben [. . .] 'Ich habe keine Sprache für die Wirklichkeit'" (You can narrate everything but your own real life [. . .] I have no language for reality).[16] Not even a writer is in possession of such language, Frisch continues, but it is being aware of this lack that makes him or her a writer. Frisch insists on this paradoxical insight and states, "Es bleibt uns nur die Fiktion" (*SQ* 29; All that is left for us is fiction). In a next step, Frisch argues that there is no fiction that is not grounded in experience: "Die Fiktion entlarvt unsere Erfahrung der Realität" (*SQ* 29–30; Fiction debunks our experience of reality). This diagnosis is immediately followed by Frisch's comment on the title of his lecture "The Writer's Journey": "Eines Tages, 1974, genau zwanzig Jahre nach der Behauptung, dass er nicht Stiller sei, mietet er sich einen Wagen in Manhattan und macht ein Journey nach Long Island, Montauk, genau gesagt, und dort bleibt er plötzlich stehen im Wind." (*SQ* 31; One day in 1974, exactly twenty years after he had claimed that he was not Stiller, he rents a car in Manhattan and makes a trip to Long Island, Montauk, to be exact, and there he suddenly stops in the wind). Frisch proceeds to quote a central passage from his novella *Montauk* that was published in 1975: "Ich lebe nicht mit der eignen Geschichte, nur mit Teilen davon, die ich habe literarisieren können" (*SQ* 31; I do not live with my own story, just with parts from it that I was able to turn into literature).

In *Montauk* (see Ruth Vogel-Klein's chapter in this volume) Frisch tries to put into words how his life as an author is refracted in his work by alternating between a first- and a third-person narrator. The narrator and notebook writer in *Stiller*, who fled to the United States and returned as someone else in search of a new start, splits himself into the characters of Stiller and White. White/Stiller writes an account of his confrontations with Stiller's family and acquaintances as well as their impressions of and experiences with Stiller. He also documents his own reflections as well as his conversations with the prison guard, his defense attorney, and his prosecutor. His accounts of these people are characterized by a strong sense of irony. In the novel, Frisch portrays Stiller as someone who constantly plays with identities, masks, and roles, a protagonist who invents a story for himself and uses it to hide his personal truth. Pursuing "das Geschäft des Schriftstellers," the writer's task, he insists on the authenticity of the written word, its autonomy from an allegedly autobiographic substrate that in its turn still informs the text.[17] *Stiller* is an aesthetic work that puts the possibility of writing about oneself, or any self, into question, a concern that the novel shares with other modernist and postwar texts.

The novel's narrative structure, the wide-ranging existential, psychological, social, and aesthetic conflicts it enacts, its thematically multilayered approach, as well as its cunning narrative complexity continue to stimulate multifaceted interpretive approaches.[18] In a draft of a dust-jacket blurb for the first edition, Frisch rejected the notion that the novel is mainly about marriage, even though two marriages in crisis served as experimental projection screens. Frisch also insists that it is not a travel book. Taking Kierkegaard's dictum "Wähle dich selbst!" (Choose yourself!) as a point of departure, Frisch suggests that the theme of the novel is individual freedom. Frisch posits that the protagonist's path can be divided into three stages of freedom: "Selbsterkenntnis auch über seine Leistungen, Leben entfremdet, Annahme seiner selbst (wähle dich selbst), Verzicht darauf" (Self-knowledge also through one's achievements, life alienates, self-acceptance (choose yourself), renouncing it).[19] Contrary to Frisch's conception, most literary critics have emphasized Stiller's marital tragedy, while also discussing the problem of self-alienation and self-acceptance. One praises the artistic treatment of the experience of time ("temps vécu") and the mirroring of perception and imagination.[20] Several Swiss critics harshly criticized what they interpreted as the author's resentment of Switzerland, condemning Stiller's comments on his native country as inappropriate.[21] German literary critics mentioned this topic rather briefly, recognizing Frisch as a moralist who operates with irony, and focusing on the protagonist who attempts to flee from himself and lacks a language for his reality. From early on, questions of identity and image that already informed earlier texts by Frisch, especially his *Tagebuch 1946–1949*, as well as his social criticism, are considered central themes of the novel.[22]

Stiller's notes from his pre-trial confinement in Zurich begin with his arrest in autumn 1952 and cover a ten-week time period until the pronouncement of a judgment. He records his experiences in the notebooks that he has been given and logs the encounters with his wife Julika, the district attorney Rolf, whom he later befriends, and Rolf's wife Sibylle, Stiller's former lover, as well as other acquaintances and relatives, encounters in which all of them present their views of the missing Stiller to him. Both the conversations and the on-site inspections in Davos and Zurich make it abundantly clear that White and Stiller are identical, even if Stiller refuses to agree: "Ich bin nicht ihr Stiller" (*S* 401; I'm not their Stiller; *INS* 41). After the pronouncement of a judgment, which sentences Stiller to self-acceptance, the sculptor retreats to Lake Geneva. Stiller presents himself to Rolf "etwas zu fröhlich" (*S* 732; a little too gaily: *INS* 316). He abandons his sculpting and sets up his own business as a pottery maker, while Julika quits ballet and dance school and starts a career as an exercise instructor. In his postscript, the prosecutor, who visits Stiller together with Sibylle roughly one and a half years later, a visit during which they learn about the renewed onset of Julika's illness and witness her lung operation, describes Stillers's and Julika's efforts to live together again, relapsing and repeating mistakes of the past, and crucifying one another. It is also Rolf who publishes his friend's account several years after the verdict without any editorial changes. The title that he affixes to the account, however, "Stillers Aufzeichnungen im Gefängnis," poses a dilemma of narrative perspective because after all, Stiller writes pretending to be James White, and the title seems to indicate that the uncertainty surrounding his identity has already been decided.[23]

In contrast to his literary precursors, for instance the fictional editors in Goethe's novel *Die Leiden des jungen Werthers* (1774) and in Hermann Hesse's *Der Steppenwolf* (1927), Rolf's relationship to Stiller is constituted by multiple layers of involvement. In his roles as betrayed husband, district attorney, and eventually generous friend, he witnesses Stiller's battles and defeats. Cautious compassion is his only option, since both he and his wife are burnt children who dread the fire. They rebuild their marriage, which has been damaged by Sibylle's affair with Stiller, with self-discipline and newly acquired mutual respect and are capable of constructing a sustainable relationship.

Innovative Narrative Perspective in Stiller

The novel's innovative characteristics include the aforementioned shifts of narrative perspective between a third-person and a split first-person protagonist. Several time frames are interwoven with the points of view of characters who are confronted with Stiller and who tell him about their impressions and experiences. Frisch breaks open Stiller's/White's confinement by having him entertain his prison guard, the reader, and himself during the waiting hours between visits with accounts of exotic landscapes and adventures. With his stories, Stiller also tries to create a communicative foundation for expressing his concern in an indirect way, albeit unsuccessfully.[24] The unavoidable clash of the split perspective of perception takes place during the field inspection of Stiller's studio, where past and present inexorably collide and where Stiller abandons his role of Mr. White. Going berserk, he smashes to pieces everything that reminds him of his former life as a sculptor. This violent fit of rage can be read as triggered by Stiller's irrevocable insight that attempting to escape his old identity and making a fresh beginning free of the burden and guilt of the past is impossible. Stiller does not directly express his own view of his life. It is White who writes down statements about Stiller, who later refrains from any communicative effort and allows Rolf to speak on his behalf. This avoidance of immediate autobiographical narration corresponds with Frisch's conviction that everything can be put into words except one's own life. Until his flight to America, Stiller had tried to craft a persona that fit and masked him, a futile effort that was accompanied by feelings of inferiority, self-inflation, and mediocrity. It is the others who form and formulate the image of Stiller, the sculptor. The others also indirectly expose the failures of his self-images and his botched attempts to craft a fitting form for himself. As Volker Hage concisely points out, whenever Stiller talks about his life, he does so by sarcastically quoting others and thereby puts the reliability of the detailed second-hand accounts into question.[25]

The Function of Stories in the Novel

One of the narrative tools the novel uses to present indirect accounts of the protagonist is the frequent insertion of stories within the story. For Stiller/White, telling stories is the only way to convey something about one's own experience, since he is incapable of putting "die schlichte Wahrheit" (the plain, unvarnished truth) on paper, as his defense attorney demands (*S* 362; *INS* 9). In his essay "Unsere Gier nach Geschichten" (Our Greed for Stories), Frisch writes: "Erfahrung bewährt sich daran, dass sie die Geschichte, die sie erfindet, glaubhaft macht. [. . .] Die Erfahrung dichtet" (Experience proves its value by making the story that it invents believable. [. . .] Experience writes poetry; *GW* 4, 262–64). Stiller/White articulates his reality in stories. They serve him as warnings, variations, and repetitions. Some of the stories in *Stiller* serve as Stiller/White's attempts to sketch his own identity before society imposes its fixed image of the missing Stiller on him again.

The first inserted story's protagonist is Isidor, a pharmacist whose actions are driven by his fear of repetition, a central motif in the novel (*S* 420). Isidor's fear drives him to despair and his marriage becomes unbearable. For Stiller, this fear takes on an existential dimension and even leads him to an alleged murder, an event that he narrates in his Texas "Grottengeschichte" (*S* 506–21). In his conversations with his prison guard Knobel, Stiller insists that this is a true story about himself. He also maintains that this event triggered his exchange of identities with Jim White, which enabled him to return as a reborn person, another man trying to find himself with the help of numerous rituals inspired by depth psychology.[26] One of Frisch's literary sources regarding his recurring motifs of a protagonist's return and identity loss is Washington Irving's short story, "Rip van Winkle" (1819). In a notebook entry from 1953, Frisch calls it a sketch of a man who never lived because he always demanded of himself to conform to the image the others had imposed on him. Frisch told Horst Bienek, who believed that Frisch's radio play *Rip van Winkle* formed the nucleus of *Stiller*, that he used Rip van Winkle material from the novel for the radio play in order to make money. However the first notebooks on *Stiller* already include sketches for a radio play.[27]

In the exaggerated fantasy stories that Stiller/White shares with the credulous prison guard, who admires him as an adventurer and a killer, he sketches a counter-reality. The story of Florence, a biracial American woman (*S* 404–7; 536–44) projects his wish for a passionate relationship with an erotically desirable, healthy woman who dances in an uninhibited way and who stands in stark contrast to Julika, whom Stiller compares to a cold sea creature, a comparison whose motivation is pondered by White (*S* 534). It is also Florence who saves Stiller's life after his botched suicide attempt that he describes to Rolf on the day before his trial comes to a verdict. By saving his life, Florence sentences him to continue to live under his former identity, his old Stiller self. This experience finally triggers Stiller's return to Switzerland, where he is taken into custody and put in jail.

Frisch's Critique of Switzerland

The prison metaphor represents one of Stiller's central perceptions of Switzerland: "Meine Zelle [. . .] ist klein wie alles in diesem Land, sauber, so daß man kaum atmen kann vor Hygiene, und beklemmend gerade dadurch, daß alles recht, angemessen und genügend ist [. . .] Alles in diesem Land hat eine beklemmende Hinlänglichkeit." (*S* 368; My cell [. . .] is small, like everything in this country, so clean one can hardly breathe for hygiene, and oppressive precisely because everything is just right [. . .] Everything in this country is oppressively adequate; *INS* 15). A society that regulates rather than questions everything triggers a feeling of constraint and loss of freedom, which is harmful to human creativity and flourishing. This perception also informs the work of Friedrich Dürrenmatt (1921–90), Frisch's friend and competitor whose stature as a Swiss representative of German letters equals that of Frisch. In a speech in honor of the Czech playwright and president Václav Havel delivered in 1990, Dürrenmatt called Switzerland a prison, causing an uproar in the Swiss media.[28]

Reading *Stiller* without an ear for the irony that permeates the whole novel would run the risk of various misinterpretations.[29] Any doubt about Stiller's reasons for leaving Switzerland and about White's true identity is erased when he writes down an account of his tirades against Switzerland, an account that is sometimes told through Julika's and Sibylle's narrative perspectives, and includes his confrontational disputes with the architect Sturzenegger, whom he considers a clown. In his portrayal of his defense attorney Bohnenblust, Stiller also ironicizes the embodiment of a stereotypical Swiss and the institutions he holds dear.[30] In *Stiller* Frisch creates an arsenal of characters and situations to illustrate his frustrations with Switzerland. The novel decries Switzerland's fabricated idylls, the deprivation of spiritual and material freedom there, its mendaciousness, and its lack of humor. Stiller also levels criticism against what he portrays as the Swiss's self-righteousness, backwardness, lifelessness, and lack of historical awareness and what he calls the impotence of their imagination. Stiller also targets himself with these relentless criticisms.

In a subtle analysis of the novel, Sonja Rüegg outlines Julika's characteristics and notices resemblances with qualities that the novel ascribes to Switzerland: On the surface, Julika, like Switzerland, is beautiful, but Stiller suspects that both lack substance. The text also emphasizes that both Julika and Switzerland remain mere ideas.[31] Frisch's criticism of Switzerland is a manifestation of his genuine concerns about the future of the country for which he feels more than he allows the reader to notice, even if they are mixed feelings.

Julika's and Stiller's Images and Self-Images

The image of Julika that Stiller sees during their first (re-)encounter in Zurich, where she visited while he was in jail, is symptomatic for the way he reduces her to an art object, an attitude for which others criticize him. Rolf provides the reader with excerpts of Stiller's descriptions of Julika's corpse, which Stiller sees in the hospital. Julika dies alone on Easter Sunday, like Stiller without having found redemption. Stiller perceives Julika not as a human being but only as an art object.[32] Her loneliness manifests itself in her face, which resembles a mask from classical antiquity and in her petrified aesthetic state, which makes her look like an object that has been sculpted by her husband:

> Ihre Haare sind rot, der gegenwärtigen Mode entsprechend sogar sehr rot [. . .] Sehr eigenartig [. . .] aber schön. [. . .] Leider hat sie die Augenbrauen zu einem dünnen Strich zusammenrasiert, was ihrem Gesicht eine graziöse Härte gibt, aber auch etwas Maskenartiges [. . .] Ihre Lippen sind für meinen Geschmack etwas zu schmal [. . .] Sie spricht sehr leise, damit der Partner nicht brüllt. (*S* 407–8)

> [Her hair is red, very red in fact, in keeping with the new fashion [. . .] Very curious [. . .] but beautiful. [. . .] Unfortunately her eyebrows have been plucked to a thin line, which gives her face a graceful hardness, but also a slightly masklike appearance [. . .] Her lips are rather thin for my taste [. . .] She speaks very softly, to prevent her interlocutor from shouting. (*INS* 47)]

While she was alive, however, Julika reacted like the wife in the Isidor story, "unfähig, ein anderes Wesen wahrzunehmen als ihren verschollenen Stiller" (*S* 411; simply incapable of perceiving any other being than her vanished Stiller: *INS* 50), unwittingly unleashing all Stiller's pent-up aggressions: he grabs and shakes her and throws her on the bed, where she remains, shutting her "uncommonly beautiful" eyes in pain. Stiller, narrating later, reveals his thoughts at the time: "Ich betrachtete sie wie einen Gegenstand, plötzlich ganz nüchtern, ein Weib, ein fremdes, irgendein Weib" (*S* 411–12; I looked at her as though she were an object, suddenly quite sober, as though she were just any unknown woman: *INS* 51).

Here the contradiction becomes tangible between Stiller describing Julika as if he had never met her before and his insinuations and assessments that imply a detailed knowledge of her. Stiller's high level of aggressiveness and brutality also suggests that what Stiller brushes aside as unfair prejudices that others harbor about his and Julika's relationship are indeed correct observations. What is at stake and presented in manifold variations is the relationship between a man who is rude, selfish, self-righteous, vulnerable, hurt, and plagued by fears of inferiority, and a woman who appears as beautiful, helpless, gentle, frigid, innocent, unhappy, and ill. Even during their first night together, Stiller explicitly refers to himself as a "stinkiger Fischer mit einer kristallenen Fee" (stinking fisherman with a fairy made of crystal). His neurotic relationship to his own body forms an obstacle for their marriage. Instead of love, Stiller, who suffers from fear of failure with women, is only able to offer a moderate level of faithfulness (*S* 500). Rolf is stunned when he reads Stiller's notes about Julika: "Das Bildnis, das diese Aufzeichnungen von Frau Julika geben, bestürzte mich: es verrät mehr über den Bildner, dünkt mich, als über die Person, die von diesem Bildnis vergewaltigt worden ist." (*S* 749; The picture which these notes give of Frau Julika amazes me; it appears to me to reveal more about the person who drew the picture than about the person who is so grossly misrepresented by it. *INS* 333).

According to Rolf's account of Stiller's and Julika's second attempt to live together, Julika refuses to fall prey again to her husband's compulsive behavior. She circumvents the torture of his continuous expectations by becoming ill and desiring to die. Rolf relates to her loneliness arising from her experience that her partner only listens to himself. He listens to Stiller's self-blame, which is at the same time aimed at Julika because she does not need him in the way he wants to be needed, and fails to understand why she should change, thus making it impossible for him to indulge in fantasies of reshaping her. In a conversation with Julika that takes place in Davos before he flees to America, Stiller shares the following self-critical insights:

> Überhaupt war ich ja voll Angst! Ich machte dich zu meiner Bewährungsprobe. Und darum konnte ich dich auch nicht verlassen. Dich zum Blühen zu bringen, eine Aufgabe, die niemand sonst übernommen hatte, das war mein schlichter Wahnsinn. Dich zum Blühen zu bringen! Dafür machte ich mich verantwortlich—und dich machte ich krank, versteht sich, denn wozu solltest du gesund werden mit einem solchen Mann; die Angst, dass du an meiner Seite unglücklich würdest, fesselte mich ja stärker als irgendeine Art von Glück, die du zu geben hast. (*S* 496–97)
>
> [I was altogether full of anxiety. I made you my test. And that's why I couldn't leave you. My crazy idea was to make you blossom out, a task no one else had undertaken. To make you blossom out! That was the responsibility I took on myself—and I made you ill, of course, for why should you become well with a husband like that; the fear that you were unhappy with me chained me faster than any kind of happiness you're able to give. (*INS* 121)]

Stiller's fear of sexual and existential impotence corresponds with Julika's frigidity, correlates with his comparison of Julika to a vase. He cannot compete with her sublimation of her own desires in the exhibitionist world of dance theater, especially since his own artistic achievements are not recognized. Frisch emphasizes the central importance of Stiller's description of bullfighting that he saw in Spain in the 1930s for his understanding of masculinity by reiterating the story in multiple refractions and with divergent interpretations. Stiller had returned from the Spanish Civil War as an injured man and not as a hero. His experience of failure drives him to self-pity. While Stiller agonizes about everything that is wrong in his life, and while both he and Julika make an effort to come together again, Rolf, whose optimism sometimes goes hand in hand with an inexorable sense of realism, sees in them "zwei Gefesselte mit der Vernünftigkeit, sich zu vertragen" (*S* 733; two people in chains who had the good sense to put up with one another: *INS* 318). The direly ill Julika and her desperate husband Stiller confess the irreversibly broken nature of their marriage to Rolf, who tries in vain to provide comfort.

The novel ends with great existential questions regarding the guilt of being alive and the difficulty of self-acceptance. In his later works, Frisch revisits and offers variations on these themes.

—Translated by Olaf Berwald

Notes

[1] References in this essay to Frisch's *Stiller* are to the edition in *Max Frisch: Gesammelte Werke in zeitlicher Folge* (*GW*) 3, ed. Hans Mayer and Walter Schmitz, 2nd ed. (Frankfurt am Main: Suhrkamp, 1986). Henceforth cited as *S* and page number in parentheses. Here, page 361. English translations are taken from *I'm Not Stiller*, trans. Michael Bullock (London/New York: Abelard-Schuman, 1958), cited as *INS* and page number in parentheses, here, page 9.

[2] Typescript in Max Frisch-Archive. See also Walter Schmitz, ed., *Materialien zu Max Frisch Stiller* 1 (Frankfurt am Main: Suhrkamp, 1978), 11, 32. The two volumes *Materialien 1* and *2* (also Frankfurt am Main: Suhrkamp, 1978) as well as *Max Frisch: Materialien*, ed. Walter Schmitz (Frankfurt am Main: Suhrkamp, 1987), represent a basic collection of critical approaches to the work of Frisch to which I am indebted.

[3] See Rolf Kieser, *Max Frisch: Das literarische Tagebuch* (Stuttgart: Huber, 1975), 87.

[4] Walter Schmitz, "Zur Entstehung von Max Frischs Roman Stiller," in *Materialien zu Max Frisch Stiller* 1, ed. Walter Schmitz (Frankfurt am Main: Suhrkamp, 1978), 29–34.

[5] Frisch also inserted descriptions of Swiss landscapes from his earlier works into the novel.

[6] Letters from Max Frisch to Helga Roloff, Max Frisch Archive. For further discussions of Frisch's impressions of the United States, compare Volker Hage, ed., *Max Frisch: In Amerika* (Frankfurt am Main: Schöffling, 1995).

[7] Roloff letters, Max Frisch Archive.

[8] Quoted from "Unser Mann in Amerika. Max Frisch und das Radio," in *Neue Zürcher Zeitung*, March 8, 2003. http://www.nzz.ch/2003/03/08/li/article8orw2_1.223124.html (accessed March 12, 2009). Altogether there are about 150 notebooks composed by Frisch throughout his life. I am grateful to the director of the Max Frisch Archive, Dr. Margit Unser, who introduced me to the notebooks.

[9] Notebook, December 17, 1950, Max Frisch Archive.

[10] Notebook, March 1951, Max Frisch Archive.

[11] Barbara Bigge has pointed out extensive correlations between Mann's novel *Der Zauberberg* and *Stiller*, which become especially conspicuous at the point when Julika is admitted to a sanatorium in Davos. For a systematic comparison of *Der Zauberberg* and *Stiller*, see Barbara Bigge, "'. . . allerlei Sonstiges.' Auf den Spuren des Zauberberg von Thomas Mann im Prosawerk Max Frischs" (Diss. University of Duisburg–Essen, 2007).

[12] Declaring Stiller a Calvinist and constructing a dialectical nexus between a rigorous American individualism and Calvin's doctrine of predestination, as Frederick A. Lubich has done, is a false generalization that ignores the historical facts. The Reformation theologian with the greatest impact on German-speaking Switzerland is Zwingli, whose role with regard to the doctrine of predestination differs widely from Calvin's. It is therefore misleading to posit a parallelism

between Stiller's/White's dual identity on one hand and Calvinism and American individualism on the other. Frederick A. Lubich, *Max Frisch: Stiller, Homo faber und Mein Name sei Gantenbein* (Munich: Fink, 1992), 23–26.

[13] Max Frisch Archive.

[14] See Hermann Hesse, *Demian. Die Geschichte von Emil Sinclairs Jugend*, in *Gesammelte Werke* 5 (Frankfurt am Main: Suhrkamp, 1970), 7: "Ich wollte ja nichts als das zu leben versuchen, was von selber aus mir heraus wollte. Warum war das so schwer?" (I wanted only to try to live in accord with the promptings which came from my true self. Why was that so very difficult?). Translation from *Demian: The Story of Emil Sinclair's Youth*, trans. Michael Roloff and Michael Lebeck (New York/Evanston: Harper & Row, 1965), xiii).

[15] "Notizheft April [19]51," Max Frisch Archive.

[16] Max Frisch, *Schwarzes Quadrat, zwei Poetikvorlesungen*, ed. Daniel de Vin and Walter Obschlager (Frankfurt am Main: Suhrkamp, 2008), 29, 35. Subsequent references to this source will be indicated with the abbreviation *SQ* and page number in parentheses.

[17] Hage, ed., *Max Frisch: In Amerika*, 64.

[18] See the "Forschungsüberblick" in Franziska Schößler and Eva Schwab's volume in the Oldenbourg Interpretationen series, *Max Frisch. Stiller. Ein Roman* (Munich: Oldenbourg, 2004), Frederick A. Lubich, *Max Frisch: Stiller, Homo faber und Mein Name sei Gantenbein* (Munich: Fink, 1992), and Claudia Müller, "*Ich habe viele Namen": Polyphonie und Dialogizität im autobiographischen Spätwerk Max Frischs und Friedrich Dürrenmatts* (Munich: Fink, 2009).

[19] Untitled note by Frisch, in *jetzt: max frisch*, ed. Luis Bolliger, Walter Obschlager, Julian Schütt (Frankfurt am Main: Suhrkamp, 2001), 102.

[20] Siegfried Unseld, "Ein neuer Roman von Max Frisch," *Morgenblatt für Freunde der Literatur*, September 23, 1951, reprinted in Schmitz, *Materialien zu Max Frisch Stiller* 2, 382–83.

[21] Werner Weber, "Der neue Roman von Max Frisch," *Schweizerische Rundfunkgesellschaft*, November 16, 1954, reprinted in Schmitz, *Materialien zu Max Frisch Stiller* 2, 387–90; Claude R. Stange, "Stiller: Zu einem Buch von Max Frisch," *Basler Nachrichten*, December 3, 1954, reprinted in Schmitz, *Materialien zu Max Frisch Stiller* 2, 408–12.

[22] For the wide range of literary genres that are used by Frisch as interpretive criteria in order to comprehend *Stiller*, compare Claudia Müller, "*Ich habe viele Namen.*"

[23] Rolf uses the more precise title "Stillers Aufzeichnungen im Gefängnis" (*S* 730) for the notebooks that he receives from Stiller.

[24] Some literary critics read Stiller's exaggerations and the inserted stories as aesthetic flaws and symptoms of a crisis of the novel.

[25] Hage, *Max Frisch: In Amerika*, 68.

[26] Compare the interpretations in *Materialien zu Max Frisch Stiller* 1, ed. Schmitz, 140–72, and Klaus Müller-Salget, *Max Frisch* (Stuttgart: Reclam, 1996), 72–78.

[27] Notebook "April 1951," Max Frisch Archive. For a careful and lucid outline of the literary genesis and thematic contexts of the radio play *Rip van Winkle*, the drama *Don Juan*, and *Stiller*, see Jürgen H. Petersen, *Max Frisch* (Stuttgart/ Weimar: Metzler, 2002).

[28] "Die Schweiz—ein Gefängnis," in Friedrich Dürrenmatt, *Meine Schweiz: Ein Lesebuch* (Zurich: Diogenes, 1998), 220–32.

[29] For a groundbreaking analysis of the role of irony in *Stiller*, see Helmut Naumann, *Der Fall Stiller: Antwort auf eine Herausforderung* (Rheinfelden: Schäuble, 1978).

[30] Sonja Rüegg offers an excellent analysis of the often ironic portrayal of Switzerland in *Stiller*, see Sonja Rüegg, *"Ich hasse nicht die Schweiz, sondern ihre Verlogenheit": Das Schweizbild in Max Frischs Werken "Graf Öderland," "Stiller," und "achtung: die schweiz" und ihre zeitgenössische Kritik* (Zurich: Chronos, 1998).

[31] Her red hair and white hat also allude to the colors of the Swiss flag, and Julika can be read as a modern version of the Helvetia figure, compare Sonja Rüegg, *"Ich hasse nicht die Schweiz,"* 277–82. For a discussion of Julika as a projection screen, compare Liette Bohler, *Der Mythos der Weiblichkeit im Werke Max Frischs* (New York: Lang, 1998), 90–104.

[32] In April 1951 Frisch wrote in his notebook: "seine Gewissensbindung an die *Kranke*; seine unverdauliche Erfahrung von der Divergenz zwischen Liebe und Geschlecht [. . .]—er opfert seine Potenz, dann rächt er sich für das Opfer. Stiller: Gewissen." (Max Frisch Archive; his being tied to the *sick woman* by his conscience; his indigestible experience of the incompatibility of love and sex [. . .]—he sacrifices his sexual potency, then he gets his revenge for the sacrifice. Stiller: Conscience.)

9: Cybernetic Flow, Analogy, and Probability in Max Frisch's *Homo Faber*

Paul A. Youngman

> *Wir [sind] denn doch keine kybernetischen Mäuse, gesteuert von "information" und "feed back" und basta.*
>
> *[After all, we are not cybernetic mice, guided by "information" and "feedback," once and for all.]*
>
> —Max Frisch, *Biografie: Ein Spiel*

THE AMERICAN AUTHOR Kurt Vonnegut proclaimed, "novels that leave out technology misrepresent life as badly as Victorians misrepresented life by leaving out sex."[1] If Vonnegut was correct, then Max Frisch's 1957 novel *Homo Faber* is a remarkably accurate representation of life. Although there is a tendency in some of the secondary literature, as noted by Ferdinand van Ingen in his article on technology and mythology in *Homo Faber*,[2] to view the protagonist Walter Faber's occupation and his obsession with all things technological as more or less coincidental, and although Frisch himself gave conflicting answers regarding Faber as a "Techniker," I suggest that technology is indeed a key to understanding this novel.[3] Faber's former lover Hanna Landsberg puts it best when she describes technology as a trick that allows humans to order the world in such a way "daß wir sie nicht erleben müssen" (so that we don't have to experience it).[4] This is Faber's goal. Throughout the text he denigrates "Erlebnisse" and the idea of "erleben." His connection to the natural world is filtered or mediated by technology, and Faber claims to prefer it that way. This essay will focus on Faber's technological desires through the lens of cybernetics—the coupling of nineteenth-century control theory and modern information theory popularized in the mid-twentieth century by Norbert Wiener—for Walter Faber is an admirer of cybernetic machines like computers because, in his words, "die Maschine erlebt nichts" (*HF* 75; the machine has no feelings: *HFAR* 76). Some machines are precision processors and calculators—something Faber, in hindsight, wishes he himself had been so that he would have been spared the "Erlebnis" of having had sex with his own daughter.

Before delving more deeply into cybernetics and its applicability to understanding the novel, a brief summary of the "facts" as Faber presents them is in order. Indeed, in his hospital notebooks, he tells his story through two reports—an appropriate form of communication for one who fancies himself "durchaus sachlich" (*HF* 91; quite realistic; my translation). The first report begins on June 21, 1957 and ends on July 8 of the same year. The second starts eleven days later, on July 19, as he lies dying in a hospital, and covers a period of approximately one week, ending in his death. In these reports, the reader learns that Faber is an engineer for UNESCO working to provide "*technische Hilfe für unterentwickelte Völker*" (*HF* 10, Frisch's emphasis; TECHNICAL AID TO UNDERDEVELOPED COUNTRIES; *HFAR* 7). Faber lives in New York, but jets around the world in Pan Am's state of the art "Super-Constellation" aircraft. He relies heavily on his Hermes-Baby typewriter and his camera and is at a loss without his electric razor. Faber believes in neither fate nor destiny, but only in mathematical probabilities—a critical aspect of his flawed embrace of Wiener's ideas. He is nicknamed Homo Faber, or man the creator, by Hanna, a former lover who never told him that he was the father of her daughter until after their child's death. It is around this child, Sabeth, that the story turns.

On a business trip to Mexico, Faber's airplane is forced to make an emergency landing in the desert of Tamaulipas. Here he and his fellow passengers spend four days awaiting rescue. This stay in the barren desert of northern Mexico marks the beginning of the unraveling of Walter Faber, for it is here that he meets Herbert Hencke, the brother of his childhood friend Joachim. Quickly calculating the odds of such a meeting, Faber decides that chance has played a role in this event, but not fate. He learns that Herbert is going to visit Joachim, who oversees a massive tobacco plantation in Guatemala. Faber uncharacteristically allows himself to be distracted from his work assignment and accompanies Herbert in finding Joachim, who, they discover, has hanged himself. Faber then returns to New York.

Commensurate with his loss of composure over these events, he decides that, on his next business trip, he will travel to Europe by ship. On board, he meets and is smitten with an attractive, twenty-something university student named Sabeth. He manages to convince her to travel with him through Europe to Greece—her ultimate destination. Along the way, they fall in love, and consummate their love one evening in Avignon. Faber also learns from Sabeth that her mother's name is Hanna, and that Hanna is an archaeologist, as his former lover Hanna Landsberg is. Faber, acting partly in denial and partly in the belief that Hanna had aborted their child, convinces himself that Sabeth could not possibly be his own child. They continue their travels, as well as their relationship, and reach Greece. After an ideal night spent on the Acrocorinth, Faber goes for a swim and leaves Sabeth sleeping. While he is in the water, he hears her screams. Sabeth has been bitten in the breast by a snake. Naked, Faber runs to her. In what appears to be a moment of recognition, she is repulsed and, backing away from him, falls off an embankment, landing on the back of her head. While Sabeth is in the hospital being treated for the snakebite, Faber is reunited with Hanna, who has come to be with her daughter. He learns that she never had the abortion. During this dark episode, he and Hanna also learn that Sabeth has died, not from the snake wound, but from massive injuries to her skull caused by the fall. In the end, after further journeys that include a return to Mexico and Guatemala, Faber goes back to Greece and dies of stomach cancer.[5]

The discussion of machines and cybernetics appears most explicitly in a passage in which Faber points out that Sabeth, his girlfriend and, as he only learns after her death, his daughter, "wußte nichts von Kybernetik." He bemoans the lack of understanding, both on Sabeth's part and on the part of people in general, about cybernetics:

> wie immer, wenn man mit Laien darüber redet, galt es, allerlei kindische Vorstellungen vom Roboter zu widerlegen, das menschliche Ressentiment gegen die Maschine, das mich ärgert, weil es borniert ist, ihr abgedroschenes Argument: der Mensch sei keine Maschine. Ich erklärte, was die heutige Kybernetik als *Information* bezeichnet: unsere Handlungen als Antworten auf sogenannte Informationen, beziehungsweise Impulse, und zwar sind es automatische Antworten, größtenteils unserem Willen entzogen, Reflexe, die eine Maschine ebensogut erledigen kann wie ein Mensch, wenn nicht sogar besser. (*HF* 74)

> [as always when you talk to laymen about it, I had to refute all sorts of childish notions about robots, the human resentment toward the machine, which annoys me because it is so short-sighted, and her hackneyed complaint that man isn't a machine. I explained what modern cybernetics means by INFORMATION—our actions or impulses as responses to information, automatic responses that are largely independent of the will, reflexes that a machine can carry out just as well as a man, if not better. (*HFAR* 75)]

For Sabeth's edification, Faber refers her to Norbert Wiener's *Cybernetics or Control and Communication in the Animal and the Machine* (*HF* 75). Mona and Gerhard Knapp hypothesize that this reference to Wiener's book as well as Frisch's other references to twentieth-century canonical works of science in the novel serve primarily a "Signalfunktion" (as signifiers) in that they simply help clarify Faber's "Denken und Bewußtsein" (thinking and consciousness), that is, that Frisch's mentions of these works are mere superficial allusions.[6] Moreover they suggest that one can assume "beim Autor eine periphere Kenntnis dieser Texte [. . .], zugleich aber ihre Quellenbedeutung als relativ gering einzuschätzen" (that the author had a cursory knowledge of these texts without assigning too much importance to them as sources).[7] I posit that the Knapps overstate their conclusion. Unlike the other scientific works Faber cites, which are all listed in a single passage and may well serve merely as modern, scientific markers of the time, the passage on cybernetics is not a mere contemporary, superficial reference as the Knapps claim, nor is it a simple coincidence as might be claimed by scholars who are part of the tendency highlighted by van Ingen. Rather, the passage is a key to understanding the downfall of Walter Faber because his misunderstanding of the nuances of Wiener's first-wave cybernetics speeds up his own demise.

Cybernetics arrived in the mid-twentieth century with some fanfare in the form of the writings of Norbert Wiener—a man as troubled by his new science of communication and control as he was excited by it. Wiener and Frisch were both writing in an era when there was a widening rift—identified by intellectuals like C. P. Snow—between humanists on the one hand and scientists and engineers on the other—an especially dangerous situation given that it was a time when science and technology were, as Snow wrote, "determining much of our destiny, that is, whether we live or die."[8] In order to prevent the establishment of two distinct cultures incapable of communicating with one another, Snow admonished intellectuals to establish a "third culture" that would bridge the gap between the techno-scientific and literary realms.[9] Wiener hoped that his vaunted cybernetics could serve as just such a bridging mechanism.

Given that it was all the rage in contemporaneous engineering circles, it is not surprising that Max Frisch, fiction writer and architect, refers to cybernetics in *Homo Faber*. In fact, by the time Frisch published his novel, Wiener's *Cybernetics or Control and Communication in the Animal and the Machine* (1948) and its more accessible adaptation for a lay reading public, *The Human Use of Human Beings* (1950), were already exerting interdisciplinary influence in the humanities and in the scientific and technological world and were the talk of the engineering fields as well as the budding field of systems control. Moreover, because cybernetics connects information, communication, and control, it seems appropriate that Frisch's protagonist, the engineer Walter Faber, embraces Wiener and cybernetics. Control is what Faber desires, and he wants to gain and maintain it in what he envisions to be a machine-like way. His problem is that he does not fully understand cybernetics. The world, according to the critic Ursula Roisch, "steht [Faber] als 'Gegenstand' gegenüber" (confronts [Faber] as an "object").[10] He does not consider himself in any way integrated with nature, which he derogatorily views as primitive and feminine.

Wiener's cybernetic program does not work as Faber wishes it would. One cannot simultaneously embrace cybernetics and confront the world as an object separate and distinct from oneself. Cybernetics is based on a level of integration between technology and the natural world that Faber would find uncomfortable at best. Wiener suggests that because our cells change many times over the course of our lives, humans are not so much discrete beings on earth as patterns of organization: "our tissues change as we live: the food we eat and the air we breathe become flesh of our flesh and bone of our bone, and the momentary elements of our flesh and bone pass out of our body every day with excreta. We are but whirlpools in a river of ever-flowing water. We are not stuff that abides, but patterns that perpetuate themselves."[11] These relatively optimistic ideas run directly counter to Faber's lament, "Überhaupt der ganze Mensch!—als Konstruktion möglich, aber das Material ist verfehlt: Fleisch ist kein Material, sondern ein Fluch." (*HF* 171; It's the same with the whole of man—the construction is passable, but the material is no good: flesh is not a material, but a curse. [*HFAR* 180–81]) Where Faber sees boundaries and limitations, Wiener sees flow and connection, and this fluid connectivity between humans and the external world allows Wiener to posit the existence of cybernetic systems. Faber chooses to ignore the metaphor of flow in Wiener's writings and construes him as saying only that humans are like machines. Admittedly, this is an analogy Wiener uses, but not in the same way or to the same extent that Faber wishes it to be true in his revealing comment on Sabeth's and other lay people's lack of scientific knowledge quoted above.

Walter Faber is a twentieth-century literary incarnation of the construct that literary scholar Katherine Hayles calls the liberal humanist subject (hereafter referred to as the humanist subject) and therefore fertile ground for a detailed discussion of a cybernetic understanding of the human relationship to the world, which is central to Frisch's novel. In her work *How We Became Posthuman: Virtual Bodies in Cybernetics, Literature, and Informatics* (1999), Hayles posits that the humanist subject is a philosophical construct that conceives of itself as a rational being with a strong sense of agency and solid grasp of reality. Moreover, born of Western, Enlightenment philosophy and values, this construct's defining boundaries are starkly drawn.[12] This leads to what Ursula Roisch calls Faber's "Subjekt-Objekt-Spaltung" (subject-object split).[13] Such conceptual boundaries have been a focus of Western philosophy, science, and art for centuries, and *Homo Faber* is no exception in its focus. Faber is the humanist subject and, as such, an embracer of his perceived apartness, so to speak. His problem is that he lives in a technological world in which the central tenets of the humanist subject, despite Norbert Wiener's vigorous defense of it, are under assault.

Much as Wiener may have bemoaned it, cybernetic thinking necessarily challenges the humanist subject's assumption of his own boundaries and agency, as well as his construction of reality. Indeed, later developments in cybernetics would eventually call into question the existence of the humanist subject as such, though Wiener's first wave did not. Wiener wished to see the humanist subject perpetuated. He saw its boundaries as porous, but as boundaries nonetheless. This idea of porous boundaries, which came under criticism by later cybernetic thinkers such as Humberto Maturana and Francisco Varela,[14] meant that, for Wiener, humans are more integrated into their surroundings than the humanist subject model would seem to allow. Within his integrative model, however, there were good and evil cybernetic systems. A "good system" maintains the humanist subject intact—autonomous, powerful, and well-defined, and allowing for the flow of information. This type of system involves a degree of flexibility in the relationship between the human and the object that an "evil system" does not evince. Of the latter, Wiener writes, "when human atoms are knit into an organization in which they are used, not in their full right as responsible human beings, but as cogs and levers and rods, it matters little that their raw material is flesh and blood."[15] Wiener's phrase "their full right as responsible human beings" is a nod to the humanist subject and its special nature—it is not just another object in the world. In an evil system, however, the loss of agency and autonomy as well as the disappearance of the border between human being and machine implied in Wiener's statement serve to erode the primacy of the humanist subject, and as we shall see later, speed up entropic decay in the system. In other words, if the human is part of a cybernetic machine-human system, and the machine is in control of that system, then the humanist subject no longer exists.

Katherine Hayles takes note of this threat. "Of all the implications first-wave cybernetics conveyed," she writes, "perhaps none was more disturbing and potentially revolutionary than the idea that the boundaries of the human subject are [philosophically] constructed rather than given."[16] When confronted with a human holding a hammer, for example, most people presume that the human ends with the outer layer of the epidermis and the hammer begins with its handle. Faber, for example, presumes that he is a discrete being, separate and distinct from his favorite objects and in control of them—his electric razor, his Hermes Baby typewriter, and his camera, among other things. Moreover, he wields technology not in an attempt to integrate with nature, but in a vain attempt to control nature and keep it at bay—his obsessive concern with the growth of his beard when he has no electricity for his razor is a case in point. The question of who or what is in control doesn't occur to Faber, the humanist subject: he simply assumes that he is. He also feels no need to concern himself with the essence of objects in the external world or the Kantian "thing in itself" because science and technology, as manifestations of control, will lead him to that essence; that is, science and technology determine, define, and mediate Faber's reality.

Cybernetics assumes a different model, one for which the metaphor of the feedback loop plays a critical role and one for which flow, analogy, and probability are central. Cybernetic systems are characterized by the fluid passing of information between the human perceiver and the object. Consciousness, or the human mode of perception, and physical objects are, as Ray Kurzweil writes in *The Age of Spiritual Machines* (1999), "fused to an irreducible duality," connected by the flow of information.[17] In cybernetic terms, our relationship with the external world is that of an informational feedback loop—a metaphor Faber attempts to embrace in the end, but his attempt is too little, too late.

One underlying assumption of cybernetics is that information processing is an aspect of human consciousness—an appealing prospect for Faber, but a prospect he largely misunderstands. In order to comprehend this assumption, a clarification of the term "information" is necessary. For the purposes of this essay I stray from the traditional, "common sense" meaning of information as an entity that literally informs, that is, as an entity that gives form and content to a message and in so doing imparts meaning. To the contrary, information by itself has no semantic value. Information, like any other object, requires an autonomous, conscious entity to process it in order to give it meaning. Information theory, then, as posited by Wiener, merely involves the transmission of messages through communication channels; it has less to do with the meaning of those messages than it does with probability.[18] Wiener, like his literary disciple Faber, holds that information is a function of probabilities that represent a choice of one message from an entire range of possible messages. Early in the text Faber muses, "[d]as Wahrscheinliche [. . .] und das Unwahrscheinliche [. . .] unterscheiden sich nicht dem Wesen nach, sondern nur der Häufigkeit nach, wobei das Häufigere von vornherein als glaubwürdiger erscheint" (*HF* 22; the probable [. . .] and the improbable [. . .] are not different in kind, but only in frequency; whereby the more frequent appears a priori more probable; *HFAR* 20). Only when confronted with subjectivity does meaning arise from the message. Faber himself, in his ruminations about his failed attempts to communicate with Sabeth about cybernetics quoted above, equates information with impulses and responses that are "größtenteils unserem Willen entzogen" (*HF* 74; largely independent of the will; *HFAR* 75) and thus machine-like and desirable. While Faber is correct in his equation of information with impulses, doing away with human will or even subjectivity is not what Wiener desired. The will is necessary to provide a semantic context subjectively applied through human consciousness. And the will allows the human a degree of control, exercising its "full right as a responsible human being," thereby establishing a productive system.[19]

What this means, of course, is that due to the subjective nature of human perception, one cannot truly know empirical reality. Subjectivity serves as a filter and, much to Faber's chagrin, no scientific or technological mediation can help reach the thing in itself. To the contrary, technological mediation serves as a further filter, as will be discussed below. The thing in itself, however, is not sought after in cybernetic theory, even though it is certainly something Faber desires to apprehend and believes he does apprehend. As Hayles aptly points out, "messages [in the context of cybernetic theory] are constituted, measured, and communicated not as things-in-themselves but as relational differences between elements in a field. Communication is about relation, not essence."[20] Further, in the key passage on cybernetics, Faber praises machines because a machine "hat keine Angst und keine Hoffnung, die nur stören, keine Wünsche in bezug auf das Ergebnis, sie arbeitet nach der reinen Logik der Wahrscheinlichkeit" (*HF* 75; feels no fear and no hope, which only disturb, it has no wishes with regard to the result, it operates according to the pure logic of probability; *HFAR* 76). The difficulty for Faber, and this is shown time and again in the text, is that the correct meaning of information, "das Wesen," does not always lie in the most probable message. He appreciates robots for their inability to dream or speculate and for their ability to be controlled "von [ihren] eigenen Ergebnissen (feed back)" (*HF* 75). Robots therefore cannot err in Faber's estimation. His flawed understanding of Wiener is no mere comic interlude, as Francis Michael Sharp has suggested it is.[21] Unfortunately for Faber and his immediate circle of friends and family, his dream is to live a life of sublime calculation—to what desired end, it is unclear. In retrospect, it is quite clear to the reader, however, that his calculations lead only to his undoing.

In addition to underestimating the importance of the human in the cybernetic system, Faber willfully overlooks the fact that "garbage in, garbage out" is axiomatic in a cybernetic world. His calculations, which he begins in San Sebastiano while traveling with Sabeth, are flawed from the beginning and lead him to conclude that Sabeth must be his friend Joachim's child and not his. He calculates and re-calculates this result until it adds up, admitting, "ich legte mir die Daten zurecht bis die Rechnung wirklich stimmte, die Rechnung als solche" (*HF* 122; I juggled the dates until the sum, as a sum, really worked out right; *HFAR* 125). And again, he reports, "Sie stimmte; ich hatte ja die Daten (die Mitteilung von Hanna, daß sie ein Kind erwartet, und meine Abreise nach Bagdad) so gewählt, daß die Rechnung stimmte" (*HF* 122; It was right; I had picked the dates (Hanna's announcement that she was expecting a baby, and my departure for Baghdad) in such a way that the sum was right; *HFAR* 125). These calculations come hard on the heels of Sabeth's revelation that her mother is named Hanna Landsberg and that she, too, studied in Zurich. Despite such coincidences, Faber disingenuously maintains that he did not for one moment think that Sabeth was his own child. He admits, "Es lag im Bereich der Möglichkeit, theoretisch, aber ich dachte nicht daran. Genauer, ich glaubte es nicht." (*HF* 118; It was within the bounds of possibility, naturally, but I never thought of it: *HFAR* 122). More precisely, he did not want to believe it. In other words, for him, unlike for the robots he so admires, wishes and hopes, the subjectivity Wiener most certainly recognized and Faber denies, have indeed played a role in Faber's conclusions. He knows precisely what he does not want to know, as Ferdinand von Ingen suggests (71). Faber, the hopeful cybernetic man, is indeed controlled by the results of his own actions but, as he well knows, his "Ergebnisse" include a great deal of subjectivity. His dreams lead him to continue his sexual relationship with his daughter and therefore indirectly contribute to her sudden death in Greece.

In addition to his willful misuse of probabilistic calculations, Faber also does not understand the relational aspect of messages in general, which Hayles has pointed out, as quoted above. The one critical message among all others Walter Faber needed to discern was: Sabeth is your daughter. Although well aware that this was one possibility, he was not able to discern this message until too late, and therefore his system of control, the very essence of cybernetics, was malfunctioning—or more likely, he did not understand cybernetic theory's requirement that the machine be integrated into a system with the responsible human. He lacked the control he longed for, in part because he did not understand how that control comes about. That is, he did not understand the relational aspect of human existence, cybernetic and otherwise.

The most obvious manifestation of his relational blind spot, so to speak, is his explicit disdain for metaphor. Early in the text, when his Super-Constellation crashes, he mocks his fellow passengers for seeing prehistoric creatures where he sees geographical features. Faber also sees none of the stone angels, demons, or ghosts the other passengers identify. He appears to lack the desire or perhaps the ability to engage in simple analogy—a mental process that is "not as merely an ornament of language" as Hayles points out, "but [. . .] a powerful conceptual mode that constitutes meaning through relation," and also "a crucial operator" in Wiener's philosophy.[22] Faber, by contrast, believes that his sense perception, mediated by technologies like his beloved camera, as discussed below, reveals the essence of objects to him. Such hubris lies at the heart of his headlong journey into oblivion. He believes too strongly in dichotomies. For Faber, there are opposites such as male-female, technology-mythology, human-machine, and there can be no fruitful interplay between them. Thus this man, who so desires a cybernetic understanding of human existence, fails to grasp a central feature of this science. Wiener's cybernetics means that all things are constituted through the process of articulating their largely fluid, informational relationship.[23]

Throughout the course of his journey, however, Faber slowly changes his understanding of analogies. The first clue that his attraction to Sabeth has affected him deeply is that he does engage in metaphor making, albeit briefly and to himself. While taking her on a tour of the machine room of the ship, he has the opportunity to help her down a ladder by grabbing her by the hips, which were "merkwürdig leicht, zugleich stark, anzufassen wie das Steuerrad meines Studebakers, graziös, im Durchmesser genau so" (*HF* 87; remarkably light and at the same time strong, gripping them was like gripping the steering wheel of my Studebaker, the same slenderness, exactly the same diameter: *HFAR* 88). Granted, the metaphor is expressed in terms of technology, but this implicitly sexual experience throws Faber's well-constructed boundaries into flux (a woman is not a car, for example) and disorients him—a conclusion supported by his claim that the experience was so disorienting that it made him feel almost senile. It is, of course, ironic that he begins to grasp that boundaries are not absolute when he begins to feel hope in light of his growing love for Sabeth because hope is precisely one of those factors by which machines, in Faber's estimation, are not burdened in their decision-making process.

Further evidence of the effects of his relationship with Sabeth occurs on their last night together, when Sabeth challenges Faber to a game of metaphor-making. Whatever they perceived, they were to put in terms of a simile. Sabeth, for example, sees a black cypress tree and says that it is like "ein Ausrufezeichen" (*HF* 151; an exclamation mark: *HFAR* 156). The smitten Faber, master categorizer and boundary-drawer, is reluctant at first, but then takes part wholeheartedly in his first public, sustained expression of essence as relation. It is as if he has given up on his favored scientific, sum-of-its-parts view of the essence of things and finally understood the relational nature of things. However, as an indication that he is not entirely willing or able to play the game on the same level as Sabeth, whose metaphors are biological or natural, he formulates his metaphors primarily in terms of the technological, just as he did with the steering wheel-hips metaphor. The sea appears to Faber as a sheet of metal. The air is like cellophane. He perceives the light on the horizon before the sun rises as fiberglass, and the first rays of that sunrise are like photographs created by an electron bombardment (*HF* 151–52).

Michael Butler sees Faber's metaphors as indicative of "a balance between the two ways of comprehending the world."[24] While this may be the case, the metaphors also emphasize a new, broader approach to perceiving the world. Faber finally grasps the cybernetic vision, albeit too late. The world consists of systems made up of machines and humans and other living organisms. There is flow between the humanist subject, including Faber, the sick animal on all fours in the bathroom of an airport, and Faber the willfully miscalculating machine, and its surroundings.[25] Finally, Faber begins to grasp cybernetics, the Greek root of which translates to "steersman." An apt etymology, as Hayles writes, of the "cybernetic man-machine: light on its feet, sensitive to change, a being that both is a flow and knows how to go with the flow" (104). Faber begins to grasp and go with the flow in his new, in-love persona, but it is too late to halt his eventual entropic decay.

Just as he begins to comprehend the relational aspect of objects as his journey goes on, he also begins to feel the marked poverty of his technologically mediated engagement with the natural world. Through most of the text, Faber ignores "Erlebnisse" in favor of technologically mediated interactions. As van Ingen writes, "überhaupt kann Faber der Natur nur technisch begegnen, mit der Natur als solcher kann er nichts anfangen" (78; Faber is only capable of facing nature with the mindset of a technician, he does not know what to do with nature as such). And while I have discussed his razor and typewriter already, his technological engagement is most clearly depicted in his preference to view the world largely through the lens of his movie camera. "Sein Filmen" is not, according to Peter Horn, "erzwungene Ersatzhandlung, es ist seine bevorzugte Art des Zugriffs." (His filming is not an enforced redirection activity, it is his preferred access mode.)[26] He prefers, as Sabeth aptly puts it, filming to seeing. The difficulty with this mediated view is that the humanist subject, through its subjectivity, is already estranged from the "thing in itself." Faber's camera provides a further layer of estrangement—a filter of sorts that inserts itself in the "irreducible duality" that exists between the humanist subject and its external world as Kurzweil describes it—until, that is, Faber has an apparent epiphany.

He finally realizes the inadequacy of the movie camera's aperture as a mediator of cybernetic flow when he decides to go to Joachim's company's headquarters in Düsseldorf to show them what has happened to their investment in Guatemala. As he shows the film of Joachim hanging by his neck to the young "Techniker" assigned to listen to his statement, he notes how strange it is that the images do not make much of an impression on him or his young colleague, declaring, "es fehlt der Gestank, die Wirklichkeit, wir sprechen über Belichtung, der junge Mann und ich" (*HF* 187; the stench was missing, it lacked reality, the young technician and I discussed lighting: *HFAR* 197). He recognizes the poverty of "reality" as it is mediated through film. And then, in the same film session, Sabeth appears as the filmed object. He recognizes, too, that his films of Sabeth also lack the synesthetic pleasure of human contact. As Alan Latta points out, "the silent film, with its reduced reality, is a metaphorical symbol of the 'Weltlosigkeit des Technikers' (as Hanna calls it)."[27] The camera interferes with one's cybernetic flow; it does not enhance one's perception, but attenuates it. By making perception all about the film or the mediated image, filming itself reduces Faber's role in the machine-human system to a mere cog no longer allowing him his "full right" as a responsible human being. He has given his perception over to the machine, which is characteristic of the "evil system" Wiener warns against.

In yet another moment of realization that equals the game of metaphor-making in importance, Faber declares, "ich filme nichts mehr. Wozu! Hanna hat recht: nachher muß man es sich als Film ansehen, wenn es nicht mehr da ist, und es vergeht ja doch alles" (*HF* 182; I'm not filming anything any more. What's the use! Hanna is right: afterward you have to look at it as a film, when it's all no longer there, and everything passes away: *HFAR* 192). Even his technologies must pass away eventually. The "Material" of those beloved technologies is also flawed and impermanent, just as the human body is in Faber's view (*HF* 171). Peter Horn, however, warns that the reader must not lose perspective on Faber's seemingly epiphanous desire to avoid "die filmische Reproduktion der Wirklichkeit" (the reproduction of reality through film).[28] The camera is not the only aperture in Faber's life or in the life of the humanist subject in the mid-twentieth century. On what would turn out to be his last flight on a Super-Constellation, for example, Faber considers his view out the window:

> Wunsch, Heu zu riechen! Nie wieder fliegen! Wunsch auf der Erde zu gehen—dort unter den letzten Föhren, die in der Sonne stehen, ihr Harz riechen und das Wasser hören, vermutlich ein Tosen, Wasser trinken— (*HF* 195)
>
> [The wish to smell hay. Never to fly again. The wish to walk on earth—there beneath the last firs standing in the sunshine, to smell their resin and listen to the water, which is probably roaring, to drink water. (*HFAR* 206)]

It would appear that he finally desires "Erlebnisse," and he no longer wants those experiences to be mediated in any way. He bemoans in the next line, "Alles geht vorbei wie im Film!" (*HF* 195; Everything goes past as though in a film: *HFAR* 206). The window of the Super-Constellation has become yet another aperture, like that of the camera, providing a filmic reproduction of reality, which he rejects with the declaration "Wunsch, die Erde zu greifen" (*HF* 195; The wish to grasp the earth: *HFAR* 206). He wants that first-wave cybernetic integration with the natural world that Wiener stressed more than the human-as-machine analogy. The question for Faber, and for Wiener for that matter, is: can he achieve such integration in the highly technological world in which he finds himself?

As if to re-emphasize his newfound need for the level of integration suggested by metaphor and analogy, Faber, after a brief scientific description of the zone of life as seen from his window, engages once again in metaphor-making, at times playing for himself and for Sabeth. The water of the Alpine lakes is like Pernod to Faber. The cracks in the glacier are beer bottle green; Sabeth would say emerald green. The cliffs for Sabeth would be like gold, for Faber like amber. Sabeth would say that the airplane's shadow looks like a bat, and Faber would lose a point because he has no metaphor for such an image. Sabeth would see cotton or cauliflower or plaster in the clouds. Faber sees a forest like a hedgehog and shadows like curtains. While this latest, more robust round of metaphor-making appears to be a further confirmation of Faber's transformation into a person who recognizes the importance of analogies, one cannot overlook the fact that this round is in fact mediated. There is no camera lens, but there is the window serving as an aperture, begging a version of the question posed above, à la Walter Benjamin: is an unmediated, "apparatfreie[r] Aspekt der Realität" even possible for modern human beings?[29] Whereas Kant was concerned about human subjectivity acting as a filter preventing humans from grasping the thing in itself, humans in the media age have even more filters in the form of various technologies. Therefore, this filtered game of metaphor-making, this mediated relationality, while a vast improvement over Faber's attitude in the desert of Tamaulipas, comes across as a diminished version of the game he and Sabeth played the evening before her demise.

As if to stress the fact that this round of metaphor-making is not as effective as the first, the passage ends with the following:

> Es ist nicht einzusehen, wieso ein solches Fahrgestell, bestehend aus zwei Pneu-Paaren mit Federung im Rohrgestell und mit Schmieröl auf dem blanken Metall, wie es sich gehört, sich plötzlich wie ein Dämon benehmen soll, wenn es den Boden berührt, wie ein Dämon, der die Piste plötzlich in Wüste verwandelt—Spintisiererei, die ich natürlich selber nicht ernstnahm; ich bin in meinem Leben noch keinem Dämon begegnet, ausgenommen dem sog. Maxwell'sche Dämon, der bekanntlich keiner ist. (*HF* 196–97)
>
> [It is extraordinary how landing gear, twin tires with telescopic suspension and lubricating oil on the shining metal, all as it should be, suddenly acts like a demon that suddenly turns the runway into desert—a figment of the imagination which I myself did not take seriously; I have never met a demon in my life, apart from the so-called Maxwell's demon, which, as everyone knows, is not a demon at all. (*HFAR* 208)]

Faber seems to have snapped out of his metaphor haze, so to speak, and returned to his old ways, explaining the parts of the Super-Constellation and deriding the idea that the essence of such a manifestation of technology could be anything other than the sum of its parts—no analogies necessary. This quotation also brings the reader back around to Wiener and cybernetics. In his youth, Faber began and never completed his dissertation on Maxwell's Demon—a thought experiment proposed by physicist and mathematician James Clerk Maxwell to show that the second law of thermodynamics is indeed correct. That is, entropy always tends to increase in a closed system, thereby forecasting a universe that is constantly winding down.

Wiener explicitly demonstrates the impossibility of the existence of Maxwell's Demon in *Cybernetics or Control and Communication in the Animal and the Machine*.[30] Proper or "good" cybernetic systems, according to Wiener, may be able to decrease the pace of entropy temporarily, but the law of entropy rules. Such systems, as Hayles tells us, include a component that is capable of "responding flexibly to changing situations, learning from the past, [and] freely adapting its behavior to meet new circumstances" (104). These are component characteristics of the humanist subject that Wiener so badly wanted to preserve, but with his human-as-machine analogy, he has protégés like Walter Faber who would so urgently like to give up these essential characteristics in hopes of making decisions free of what Faber considers "noise"—the opposite of information—like hope, fear, and other emotions. Faber would relinquish his humanity and become part of the "evil" cybernetic system that Wiener regrets is a possibility within his philosophy. In such a system, entropy, the true evil in Wiener's philosophy, occurs at a faster rate due to the lack of those very factors Faber considers noise, because it is precisely those factors, allowing for the flexibility described above, that are necessary to slow the rate of entropic decay.

If a human, like Faber, is willing to give up those essentially humanist subject characteristics, then machines can become dominant. This is Faber's misunderstanding of Wiener and first-wave cybernetics; it is also his flaw. Rather than embracing the correct type of system, Faber grabs the bad, the human as machine, the one in which there is little flexibility, minimal flow, and no call for analogy; and he maintains his hold on such ideas until it is too late. In so doing, he speeds up the pace of entropic decay in his life, and no metaphor-making will slow it down. His lauding of medical science's ability to overcome various illnesses, his bemoaning of the transience of the flesh, and, most importantly, his pursuit of a young woman who turns out to be his daughter are all manifestations of a man trying to overcome entropy, of a man trying to find a functioning Maxwell's Demon. As Horn writes, "Er begreift endlich, daß weder physikalisch (Maxwellscher Dämon) noch mythisch (die Verjüngung durch die Liebe zur Tochter) die anthropologische Zeit umgekehrt werden kann: er begreift, daß er sterben muß" (69). What he finds in his desire to become machinelike is that he has become part of a bad system.

Whereas Wiener writes that "the dominance of the machine presupposes a society in the last stages of increasing entropy [. . .]. Fortunately we have not yet reached such a state,"[31] one could write of Faber, "the dominance of technology presupposes a human in the last stages of increasing entropy. Unfortunately Faber has indeed reached such a state." According to Wiener, the flow of information through an organism is interrupted "when the boundaries cease to define an autonomous self, either through manipulation or engulfment."[32] Walter Faber, the man who dreams of control, has been technologically engulfed. To suggest that the role of technology is merely coincidental or that cybernetics is a convenient marker of the times is to miss the point of Faber's engulfment.

Notes

[1] Kurt Vonnegut, *A Man Without a Country* (New York: Seven Stories Press, 2005), 17.

[2] Ferdinand von Ingen, "Max Frischs Homo Faber Zwischen Technik und Mythologie," *Amsterdamer Beiträge zur neueren Germanistik* 2 (1973): 63–64.

[3] In a 1975 interview with Heinz Ludwig Arnold, Frisch suggests that Walter Faber is "der vermeintliche Techniker-Typ" (Arnold 50). In the same year, in an interview with Rudolf Ossowski, he describes Faber as "kein Techniker, sondern er ist ein verhinderter Mensch, der von sich selbst ein Bildnis gemacht hat, der sich ein Bildnis hat machen lassen, das ihn verhindert, zu sich selber zu kommen" (Ossowski 121).

[4] Unless otherwise stated, all references to Frisch's *Homo Faber* are from *Homo Faber: Ein Bericht* (Frankfurt am Main: Suhrkamp, 1957) and will be indicated with the abbreviation *HF* and page number. Here, page 169. Translated passages are taken from *Homo Faber: A Report*, translated by Michael Bullock (New York: Harcourt Brace Jovanovich, 1959), which will be indicated with the abbreviation *HFAR* and page number. Here, page 178.

[5] See Paul A. Youngman "Robbing the Cradle: Mesoamerica, Greece, and the Power of Place in Max Frisch's *Homo Faber*," *Southeastern Council on Latin-American Studies Annals* 36 (2004): 130–31.

[6] Gerhard and Mona Knapp, *Max Frischs Homo Faber Grundlagen und Gedanken zum Verständnis erzählender Literatur* (Frankfurt am Main: Diesterweg, 1987), 29. The other works Frisch mentions include Ernst Mally's *Wahrscheinlichkeit und Gesetz* (1938), Hans Reichenbach's *Wahrscheinlichkeitslehre* (1935), Richard von Mises's *Wahrscheinlichkeit, Statistik und Wahrheit* (1936), and Alfred North Whitehead and Bertrand Russell's *Principia Mathematica* (1925–27).

[7] Knapp, *Max Frischs Homo Faber*, 29.

[8] Charles Percy Snow, *The Two Cultures* (1959; Cambridge: Cambridge University Press, 1993), 98.

[9] Snow, *The Two Cultures*, 3.

[10] Ursula Roisch, "Max Frischs Auffassung vom Einfluß der Technik auf Menschen—nachgewiesen am Roman 'Homo Faber,'" *Weimarer Beiträge* 6 (1967): 965.

[11] Norbert Wiener, *The Human Use of Human Beings: Cybernetics and Society*, 2nd ed. (Garden City, NY: Doubleday, 1954), 96.

[12] Katherine N. Hayles, *How We Became Posthuman: Virtual Bodies in Cybernetics, Literature, and Informatics* (Chicago: University of Chicago Press, 1999), 85–86.

[13] Roisch, "Max Frischs Aufassung vom Einfluß der Technik," 966.

[14] See for example Humberto R. Maturana and Francisco J. Varela, *Autopoiesis and Cognition: The Realization of the Living* (Dordrecht/Boston: Reidel, 1980).

[15] Wiener, *The Human Use of Human Beings*, 185.

[16] Hayles, *How We Became Posthuman*, 84.

[17] Ray Kurzweil, *The Age of Spiritual Machines: When Computers Exceed Human Intelligence* (New York: Viking, 1999), 62.

[18] Norbert Wiener, "Thermodynamics of the Message," In *Norbert Wiener: Collected Works with Commentaries*, vol. 4, ed. Pesi Mesani (Cambridge: MIT Press, 1985), 206–11.

[19] Wiener, *The Human Use of Human Beings*, 185.

[20] Hayles, *How We Became Posthuman*, 91.

[21] Francis Michael Sharp, "Max Frisch: A Writer in a Technological Age," *Twayne's Companion to Contemporary World Literature*, vol. 2, ed. Pamela A. Genova (New York: Twayne Publishers, 2003), 1407.

[22] Hayles, *How We Became Posthuman*, 91.

[23] Hayles, *How We Became Posthuman*, 92.

[24] Michael Butler, *The Novels of Max Frisch* (London: Oswald Wolff, 1976), 95.

[25] Alan Latta, "The Nature and Variety of Signifying Elements in Max Frisch's Novel *Homo faber*: An Approach," *Germanic Review* 65 (1990): 147.

[26] Peter Horn, "Entropie der Liebe: Zu Max Frischs *Homo Faber*," in *Zwischen den Wissenschaften: Beiträge zur deutschen Literaturgeschichte*, ed. Gerhard Hahn and Ernst Weber (Regensburg: Pustet, 1994), 58.

[27] Latta, "The Nature and Variety of Signifying Elements," 149.

[28] Horn, "Entropie der Liebe," 59.

[29] Walter Benjamin, "Das Kunstwerk im Zeitalter seiner technischen Reproduzierbarkeit," In *Gesammelte Schriften* vol. 1, eds. Rolf Tiedemann and Hermann Schweppenhäuser (Frankfurt am Main: Suhrkamp, 1980), 459.

[30] Norbert Wiener, *Cybernetics or Control and Communication in the Animal and the Machine* (Cambridge: MIT Press, 1948), 84.

[31] Wiener, *The Human Use of Human Beings*, 181.

[32] Wiener, *The Human Use of Human Beings*, 107.

10: The Ends of Blindness in Max Frisch's *Mein Name sei Gantenbein*

Olaf Berwald

In an interview published in *Die Zeit* in 2010, Swiss actor Bruno Ganz, one of the most influential artists in the German-speaking world over the last fifty years, insists on the unreliability and fluid status of personal identity:

> Ich halte es nicht für einen allzu gesicherten, fest umrissenen Zustand, der zu sein, der ich bin. Ich denke, Identität besteht aus allen möglichen ungeklärten Teilen. Und was ist eigentlich dieses "Ich"? Ich versuche, das fliessend zu halten, weil ich Angst vor festen Grenzen habe. Andererseits merke ich schon, dass es so etwas wie "mich" gibt. Oder Dinge, die sich einfach immer wieder ereignen, wenn ich dabei bin.[1]

> [I do not consider being who I am a well secured and rigidly defined condition. I believe that identity consists of all kinds of possible unexplained components. And what is this "I" in the first place? I try to keep it fluid because I am afraid of static boundaries. On the other hand I notice that there is something like "me." Or things that happen time and again when I happen to be around.]

Arguing against a static conception of autobiographical coherence, Ganz, whose early theater career at the Zurich Schauspielhaus had been supported by Frisch when he urged the city of Zurich not to close the Schauspielhaus, puts the fragility of selfhood and a productive fear of fixed boundaries at the heart of self-understanding. His concise summary of an ontological dilemma not only provides a glimpse into the mind of an actor who has explored a wide range of human possibilities—playing such diverse roles as Goethe's Faust, an angel longing for corporeal experience in Wim Wenders's film *Der Himmel über Berlin* (Heaven Above Berlin, released in the United States as *Wings of Desire*, 1987) and portraying Hitler in *Der Untergang* (The Downfall, 2004)—it also points at a core existential problem that Max Frisch explores throughout his novels and plays. Ganz's sustained skepticism about the myth of human wholeness and his playful Socratic curiosity regarding the psychological and social boundaries that constitute and imprison us provide a precise lens through which Frisch's final full-length novel can be read with the care it requires.

Celebrated by some of his colleagues and critics as his most radical prose project, and listed atop German bestseller lists from November 1964 until February 1965,[2] Frisch's novel *Mein Name sei Gantenbein* (literally: Assume My Name Is Gantenbein, 1964), whose English edition is aptly if freely titled *A Wilderness of Mirrors*, abandons any attempt at approximating the literary convention of linear plotlines.[3] Storytelling itself, or rather its failure to provide shelter from existential insecurity, emerges as the thematic thread and "protagonist" of this novel that portrays life as a serial production of exchangeable illusions. Reminiscent of a Bach fugue or a jazz composition, or, as Wilma Iggers suggests in her 1965 review of the novel's English version, "reminiscent of Leonardo's multiple sketches of persons, or of Picasso's composite portraits,"[4] *Mein Name sei Gantenbein* offers numerous variations on an inexorable question while abstaining from offering any answer: how is human freedom possible for an individual and for a couple? While Frisch's previous novels *Stiller* (1954) and *Homo faber* (1957), works that are discussed by Beatrice Sandberg and Paul Youngman in their essays in this book, operate with recognizable if disillusioned and split individual narrative voices in the form of notebooks composed by Anatol Stiller in prison, and by Walter Faber, hospitalized awaiting stomach cancer surgery, the boundaries between narrators and their invented figures in *Mein Name sei Gantenbein* are constantly shifting and remain permeable throughout the book.

The reader can never determine beyond reasonable doubt whether Gantenbein, a writer who after a car accident pretends to be blind in order to save his marriage, is the main narrator or the invention of another narrator or antagonist, among them the sturdy architect Svoboda and the art historian and Hermes expert Enderlin, who focuses on the uncanny and lethal dimensions of the Hermes myth, "das Unberechenbare und [. . .] das Unheimliche in aller Heiterkeit, denn Hermes ist ja auch der Gott, der die Scheidenden holt, lautlos wie immer, unversehens, allgegenwärtig" (*G* 132; the incalculable and [. . .] the sinister element in all gaiety, for Hermes is also the god who fetches the departing, silent as always, unexpected, omnipresent: *WM* 139). These three figures—Gantenbein, Svoboda, and Enderlin—and the narrator might very well be each other's inventions, connected through their failed love, as exchangeable lovers or husbands, for Lila, who is an actress or, according to two tentative revisions, a scientist or a countess who is addicted to cocaine.

Rather than embracing storytelling as a protective shield against psychological disintegration, the narrative voices in *Mein Name sei Gantenbein* appear to consent to the dissolution of their personal identities. With vertiginous shifts between and fusions of narrative perspectives, the novel presents a narrator's and his invented characters' fantasies about liberation from the repetitiveness of emotionally malnourished middle-aged life. As Frisch outlines in a letter of February 9, 1964 to one of his Suhrkamp editors, the novelist Martin Walser, *Mein Name sei Gantenbein*, rather than developing a character, consists in the polyphonic experiment of "encircling" characters with their projections and associations, "ein Ego einzukreisen durch seine Assoziationen."[5] Sharing philosophical correlations with Pessoa's and Pirandello's works,[6] as well as with Frisch's own later plays *Biografie: Ein Spiel* (1968/1984) and *Triptychon* (1978), which are discussed in detail by John Pizer in his essay in this volume, the *Gantenbein* project conceives of a human life as an arbitrary construct open to minor cosmetic revisions but ultimately incapable of achieving release from firmly framed patterns.

One of the recurring topoi that structure the novel is the apartment of Camilla Huber, a prostitute who officially works from her home as a manicurist. Theo Gantenbein is one of her regulars, but all he wants are manicures during which the allegedly blind malingerer can share stories with Camilla while they both adhere to an unspoken pact not to reveal each other's masks to the outside world. Camilla passionately craves "wahre Geschichten" (*G* 103; true stories) that are based on real events, while for Gantenbein, everything he can imagine to happen is good enough to qualify for being relevant (*G* 106). During their last meeting before she is murdered, possibly by Gantenbein himself (the crime remains unresolved), Gantenbein challenges Camilla to tell him how she would live her life if she knew that she had only one more year to live. She immediately tells him that she would discontinue her current career. Gantenbein's question at first empowers her. She seems to become the author of her own life story, rather than a passive if avid listener:

> Es ist das erste Mal, dass Camilla keine Geschichte braucht; sie erfindet sich selber eine, scheint es, wortlos:—ihr letztes Jahr auf Erden, eine Geschichte mit Wandlung vermutlich, eine Geschichte, die aufgeht in Sinn, eine tröstliche. (*G* 145)
>
> [It's the first time Camilla doesn't need any story; she is making one up herself, it seems, without words: her last year on earth, a story that probably includes a transformation scene, a story with a meaningful ending, a comforting story. (*WM* 152)]

Neither Theo Gantenbein nor Frisch offers the listener or reader the kind of story that Camilla tries to invent for herself, a consoling tale of meaningful transformation. On the contrary, *Mein Name sei Gantenbein* can be read as Frisch's sustained attempt to destabilize and render absurd any expectation of life's coherence or purpose. For Gantenbein, comprehensive stories, rather than offering freedom from existential confusion and emptiness, constitute prisons that encapsulate the mind. The final story that Gantenbein shares with Camilla illustrates what self-liberation from the constraints of a life's storyline might look like. Gantenbein describes how a corpse was floating down the river Limmat in Zurich. In too great of a state of disintegration to be pulled onto land in one piece, the corpse gets stuck between barrels near a bridge, before it floats away further. It almost gets away without being captured and identified by the police (*G* 283–88). According to Gantenbein, the corpse had almost succeeded in disappearing into irrecoverable namelessness without having been provided with a story or history, "Abzuschwimmen ohne Geschichte" (*G* 288; floated away without a story: *WM* 303), but its complete disintegration into namelessness is prevented by a vigilant police officer who retrieves it.

Even a text like *Gantenbein* that confronts the reader with a maze of interlaced narrative perspectives and dismisses the idea of mappable plot developments has traceable origins. In a handwritten notebook entry from January 22, 1960 on the last page of a notebook Frisch wrote in Berlin, he sketched the idea for a story titled "Der Blinde." The blind protagonist is asked by his companion, a famous dancer, to attend all her rehearsals and performances. Everyone suspects that he only pretends to be blind.[7] This constellation would later undergo an inversion: while the main character in Frisch's outline from early 1960 is genuinely blind but is met with suspicion regarding his medical condition, Theo Gantenbein in the 1964 novel can see but chooses to portray himself as a blind man for the outside world, including his partner Lila.

Frisch's slow and Socratic approach to conceptualizing his novel is manifest in a discussion with his audience during a public reading of drafts from the *Gantenbein* work-in-progress that was documented by Rudolf Hartung in the newspaper *Der Tagesspiegel* on January 17, 1962, two years before the novel was published. Frisch told his audience that the Gantenbein novel was "ein Buch, von dem ich noch nicht allzuviel weiss" (a book about which I do not know very much yet).[8]

Frisch's correspondence with one of his closest friends, the dramaturge and theater director Kurt Hirschfeld, includes an intimate discussion of *Mein Name sei Gantenbein*. In a letter to Hirschfeld from July 2, 1964, Frisch highlights the mental and physical suffering that is in his view constitutive of the novel's bleakness beneath the surface of playfulness, its "lustig getarnte Trostlosigkeit." Referring to *Gantenbein* as a book of "disconsolation" camouflaged with humor, Frisch welcomes Hirschfeld as his "ideal reader" and calls him the only reader capable of deciphering the pain that went into and is worked through in the novel: "Also der ideale Leser? Insofern es ideal ist, wenn Not und Not sich in die Augen schauen, so dass Literatur aufhört Literatur zu sein." (The ideal reader? To the degree that it is ideal when misery and misery look each other in the eye so that literature ceases to be literature.)[9] In his first response, written two days later, Hirschfeld counters the bleakness of Frisch's outline of his novel by arguing for what Hirschfeld reads as *Gantenbein*'s socially and politically transformative potential and calls the novel an unswerving defense of freedom against societal norms, "die unentwegte Apologie der Freiheit gegen die Hörigkeit, gegen die Tabus der von Menschen und der Gesellschaft gesetzten, keineswegs endgültigen, sondern höchst bedingten Situation."[10]

In another letter to Frisch from July 23, 1964, Hirschfeld adds a poetological comment that favorably compares the novel to its predecessors. According to Hirschfeld, *Mein Name sei Gantenbein* intensifies the splits inside a character's mind that Frisch had already explored in *Stiller* and *Homo Faber* and takes these soundings of the arbitrary nature of identity to aesthetic extremes that make it "von den Romanen das Reifste und Beste und Richtigste, weil es eigentlich die in den andern Büchern angelegten Linien in extremis weiterführt" (the most mature and the best and most fitting of [Frisch's] novels because it consistently develops and radicalizes features that are sketched out in [Frisch's] earlier books).[11]

Even (and especially) a text that conducts radical aesthetic experiments and breaks with expectations of identifiable plotlines or coherent characters needs referential points in literary history. An integral literary ally at work in *Gantenbein*, and in all of Frisch's mature works, is Georg Büchner's novella *Lenz* (1835), arguably one of the most haunting psychological portraits of a disintegrating and suicidal mind in modern literature. In one of the episodic outlines in Frisch's novel, a naked patient escapes from a hospital and runs onto a theater stage during a performance. Questioned about his motives, he states that an indomitable desire to scream prompted him to run through the city naked: "Er habe einen Schrei ausstossen wollen, sagte er, dabei saß er vollkommen ruhig, vernünftig, höflich-alltäglich." (*G* 17; He had wanted to scream, he said; yet he sat there perfectly quietly, sensibly, behaving with everyday politeness. *WM* 17) In the final passage of Büchner's *Lenz*, the suicidal protagonist's indifferent demeanor is described with some of the same adverbs used by Frisch, "ganz ruhig," "vollkommen gleichgültig," and "ganz vernünftig." In another passage in *Gantenbein*, the dissolution of erotic and intellectual curiosity that marks the end of a meaningful marriage carries an explicit reference to the concluding passage in Büchner's novella *Lenz*, "Da lebt Ihr so hin." (*G* 121; Thus you live away your lives. *WM* 128) A comparison with the final sentences in Büchner's novella can serve to highlight not only the explicit reference to *Lenz* employed by Frisch but also Büchner's hauntingly understated lines that precede the final remark and that have been left out by Frisch so that his reader can complete them:

> Er schien ganz vernünftig, sprach mit den Leuten; er tat Alles wie es die Andern taten, es war aber eine entsetzliche Leere in ihm, er fühlte keine Angst mehr, kein Verlangen; sein Dasein war ihm eine notwendige Last.—So lebte er hin.[12]

> [He seemed quite rational, he talked to people; he did everything as others did, but there was a terrible emptiness within him, he felt no fear, no longing any more; he saw his existence as a necessary burden.—Thus he lived for the rest of his days.]

While Büchner's novella contains a famous discussion of literary naturalism *avant la lettre*, Frisch's novel's aesthetic self-justification is offered as a passing reflection of a narrator who attempts to read:

> Ich versuchte zu lesen. (Manchmal scheint auch mir, daß jedes Buch, so es sich nicht befasst mit der Verhinderung des Kriegs, mit der Schaffung einer besseren Gesellschaft und so weiter, sinnlos ist, müssig, unverantwortlich, langweilig, nicht wert, daß man es liest, unstatthaft. Es ist nicht die Zeit für Ich-Geschichten. Und doch vollzieht sich das menschliche Leben oder verfehlt sich am einzelnen Ich, nirgends sonst.) (*G* 62)

> [I tried to read. (I, too, often have the feeling that any book which isn't concerned with the prevention of war, with the creation of a better society and so on, is senseless, futile, irresponsible, tedious, not worth reading, inadmissible. This is no time for ego stories. And yet human life is fulfilled or goes wrong in the individual ego, nowhere else.) (*WM* 65)]

This key passage on the necessary tensions between ethics and aesthetics illustrates Frisch's emancipation from his mentor Brecht. Acutely aware of running the risk of being accused of introspective solipsism, Frisch and his narrators expose themselves to the hard question of what it means to be, and to what extent it is still possible to live as an individual. For Frisch, immersing oneself in the political sphere while turning away from the conflicted status of solitary autonomy and the possibility of love would be as hypocritical a mode of escapism as avoiding the political altogether. According to Frisch, it is impossible to understand the need for social change without considering the psychological afflictions of the individual.

In *Gantenbein*, narrative perspectives are permeable. They oscillate from first-person voices to third-person ones that constantly question the very possibility of telling and living coherent life stories. Frisch's narrative voices in *Gantenbein* are perplexed by their inability to translate or at least integrate an experience ("Erfahrung") into a corresponding story ("Geschichte"). Rather than offering coherent plotlines, the novel offers multiple layers of invented selves and their failures to comprehend and live with themselves and others. An existential helplessness drives the characters, who are themselves inventions of their narrator, to produce fictional alternatives to who they currently are. To examine the emptiness in their lives they imagine themselves in continuously altered roles, only to come to the conclusion that they are incapable of sustainable self-transformation. In his posthumously published late notebook, *Entwürfe zu einem dritten Tagebuch* (2010), Frisch describes with laconic conciseness the productive philosophical conflict that nourishes his writing: "Ich bin auf Erfahrungen angewiesen, die mich begrifflich hilflos machen und von daher narrativ." (I depend on experiences that make me epistemically helpless and therefore force me to write.)[13] The anonymous main narrator, one of whose invented voices is that of the writer Theo Gantenbein, shares his author's admission that the contradiction between experience and its narration remains unbridgeable: "man kann nicht leben mit einer Erfahrung, die ohne Geschichte bleibt [. . .] (*G* 11; you can't live with an experience that remains without a story [. . .]: *WM* 11).

Later, he adds the following:

> "zwei oder drei Erfahrungen, wenn's hochkommt, das ist's, was einer hat, wenn er von sich erzählt, überhaupt wenn er erzählt: Erlebnismuster—aber keine Geschichte", sage ich, "keine Geschichte". [. . .] "Man kann sich selbst nicht sehen, das ist's, Geschichten gibt es nur von außen", sage ich, "daher unsere Gier nach Geschichten!" [. . .] "Jeder Mensch erfindet sich früher oder später eine Geschichte, die er für sein Leben hält", sage ich, "oder eine ganze Reihe von Geschichten", sage ich [. . .] (*G* 44–45)
>
> "two or three experiences at the outside, that's what a man has had when he tells stories about himself, when he tells stories at all: a pattern of experience—but not a story," I say, "not a story." [. . .] "One can't see oneself, that's the trouble, stories only exist from outside," I say, "hence our greed for stories." [. . .] "Sooner or later everyone invents for himself a story which he regards as his life," I say, "or a whole series of stories," I say [. . .] (*WM* 46–47)]

For the narrative voices in *Mein Name sei Gantenbein*, inventing stories constitutes an unfinishable search process. The characters in Frisch's novel are constantly trying on masks and providing running commentaries on their need to disguise themselves, for example with a blind man's dark glasses; they "probiere[n] Geschichten an wie Kleider" (*G* 20; try on stories like clothes: *WM* 21) in order to at once alleviate the pressures of their self-isolation and to gain the distance needed to examine it. Especially in our current age of Facebook, which is marked by an excessively pictorial auto-archival drive and constant "status updates," *Gantenbein's* soundings of human facelessness and humans' resulting addiction to crafting version after version of autofictional masks remain acutely relevant.

Despite its persistent focus on anthropological and psychological layers of storytelling, *Mein Name sei Gantenbein* offers the reader more than a metanarrative on preliminary identities sketched into ephemeral existence by acts of telling. Carefully woven together, the episodes in the novel conduct thought experiments that inexorably elucidate the question of individual freedom under extreme circumstances. The main narrator puts both himself and invented versions of himself under a microscope. Recounting a seemingly harmless experience that he had in 1942 as a young Swiss soldier who suddenly encountered a German hiker on a mountaintop, he negotiates the question of individual guilt by wondering why he did not act on a sudden impulse to push the hiker off the mountain: "Ich habe diesen Mann über die Felsen gestoßen. Ich wußte: Ich habe es nicht getan. Aber warum eigentlich nicht?" (*G* 51; I pushed that man over the rocks. I knew I hadn't done it. But why didn't I? *WM* 53) Embarrassed by the contradictory inner workings of his mind, and responding with the performative use of irony, the narrator wonders why a murder that he only committed in his imagination continues to occupy his memory, while everything that he in fact did undertake or commit in his life appears boring to him (*G* 54). The narrator admits: "Eine Tat nicht vergessen zu können, die man nicht getan hat, ist lächerlich. Ich erzähle ja auch niemand davon." (*G* 55; Not to be able to forget an act one never performed is ridiculous. And I never tell anyone about it. *WM* 57).

Illustrating his position that humans are measured only by the virtuosity with which they perform their roles, the narrator outlines the story of an anonymous ambassador of a superpower who experiences a breakdown when he realizes that he is not the noble diplomat the world believes him to be. But instead of quitting his career, he decides to play his role without ever sharing his self-doubts with anyone and without leaving behind any trace of his own skepticism about his capabilities. Far from undermining his work, the ambassador's irrevocable loss of belief in himself enables him to achieve hitherto unimaginable diplomatic successes, and his worldwide obituaries will be filled with admiration:

> Seine Selbsterkenntnis bleibt sein Geheimnis. Er erfüllt sein Amt. [. . .] Er spielt also, versetzt nach Washington oder Peking oder Moskau, weiterhin den Botschafter, wissend, daß er spielt [. . .] indem er eigentlich bloß spielt, leistet er nicht nur Ordentliches wie bisher, sondern Außerordentliches. (*G* 108)

> [His self-knowledge remains his secret. He fulfils his office. [. . .] So he continues to play the part of an ambassador, transferred to Washington or Peking or Moscow, knowing that he is acting a part

> [. . .] while he is really only acting a part he not only achieves good solid results as heretofore, but exceptional results. (*WM* 113–14)]

Frisch's narrators in the novel's laboratory of existential thought and life experiments are mostly focused on imperfect performances, indecisiveness, and failed attempts at a fulfilling life. Mistakenly assuming that he has only one more year to live, Enderlin, an earnest and diligent art historian, is torn between accepting a job offer from Harvard and ignoring it (*G* 131). Contemplating the divergent options for the Enderlin plot development, the narrator remains transfixed by the undecidability, or rather the exchangeability, of Enderlin's impulses to stay in Switzerland or to leave for Harvard:

> Ich kann mir beides vorstellen: Enderlin fliegt. Enderlin bleibt. [. . .] Handlung und Unterlassung sind vertauschbar [. . .] Der nämlich bleibt, stellt sich vor, er wäre geflogen, und der nämlich fliegt, stellt sich vor, er wäre geblieben, und was er wirklich erlebt, so oder so, ist der Riß, der durch seine Person geht, der Riß zwischen mir und ihm, wie ich's auch immer mache [. . .] (*G* 117–18)

> [I can imagine both: Enderlin departs. Enderlin stays. [. . .] action and inaction are interchangeable [. . .] The one who stays imagines how it would have been if he had flown, and the one who flies imagines how it would have been if he had stayed, and what he really experiences, either way, is the split that runs through his person, the split between me and him, whatever I do, either way [. . .] (*WM* 123–24)]

Weaving the richly charged key term "Riss" ("tear," "crack," "fracture," "crevice," "fissure") into this passage, Frisch highlights conceptual affinities with Freud's late essay "Die Ichspaltung im Abwehrvorgang" (1939), in which Freud posits that unresolved and early childhood conflicts between impulsive desires on the one hand and internalized feelings of guilt and inhibition on the other result in lifelong "Risse im Ich," cracks in the ego that never heal and become more pronounced in adult life. Stylistic parallels between Freud's and Frisch's playfully hesitant, Socratic modes of essayistic writing cannot be examined here but deserve further scholarly attention.

Arguing that love as a transformative encounter cannot be captured in writing, the narrator writes against the intrinsic epistemic arrogance of descriptive prose and its fantasies of being able to level off the contours of unrepeatable life moments. He mourns the loss of erotic immediacy that could resist being encapsulated by descriptive patterns: "Keine Wiederholung—Keine Geschichte—Sie wollten, was nur einmal möglich ist: das Jetzt." (*G* 66; No repetition—No story—They wanted what is possible only once: the now. *WM* 69) It has to be kept in mind that the narrator continues to employ the craft of storytelling even while denouncing language as a form of imprisonment that endangers the spontaneity of love. Praising intense mutual love as an experience that provides the very opposite of accumulating knowledge and control, the narrator reminisces: "Einander nicht zu kennen in einem Grad, der alles Kennenkönnen übersteigt, war schön." (*G* 70; Not to know one another to a degree that went beyond all possibility of knowing one another was beautiful. *WM* 73) Lila, the fictional vanishing point of all male characters' attempts at self-definition, is presented as a woman whose face defies any attempt at description to such an extent "dass alle Beiwörter, die ich gesammelt habe, einfach abfallen von ihrem Gesicht" (*G* 258; to make all the adjectives I have collected simply fall down from her face: *WM* 271–72). The narrator concludes that any sentences he employs to capture Lila remain helpless sketches that are incapable of capturing her as a living woman: "Einzige Gewißheit über Lila: so wie ich sie mir vorstelle, gibt es sie nicht" (*G* 252; The only certainty about Lila: she doesn't exist in the way I imagine her; *WM* 264). During a chess game with the medical doctor Burri, Gantenbein posits the conceptual unattainability of women for anyone who loves them: "Die Frau ist ein Mensch, bevor man sie liebt, manchmal auch nachher; sobald man sie liebt, ist sie ein Wunder, also unhaltbar—" (*G* 189; The woman is a person before one loves her, sometimes afterwards as well; as soon as one loves her she is a miracle and hence untenable; *WM* 198). In her feminist critique of *Mein Name sei Gantenbein*, Georgina Paul suggests that Frisch's novel is organized around what she calls "the male subject's anxiety vis-à-vis the increasing independence of woman and her evasion of his control."[14] While the novel can be fruitfully read as both illustrating and undermining male aggressiveness and helplessness towards female objects of desire, Paul's diagnosis repeats the same conceptual mistake that she attacks, clinging to one-dimensional readings of a text or a character. More convincing as a passing comment than an exhaustive conclusion is Chloe Paver's suggestion that the narrator is an experimental manipulator whose "successive projection, revision, and cancellation of fictions" constitutes a desperate "attempt to maintain control over his fictions."[15] Perhaps Frisch's narrator serves as a prototype for the conflicted desire that sustains the profession of writing and of literary scholarship, pursuing at once interpretive undecidability and recurring dreams of conceptual control.

One of the salient points of Frisch's novel is that turning humans into one-dimensional plot devices is a violation of their integrity and complexity. The novel correlates with Frisch's lifelong critique of conceiving of others and ourselves in terms of fixed images. As he writes in his seminal *Tagebuch 1946–1949*, careful and caring understanding of another human being begins when we overcome mutual "Bildniszwang," the obsession with fitting one another into imagined frames of expectation:

> Man macht sich ein Bildnis. Das ist das Lieblose, der Verrat. [. . .] Wir [. . .] ahnen nur selten, wie sehr der andere seinerseits eben der Spiegel unseres erstarrten Menschenbildes ist, unser Erzeugnis, unser Opfer.[16]
>
> [One produces an image. This is where the lack of love emerges, the betrayal. [. . .] We [. . .] rarely feel the extent to which the other is in turn the mirror of our petrified image of man, our product, our victim.]

The main object of male desire in the novel, the elusive Lila, an actress or, in the narrator's shifting recalibrations of his dreamlife, a scientist, or a drug-addicted countess, remains an unfinishable sketch, as mentioned above. Imagining himself as a stranger entering his own home, which he barely recognizes as his own, the narrator also remains a riddle to himself. In a recurrent post-mortem fantasy, he pictures himself visiting a recently abandoned apartment: "Lang kann's nicht her sein, seit hier gelebt worden ist" (*G* 17; It can't be a long time since someone lived here: *WM* 18); later, he continues: "Der Herr meines Namens ist verreist" (*G* 19; The gentleman of my name has gone away: *WM* 19). In a related episode that Frisch developed into a filmscript in 1966, a film that finally came out in 1992 under the title *Zürich: Transit*, the narrator reads the incorrect news of his death in a newspaper during a transatlantic flight. Hesitating and finally deciding not to reveal the news as false, he witnesses his own funeral and feels liberated by not informing his relatives and the public that declaring him dead has been a mistake, and by standing by and allowing his identity to be erased (*G* 224–31).

Paradoxically, far from merely enacting the ludic dimension of assuming roles in life, "ein Leben als Spiel" (*G* 20; life as a game: *WM* 21), the obsession with playing a blind man that the narrator shares with his invention, Gantenbein, is motivated by a longing for authenticity in social relationships. The narrator has Gantenbein cling to the hope that, in interactions with another person, the other's need for falseness dissipates when it is assumed that one is blind and therefore incapable of noticing symptoms of lies, so that understanding and trust have a chance of becoming more genuine:

> Vor allem aber, so hofft Gantenbein, werden die Leute sich vor einem Blinden wenig tarnen, so daß man sie besser kennenlernt, und es entsteht ein wirklicheres Verhältnis, indem man auch ihre Lügen gelten läßt, ein vertrauensvolleres Verhältnis— (*G* 40)
>
> [Above all, however, Gantenbein hopes, people won't camouflage themselves much against a blind man, so that one will get to know them better, and a more real relationship will come into being as a result of granting validity to their lies, a more trusting relationship— (*WM* 42)]

Pursuing this logic of negative inversion to its extreme, Gantenbein defines a couple as two humans who succeed in protecting secrets from each other, "erst das Geheimnis, das ein Mann und ein Weib voreinander hüten, macht sie zum Paar" (*G* 94; it is the secret that a man and a woman keep from each other that makes them a couple: *WM* 99). Jealousy constitutes a thematic thread that permeates the whole narrative. Gantenbein is haunted by the traumatic insight that there is no such thing as a comforting interwovenness of two lovers and the world they inhabit. He experiences the dissolution of his fantasies of oneness as a traumatic wound: "Schock: die Welt deckt sich mit dem Partner, nicht mit mir, die Liebe hat mich nur mit meinem Wahn vereint" (*G* 244; a shock: the world is identical with my partner, not with me, love has made me merely one with my madness: *WM* 256). On the other hand, Gantenbein admits to an addiction to being humiliated by betrayal in order to feel confirmation that he is part of a reality outside his self-induced imaginary world:

> Ich lechze nach Verrat. Ich möchte wissen, dass ich bin. Was mich nicht verrät, verfällt dem Verdacht, daß es nur in meiner Einbildung lebt, und ich möchte aus meiner Einbildung heraus, ich möchte in der Welt sein. Ich möchte im Innersten verraten sein. (*G* 244)
>
> [I am hankering after betrayal. I should like to know that I exist. That which does not betray me is subject to the suspicion that it exists only in my imagination, and I should like to come out of my imagination, I should like to be in the world. I should like to be betrayed in my innermost being. (*WM* 256)]

A recurring reminder of the novel's open exhibition of its continuous rehearsal mode is offered whenever the narrator suddenly comments on his conflicted emotional investment in his invented characters: "Ich habe Enderlin aufgegeben." (*G* 145; I have given Enderlin up. *WM* 152). "Gantenbein macht mich unsicher." (*G* 188; Gantenbein makes me unsure of myself. *WM* 197). "Svoboda beschäftigt mich noch immer." (*G* 231; I'm still preoccupied with Svoboda. *WM* 243). Critics and scholars have been attracted to Frisch's novel as a laboratory of psychological drafts, erasures, and overwritings. In one of the earliest discussions of *Mein Name sei Gantenbein*, Dieter Lattmann stated on a German radio program on September 14, 1964, "Existenzen werden durchgespielt als Möglichkeiten" (lives are rehearsed as alternative options).[17] In his review, "Max Frischs Entwürfe zu einem Ich" (Max Frisch's sketches towards a self), which appeared in the *Salzburger Nachrichten* on January 9, 1965, Adolf Haslinger writes that the narrative "bricht aus jeder chronologischen Orientierung immer wieder in die neue Probe einer Möglichkeit aus" (time and again breaks out of any attempt at chronological navigation and into a new rehearsal of an option). An unwittingly comical propagandistic summary of Frisch's novel is offered by Christoph Funke, who concludes in his review that appeared in the GDR's newspaper *Der Morgen* on September 17, 1966: "Max Frisch hat ein interessantes Buch geschrieben. Es ist auch für uns nützlich, auch wenn es oft nur Fragen stellt, wo wir die Antworten schon erfahren haben." (Max Frisch has written an interesting book. It is also useful to us, although it often only poses questions whose answers we have already experienced.) Apparently, as far as Funke and his employers were concerned, in the Eastern Bloc no one had to suffer from psychological crises or escape into preliminary sketches of themselves.

In his stimulating and influential monograph, *Max Frisch: Gantenbein; Das offen-artistische Erzählen* (1976) whose analytical rigor continues to set a high standard for Frisch research, Heinz Gockel offers a compelling outline of the pictorial dialectic of image and counter-image that purposefully disables character formation and plot development in Frisch's novel:

> Das Gegenbild ist nicht mehr eine neue Position gegen das Vorangegangene, sondern die Ausfaltung und Konkretisierung der im vorangegangenen Bild angelegten Widersprüchlichkeit. [. . .] Gegenbild und Bild erweisen sich gleichermaßen als Varianten der Widersprüchlichkeit. Enderlin ist nicht Gegenfigur zu Gantenbein, sondern Gantenbein und Enderlin sind mögliche Figurationen des im Aufbau der Figur angelegten Widerspruchs.[18]

> [The counter-image is not a new position in relation to the one that preceded it, but unfolds the contradictions that were outlined in the previous image and renders them more concrete. [. . .] Counter-image and image are equally variations on contradictions. Enderlin is not a mere contrast to Gantenbein; instead Enderlin and Gantenbein are both possible figurations of the contradiction that is built into the character.]

Following Gockel's philosophically alert presentation of Frisch's novel's conceptual core structure of character inventions as a self-proliferating series of contradictions, Frederick Lubich succinctly describes the interlacing of character inventions by the narrator—as well as by his inventions themselves: "Der namenlose Ich-Erzähler löst sich in verschiedenen Identifikationsfiguren auf, die ihrerseits eigene Sinnbilder und Lebensgeschichten entwerfen, sodaß schließlich das Ich des Erzählers vielfach gespiegelt und gebrochen in Erscheinung tritt." (The anonymous first-person narrator dissolves into various characters who, for their part, devise their own allegories and life stories so that eventually the narrator's self appears mirrored and refracted in multiple ways.)[19]

Highlighting Frisch's indebtedness to Kierkegaard, Gockel refers to Frisch's conversation with Horst Bienek in 1961, during which

Frisch discussed his ongoing work on the *Gantenbein* project with an emphasis on the arbitrariness of existential choices: "Man könnte mit einer fixen Summe gleicher Vorkommnisse, bloß indem man ihnen eine andere Erfindung seines Ichs zugrundelegt, sieben verschiedene Lebensgeschichten nicht nur erzählen, sondern leben. Das ist unheimlich." (One could not only tell but live seven different life stories with a certain number of similar events, simply by basing them on a different construction of one's "I." That is uncanny.)[20] The experience of the uncanny that the author and his narrators evoke and examine is triggered by an inescapable undecidability between alternative sketches of a life that appear to be equally repetitive. Gantenbein has premonitions about being interrogated and told: "Sie erzählen lauter Erfindungen." (What you are telling us is a lot of inventions.) His response is disarmingly pointed: "Ich erlebe lauter Erfindungen." (*G* 283; What I experience is a lot of inventions. *WM* 298).

The final half page of *Mein Name sei Gantenbein* seemingly breaks through the narcissistic walls of mirrors that have turned the narrator's universe into a prison cell. The narrator's sudden declaration of freedom and contentment with an idyllic Mediterranean landscape, which culminates in the life-affirming phrase, "alles ist Gegenwart" (*G* 288; everything is the present: *WM* 303), have been interpreted by the prolific Frisch scholar and editor Walter Schmitz as a sudden breakthrough into reality.[21] Hardly anyone has enriched Frisch scholarship more than Schmitz, yet it speaks to the productive ruses that permeate *Mein Name sei Gantenbein* that they trigger respectful disagreement among readers. In my reading, even the deceptive praise of a *locus amoenus* with which the novel ends does not offer any release from the gallery of self-contained mirrors through which the narrator and his character drafts chase each other. There is no "Bildbefreiung," no liberation from the inexorable experimental hall of mirrors in which the novel captures its voices and its readers. Far from delivering relief from existential pain, the novel's final scene might as well be read as yet another Rorschach exercise in pictorial projection. Even what declares itself at the end of the novel as a fresh beginning outside any narrative frame remains encapsulated in a vertiginous denial of facing reality and perpetuates storytelling as a mode of self-imprisonment. Nothing is resolved in the novel, whose freeze-frames offer variations on Frisch's observation, in his *Tagebuch 1946–1949*, of "wie sehr der andere seinerseits eben der Spiegel unseres erstarrten Menschenbildes ist, unser Erzeugnis, unser Opfer" (the extent to which the other is in turn the mirror of our petrified image of man, our product, our victim).[22]

Yet Frisch's novel has a liberating dimension exactly because it refuses to fabricate illusions of freedom. Demanding active and creative readers, *Mein Name sei Gantenbein* has a radically Socratic dimension that is best exemplified in Gantenbein's imaginary stint as a blind tour guide in Greece whose cunning helplessness turns his audience into narrators whose words at first are clumsy but who begin to look at their surroundings with fresh eyes. Some members of the group "empfinden ein solches Erbarmen mit ihm, daß sie, um Worte zu finden, die ihm eine Vorstellung geben von der Weihe des Ortes, selber zu sehen anfangen. Ihre Worte sind hilflos, aber ihre Augen werden lebendig." (*G* 181; feel so sorry for him that, in their search for words that will give him an idea of the sacred atmosphere of the place, they themselves begin to see. Their words are lame, but their eyes come to life. *WM* 190–91) The ruse of blindness and the anonymous corpse that almost floated away down the Limmat without a name tag or story in *Mein Name sei Gantenbein* remain necessary provocations in an era that remains entranced by planted images and slogans designed to suffocate independent thought and unscripted human interaction. Will we be able to step out of this novel?

Notes

[1] See http://www.zeit.de/2010/39/Traum-Bruno-Ganz (accessed July 2, 2012).

[2] Max Frisch Archive.

[3] References to *Mein Name sei Gantenbein* in this chapter are based on the following edition of the novel, Max Frisch, *Mein Name sei Gantenbein* (Frankfurt am Main: Suhrkamp, 2007), which will be henceforth cited using the abbreviation *G* and page number. Translations are taken from *A Wilderness of Mirrors*, translated by Michael Bullock (London: Methuen; New York: Random House, 1965), which will be cited using the abbreviation *WM* and page number. I am grateful to Margit Unser, director of the Max Frisch Archive, for her generous support during my visit at the archive and for allowing me to quote from unpublished letters.

[4] Wilma Iggers, "Max Frisch. *Mein Name sei Gantenbein*," *Books Abroad* (Spring 1965).

[5] Max Frisch Archive.

[6] For correlations between dissolutions of selfhood and of conventional temporal structures in Frisch's *Mein Name sei Gantenbein* and Luigi Pirandello's novellas and plays, see Giorgio Zampa's review of Frisch's novel in *La Stampa*, January 13, 1965, titled "Il difficile 'Gantenbein' di Max Frisch è la più disperata negazione della realtà" (The difficult "Gantenbein" by Max Frisch and the more desperate negation of reality): "Dissociazione dell'io [. . .] polivalenza del protagonista, compenetrazione di piani temporali, simultaneità di emozioni, a tutto questo siamo abituati da un pezzo: addirittura dai tempi di Pirandello" (The dissociation of the self [. . .] the protagonist's polyvalence, the permeation of temporal levels, the simultaneity of emotions, we are used to all this: straight from Pirandello's times).

[7] Max Frisch Archive.

[8] Rudolf Hartung, "Die Wahrheit läßt sich nur erfinden. Max Frisch las in der Kongreßhalle." *Der Tagesspiegel*, January 17, 1962, 4.

[9] Max Frisch Archive.

[10] Max Frisch Archive.

[11] Max Frisch Archive.

[12] Georg Büchner, *Lenz*, in G. B. *Dichtungen*, ed. Henri Poschmann (Frankfurt am Main: Deutscher Klassiker Verlag, 2006), 223–50; here 250. Translation taken from *Complete Plays, Lenz and Other Writings*, translated by John Reddick (London: Penguin, 1993), 164.

[13] Max Frisch, *Entwürfe zu einem dritten Tagebuch*, ed. Peter von Matt (Berlin: Suhrkamp, 2010), 176.

[14] Georgina Paul, *Perspectives on Gender in Post-1945 German Literature* (Rochester, NY: Camden House, 2009), 111.

[15] Chloe E. M. Paver, *Narrative and Fantasy in the Post-War German Novel: A Study of Novels by Johnson, Frisch, Wolf, Becker, and Grass* (Oxford: Clarendon Press, 1999), 52 and 74.

[16] Max Frisch, *Tagebuch 1946–1949* (Frankfurt am Main: Suhrkamp, 2007), 28–29. English translation by the author.

[17] Dieter Lattmann, "Für Sie gelesen—aus neuen Büchern," Bayerischer Rundfunk, September 14, 1964. Transcription (Max Frisch Archive), 17.

[18] Heinz Gockel, *Max Frisch: Gantenbein; Das offen-artistische Erzählen* (Bonn: Bouvier, 1976), 16. English translation by the author.

[19] Frederick A. Lubich, *Max Frisch: "Stiller," "Homo Faber" und "Mein Name sei Gantenbein"* (Munich: Fink, 1990), 82.

[20] Gockel, *Max Frisch: Gantenbein*, 18. First published in Horst Bienek, *Werkstattgespräche mit Schriftstellern* (Munich: Hanser, 1962), 24–25. English translation by the author. For a discussion of Kierkegaard's influence on Frisch, see Gockel, 122–39.

[21] Walter Schmitz, *Max Frisch: Das Spätwerk (1962–1982); Eine Einführung* (Tübingen: Francke, 1985), 64.

[22] Frisch, *Tagebuch 1946–1949*, 29.

11: Max Frisch's *Montauk. Eine Erzählung*

Ruth Vogel-Klein

In Frisch's narrative *Montauk* (1975), various memories and episodes from the narrator's life are alternately presented from a first-person and a third-person point of view. Throughout the text, the writing process of this specific book, and of literature in general, are negotiated in a self-referential discourse. The time frames change frequently. Fragmentary and constantly shifting memories that reach back into childhood are interwoven with a present-day plot set in the United States. This plot shows the sixty-two-year-old narrator "Max" in 1974 with Lynn, a young American woman whom he met at his New York publisher's office and with whom he spends a few days in New York City and a weekend at the shore, in Montauk, on the far eastern end of Long Island.

The work's narrative structure is highly complex. The pages written in the past tense are partially grouped according to thematic clusters and partially follow a loose associative pattern. The thematic segments present aspects of the life of "Max," a Swiss writer, in brief episodes or diachronically under thematic titles such as "architecture" or "fame," and shed light on his experiences and character traits. Another technique of weaving the diverse segments together uses subtle associations that are triggered by persons, places, objects, time references, questions, single words, and quotations, associations that establish parallels between the present and a remembered past. Particularly memories of other people are interwoven in an associative manner. They provide connections to the narrated time in *Montauk*. The narrator discusses several women: his two wives, Trudy and Marianne; Käthe, his fiancée in his student days; and the poet Ingeborg Bachmann. The frequently used singular personal pronoun "sie" (she) cannot always clearly be connected to one specific woman. The narrator also discusses family relations and friendships. The happiness of bygone days is constantly overshadowed by the question which actions, attitudes, and words in these relationships have been unfair, selfish, or culpable. The first- and third-person narrator at times accuses himself, but he also defends himself by accusing others. Often these recapitulations are tinged with acrimony, which is completely absent from the narrative present.

It remains unclear whether Max and Lynn are lovers. They are a couple drawn to each other by fondness and affection, and they share untarnished days together. This present is defined as weightless, and indeed nothing extraordinary happens. Frisch frequently employs this weightless narrative present as a foil in order to sharpen the contours of past experiences all the more intensely and painfully. The weekend in Montauk and the days together in New York City owe their significance mainly to the fact that they elude the patterns of past conflicts and hurt that the narrator remembers. Given the American context of the book, Frisch inserts English quotations and questions into the German text, creating additional disruptions in the complex narrative structure.

Biographical Contexts

In 1974 Frisch traveled to New York for a reading tour organized by his American publisher Helen Wolff.[1] He was accompanied by Alice Locke-Carey, a young employee of the publishing house with whom he also spent a private weekend in Montauk on Long Island. In *Montauk*, Alice's name is changed to Lynn. It is the only fictional name in the novella. While he was writing *Montauk* from 1974 to 1975, Frisch continued to live with his significantly younger wife, Marianne Frisch-Oellers, despite several crises in their marriage. They filed for divorce in 1979. In 1980 Frisch resumed his relationship with the young American, Locke-Carey. The Austrian poet Ingeborg Bachmann, who had been Frisch's lover between 1958 and 1962, had been killed in a fire in 1973, two years before the publication of *Montauk*.

Numerous studies focus on biographical contexts in *Montauk*. In the correspondence between the novelist and editor Uwe Johnson, Johnson's wife Elisabeth Johnson, Marianne Frisch-Oellers, and Max Frisch, the literary genesis of *Montauk* is discussed along with the author's right to use his personal life, including insights into the lives of others, as material for a literary work.[2] Ingeborg Bachmann's correspondence with the composer Hans Werner Henze[3] and with the poet Paul Celan, as well as letters exchanged by Celan and Frisch, also provide information about the biographical background of *Montauk*.[4] In a magazine article published in 2009, Frisch's German publisher Siegfried Unseld describes Max Frisch in New York,[5] and Frisch's friend, the painter Gottfried Honegger, in whose house he wrote the novella, has published autobiographical poems that also shed light on Frisch's life at the time.[6] Another noteworthy memoir by Frisch's daughter Ursula Priess, *Sturz durch alle Spiegel* (2009), provides a different perspective on the impact of *Montauk* on Frisch's family.[7] Priess criticizes passages in *Montauk* in which she is mentioned.[8] Richard Dindo's film, *Max Frisch, Journal I–III* (1981), includes several interviews with people who are depicted in *Montauk*.

The Sketchbook as Structural Model

For a reader who is not familiar with Frisch's works, the literary structure of *Montauk* might be surprising. Even at first glance, the text's porosity is striking. Short paragraphs or longer passages are only separated by blank lines. Capitalized lines alternately serve as titles, questions, or form independent fragments. This fragmentary structure of the written page corresponds to ruptures within and between the narrative layers. The narrated present in Montauk and New York City is time and again interrupted by flashbacks. Various temporal layers are entangled with each other and often cannot be isolated by the reader. As Knapp points out, the fragmentary narrative structure creates the fiction of subjective experience.[9] Often characters that emerge from different events in the past are not identified with names but only referred to with a personal pronoun. During a first reading of the text, a full comprehension of the disjointed narrative layers and the arsenal of characters is fairly impossible, but a more thorough examination can result in a more complete deciphering of the work.

Montauk shares structural affinities with Frisch's *Tagebuch 1946–1949* and *Tagebuch 1966–1971*.[10] This similarity goes beyond Frisch's general tendency to embrace a literary diary form, as he does in *Blätter aus dem Brotsack*, *Tagebuch 1*, *Stiller*, and *Homo Faber*. Frisch remarks: "Die Form des Tagebuches, so wie ich es für mich entwickelt habe [. . .] ist eigentümlich für den Verfasser meines Namens" (The form of the diary as I have developed it for myself [. . .] is idiosyncratic for the author who bears my name).[11] In his first *Tagebuch* Frisch develops a poetics of the fragment that is also relevant for *Montauk*, "arguing for the sketch as a manifestation of a worldview that refuses closure."[12] Rolf Kieser writes that Frisch passionately demands an open structure and that for him a sketch is the only appropriate art form.[13] In another *Tagebuch* entry that Frisch later integrated into his poetics lectures (which were published in 2008 as *Schwarzes Quadrat*), he argues for disrupting linearity as a precondition for self-awareness: "Wir können nur, indem wir den Zickzack unserer jeweiligen Gedanken bezeugen und sichtbar machen, unser Wesen kennenlernen, seine Wirrnis oder seine heimliche Einheit . . ." (We can only acquaint ourselves with our essential core, its confusion or its secret unity by bearing witness to and making visible the zigzag of our specific thoughts . . .).[14]

Analyzing *Montauk* as a continuation of the *Tagebücher* offers instructive perspectives. As mentioned before, the affinity manifests itself in the fragmentary form, the diverse brief entries and isolated memories, and the subheadings and blank lines between heterogeneous textual elements. The novel on the one hand and the *Tagebücher* on the other are similarly concise.[15] Themes the two have in common include repetition, literary translation of experience into language, role and identity, and the question of self-representation. The principle of "inner time," which plays a foundational role for the interweaving of motifs, is another shared aspect.[16] There are also specific similarities between *Montauk* and *Tagebuch 2*, including the thematic threads of aging, death, marital crisis, emancipation, memories of the Jewish fiancée and the affluent school friend, and references to literary works such as Montaigne's *Essais*. The sketchbook character of *Montauk* seduced director Richard Dindo into selecting *Max Frisch, Journal I–III* (1981) as the title for his "filmischen Lektüre" of *Montauk*. It should be noted here that Frisch later distanced himself from Dindo's pictorial transposition of his text and from the interviews in the film with various people who appear in *Montauk*.[17]

Frisch's *Tagebuch 2* and *Montauk* share the same questions that keep the texts moving forward. But they diverge with regard to the form and function with which they endow these questions. While in *Tagebuch 2* the reader is provided with general questionnaires about personal topics as well as with fictional dialogues on political matters in which the narrator, as Rolf Kieser writes, "als sokratisch Fragender [. . .] über den Marktplatz der Zeit [geht]" (walks across the market square of time [. . .] asking questions like Socrates),[18] *Montauk* focuses on questions that are peculiar to the writer and his personal history. These questions in *Montauk* have a specific structural function. Although the answers sometimes seem evasive, the interview situation allows Frisch to address different points of his biography in a fragmented yet concise way, unrestrained by chronological linearity.

Even though *Montauk* has to be read as a continuation of the *Tagebücher*, it lays the foundations for a new form of self-presentation. While Frisch's *Tagebücher* did not intend to focus on the private sphere, as Meike Heinrich-Korpys emphasizes,[19] *Montauk* consciously insulates itself against contemporary events in the outside world in order to dedicate itself fully to the narrator's own story, although its literary ambition is to transcend the strictly individual sphere.[20] The focus moves far away from world events, and the objective chronological pattern almost completely disappears. In the segment on "Schreiben in Ich-Form" in *Tagebuch 2*, Frisch discusses the many insertions on politics as an autobiographer's hide-and-seek game.[21]

The "Ich/Er" in *Montauk*, on the other hand, occupies himself with autobiographical introspection. The narrative from 1975 focuses on the narrator's life, and those elements of the *Tagebücher* that do not correspond to open autobiographical self-presentation, such as fictional texts, accounts of political events, documents, and lengthy quotations from works by others, are absent from *Montauk*. The two works also differ in the way they present temporality. The structure of *Montauk* is determined by tensions between the narrative present and different layers of the past, that is, from the writer Max Frisch's life from his childhood until 1974, the year of the narrated weekend in Montauk. While not always made explicit, the connection between present and past becomes apparent if one reads carefully. This becomes especially clear if we analyze Frisch's then wife Marianne's implicit participation in the narrative present with Lynn.[22] Claudia Müller's assumption that the female voices in *Montauk* represent parallel yet unrelated stories[23] is a bit too simplistic. Barbara Saunders offers the beautiful definition of Lynn as a "catalyst of [Frisch's] memories."[24]

Narrative Perspectives and the Question of Autobiography

The extent to which *Montauk* can be considered an autobiography has often been debated among scholars. We need to ground this discussion in the long-established insight that any literary work, including an autobiographical narrative, is a work of artistic figuration and not a copy of reality. As Rudolf Hartung writes in his study of *Montauk*, the truth about one's own self and life can neither be located outside nor before literature: "Erst die Literatur bringt mitteilbare Erfahrung und die Erkenntnis dieser Erfahrung hervor." (Only literature produces experience that can be communicated and knowledge of this experience.)[25] The question of the autobiographical status of *Montauk* can be answered using criteria developed by French literary scholar Philippe Lejeune. Lejeune posits that author, narrator, and protagonist are identical in an autobiography.[26] This identity is present in *Montauk*: there is no doubt that Max Frisch is the narrator and that the narrated events are taken from his biography. Numerous indications in the text prove this identity: mentions of Switzerland as the narrator's home country; the use of names of Frisch's actual relatives, lovers, and friends; references to houses in which Frisch had lived, quotations from and references to his own works. The name "Frisch" appears, and the main character's first name is "Max."

But *Montauk* does not only have an auto-diegetic narrator, to use Genette's terminology;[27] it also has a narrator who presents "Max's" life from a third-person point of view. To some degree it is possible to distinguish the two narrative personas from each other, but these schematic definitions are frequently disrupted, often with a shift in perspective in the middle of a sentence (*M*, 102, 107). "Er" is Lynn's partner who experiences himself in a new way in this relationship. "Er" is also the jealous husband who undergoes a marital crisis. "Ich" stands for the writer Max Frisch, both as public figure and as private person with his childhood and his memories.[28] The distinction suggested by Gerhard Knapp, according to whom the "Ich" is a "Realfigur," while the "Er" is a "Kunstfigur," operates with an overdrawn dichotomy and does not do justice to the complex dual narrative identity that is at work here.[29]

The narrative in the third person and the shifts between the first- and third-person narrator in *Montauk* have been misinterpreted by Frisch scholars as an indicator of fictionality. According to Lejeune these techniques are characteristic for autobiographies.[30] The account in the course of which the "ich" is replaced with a third person continues to refer to the same person while creating a discrepancy that allows for the emergence of questions pertaining to self-presentation, the complexity of identity, internal versus external points of view, as well as life and writing.[31] Through its shifts between its narrative voices, a tension is sustained in *Montauk* that repeatedly disrupts the illusion of a coherent story and that has a defamiliarizing effect. In his interview with Heinz Ludwig Arnold, Frisch confessed: "Wenn ich als Tagebuch-Ich auftrete, so tarne ich mich mehr, als wenn ich in der Er-Form auftrete, im Roman." (I camouflage myself more when I appear in a diary in the first person than by presenting myself in a novel in the third person.)[32] But the configuration in *Montauk* is somewhat different. What is at stake in the narrative is not a fictional "er" but an autobiography narrated in the third person.

Its relationship with the reader offers another argument for an autobiographical reading of *Montauk*. According to Lejeune, the reader is entangled ("embrayé") in any autobiographical text because he or she maintains a relationship with the author. The author of an autobiography has the specific agenda of earning the respect of the reader, whose reaction is as important to him as the reactions of our fellow human beings are to us in real life. The reader's relationship to the author in a work of fiction on the other hand is cut off ("débrayé"). The reader responds freely, his reactions are irrelevant to the author.[33] The reader of *Montauk* is tied into the text. The author/narrator frequently employs strategies of justification when the question of his guilt is at stake. This is especially apparent in the segments about his oldest daughter, about Ingeborg Bachmann, and about his second wife, Marianne. The explanatory style goes hand in hand with an apologetic tone that is intended to move the reader to declare "Max"—rather than a fictional character—innocent.

Has the Janus-faced narrator in *Montauk*, who wants to be declared free of guilt, agreed to an "autobiographical pact" with the reader as defined by Philippe Lejeune?[34] It has to be kept in mind that such a narrative always remains subjective and relative and may not be confused with documentary writing.[35] The narrator in *Montauk* explicitly announces his intention to write an autobiographical and not a fictional work:

> dieses Wochenende zu erzählen: autobiographisch, ja, autobiographisch. [. . .] ohne auszuweichen in Erfindungen. Ohne seine Schriftstellerei zu rechtfertigen durch Verantwortung gegenuber der Gesellschaft; ohne Botschaft. Er hat keine und lebt trotzdem. (*M*, 155)

> [to describe this weekend: in an autobiographical way. Completely autobiographical [. . .] without taking refuge in inventions of any kind; without seeking to justify his writing as a duty toward society. A story without a message. He has none to give, and yet he is alive. (Skelton, 106)]

This passage contains a reference to Frisch's presentation of his life in his literary work in the form of "Erfindungen," inventions, especially in *Tagebuch 2*, where the political realm is given much weight. Here, in *Montauk*, the narrator postulates an autobiographical truth that is supposed to differ from his former texts. In another passage he radically devalues his fictional work and contrasts it with his new ambition to tell the truth:

> Ich habe mir mein Leben verschwiegen. [. . .] Ich habe mich in diesen Geschichten entblößt, ich weiß, bis zur Unkenntlichkeit. Ich lebe nicht mit der eigenen Geschichte, nur mit Teilen davon, die ich habe literarisieren können. (*M*, 156)

> [[. . .] I have been concealing my life from myself. [. . .] I have, I know, I laid myself bare—to the point of non-recognition. I live, not with my own story, but just with those parts of it that I have been able to put to literary use. (Skelton 106–7)]

Montauk is supposed to finally present the "eigene Geschichte," the real story, leaving behind fiction as an obstacle to self-knowledge. The epigraph taken from Montaigne's *Essais* that Frisch inserts at the beginning of his book also embraces an autobiographical project. However, as a quotation from another author that is purposefully only rendered with omissions by Frisch,[36] the weight of the Montaigne quotation differs from that of the self-confessions:

> Dies ist ein aufrichtiges Buch, Leser, es warnt dich schon beim Eintritt, dass ich mir darin kein anderes Ende vorgesetzt habe als ein häusliches und privates [. . .] ich bin es, den ich darstelle. Meine Fehler wird man hier finden, so wie sie sind [. . .] (M, 5)

> [This book was written in good faith, reader. It warns you from the outset that in it I have set myself no goal but a domestic and private one [. . .] for it is myself that I portray. One will find my faults here just as they are [. . .] (Skelton, modified, unpaginated)]

It would be simplistic to reduce this epigraph to its apparent meaning and to read it as clear proof of the author's autobiographical intention.[37] According to Michael Butler, "to read the book as a guide to Frisch's private life would indeed be an idle occupation."[38] The intertextual correlation with Montaigne suggests an additional layer of meaning. As

Hugo Friedrich elaborately demonstrates, Montaigne was not primarily interested in autobiography when he composed his *Essais* but rather in a philosophical project.[39] Gerhard vom Hofe confirms this in an excellent article in which he outlines the relation between *Montauk* and the *Essais*. On the one hand, it is a structural correlation. Autobiographical notes, memories, reports of exemplary events and observations culminate in general reflections. On the other hand, the texts share thematic terrain, for example self-examination in the face of the experience of aging, skepticism and melancholy, self-devaluation, contemplation of one's own mistakes against the backdrop of the human condition in general.[40] It can therefore be concluded that by quoting the great French philosopher, Frisch was attempting to abandon a memory pattern that is tied to purely personal memory. He wanted his book to be part of a philosophical tradition that takes the individual as its point of departure and arrives at insights into the *conditio humana*. The gesture of modesty that characterizes Montaigne's preface is echoed in Frisch's self-presentation, but Frisch's emphasis on self-deprecation goes beyond Montaigne's rhetorical gesture. Excerpts from the epigraph permeate Frisch's narrative as leitmotifs, especially when, as he often does, Frisch evokes the programmatic honesty of the book.

The label "Erzählung" attached to the book by Frisch in its title seems to contradict all these elements that suggest a non-fictional autobiographical text. There are two plausible explanations for this contradiction. Frisch scholars repeatedly state that by explicitly subsuming the book under the genre "Erzählung" Frisch was emphasizing the elaborate literary structure of the text, and this finding is certainly correct. In this complex artistic form Max Frisch appears as a "Kunstfigur."[41] Barbara Saunders convincingly comments: "In *Montauk* his chosen style and theme must be seen as a personal [. . .] a contemporary attempt to come to terms with the autobiographical tradition, not as [a . . .] rejection of his achievements."[42] It is also possible that with the term "Erzählung" Frisch had in mind a form of short prose that offers more coherence than his *Tagebücher*. The genre term "Erzählung" does not denote fictionality[43] but only an auctorial intention not to be confused with a documentary form of life-writing. We know from the manuscript drafts of the work that Frisch did not use the word "Erzählung" until rather late in the composition process. Not until the seventh of the eleven preserved manuscripts of *Montauk* did he use the term.[44]

It is possible that Frisch was trying to create room for flexibility. By opting for the genre term "Erzählung" he was able to make use of private matters from his life and the lives of those close to him as material for a literary work without being indiscrete. In this context, Michael Butler sees an ironic element in the subtitle.[45] Frisch's correspondence with Uwe Johnson and the early drafts of the text show that Frisch repeatedly had skeptical thoughts about the degree to which one is allowed to portray other people without exposing them. Reflections of this kind can already be found in *Tagebuch 2*.[46] Of special importance in this regard were numerous details about his second wife Marianne's private life. Lioba Waleczek notes that before the publication of *Montauk* Frisch und Marianne were engaged in a dispute: she was opposed to the publication. Twenty-five years later, she told Lioba Waleczek that there was a "fundamental disagreement" between her and Frisch regarding what should be protected as "private" and what can become "public."[47] Frisch had asked his friend Uwe Johnson, who also was a good friend of Marianne's, to mediate between him and his wife in this matter. The couple asked Johnson for a written statement. To this end, Johnson wrote a letter to Marianne about *Montauk*. Siding with Frisch, and underscoring the subtle interweaving of autobiographical material and narrative layers of fictionality in *Montauk*, he tried to dispel any arguments against the publication of the text.[48] Johnson also expressed his hope that Marianne would not try to have the work censored, and she immediately replied that she would not.[49] Johnson uses the complex narrative structure of *Montauk*, which is indeed reminiscent of fictional texts and relatively untypical for an autobiography, as a means to downplay the autobiographical content of the work. Far from being a neutral document, Johnson's often-quoted letter exaggerates the "fictional" aspect of the book in an attempt to persuade the skeptical Marianne to allow its publication. Ultimately, even Johnson read *Montauk* as an autobiographical text. Otherwise there would have been no need for him to justify (with arguments that are not very convincing) the author's "indiscretion" regarding his wife.[50] Klaus Müller-Salget's diagnosis that *Montauk* consists of a "stylized stream-of-consciousness,"[51] provides a more nuanced description than Johnson's letter, for which Frisch thanked him, calling it "ein Akt letzter Hilfe."[52]

Gerhard vom Hofe regards *Montauk* as an "autobiographical correction" in the nexus of Frisch's work as a whole. Vom Hofe argues that in contrast to Frisch's earlier works, *Montauk* abandons the "poetics of fictional variations of the self" and any hope for fundamental change. According to vom Hofe, Frisch's revision of his former aesthetic principles is based on his experience of aging. A retrospective gaze becomes prevalent and the "Ich" no longer has any recourse to future life options and variations.[53] In the aforementioned interview with Heinz Ludwig Arnold that was conducted during the time period in which he worked on *Montauk*, Frisch described his writing as an attempt to anchor himself in the present: "Ich schreibe, um zu bestehen; ich schreibe, um mir klar zu werden [. . .]" (I write in order to endure. I write in order to enhance my awareness [. . .]).[54]

Inhabiting Quotation Marks

The subheading "Leben im Zitat" (*M*, 103; Living in quotations: Skelton 69) that follows a quotation from *Homo Faber* refers to several different semantic elements. On the one hand, Frisch quotes his own works in *Montauk*.[55] The content of these quotations are generally integrated into the new text as observations. The narrator backs up his views with the help of his own works and interweaves them with *Montauk*. The unity of the author's life manifests itself in a past that consists of his works. Past literary works and quotations provide the formula for experiencing the present. On the other hand, the authenticity of this experience of the present is threatened by the quotation. The inextricable entanglement of literature and life de-emphasizes life in favor of its written form. Walter Schmitz describes the autobiographical project in *Montauk* as "the sum of his self-quotations" and argues that the quotations represent his past and guilt rather than redemption:

> Die Autobiographie, die der Schriftsteller erkundet, ergibt sich als die Summe seiner Selbstzitate, und die Zitate verraten die Rollen, in denen das Ich sich auszudrücken vermag. [. . .] Das Zitat [. . .] ist die Sprache der Vergangenheit, nicht der Zukunft, der Schuld, nicht der Erlösung.[56]
>
> [The autobiography that is explored by the writer emerges as the sum of his self-quotations, and the quotations give away the roles in which the "I" is able to express itself. [. . .] Quotation [. . .] is the language of the past and not of the future, of guilt and not of redemption.]

In a similar vein, Hans Bänziger describes Frisch's confrontation with the quoted past as an introspective mode of torment, "skrupelhaft-quälerisch.[57] At times the narrator in *Montauk*, who frequently refers to himself in the third person, varies the ambiguous relationship between life and quotation:

> Er hat reichlich über Eifersucht geschrieben. Schon deswegen hat er sich in den letzten Jahren jede Eifersucht versagt. Es wäre keine neue Erfahrung für ihn [. . .] es fiele ihm als Schriftsteller dazu nichts ein, nichts Neues. (*M*, 121)
>
> [He has already written a great deal about jealousy. For that very reason he has in recent years sternly forbidden himself any feelings of jealousy. It would not be a new experience for him [. . .] as a writer, he would have nothing to say about it, nothing new. (Skelton 82)]

But the narrator cannot escape his quotations and repetitions, and his role as writer does not save him from renewed jealousy. Only a few pages after this passage an elaborate story about jealousy unfolds, and the narrator emerges as a betrayed, bitter, and angry husband (*M*, 123–27).

Ursula Haupt alerts the reader to a different kind of "Leben im Zitat." The autobiographical descriptions of Lynn in *Montauk* display striking similarities to descriptions of Sabeth in Frisch's novel *Homo Faber*. At times the word choices are identical. Even the age difference between Lynn and Max is compared to that of a father and his daughter.[58] Madeleine Salzmann discusses the recurring incest motif in *Montauk* by showing connections between Sabeth and Lynn in addition to passages about Lynn and the narrator's daughter.[59] Here the literary quotation from the past is inserted into the narrator's current life. Walter Schmitz writes that in Montauk, "das Leben wird zur Wiederholung seiner vorweggenommenen Beschreibung" (life becomes the repetition of its description that has been crafted beforehand).[60]

In *Montauk*, inhabiting a quotation not only refers to quotations of writings but to the experience of life as an inescapable spiral of repetitions.[61] Gerhard Knapp goes so far as to subsume all of the over fifty analepses that he finds in the work, "über fünfzig Einblenden," in which experiences of the past are presented, under the heading "déjà vu."[62] Klaus Müller-Salget highlights the superimposition of elements from the narrative present and the various temporal layers of the past as a constitutive structure of the book.[63]

Often a specific place serves as a point of contact for the recurring memory, for example the ocean as projection screen of the present and the past. But even experiences with people seem to repeat themselves. Barbara Saunders notes: "In *Montauk* Frisch concentrates explicitly upon the deterministic effect of certain recurrent patterns of his life which continue to influence his emotional responses as a 64-year-old man."[64] In Frisch's narrative, "déjà vu" operates with the narrator's subjective perception as a connective element. The phenomenon of "déja vu" suggests a surprising similarity and almost an identity of past and present perceptions, a kind of *télescopage* that connects and fuses the temporal layers.

Max Frisch, who quotes a passage from his novel *Stiller*—"my greatest fear: repetition" (*M*, 18)—nevertheless creates in *Montauk* a poetics of repetition and quotation. A principle of unity in the fragmentary narrative consists in the recurrence of the same or of similar experiences. The literary quotation from earlier works is used in order to express a comparable experience in the present while the artful connection of associative elements in the form of "déjà vu" draws lifelines that provide the memories in logical disorder. The element of repetition corresponds to the mutual mirroring of life phases, be it as a vicious cycle or as a principle of life that offers coherence.

Textual Genesis[65]

The narrative was composed within one year, between the summers of 1974 and 1975. The galley proofs are dated July 3, 1975. The writing process can be reconstructed because Frisch gave his various typescript versions to the Max Frisch Archive that he founded in Zurich in 1981.[66] There are six complete drafts and five incomplete ones consisting mostly of newly reworked segments and pages. In his interview with Heinz Ludwig Arnold, Frisch talked about his working method during the time he was writing *Montauk* (which he did, as mentioned above, in the studio of his friend, the painter Gottfried Honegger), comparing his composition process with that of a contruction worker.[67] All the drafts, even the first one, were typed, because for the architect Frisch, the visual aspect of the page was important. Several months later, in November 1974, Frisch reported to his friends Uwe und Elisabeth Johnson that he had completed his book.[68] But the manuscript was not ready yet. In a letter from January 11, 1975, Frisch asked his friends to "improve" the text.[69]

Uwe Johnson had served as Frisch's editor for the second *Tagebuch.* Their correspondence during that collaboration, in the course of which Frisch accepted many of Johnson's suggestions, amounts to about 160 pages.[70] The editorial changes in *Montauk* were less extensive than in *Tagebuch 2.* Johnson verified the date of Montaigne's preface and proofread the typescripts. His wife Elisabeth appears to have made a major contribution to the critical reading of the text.[71] The typescripts display traces of the corrections, most of which are confined to linguistic and stylistic matters and are not very far-reaching. Unfortunately, the preserved correspondence between Frisch and the Johnsons does not contain Elisabeth Johnson's letters about *Montauk*, to which Frisch refers once and in which matters of principle and content were apparently discussed.[72] Frisch dedicated a copy of the book to the Johnsons, "in großer Dankbarkeit" (with great gratitude).[73]

What are the major findings of a comparison of the various drafts of *Montauk*? The narrative structure, which is characterized by interrupted narrative threads, flashbacks, and shifting narrative perspectives, can already be found in the first preserved version.[74]

Based on Philippe Lejeune's theory, this discussion of selected elements of the textual genesis of *Montauk* does not assume that the early typescripts are more truthful and then gradually lose their alleged authenticity in later versions.[75] Each phase has its own coherence and internal logic, and the narrator's self-perception changes in the course of the different versions of an autobiographical text.

It is instructive to analyze deletions and omissions. The first draft of *Montauk* was substantially shorter than the final narrative. Many of the longer segments were inserted later: "Money," "Architecture," "Renown,"

"The Jewish Bride," "Memoirs." Two of the episodes had been already completed when Frisch began to write *Montauk*. The story of his friendship with Werner Coninx ("W.") was composed in 1973. It was revised in 1974 and separately published in 1975 under the title "Autobiographisches."[76] Frisch wrote the memory of his paralyzed school friend Therese Haller, Thesy, for *Tagebuch 2* but Uwe Johnson dissuaded him from including it.[77] Frisch did not originally plan to integrate these two episodes into *Montauk*.

The insertions into the later versions amount to more than a quarter of the book. Their inclusion alters the importance of what was present in the first version. The two narrative threads that carried the weight in the first draft were the narrative present with Lynn and the constantly recurring memories of Marianne. A careful reading of the final version still reveals to some degree this original parallel structure. The presentation of the relationships with Lynn and Marianne can be read in a complementary way. There are numerous explicit as well as implicit correlations.[78] The later narrative insertions render the fundamental nexus of the two stories (Max/Marianne and Max/Lynn) less visible.

A third important narrative thread that was an integral part of the book from the beginning is the love story between the narrator and Ingeborg Bachmann. This story does not assume importance comparable to the Max/Lynn story, but like the story of Marianne, it forms a stark contrast to the carefree and emotionally less involved experience of the present. In the later drafts, Frisch not only intended to narrate "sein Leben als Mann" with women but also to give a more comprehensive overview of his life, friendships, and professional matters.

In the course of the various versions, Frisch not only inserted narrative segments but also deleted or moved some episodes or sentences, so that the logic of specific episodes and reflections was fundamentally altered. The episodes involving Ingeborg Bachmann and Marianne Frisch underwent more revisions than any other segments of the book.

Frisch heavily edited those pages of the typescript that present the narrator's conflicts with the women he loved and the wounds they inflicted on him. Severe allegations were toned down, the sequence of bitter memories was restructured, shortened, and integrated into the rhythm of the narrative. It is striking that in contrast to these numerous alterations, Frisch made very few changes in the passages that describe Ingeborg Bachmann in a positive way. His admiration was not subjected to corrections. The nostalgic and endearing segments about Marianne were also left unchanged for the most part, while multiple versions of the narrator's conflicts with her can be found in the same typescript. Apparently it was only possible for Frisch to transform emotionally challenging material into a literary text in successive phases.

A comparison of the deletions and omissions in the different versions reveals an incremental condensation of the material and an increasingly coherent and unified style. Similar memories are integrated into a sequence, and numerous interjections in capital letters are deleted or reduced. Frisch also deleted or cut back passages in which questions of discretion are discussed, a topic that often recurs in the early drafts and is still present in the final version. In one of the drafts, Frisch declares that he never turned himself into an object of literary representation because that would have required honesty: "Ich habe mich nie dargestellt. Um das zu dürfen, müsste man aufrichtig sein [. . .]" (I have never represented myself. In order to be allowed to do that one would have to be honest [. . .]).[79] But despite his announcement of the intention to be discreet, Frisch discloses information about the personal life of others. Even though one can detect strategies of encryption and omission in the typescripts, Frisch did not adhere to his plan to show respect and restraint.

The process of writing *Montauk* also involved a search for a fitting literary structure. Different rearrangements of narrative sequences indicate that Frisch, who had inserted six "narrative blocks" into the first version, was striving for a balanced form. Claudia Müller points out that the Lynn, Marianne, and Ingeborg Bachmann characters alternately make their appearances in the text, and she even compares this literary technique with a musical composition.[80]

Gender Aspects

Reflections on femininity and masculinity are a recurring component of *Montauk*. This is not a new theme for Frisch. As Walter Schmitz points out, masculine identity is a central theme in Frisch's work.[81] The account of the relationship between man and woman provides the foundation of the emerging narrative in *Montauk*. Taking the book *My Life as a Man*, which he received as a present from its author Philip Roth, as a point of departure, the narrator states his desire to find out what he can learn about his "life as a man" while composing a literary work (*M*, 24). The question of the narrator's own behavior is at the center of all his memories of women. He self-critically analyzes but at the same time subtly defends himself.

Frisch wrote *Montauk* in the middle of the 1970s, a period in which the women's movement was asserting itself in society. Traces of this topic can be found in the text. The role of man is confronted with concepts such as emancipation and self-realization of women. Surprisingly, financial matters are often an indicator of the state of the narrator's relationship with a woman. He records who is taking care of the expenses, whether each woman is financially independent, and what kinds of power structures these financial relations reflect. What is really at stake, however, are the balance sheets of failure in human relationships. The narrator describes his relationships with women as a function of his own flawed conduct and attitude:

> Manchmal meine ich sie zu verstehen, die Frauen, und im Anfang gefällt ihnen meine Erfindung, mein Entwurf zu ihrem Wesen [. . .] Natürlich habe ich nicht für alle Frauen den gleichen Entwurf. Zum Beispiel, dass sie die Stärkere ist oder dass ich der Stärkere bin. [. . .] ich erfinde für jede Partnerin eine andere Not mit mir. [. . .] Es sind nicht die Frauen, die mich hinters Licht führen; das tue ich selber. (*M*, 118–19)
>
> [Women: sometimes I believe I understand them, and at the outset they are pleased with my inventions, with my sketch of their character [. . .] Naturally, I do not produce the same model for every woman. [. . .] for each partner I invent a new difficulty in relation to myself—for instance, that she is the stronger character, or, alternatively, that I am. [. . .] It is not the women who make a fool of me. I do that myself. (Skelton 80–81)]

Not without irony and a certain degree of self-stylization Frisch continues to work on the theme of liberating oneself from the practice of creating fixed images, a theme that played an important role in the first *Tagebuch*. In a self-critical manner the narrator presents himself as a kind of Pygmalion who invents specific qualities that he attributes to each of the women as if they were literary characters. A constant theme is the "Not" (misery) that his female partners experience with the narrator, their difficulties with him. Obsessed with failure, the narrator persuades all his female partners that their relationships with him are miserable. The repetition of this destructive behavioral pattern makes fulfilling communication between man and woman impossible.

Although Frisch points to an impasse here, there are other segments in *Montauk* where he traces an inner development of the narrator over the course of time. In the early relationships he describes himself as an immature and selfish young man who is afraid of commitment. Moral insecurity characterizes the passage about the model for Hanna in *Homo Faber*, who wishes for a child:

> Die jüdische Braut aus Berlin (zur Hitler-Zeit), heißt nicht Hanna, sondern Käte [. . .] gemeinsam haben sie nur die historische Situation und in dieser Situation einen jungen Mann, der später über sein Verhalten nicht ins klare kommt. (*M*, 166–67)
>
> [My Jewish fiancée from Berlin (during the Nazi period) was not named Hanna, but Käte [. . .] All they had in common was the historical situation and, within this situation, a young man who later was unable to explain his behavior. (Skelton 114)]

According to this account, the marriage proposal was not motivated by the wish to make a commitment out of love but by a sense of ethical obligation at the time of the Nazi dictatorship's racial laws.[82] In retrospect, this story appears as a story of guilt, just like the story of Frisch's bourgeois marriage with the architect Gertrud Constanze von Meyenburg, known by Frisch as Trudi (*M*, 175). The traditional male role of father and provider for the family is not questioned per se. Rather Frisch's unfaithfulness and separation from the family appear to evoke guilt not only with regard to his wife but also his daughter. His self-criticism and confession of guilt are unmistakable: "Ich leugne nicht meine Schuld; sie ist mit langen Briefen, die der erwachsenen Tochter meine damalige Scheidung erklären, nicht zu tilgen." (*M*, 54; I do not deny that the fault was mine, not to be wiped out with letters to my grown-up daughter explaining why, years before, I had got a divorce. [Skelton, 35]) The narrator's guilt is mirrored in another episode about guilt under the title "Memoiren." Therese Haller, Frisch's paralyzed childhood friend mentioned earlier, lives in the same house as Frisch and Trudi but never receives a visit from the narrator, although she is lonely. Lynn summarizes this as follows: "Max, you are a monster" (*M*, 79). Even though the term "monster" is not used by the narrator himself, an unmistakably negative assessment is upheld.

The narrator views his awareness of his role as a man as having evolved in his later relationships with women. About the keyword "women's liberation" he writes affirmatively, in the dialogic context of the book, which was written in 1974, describing it as the most urgent project for society (*M*, 90).[83] After a brief transition, he remembers Ingeborg Bachmann as a self-confident poet.[84] She had planned the first rendezvous with the narrator, she found his address and visited Paris for a premiere of one of his plays (*M*, 90). In a later passage her mature attitude toward money is mentioned (*M*, 182). Bachmann appears not only as an emancipated woman but as an independent female artist. A letter from the narrator to Bachmann about women's writing marks the beginning of the love story. Having listened to Bachmann's radio play *Der gute Gott von Manhattan* (The Good God of Manhattan), a work that thematizes a consuming passion that kills a woman, he wrote to Bachmann, whom he had not met yet at the time, that it is necessary that not only male but also female authors represent women in their texts (*M*, 90). Free of envy, Frisch expresses his admiration for her intellectual brilliance, listing her remarkable achievements as a doctor of philosophy, a Wittgenstein and Heidegger expert, and a highly gifted poet who was invited to give the first poetics lectures at Frankfurt's Goethe University. Their love story, however, failed dramatically in the eyes of the narrator (*M*, 151), though he does not clearly assign responsibility for this failure. On the one hand, the narrator characterizes himself as a fool (*M*, 149). He evokes the power she had over him, and describes how his extreme jealousy once led him to take his car for a dangerous night-long drive while heavily intoxicated in order to catch her by surprise with one of her lovers (*M*, 146). Overall he does not admit to any guilt but to madness triggered by his love for her (*M*, 142). On the other hand, these brief moments of self-criticism are countered by lengthy presentations of the injuries and humiliations inflicted on him by Bachmann. We read that she denied his existence in front of others, that she had other lovers, and that he once opened a letter to her written by one of them, a letter that included a secret marriage proposal (*M*, 142–51). Classical gender roles seem inverted here: the woman is the dominant personality and demands an open relationship free of commitment. The man submits to the brilliant woman and accepts everything that hurts him.

Frisch's marriage to the much younger Marianne is depicted as adhering to a different gender-role pattern. From the narrator's point of view this relationship was characterized by partnership. The man also did his part in grocery shopping and doing the dishes, they renovated a house together, traveled together, sharing beautiful experiences (*M*, 94, 186–97). Such positive memories, however, stand in contrast to a series of conflict-driven episodes in which the narrator uses his writing to reject the undermining of his masculinity by his wife. Here the reader is woven into the narrator's strategy of justification. It is indispensable to recognize the narrator's subtle defense strategy. Employing what Wayne Booth calls "unstable irony,"[85] he crafts an ambiguous discourse that allows him to pretend to admit having committed mistakes while at the same time denying any fault.

One passage will serve as an illustration of this strategy. In a central scene, Marianne accuses the narrator of not having contributed to her "self-realization" (*M*, 94). The husband responds by seemingly agreeing while simultaneously completely subverting this admission. He accuses himself of "MALE CHAUVINISM" (English in the original), an accusation that is already devalued as a mere catchword by its rendering in a foreign language and in capital letters. The narrator concludes that having done everything for his wife constituted the most convenient and the worst way of treating a woman: "Ich habe sie auf Händen getragen: die bequemste Art, umzugehen mit einer Frau, und die schlimmste Art. Das sehe ich ein." (I lavished every attention on her: the easiest way of treating a woman, and the worst. I can see that. [Skelton, 63]) However, in a subtle inversion, the narrator's alleged confession of guilt that ends this passage turns into an accusation of the woman. He claims that his behavior caused her to forget that she had to take her life into her own hands. This confession of guilt sounds hollow, and the narrator has the last word: a woman should initiate her own self-realization, rather than waiting for a man to deliver it to her. This argument counters her reproach but the argumentative technique is ambivalent.[86]

The narrator, however, declares himself implicitly responsible for one central problem in the marriage, his age, which Frisch painstakingly put on display throughout his *Tagebuch 2* and which constitutes a leitmotif in *Montauk*. Descriptions of his aging body and doubts about whether he has become an inadequate partner alternate with the narrator's attempt to define himself as a "dirty old man" (M, 14, 55). The narrator, who is sixty-three years old, remarks that he has almost reached the average life expectancy, and he writes that he does not want to live to a very old age, acknowledging the need not to tie a younger woman to his lack of a future (*M*, 203).

Even though the age difference between Frisch and Lynn is the same as between him and Marianne—in both cases they are one generation apart—with regard to the young American woman it is not as decisive (*M*, 37–39). "Life as a man" with a young woman still seems possible in Lynn's case because it is a relationship without any future that means nothing but a liberated present. The plotline with Lynn presents a guilt-free relationship between man and woman (*M*, 189). The narrator emphasizes that he does not blame himself and that he is not hurt when the "junge Fremde" (young stranger), as which he sometimes perceives her, tells him, "Max, you are wrong" (M, 161). The Lynn character has a job and leads an independent life. She is not the passive object of seduction, and emancipation is described as a given (*M*, 100). But what matters most is that Lynn does not participate in any constellations that correspond to the dependency, the crises, conflicts, and inhibitions, in sum, the suffering that according to Marcel Reich-Ranicki characterizes the narrator's relationships with the other women in *Montauk*:

> Idyllen sind es nicht. Vielmehr ist hier immer wieder die Rede von Spannungen und Verstrickungen, von Skrupeln und Hemmungen, von Krisen und Konflikten. Gezeigt wird, wie Abhängigkeit entsteht und wohin sie führen kann. Es sind also Leidensgeschichten.[87]
>
> [These are not idylls. What is rather made explicit here time and again are tensions and entanglements, qualms and inhibitions. It is shown how addiction develops and where it can lead. These are therefore stories about suffering.]

Reich-Ranicki writes that the episode about the narrator's friendship with W. that began during his school days serves as a parable for individual guilt and innocence.[88] W. stands for Werner Coninx (1911–80), Frisch's closest friend during his high-school and university years, who came from a privileged background and who provided Frisch with intellectual mentorship and paid for Frisch's university studies. It is noteworthy that in this case, a relationship is described as undergoing a transformation. At the end of the narrator's memories concerning his friendship with W.,

W., who in the past was the more giving friend, appears as the weaker of the two. He never had to make a living but increasingly struggled to give meaning to his life, while the narrator had gained financial and intellectual independence.

In the end, *Montauk*, despite Frisch's statement that he wrote it in a conciliatory state of mind and that in doing so succeeded in accepting "sechzig Jahre meines Lebens [. . .] einschließlich der Fehler: ohne mich oder die andern zu richten" (sixty years of my life, including the mistakes: without condemning myself or the others), falls far short of offering a convincing balance sheet of all his stories of love and friendship. Instead, it appears to consist of retroactive wishful thinking, or, to quote a phrase chosen by Volker Hage as the title of his book offering "portraits of German and American authors," including Frisch, it appears to be "alles erfunden."[89]

—*Translated by Olaf Berwald*

Notes

[1] Lioba Waleczek, *Max Frisch* (Munich: dtv, 2001), 117.

[2] *Der Briefwechsel Max Frisch / Uwe Johnson 1964–1983*, ed. Eberhard Fahlke (Frankfurt am Main: Suhrkamp, 1999), see for example 102–17.

[3] *Briefe einer Freundschaft, Ingeborg Bachmann—Hans Werner Henze*, ed. Hans Höller (Munich: Piper, 2004).

[4] *Herzzeit: Ingeborg Bachmann—Paul Celan; Der Briefwechsel, mit den Briefwechseln zwischen Paul Celan und Max Frisch sowie zwischen Ingeborg Bachmann und Gisèle Celan-Lestrange*, ed. Bertrand Badiou, Hans Höller, Andrea Stoll, and Barbara Wiedemann (Frankfurt am Main: Suhrkamp, 2008).

[5] Siegfried Unseld, "Ein Fest für Max Frisch," in *Der Spiegel*, September 26, 2009.

[6] Gottfried Honegger, *Elf Porträtskizzen: Vierzehn Texte zur Erinnerung* (Steinhausen: Hotz, 2007).

[7] Ursula Priess, *Sturz durch alle Spiegel* (Zurich: Ammann, 2009).

[8] At the time of the completion of this chapter, Frisch's "Berlin Journal," edited by Peter von Matt, a journal that Frisch dedicated to "Alice" (Locke-Carey), had not yet been published.

[9] Gerhard P. Knapp, "Noch einmal: Das Spiel mit der Identität. Zu Max Frischs *Montauk*," in *Max Frisch, Aspekte des Prosawerks*, ed. Gerhard P. Knapp (Bern, Frankfurt am Main: Lang, 1978), 285–307; here 291.

[10] Max Frisch, *Tagebuch 1946–1949* (Frankfurt am Main: Suhrkamp, 1985), referred to as *Tagebuch 1* and abbreviated as *Tb 1*. Max Frisch, *Tagebuch 1966–1971* (Frankfurt am Main: Suhrkamp, 1972), referred to as *Tagebuch 2* and abbreviated as *Tb 2*. The first edition of *Tagebuch 1* appeared in 1950. For discussions of Frisch's literary use of autobiography, see Gerhard vom Hofe, "Zauber

ohne Zukunft. Zur autobiographischen Korrektur in Max Frischs Erzählung *Montauk*," in *Euphorion* 70, no. 4 (1976): 376–96; Horst Steinmetz, *Max Frisch, Tagebuch, Drama, Roman* (Göttingen: Vandenhoeck & Ruprecht, 1973), 72; Gerhard Knapp, "Noch einmal: Das Spiel mit der Identität," 297; and Anton Krättli, "Leben im Zitat, Max Frischs *Montauk*," in *Über Max Frisch II*, ed. Walter Schmitz (Frankfurt am Main: Suhrkamp, 1976), 429.

[11] Horst Bienek, *Werkstattgespräche mit Schriftstellern* (Munich: dtv, 1965), 26. Quoted from Rolf Kieser, *Das literarische Tagebuch* (Frauenfeld: Huber, 1975), 44–45.

[12] Max Frisch, *Tagebuch 1946–1949* (Frankfurt am Main: Suhrkamp, 1958), 119. Quoted from Kieser, *Das literarische Tagebuch*, 43.

[13] Kieser, *Das literarische Tagebuch*, 42.

[14] Max Frisch, *Schwarzes Quadrat: Zwei Poetikvorlesungen*, ed. Daniel de Vin and Walter Obschlager (Frankfurt am Main: Suhrkamp, 2008), 25.

[15] Kieser, *Das literarische Tagebuch*, 35.

[16] Meike Heinrich-Korpys, *Tagebuch und Fiktionalität: Signalstrukturen des literarischen Tagebuchs am Beispiel der Tagebücher von Max Frisch* (St. Ingbert: Röhrig, 2003), 241.

[17] "Als Sie mir neulich in Paris die Fotos von Montauk gezeigt haben, habe ich [. . .] bemerkt, was auch bei andern Objekten genauso problematisch sein wird: Wozu muss man das sehen? Was im Wort eine andere und eigentliche Wirklichkeit gewonnen hat durch die Imagination des Lesers. Dabei handelt es sich erst um Objekte, noch nicht um Personen." (When recently in Paris you showed me the pictures of Montauk, I [. . .] realized something that will be equally problematic with other objects: Why should one have to see it? That which through the reader's imagination has gained a different and genuine reality in the word. And here we are not even talking about persons yet, but merely about objects; letter from Max Frisch to Richard Dindo, June 29, 1978, in *Jetzt: Max Frisch*, ed. Luis Bolliger, Walter Obschlager, Julian Schütt (Frankfurt am Main: Suhrkamp, 2001), 226. Unless otherwise noted, all translations of quotations are by Olaf Berwald. In this letter Frisch revokes his agreement to collaborate on the film project.

[18] Kieser, *Das literarische Tagebuch*, 67.

[19] Heinrich-Korpys, *Tagebuch und Fiktionalität*, 103. Compare also Rolf Kieser, *Das literarische Tagebuch*, 23–25.

[20] Max Frisch, *Montauk: Eine Erzählung* (Frankfurt am Main: Suhrkamp, 1975), 28. Translations taken from *Montauk*, translated by Geoffrey Skelton (New York/ London: Harcourt Brace Jovanovich, 1976), Throughout this chapter, references to this German edition are given parenthetically as *M*, and the translation as Skelton, followed by page numbers.

[21] Max Frisch, *Tagebuch 2*, 311.

[22] Ruth Vogel, "Montauk, l'ecriture et la vie, ou Marianne à Montauk," in *Relire Max Frisch*, ed. Régine Battiston-Zuliani and Philippe Forget (Paris: Editions du Temps, 2001), 143–55.

[23] Claudia Müller, *"Ich habe viele Namen": Polyphonie und Dialogizität im autobiographischen Spätwerk Max Frischs und Friedrich Dürrenmatts* (Munich: Fink, 2009), 59–60, 165–74.

[24] Barbara Saunders, "Confronting 'Fictions,' Past and Present: Max Frisch's *Montauk* as Autobiography," in *Forum for Modern Language Studies* 3, no. 18 (July 1982): 221.

[25] Rudolf Hartung, "'Schreibend unter Kunstzwang.' Zu der autobiographischen Erzählung *Montauk* von Max Frisch," in *Über Max Frisch II*, ed. Walter Schmitz (Frankfurt am Main: Suhrkamp 1976), 435–42; here 440. Quoted from Knapp, "Noch einmal: Das Spiel mit der Identität," 299.

[26] Philippe Lejeune, *Le pacte autobiographique* (Paris: Seuil, 1996), 13–45.

[27] Gerard Genette, *Der Erzähler*, German translation by Andreas Knop (Munich: Fink, 1994), 174–81. Originally published in *Figures III* (Paris: Le Seuil, 1972).

[28] Klaus Müller-Salget, "Max Frischs *Montauk*—eine Erzählung?" in *Zeitschrift für deutsche Philologie* 97 (Sonderheft 1978): 108–20; here, 118.

[29] Gerhard Knapp, "Noch einmal: Das Spiel mit der Identität. Zu Max Frischs *Montauk*," 290. Compare Saunders's criticism of Knapp in her "Confronting 'Fictions,'" 216.

[30] Lejeune, *Pacte autobiographique*, 16. Lejeune's examples of autobiographies that alternate between first- and third-person narration include André Gorz, *Traître* (Paris: Gallimard, 1958), Claude Roy, *Nous* (Paris: Gallimard 1980), and Roland Barthes, *Roland Barthes* (Paris: Seuil, 1975).

[31] Philippe Lejeune, "L'autobiographie à la troisième personne," in Philippe Lejeune, *Je est un autre* (Paris: Seuil, 1980), 34. I would like to thank Philippe Lejeune for alerting me to this article. I am also indebted to him and to Catherine Viollet for their inspiring questions following my various presentations on *Montauk* in the Paris research group under their direction, "Genèse et autobiographie."

[32] Heinz Ludwig Arnold, *Gespräche mit Schriftstellern* (Munich: Beck 1975), 43. The conversation with Max Frisch took place from November 24 to 27, 1974, during the time Frisch was writing *Montauk*.

[33] "Dans l'autobiographie, la relation avec l'auteur est *embrayée* (il vous demande de le croire [. . .]), tandis que dans le roman elle est *débrayée* (vous réagissez librement au texte, à l'histoire, vous n'êtes plus une personne que l'auteur sollicite)." (In an autobiography the relation with the author is engaged (he asks you to believe him [. . .]), while in a novel it is disengaged (you react freely to the text [. . .]); quoted from Lejeune's website: http://www.autopacte.org/pacte_autobiographique.html, last consulted on November 2, 2009).

[34] "Si vous, lecteur, vous jugez que l'autobiographe cache ou altère une partie de la vérité, vous pourrez penser qu'il *ment*. En revanche il est impossible de dire qu'un romancier ment: cela n'a aucun sens, puisqu'il ne s'est pas engagé à vous dire la vérité." (If you, the reader, judge that the autobiographer is hiding or altering a part of the truth, you could think that he is lying. On the other hand it is impossible to say that a novelist is lying: This does not make any sense, since he is not in the business of telling you the truth. [Quoted from Philippe

Lejeune's website. Text written in 2006. http://www.autopacte.org/pacte_autobiographique.html, last consulted on November 2, 2009.])

35 For an insightful and innovative analysis of the problem of autobiography in *Montauk*, see Madeleine Salzmann, *Kommunikationsstruktur der Autobiographie: mit kommunikations-orientierten Analysen der Autobiographien von Max Frisch, Helga M. Novak und Elias Canetti* (Bern, Frankfurt am Main: Lang, 1988), 33.

36 Heinz Gockel, "Montauk, Eine Erzählung," in *Duitse Kroniek* 29 (1977): 53.

37 Secondary literature has at times reduced Montaigne's project to autobiography; see Gerhard Knapp, "Noch einmal: Das Spiel mit der Identität," 289; and Hans Mayer, "Die Geheimnisse jedweden Mannes," in *Über Max Frisch*, ed. Walter Schmitz (Frankfurt am Main: Suhrkamp, 1976), 446–47. Salzmann's definition of this "Fremdtext" by Montaigne as an autobiographical pact has to be taken with a grain of salt, see Salzmann, *Kommunikationsstruktur*, 44.

38 Michael Butler, *The Novels of Max Frisch* (London: Wolf, 1976), 153.

39 Hugo Friedrich, *Montaigne* (Paris: Gallimard, 1968), 15, 232.

40 Vom Hofe, "Zauber ohne Zukunft," 382–84.

41 Mayer, "Die Geheimnisse jedweden Mannes," 445.

42 Saunders, "Confronting 'Fictions,'" 215.

43 Claudia Mauelshagen mentions the "Wirklichkeitsaussage des Textes." But her use of the term "Rezeptionsunsicherheit" is incapable of distinguishing between author and narrator. See Claudia Mauelshagen, "Montauk zwischen Faktualität und Fiktionalität," *Literatur und Linguistik: Beihefte*, ed. Joachim Göschel (Stuttgart: Steiner, 2001), 127–38; here 135.

44 Dedicated to Uwe and Elisabeth Johnson, this typescript is dated March 1975. Max Frisch Archive.

45 Butler, *Novels of Max Frisch*, 153.

46 Frisch, *Tagebuch 2*, 311.

47 Waleczek, *Max Frisch*, 115.

48 Uwe Johnson to Marianne Frisch-Oellers, January 18, 1975, in *Max Frisch/Uwe Johnson: Der Briefwechsel, 1964–1983*, ed. Eberhard Fahlke (1999; Frankfurt am Main: Suhrkamp, 2001), 104–5.

49 Marianne Frisch-Oeller's letter to Uwe Johnson, January 28, 1974, in *Frisch/Johnson*, 114.

50 Johnson's attempted justification, in his letter to Marianne Frisch-Oellers from January 18, 1975: "Wer mit einem Schriftsteller umgeht, tut dies ohnehin in der Vorraussicht, sich einst als Erfahrung in einer Geschichte versteckt zu finden. [. . .] Wenn einer sich freundliche Bemerkungen in einem der veröffentlichten Tagebücher gefallen lässt, schlicht als Wahrheit [. . .] wird [er] Erwähnungen voraussehen dürfen, die er auffassen möchte als unfreundlich." (Everyone who interacts with a writer does so anyway in full awareness that one day one will find oneself disguised as an experience in a story. [. . .] If one tolerates friendly comments in one of the published sketchbooks, reading them as the plain truth [. . .] [one] can be expected to anticipate references that one might consider unfriendly). *Frisch/Johnson*, 106–7. In her written response from January 28,

1975, Marianne Frisch points out the incoherence of Johnson's argument. See *Frisch/Johnson*, 113.

[51] Müller-Salget, "Max Frischs *Montauk*—eine Erzählung?," 114.

[52] See *Frisch/Johnson*, 11: "Lieber Uwe, Ihr Brief an Marianne: ein Akt letzter Hilfe. Ich danke Ihnen dafür. Wie sie sich auch dazu verhalten mag: ich bin mir jetzt im klaren, dass ich das Skript weiter ausarbeite, verstärke, erweitere—mit dem Entschluss zur Publikation." (Dear Uwe, Your letter to Marianne: an act of final aid, for which I thank you. However she will react: I have decided now to elaborate on the manuscript, to strengthen and expand it—for publication). Letter from Frisch to Johnson, January 20, 1975.

[53] Vom Hofe, "Zauber ohne Zukunft," 379.

[54] Arnold, *Gespräche mit Schriftstellern*, 44.

[55] For example *Stiller* (18), *Mein Name sei Gantenbein* (156), *Homo Faber* (103).

[56] Walter Schmitz, *Max Frisch: Das Spätwerk, 1962–1982* (Tübingen: Francke 1985), 109–10.

[57] Hans Bänziger, "Leben im Zitat. Zu *Montauk*: Ein Formulierungsproblem und dessen Vorgeschichte," in *Max Frisch: Aspekte des Prosawerks*, ed. Gerhard Knapp (Bern, New York: Lang, 1978), 264–87; here 284.

[58] Ursula Haupt, *Weiblichkeit in Romanen Max Frischs* (Bern, New York: Lang, 1996), 102.

[59] Salzmann, *Kommunikationsstruktur*, 50. See also the innovative study by Lübbert R. Haneborger, *Max Frisch—Das Prosa-Spätwerk, Montauk, Holozän, Blaubart* (Norderstedt: Books on Demand, 2008), 41.

[60] Schmitz, *Max Frisch: Das Spätwerk*, 106.

[61] About the principle of repetition in Frisch's work until 1975, see especially Daniel de Vin, *Max Frischs Tagebücher: Studie über Blätter aus dem Brotsack (1940), Tagebuch 1946–1949 (1950), und Tagebuch 1966–1971 (1972) im Rahmen des bisherigen Gesamtwerks (1932–1975)* (Cologne/Vienna: Böhlau, 1977), 146–66.

[62] Gerhard Knapp, "Noch einmal: Das Spiel mit der Identität," 301.

[63] Knapp, "Noch einmal: Das Spiel mit der Identität," 114.

[64] Saunders, "Confronting 'Fictions,'" 212–24.

[65] The following discussion of the textual genesis is based on my detailed article, "Dies ist ein aufrichtiges Buch, Leser. Was verschweigt es und warum? Max Frisch: *Montauk*, Einblick in die Typoskripte," *editio* 16 (2002): 117–34.

[66] For my archival research in the Max Frisch Archive in Zurich, I received several research stipends from the Pro Helvetia Foundation. I am grateful to the former director of the archive, Walter Obschlager, and to its new director, Margit Unser, for their support.

[67] The cover page of the first typescript version that has been preserved has the title: "1 Version," followed by the handwritten addition and dedication: "Entwurf, geschrieben in Gockhausen (CH) im Sommer 1974 bei Gottfried Honegger. Ich danke DIR, Gottfried Max."

[68] *Frisch/Johnson*, 93.

[69] *Frisch/Johnson*, 101–2.

[70] *Frisch/Johnson*, 242–404.

[71] Uwe Johnson reminded Frisch that he and his wife dedicated "viel Überlegung und tägliches Leben" (much thought and daily lived experience) to proof-reading *Montauk*, "insbesondere Elisabeth, der Sie mit ihrem eigenen Motto der Aufrichtigkeit quälend zusetzten" (Elisabeth in particular, who took your maxim of honesty, which is also her own maxim, painfully to heart). Letter from Uwe Johnson to Max Frisch, August 13, 1975, *Frisch/Johnson*, 136).

[72] Letter from Max Frisch to Uwe Johnson, July 20, 1975, *Frisch/Johnson*, 131.

[73] As mentioned above, Frisch also dedicated one typescript to Uwe and Elisabeth Johnson: "Für Uwe und Elisabeth herzlich Max Frisch 23.III.1975."

[74] Inserted photocopies of additional passages and alterations in the pagination indicate that the typescript marked "September 74," the earliest complete version in the archive's possession, already constitutes a reworked draft.

[75] According to Lejeune, an autobiographical work is not a transcription of given facts into a coherent text, but a creative process in which the self unfolds. See Philippe Lejeune, *Brouillons de soi* (Paris: Le Seuil, 1998), 146: "un travail que l'on n'envisagera plus uniquement comme la traduction, plus ou moins fidèle, d'une vérité préexistante, mais comme la création du moi dans le langage [. . .]" (a work that one does not consider exclusively a more or less accurate translation of a preexisting truth anymore, but rather a creation of the self within language [. . .]).

[76] Frisch added the episode about W. titled "Memoiren (Montauk) Berlin März 1973" to the *Montauk* versions, see Max Frisch, "Autobiographisches," in *Neue Rundschau* 86, no. 2 (1975): 269–79. There are minor differences between this and the final version of *Montauk*.

[77] *Frisch/Johnson* 367–72.

[78] See my essay on the final version: Ruth Vogel, "Montauk, l'ecriture et la vie, ou Marianne à Montauk," in *Relire Max Frisch*, eds. Régine Battiston-Zuliani and Philippe Forget (Paris: Editions du Temps, 2001), 143–55.

[79] Typescript, September 1974, Max Frisch Archive.

[80] Claudia Müller, *"Ich habe viele Namen,"* 59–60, 165–74.

[81] Walter Schmitz, *Max Frisch: Das Spätwerk*, 103. See also Lioba Waleczek, *Max Frisch*, 99.

[82] For a discussion of the Jewish fiancée Hanna and the representation of the Shoah in *Homo Faber*, see Walter Schmitz, "'Was hat unsereiner denn eigentlich getan?' Die Erinnerung an die Shoah im Werk Max Frischs," in *Die ersten Stimmen: Deutschsprachige Texte zur Shoah 1945–1963*, ed. Ruth Vogel-Klein (Würzburg: Königshausen & Neumann, 2010), 243–69.

[83] Compare the ironically charged passage on gender equality written in 1971 and published in *Tagebuch 2*, 371.

[84] In Richard Dindo's 1981 film of *Montauk*, *Max Frisch, Journal I–III*, Frisch emphasizes the importance of a radical change in gender relations: "Die Beziehung

zwischen den Geschlechtern, das wissen Sie, hat mich immer schon beschäftigt. Wenn sie gelingen sollte, ich meine die Emanzipation der Frau, und das wäre ja auch eine Emanzipation des Mannes, ich kann mir vorstellen, das würde die Gesellschaft mehr verändern als etwa die Verstaatlichung der Schwerindustrie, der Banken, was ich mir beiläufig auch wünsche. Weil das, meine ich, am Fundament verändert." (As you know, gender relations have always been an important problem for me. If it succeeds, I mean the emancipation of women, which would of course also be an emancipation of men, I can imagine that it would transform society more than, for instance, the nationalization of heavy industry and the banks, which I incidentally also desire. Because it [the emancipation of women] transforms the foundations.) See Fritz J. Raddatz, *Zeitgespräche* (Frankfurt am Main: Suhrkamp, 1982), 45–46.

[85] See Wayne Booth, *A Rhetoric of Irony* (Chicago: University of Chicago Press, 1974).

[86] It has to be taken into account that in Richard Dindo's film, Marianne Frisch insists that she never talked about her self-realization in the way portrayed in the novel. According to her, this passage is purely fictional.

[87] Marcel Reich-Ranicki, *Max Frisch* (Zurich: Ammann, 1991), 86.

[88] Reich-Ranicki, *Max Frisch*, 87.

[89] Volker Hage, *Alles erfunden: Porträts deutscher und amerikanischer Autoren* (Reinbek: Rowohlt, 1988), 83.

12: Man, Culture, and Nature in Max Frisch's *Der Mensch erscheint im Holozän*

Walter Obschlager

In Max Frisch's early work, nature is often presented in a sentimental and Romantic manner. In his *Tagebuch 1946–1949*, for example, Frisch describes the golden autumn landscapes, and a morning break at a lake with "versponnener Sonne" (a hazy sun) and "verblauenden Ufern" (the banks turning bluish).[1] From his early works on, Frisch used images of water to symbolize a longing for vastness and distance, for movement, transformation, and therefore aliveness. Already young Jürg Reinhart, the protagonist in the eponymous novel published in 1934, is fascinated with the ocean. At the beginning of the novel, Frisch writes:

> Und wenn man dann aufsprang und diese hellgrünen Holzlättchen verstellte, sah man zwischendurch das Meer; es lag in silbriger und makelloser Zartheit, und makellos war auch die Riesenmuschelbläue, die es überwölbte. Jauchzen hätte man wollen.[2]

> [And when one jumped out of bed and moved these light-green wooden battens, one could see the ocean in between; it lay in silvery and pristine delicateness, and the gigantic sea-shell blue that arched over it was also pristine. One felt like cheering.]

But soon Reinhart experiences the sea as a dangerous force of nature. As Reinhart is tacking along the coast of Dalmatia with his improvised sailboat, the wind intensifies dramatically and drives him and his boat out into the open ocean:

> Es ging immer rasender in dieser neuen Richtung. [. . .] er [. . .] blickte gradaus, was wohl kommen würde. Und sein Herz hämmerte. Denn dieser Wind hatte ihm den Willen aus der Hand gerissen, und er klammerte sich mit adergeschwollenen Fäusten ans Steuerruder. (*JR* 245–46)

> [It went furiously faster and faster in this new direction. [. . .] he [. . .] looked straight ahead to see what might come. And his heart

> was hammering. For this wind had torn his willpower out of his hand, and he clung to the rudder with hands with swollen veins.]

In this early passage a conflict that pits force against force is unfolding. Reinhart must suddenly fight for his life and liberate himself from the forces of nature. The sea has shown its other side, its unpredictability and violence.

Mountains, too, are conspicuously often at the center of Frisch's journalistic writings from the 1930s. These texts describe hiking and climbing tours, skiing outings, and experiences in the high mountains such as a crossing of the Alps by foot. These encounters with nature are consistently presented as peaceful. At the outset of all of these texts, the author as wanderer appears to consider them exclusively pleasant aesthetic experiences, while the tone changes at the end of Frisch's newspaper article, "Skizzen aus dem Eifischtal" (Sketches from the Eifisch Valley), published in *Neue Zürcher Zeitung* on July 8, 1932, when he describes how a waterfall can evoke the uncanny:

> Unerwartet steht man davor: gelber Absturz, Lehm, Sand [. . .] und fast lotrecht fällt es vor uns siebzehnhundert Meter hinab. [. . .] Und herauf aus diesem Riesentrichter weht Rauschen von Wasserstürzen. Man sieht sie nicht, ganz tief. Man schaut und horcht und steht am Rand, und es ist, als hätte man eine Zange um die Brust.[3]

> [All of a sudden you stand in front of it: a yellow cascade, clay, sand, and before our eyes it falls almost vertically 1700 meters. [. . .] And up out of this gigantic funnel the roar of crashing water blows. One does not see it, very deep. One looks and listens and stands on the edge, and it is as if one had pliers around the chest.]

Frisch's newspaper features about mountaineering from this time period offer numerous similar examples. It is therefore not surprising that the short novel *Antwort aus der Stille* (An Answer from the Silence, 1937) culminates in an inexorable struggle with nature. Suddenly nature in the form of an unscaled north face becomes a powerful enemy that has to be defeated. The protagonist, who has recently been engaged to be married, is about to start a career as a teacher and also serves in the Swiss standing army as an officer. Faced with personal and professional decisions, he realizes that he is about to relinquish the ideas and ideals of his youth regarding a truly lived life. At this moment he decides to pursue those ideals one last time by conducting an extreme trial of courage, a fight to the death with the mountain: "Einmal muss man es wagen, die Tat oder den Tod, denn ein Leben, wie es sich anlässt, kann und will er nicht ertragen, das hat er sich geschworen, dieses Leben eines Durchschnittsmenschen—nie und nimmer!" (There comes a point when you have to take the risk: the deed or death, for he has sworn to himself that he cannot and will not bear the kind of life that is before him, the life of an average man—never!)[4]

While the protagonist stays alive, he does not come out of the fight unharmed. The man who returns after three days and nights is not the same anymore. Frostbite on all his limbs are the external results. His inner self has experienced an almost religious change to humility and modesty. The forces of nature he has experienced on the mountain have shown him his mortality: "Die Naturgewalten haben ihn zurechtgestutzt." Now he realizes "[d]ass es ein unsagbar ernstes Glück ist, leben zu dürfen, und dass wohl nirgends die Leere sein kann, wo dies Gefühl auch nur einmal errungen worden ist, dies Gefühl der Gnade und des Dankes" ([t]hat being granted the opportunity to live is an unutterably serious piece of good fortune and that there can surely be no emptiness when this feeling has really been won, if only once, this feeling of grace and gratefulness).[5]

Twenty years later, in his novel *Homo Faber* (1957) Frisch illustrates that man and culture are engaged in an antagonistic relationship and irreconcilable conflict with nature. The engineer Walter Faber considers the subjugation of nature the only means toward the survival of mankind. One of his arguments is the threat of overpopulation. He is in favor of abortion. According to Faber, uncontrolled reproduction would not result in the preservation of mankind but its obliteration. He supports abortion as an inevitable cultural practice, "nur der Dschungel gebärt und verwest, wie die Natur will. Der Mensch plant" (only the jungle gives birth and moulders away as nature decrees wants. Man plans). Faber defines man as being in control of nature, as "Beherrscher der Natur."[6]

Since his beginnings, man has continuously been endangered by nature. In the process of fighting nature he developed modes of behavior and institutions that increased his chances of controlling nature. What we call culture is the result of this process. It is always linked to the appropriation of nature. We call the theoretical and practical appropriation of nature science and technology. According to Sigmund Freud, the main task of culture and its very reason for existence is to protect us against nature's destructiveness:

> Da sind Elemente, die jedem menschlichen Zwang zu spotten scheinen, die Erde, die bebt, zerreisst, alles Menschliche und Menschenwerk begräbt, das Wasser, das im Aufruhr alles überflutet und ersäuft, der Sturm, der es wegbläst, da sind die Krankheiten, die wir erst seit kurzem als die Angriffe anderer Lebewesen erkennen, endlich das schmerzliche Rätsel des Todes, gegen den bisher kein Kräutlein gefunden wurde.[7]

> [There are the elements, which appear to mock any kind of human constraint: earth, which heaves and splits open, burying all things human and all the works of humankind: water, which when in

> tumult swamps and drowns everything; storms, which blow everything away; there are the diseases, which we have only recently come to recognize as attacks by other living creatures, and finally there is the painful riddle of death, against which no remedy has yet been found [. . .]]

A strikingly high number of Frisch texts are organized around the basic constellation of nature versus culture. As early as 1932, Frisch outlined this problem with stunning radicalism in an article in the *Neue Zürcher Zeitung*. The twenty-one-year-old author gives an account of his experience in a student work camp in a mountain community in the Swiss canton of Valais (in German: Wallis). Young people are there to help with the construction of a forest road. The goal is to make a steep and heavily overgrown mountainside accessible to the locals. In the article, published on September 29, 1932, Frisch highlights the violent aspect of this undertaking and describes the new road as a wound that is incised into the forest: "Mühsam schneiden wir jetzt einen Pfad hindurch und weiten ihn zum Weg und zwingen endlich eine zweieinhalb Meter breite Strasse hinein in diesen harten Berg. Das sieht aus wie eine Wunde." (Working strenuously we are cutting a path through it now and expand it into a lane and finally force a two-and-one-half-meter-wide road into this hard mountain. This looks like a wound.)[8]

The reflections that follow in this early Frisch text surprisingly point at correlations between the relationship between inhabitants of cities and of rural mountain areas on the one hand, and the contrast between nature and culture on the other. During physical labor Frisch experiences a growing inner void. Because he is forced to put all his energy into his arms and legs, he withdraws it from his soul. Any intellectual effort becomes pointless. Hard physical labor and thinking, he reasons, are mutually exclusive:

> Sieben Stunden bringt man es auf keinen weitzügigeren Gedanken. Jede aufgenommene Idee verliert man, und die Gefühle verflachen oder sie bleiben an einem süssen Blödsinn kleben wie Bienen am Honig. Leerlauf der Seele. (*GW* 1:23–24)

> [For seven hours you are incapable of forming any thoughts that are more far-reaching. You lose any idea that you had adopted, and emotions flatten out or are glued to a sweet nonsense like bees to honey. Idling cycle of the soul.]

It is as if direct physical contact with nature puts man at risk of being taken over by and transformed into it. That which elevates him above nature, mind and consciousness, increasingly seems to diminish. The young Frisch is terrified when he observes this process unfolding in himself, and he believes to see its results embodied in the people who live in the mountains.

A girl stares at him "as with the eyes of a cow," and he is in panic about his inability to distinguish between human and animals: "Wie jetzt diese Melker und dieses Rindvieh in mir den Städter anglotzen. Ich sehne mich zurück nach der Stadt, nach dem bewussten Leben, nach dem Ich." (How these milkers and cattle stare at the city dweller in me. I am longing to return to the city, to conscious life, to the "I": *GW* 1:25).

The sad protagonist in Frisch's narrative *Wilhelm Tell für die Schule* (1971) undergoes a similar experience. On a business trip through medieval Switzerland, a *Reichsvogt* in the service of the Habsburg empire, Ritter Konrad oder Grisler, on whom Friedrich Schiller based the Gessler character in his play *Wilhelm Tell* (1804), passes an alpine pasture where not only cows stare at him but a cowherd does too (*GW* 6:416). The knight feels suffocated by the high mountains that encircle him and feels threatened by the constant wind and the violent storm on a lake, from which he barely escapes. Nature and the inhabitants of these narrow valleys appear one and the same to him: he perceives both as similarly dull and threatening. Even the arrow that will eventually kill him can be seen as a force of nature, fired off from the bushes by a robust, red-bearded nature-boy who remains invisible to his victim.

According to Freud, humans are exposed to three kinds of danger: to nature's destructive forces, to their own bodies, which are destined "zu Verfall und Auflösung" (for decay and dissolution), and to their relationships.[9] These fundamental experiences form the main theme in Frisch's narrative *Der Mensch erscheint im Holozän* (Man in the Holocene, 1979).[10] Oppressive physical forces of nature that threaten the protagonist are once again emphasized. A storm has raged for days in a remote valley. Roads are submerged, the power supply is cut off, and whole mountain slopes are at risk of forming a landslide. An old man named Geiser has barricaded himself in his house and begins to organize his resistance against the lightning, hail, and inexorable rainfall. At first glance a strange endeavor given the extreme circumstances, his attempt to build a pagoda out of crispbread on his kitchen table is not primarily a way of passing time. It rather serves a twofold purpose. On the one hand, Geiser tries to block out any distress he experiences, "nichts zu denken und keinen Donner zu hören, keinen Regen, kein Plätschern aus der Traufe, kein Gurgeln ums Haus" (*MH*, 207; to think of nothing, to hear no thunder, no rain, no splashing from the gutter, no gurgling around the house: *MHAS*, 3). Geiser's game of building a pagoda out of crispbread is also a symbolic act with which he counters nature's invasion with a deed that evokes civilization and technology. A house represents shelter from the outside world. To build a house has always been a gesture of resistance against the power of nature. That Frisch has his protagonist build a pagoda, a sacral structure, might have to do with its specific challenge with regard to statics or simply with the shape of crispbread rather than with the historical fact that since the Ming dynasty, feng shui pagodas served the purpose of warding off evil spirits. This protagonist is not interested in paranormal apparitions and myths.

"Herr Geiser glaubt nicht an Sintflut" (Geiser does not believe in the flood), the narrator states after having inserted a quotation from the Book of Genesis into the text (*MH*, 219; *MHAS*, 16). This implies that Herr Geiser does not believe in a punishing God. The idea of forces of nature in the form of angry gods or as a fate assigned by an all-powerful God has become obsolete since the early modern period. Since the enlightenment period, nature is seen in an increasingly desacralized and demythicized way such that it simply belongs to a branch of scientific knowledge. Herr Geiser asks himself whether there will still be a God when there is no longer a human alive who cannot conceive of creation without a creator (*MH*, 212). He searches for safety and reassurance in the encyclopedia rather than in the Bible.

The repeated collapse of Geiser's crispbread pagoda triggered by his coughing or the trembling of his hand corresponds to increasing technological failures outside the house. Retaining walls have collapsed, the road to the valley is submerged, the power supply is cut off, the fog makes the use of rescue helicopters impossible, and even the field glasses with which one could identify fissures in the terrain become useless because the fog condenses on them. While the villagers do not believe that the whole village would be buried if a landslide occurred, Herr Geiser knows from the *Geschichte des Kantons Tessin*, a book that he finds in his library, that these kinds of catastrophes have occurred: "Man muss auf alles gefasst sein" (*MH*, 232: One must be prepared for everything: *MHAS*, 33). He tries to control his fear of imminent chaos and the unpredictability of the forces of nature by condensing phenomena into concepts. He develops categories for different kinds of thunder and names the manifold forms of rain. Through his ability to intervene against nature in the world that he inhabits, man is capable of distancing himself from his environment. As an encyclopedia entry for the term "Mensch" that Geiser cuts out puts it: "Dieses Abstandnehmen zu der Welt ist die Voraussetzung dafür, sich ihrer zu bemächtigen" (*MH*, 249; This objective attitude toward the world is what gives M. his ability to conquer it: *MHAS*, 53). What is at stake is a way to overcome fear by using science, a method that has played a decisive role in mankind's process of civilization.[11] Herr Geiser works hard to maintain control and to maintain oversight of what is happening to him. Part of this effort consists in compiling an inventory of his grocery provisions, checking his emergency medication, and observing the terrain as the storm goes on. He even contemplates and prepares for a possible escape, "Herr Geiser hat an alles gedacht" (*MH*, 217; Geiser has thought of everything: *MHAS*, 15). Only man has the ability to plan, according to Walter Faber's dictum about the need to assert oneself against nature.

Ever since Francis Bacon wrote of his dream of the subjugation of nature by science and technology, his famous pronouncement "Knowledge is power" has fascinated and inspired mankind.[12] Herr Geiser considers knowledge reassuring even if it is of no use at the moment. His attempt to surround himself with a protective shield of knowledge by copying and cutting out encyclopedia entries clearly contains an irrational element. The notes he pins to the wall are reminiscent of magical circles used in rituals by witches and magicians in order to demarcate a space that grants anyone who stands inside the circle protection. Nature's intrusion into Geiser's house, however, appears to be unstoppable. It is not the water in his basement that makes him fearful. He considers this a typical side effect of increased rainfall. Repeatedly he encounters salamanders in his bathroom and living room. He does not want to touch them but is looking for more precise information about them and observes one of them closely with a magnifying glass:

> Sein übergrosser Kopf, die schwarzen Augen ohne Blick. Plötzlich bewegt er sich. Sein ungelenker Gang in einer Art von Liegestütz, der Schwanz bleibt dabei unbeweglich. Er strampelt sich stur in eine Richtung, wo er nie weiterkommt. Plötzlich hält er wieder inne, Kopf in die Höhe gereckt. Dabei ist zu sehen, wie sein Puls schlägt. Ein entsetzlicher Stumpfsinn in allen Gliedern. (*MH*, 256)
>
> [Its overlarge head, the black, unfocused eyes. Suddenly it moves. Its clumsy walk, rather in the style of someone doing push-ups, tail held rigid. It crawls doggedly in a direction in which it will never make any progress. Suddenly it lies still again, its head raised. One can see its pulse beating. An awful dullness in all limbs. (*MHAS*, 61)]

This description presents the nucleus of the narrative. It becomes evident that, behind the onslaught of physical forces of nature, something more uncanny and much more threatening appears to Geiser. It is a form of life that lacks what distinguishes a human being: mind, spirit, consciousness, a self. The impression of the animal's unfocused eyes without a gaze, its clumsy walk, the stubbornness of its movements culminates in a vacant terror that the observer summarizes in his last sentence: "Ein entsetzlicher Stumpfsinn in allen Gliedern." Through the magnifying glass the small animal appears increasingly larger until it becomes a monster. Geiser's imagination soon transforms it into a dinosaur, a term that, as Geiser copies from the encyclopedia, in the original Greek means "terrifying lizard." The numerous zoological images from encyclopedias that are pinned to the wall make Geiser's growing fear of an overpowering nature manifest. In this context, one of Geiser's handwritten encyclopedia excerpts that is given not once but twice in the text plays a central role: "Verwandlung von Menschen in Tiere, Bäume, Steine etc. Siehe:

Metamorphose/Mythos" (*MH*, 225, 251; Changing of human beings into animals, trees, stone, etc. See: Metamorphosis/Myth: *MHAS*, 24, 56). This note exists in two copies, arguably also an indication that the diligent note-taker has lost oversight over the snippets of knowledge that he is collecting on his walls. The note shows striking differences from the other ones. Apart from the three passages from the Bible, Geiser exclusively uses scientific texts, from mathematics, meteorology, geography, physics, and medicine to biology and zoology. This quotation is inserted for the first time when Geiser becomes aware of his forgetfulness and admits to himself: "Man verblödet—!" (*MH*, 224; One is becoming stupid!: *MHAS*, 24). It recurs for the second time immediately before Herr Geiser finds himself standing with a candle in his hand, not remembering why he is wearing his hat (*MH*, 252). Geiser repeatedly quotes the sentence on human transformation, which displays his diffuse and latent fear of losing the quality that distinguishes him from mere nature, the world of animals, plants, and minerals.

With striking frequency, Frisch's works evoke images of amphibians and reptiles in the context of age and human aging. There is a scene in *Homo Faber* in which Walter Faber looks at Hanna and notices that she is aging rather well, except for the skin beneath her chin, which reminds him of lizard skin.[13] This comparison recurs in a passage from *Tagebuch 1966–1971* in which Frisch characterizes an old man with inexorable precision by focusing on his physical appearance, comparing him to an amphibian:

> Er schlurft, die Fersen heben sich kaum noch vom Boden; er macht nur noch Schrittchen, als gehe er überall auf Glatteis [. . .] seine Zigarre ist immer nass, die Asche fällt auf seinen Bauch oder auf die Schenkel [. . .] Wenn mehrere zusammensitzen, so denkt man an Lurche; sie haben nichts mit uns zu tun. (*GW* 6:107–8)

> [He scuffs his feet, his heels barely leave the ground anymore. He only makes small steps as if he walked on ice everywhere [. . .] his cigar is always wet, the ashes fall on his belly or his thighs. [. . .] When several of them sit together, they make you think of amphibians. They have nothing to do with us.]

When Herr Geiser later finds himself stretched out on the ground, he does not remember what happened. His glasses and hat lie next to him, he appears as an animal that helplessly lies on its back. While he manages to sit up, it takes him a long time "aufzustehen wie ein Mensch" (*MH*, 213; to rise to his feet like a human being: *MHAS* 92). In front of the mirror he realizes that his face does not show any injury. His left eyelid, however, is paralyzed, and now he looks like an amphibian. He makes an effort to keep his composure and to differentiate himself from the animal by remembering the year of his birth, his mother's maiden name, the name of the street and the street number where he was born, "was ein Lurch alles nicht weiss" (*MH*, 287; all of which an amphibian doesn't know).[14]

As tools and appliances in the house repeatedly malfunction, Herr Geiser undergoes a process of increasing uncertainty. More and more frequently he forgets what he has just done or what he wanted to do. Although he recognizes the handwritten notes on the walls, he no longer remembers why he started to cut out illustrations of reptiles and amphibians and hang them on the wall (*MH*, 285). According to the very beginning of the narrative, the storm was not terrifying but "schlimm wäre der Verlust des Gedächtnisses" (*MH*, 211; What would be bad would be losing one's memory: *MHAS*, 6). It remains open whether the narrator makes this statement, or whether this passage renders Geiser's own fearful thought. But it can be stated with certainty that, as he grew older, Max Frisch contemplated the fear of memory loss with increasing intensity. This was probably triggered by an experience he had when he was forty-eight years old, which he fictionalized in his narrative *Montauk* (1975). He is sick and hospitalized with hepatitis. At first he rather enjoys the situation, but suddenly he is haunted by fear of losing his memory, for the first time, as he notes. During this time he was living with Ingeborg Bachmann, the narrator in *Montauk* remembers, pointing out that while waiting for Bachmann to visit him, he underwent a radical language crisis and was afraid of losing his memory:

> In der Nacht ein Satz, den ich ihr sagen muss: Der Satz. [. . .] Um ihn nicht zu verlieren, wiederhole ich den nächtlichen Satz von Viertelstunde zu Viertelstunde; ohne jedesmal denken zu können, was er heisst. Eine Gruppe von Wörtern. [. . .] Ich muss aber den Satz notieren, bevor ich in Schlaf falle. [. . .] das Subjekt ist nicht zu entziffern, ich rate vergeblich, und es fehlt jedes Verbum. Ich habe Angst.[15]
>
> [During the night a sentence that I must say to her: The sentence. [. . .] So as not to forget, I repeated to myself, every quarter of an hour, the sentence that had come to me in the night. I did not always know what it meant: It was just a group of words. [. . .] However, I had to jot the sentence down before I went off to sleep. [. . .] the subject so undecipherable I could not even guess at it, and no sign of a verb. I felt frightened.]

Years later, in a sketch included in *Tagebuch 1966–1971*, Frisch illustrates the object of his fear by telling the story of a professor of architecture. This text reads like a prelude to *Der Mensch erscheint im Holozän*: the man Frisch describes in this passage teaches statics at the university. One morning he appears at the police station with the intention to turn himself in without any plausible reason. Finally he becomes uncertain whether it has to be done that day, and he walks home. When, during his second attempt to turn himself in, he is asked what he wants, his face expresses despair, and it collapses like a building: "Nur sein Gesicht ist eingestürzt." (Only his face has collapsed.)[16] In one instance, the man does not recognize his sister when he goes to pick her up from the airport, and another time he insists that he has never visited Brussels even though his wife can show him letters and photographs from their visit to that city (*Tb* 2, 373). But his memory does not simply deteriorate; its decline proceeds in a different, chaotic way. He loses his memory by losing control over it. Incoherently and unintentionally he remembers seemingly unimportant events and experiences that he thought he had successfully forgotten. Like Herr Geiser, he is afraid of cracks, not in mountain slopes or bedrock but in the concrete of bridges and buildings. He admonishes his students about the lethal risks of incomplete calculations ("jede Last, die wir in unserer Rechnung vergessen, rächt sich"), shows them slides as evidence and warns them against the instability of these structures: "Risse über dem Auflager, Schub, Torsion im Pfeiler, Einsturz. Dann sagt er jedesmal: Sehen Sie!" (*Tb* 2, 367; cracks above the support: shearing, torsion in the pillar, collapse. Then he always says, "You see?": *Sb* 2, 310). The author of a widely used textbook on statics, he is now convinced that everything he has ever taught about the subject was wrong:

> Die sichtbare Tatsache, dass die Bauten seiner Schüler (Siedlungen, Hallen für Kongresse, Krankenhäuser, Büro-Türme aus Stahl und Glas) allesamt nicht einstürzen, ändert nichts an seiner Selbsterkenntnis:—er verstehe nichts von Statik, habe nie verstanden, was er gelehrt habe— (*Tb* 2, 374)
>
> [The visible fact that his pupil's [*sic*] buildings (housing developments, congress halls, hospitals, office towers of steel and glass) have none of them collapsed so far does nothing to alter his inner feeling: that he understands nothing of statistics [*sic*], had never understood the things he taught (*Sb* 2, 317)]

For a while he denies knowing anything, and finally he falls completely silent.

"Ohne Gedächtnis kein Wissen," "No knowledge without memory," Herr Geiser remarks (*MH*, 210; *MHAS*, 6), only to have a premonition a little later that apparently brain cells become dysfunctional. The small cracks he searches for in the terrain outside have for a long time been forming inside him. The memory loss from which Geiser suffers more and more, and which is described in minute detail, is a growing incapacity to remember, structure, and share received pieces of information or thoughts. Fittingly, there is even an encyclopedia entry about memory loss in Geiser's collection of notes. Something that might not be apparent at first sight because the author introduces it in a subtle and casual manner presents an equally dire threat for Geiser. He is not only haunted by memory loss but also by remembering. He suffers from a similar process of losing control of his memory as the professor of statics mentioned above: "Er ist nicht mehr Herr über sein Gedächtnis." Everything he had, for whatever reason, repressed from his consciousness and banned from his memory returns without having been invited back.

Among the memories that force their way back into Geiser's mind, the fragmentary "Matterhorngeschichte" is recounted in the most detailed manner. On the surface it is a story about a struggle with nature, a matter of life and death. But the context makes it clear that Geiser's brother Klaus, or more precisely, the relationship of the two brothers, has triggered this memory. Fifty years before, Klaus had put his own life at risk to save Geiser's life while descending from the Matterhorn. Soon afterward, they apparently lost touch with each other. Geiser tells himself that it happened long ago, just like the sandstorm at the outskirts of Baghdad in which Klaus presumably died (*MH*, 285). Geiser's need to retell the Matterhorn story over and over again—his grandchildren are already tired of hearing it—presumably indicates a repressed and latent feeling of guilt with regard to his brother that might be based on a fraternal relationship that he yearns for and that he never fully experienced. Herr Geiser reassures himself that Klaus was a good brother, another reflection that connotes regret about having irretrievably missed something (*MH*, 293).

According to Sigmund Freud in *Das Unbehagen in der Kultur* (Civilization and its Discontents, 1930), in addition to the outside world and our own bodies, our relationships to other humans constantly threaten to become sources of our suffering, and isolation from others can become a strategy of self-protection.[17] The narrative does not mention why Herr Geiser left Basel and moved to his remote valley. He himself considers this question irrelevant. It appears that he does not want to know the answer. Not only Geiser's loss of control of his memory is similar to that of the professor of statics mentioned earlier, but his behavior is similar to the professor's, too. He is afraid of memories of a personal nature. In this vein, he posits that reading novels has become obsolete because they operate with the unsustainable illusion that humans can form reliable relationships and still inhabit firm and reliable ground, "als sei das Gelände dafür gesichert" (*MH*, 211; as if the terrain for these things were secured; *MHAS*, 8, translation modified).

Just as the reader only gets a glimpse of the relationship of the two brothers in the "Matterhorngeschichte," Geiser's memories, as they are recounted in the text, include few allusions to his other family relations. It is impossible for the reader to discern whether Geiser's feelings towards his daughter and son-in-law are partially hostile or at least ambivalent, or whether his self-isolation is primarily a symptom of his disintegrating mind, or whether these two possible explanations of his refusal or inability to connect with his family can be combined. He tells himself that Corinne is a loving daughter, but he does not pick up the phone when it rings the whole morning even though he assumes that it is she, calling him from Basel. Later, when she appears at his house, she delivers greetings from her husband, Geiser's son-in-law, who is now in charge of a company in Basel, having tripled its profits, and whom Geiser remembers as a know-it-all.

Geiser remembers how his late wife, Elsbeth, tried to persuade herself that the remoteness of the valley into which they had moved was easily endurable: "Man ist nicht am Ende der Welt!" (*MH*, 223; One is not at the end of the world: *MHAS*, 22). The frequency with which Geiser repeats this statement has an air of whistling in the graveyard, as if doubts had to be drowned out very early on and continue to burden him. Apparently, Herr Geiser's memories of his wife make him nervous. He not only asks himself what she would say about his notes on the walls but also whether she would have tolerated him putting nails in the walls. Her painted portrait on the wall makes her an eyewitness of his strange behavior, and Herr Geiser decides to remove the painting with the justification that he needs more space for his notes. This way, the painting ends up behind a cupboard, out of his sight, where it no longer calls up memories.

Geiser stays away from the rest of the world in order to protect himself, a continuous isolation that he embraces more rigorously the more his deterioration progresses and his alienation increases. He closes the shutters and ignores the ringing bell at his locked door. He chases away three men, who try to spy on him by looking into the house with their flashlights. "Herr Geiser will keinen Besuch," "Geiser wants no visitors," the text states laconically (*MH*, 284; *MHAS*, 93).

The premonitions Geiser suffers while looking at the mountainsides precisely summarize what happens to him: "So fangen Erdrutsche an, wobei solche Risse lautlos entstehen und sich wochenlang nicht mehr erweitern oder kaum, bis plötzlich [. . .] der ganze Hang unterhalb des Risses rutscht und auch Wälder mit sich reisst und alles, was nicht Grundfels ist." (*MH*, 232; That is the way landslides begin, cracks appearing noiselessly, not widening, or hardly at all, for weeks on end, until suddenly, when one is least expecting it, the whole slope below the crack begins to slide, carrying even forests and all else that is not firm rock down with it. *MHAS*, 32–33) Geiser's downfall begins in a similarly soundless, slow, and indiscernible manner. Preparing for threats from the outside, he incrementally loses his inner balance until finally he abruptly and unexpectedly falls.

Geiser's assumption that he has fallen down the stairs turns out to be incorrect. He does not find himself at the bottom of the stairs but on the floor next to the table, possibly several hours after his accident (*MH*, 285). His daughter Corinne arrives, and Geiser notices that she smiles like a nurse and has tears in her eyes. When she opens the shutters, the sudden draft blows the notes from the walls in a whirl. They fly to the ground in a chaotic mess, like surprised defenders of a fortress that had been besieged for a long time. At this moment, the key motif of Geiser's failed attempt at building a pagoda with pieces of crispbread recurs: "Es wird nie eine Pagode" (*MH*, 295; There will never be a pagoda: *MHAS*, 106), Geiser reiterates, as if at this moment he grasps the fundamental inferiority of man to nature. He is about to submit to nature, to dissolve into that which neither needs his name nor his memory. A final encyclopedia entry is presented to the reader: one that defines a stroke. Geiser has disappeared from the narrative without any sound. Against the deceptively idyllic backdrop of late summer in the remote valley, where at night one occasionally sees shooting stars or hears a screech owl, nature has the final word (*MH*, 299; *MHAS*, 111).

It is useful here to look back at the beginning of the narrative: Geiser attempts to build a pagoda with slices of crispbread—a symbol of a house in general, a gesture of resistance and symbolic counterpoint against the forces of nature that he feels oppress him. With this symbolic description the author brings the context in which Geiser's story unfolds into focus. What Frisch's narrative alludes to is the moment in the history of mankind in which *homo sapiens* as hunter and gatherer begins to decisively alter his behavior and his attitude toward nature. He not only disentangles and distances himself from nature but confronts it. Adaptation increasingly turns into resistance, appropriation, and conquest. At the end of the Pleistocene, the last ice age, he settles down, erecting huts and houses, cultivating the land, and taming and breeding animals. He initiates the process of civilization, which leads to the emergence of increasingly complex societies and forms the basis for the development of science and technology. For Frisch and several of his literary characters, including for example Don Juan, Walter Faber, and Herr Geiser, nature always represents darkness and emptiness from which man remains in the process of liberating himself. This same man appears at the beginning of the current post-glacial period, the Holocene. Having declared the subjugation of nature his goal, he becomes a technician and scientist and yet still has to endure the scandalous fact that he remains at the mercy of nature or, as Freud puts it, "dass alles Lebende aus inneren Gründen stirbt, ins Anorganische zurückkehrt" (that all living forms die for internal reasons and return into the realm of the inorganic).[18]

—*Translated by Olaf Berwald*

Notes

[1] Max Frisch, *Tagebuch 1946–1949*, in *Gesammelte Werke in zeitlicher Folge (GW)* 2, ed. Hans Mayer and Walter Schmitz, 2nd ed. (Frankfurt am Main: Suhrkamp,

1986), 4:404. English translations taken from Max Frisch: *Sketchbook 1946–1949*, trans. Geoffrey Skelton (New York, London: Harcourt Brace Jovanovich, 1977), here 45. Translation modified. Throughout this essay, unless a published translation is cited, all translations are by Olaf Berwald.

[2] Frisch, *Jürg Reinhart*, *GW* 1:227. Subsequent references to this work will be given in text using the abbreviation *JR* and page number in parentheses.

[3] Frisch, "Skizzen aus dem Eifischtal," *Neue Zürcher Zeitung*, July 8, 1932.

[4] Frisch, *Antwort aus der Stille: Eine Erzählung* (Frankfurt am Main: Suhrkamp, 2009), 18. The English translation is taken from *An Answer from the Silence: A Story from the Mountains*, trans. Mike Mitchell (Calcutta/London/New York: Seagull, 2011), 8–9.

[5] Frisch, *Antwort aus der Stille*, 145; trans. Mitchell, *An Answer from the Silence*, 101.

[6] Frisch, *Homo Faber*, *GW* 4:105–7. English translations of this work are taken from *Homo Faber: A Report*, trans. Michael Bullock (New York: Harcourt Brace Jovanovich, 1959), here 109.

[7] Sigmund Freud, *Die Zukunft einer Illusion*, in *Studienausgabe* 9 (Frankfurt am Main: Fischer, 1974), 148. Translation taken from *The Future of an Illusion*, trans. J. A. Underwood and Shaun Whiteside (London: Penguin, 2008), here 16.

[8] Frisch, "Wir bauen eine Strasse," in *Neue Zürcher Zeitung*, September 29, 1932, also in *GW* 1:22.

[9] Freud, *Das Unbehagen in der Kultur*, in *Studienausgabe* 9 (Frankfurt am Main: Fischer, 1974), 208–9.

[10] Frisch, *Der Mensch erscheint im Holozän*, in *GW* 7. Subsequent references to this text will be given using the abbreviation *MH* and page number in parentheses. Translations are taken from *Man in the Holocene: A Story*, trans. Geoffrey Skelton (New York/London: Harcourt Brace Jovanovich, 1980; reprinted Champaign, IL/London: Dalkey Archive Press, 2007). Subsequent references to this translation will be given using the abbreviation *MHAS* and page number in parentheses.

[11] See Wolf Lepenies, *Das Ende der Naturgeschichte* (Frankfurt am Main: Suhrkamp, 1978), 208.

[12] See Francis Bacon, *Neues Organon* (Hamburg: Meiner, 1990).

[13] Frisch, *Homo Faber*, *GW* 4:138.

[14] This is mistranslated by Skelton as "the things a newt knows," *MHAS*, 97.

[15] Frisch, *Montauk*, *GW* 6:210. Translation taken from *Montauk*, trans. Geoffrey Skelton (New York/London: Harcourt Brace Jovanovich, 1976), 98.

[16] Frisch, "Statik," in *Tagebuch 1966–1971*, *GW* 6:368. Subsequent references to this source will use the abbreviation *Tb* 2 and page number in parentheses. Translations taken from *Sketchbook 1966–1971*, trans. Geoffrey Skelton (New York: Harcourt Brace Jovanovich, 1974), here 312. Subsequent references to the translation will use the abbreviation *Sb* 2 and page number in parentheses.

[17] Freud, *Das Unbehagen in der Kultur*, 209.

[18] Sigmund Freud, *Jenseits des Lustprinzips*, in *Studienausgabe* 3 (Frankfurt am Main: Fischer, 1974), 248.

13: "My life as a man. Everyman": Max Frisch's *Blaubart. Erzählung*

Daniel de Vin

In a notebook entry from 1982 posthumously published in *Entwürfe zu einem dritten Tagebuch* (Drafts for a Third Sketchbook, 2010), Max Frisch comments on the recent publication of his story or short novella *Blaubart* (Bluebeard): "Was habe ich geschrieben? Eine Fratze." (What have I written? A grimace.)[1]

According to the notes in the critical edition of Frisch's collected works, *Blaubart* was written in Zurich between October and December 1981. In February and March 1982 it appeared serially in the *Frankfurter Allgemeine Zeitung* before being published as a book in March 1982. The *Frankfurter Allgemeine* announced the work to its readers as an unconventional narrative that begins like a crime story and consists of a multitude of mosaic stones. The newspaper further stated that the protagonist, the fifty-four-year-old medical doctor Felix Schaad, is confronted with a role-play that complicates his true identity, just like Anatol Ludwig Stiller and Theo Gantenbein, the protagonists in Frisch's previous novels *Stiller* and *Mein Name sei Gantenbein*.[2] I precisely recall reading segments of *Blaubart* as they appeared in the *Frankfurter Allgemeine*, and I remember the high expectations I had as well as the lightness of this new text, and my confusion, which increased from day to day: could this really be all that there was to this work?

It will be useful to begin with an overview of the most important book reviews of *Blaubart* that appeared in the spring of 1982. They were written by Klara Obermüller ("Die Wahrheit und nichts als die Wahrheit"), Christoph Kuhn ("Die Wahrheitsfindung und die andere Schuld"), Joachim Kaiser ("Vom Schuldgefühl des Mannes"), Marianne Zelger-Vogt ("Vor Gericht"), Marcel Reich-Ranicki ("Max Frischs ungedeckter Scheck"), Peter Wapnewski ("Leben mit Mord"), Klaus Schuhmacher ("Nur Billard kann dem Angeklagten noch helfen"), Friedrich Luft ("Mit einem Freispruch zu leben ist schwer"), Reinhard Baumgart ("Kahlschlag"), Hans Mayer ("Ritter Blaubart und Andorra"), Heinz Ludwig Arnold ("Im Zweifel gegen den Autor"), Sibylle Cramer ("Mein Name sei Blaubart"), Elsbeth Pulver ("Ein moderner

Jedermann"), and also by fellow novelists and poets Martin Walser ("Der Mensch erscheint im Kriminalroman"), and Günter Kunert ("Die Schuld eines Nichttäters").[3] The mere titles of this series of reviews by an illustrious group of critics and writers provide numerous useful keywords that reveal the following: a man is standing trial and is cross-examined; he is accused of murder but he did not commit the crime; he is released yet nevertheless feels guilty. There are references to earlier works by Frisch such as *Andorra*, *Mein Name sei Gantenbein*, and *Der Mensch erscheint im Holozän* (Man in the Holocene). The core questions are: What is truth? What is guilt?

Having been alerted to a murder trial in Zurich by Peter Noll, one of his closest friends and a law professor, Frisch attended the trial against the goldsmith Heinz Keller, who was accused of having killed his wife but acquitted for lack of evidence, for a total of sixty hours. Frisch's interest in how courts determine the truth of a case and his observations of the Keller trial triggered the writing of the book. The narrative begins after the trial, after an acquittal of the accused, Felix Theodor Schaad, a middle-aged specialist in internal medicine, for lack of evidence ("Freispruch mangels Beweis"). Frisch's text asks how anyone could endure experiencing an entire life as a continuous interrogation. Schaad experiences his acquittal as a punishment and starts to put himself on trial until he is silenced by the babble of voices in his head. Critics have pointed out that far from being violent like his literary predecessors in the long tradition of rewritings of the Bluebeard legend about a serial wife-killer, Frisch's Blaubart displays average behavior and appears normal. This observation leads Kunert to read the title as an ironic allusion. According to Walser, Felix Schaad joins Franz Kafka's protagonist Josef K. in suffering from feelings of unexplained guilt and being complicit in his own obliteration.

Most of the reviewers listed above are genuine Frisch experts and therefore discuss *Blaubart* in the context of Frisch's whole work. Obermüller and Mayer describe Schaad, respectively, as a close relative of the protagonists in Frisch's novels *Stiller* and *Mein Name sei Gantenbein*, and as an inhabitant of Frisch's fictional Andorra. Mayer also points out correlations with Frisch's play *Biedermann und die Brandstifter* (The Arsonists) and suggests that *Blaubart* forms a narrative triptych with his late narratives *Montauk* and *Der Mensch erscheint im Holozän*. Kuhn and Kaiser point at correlations between *Blaubart* and Frisch's play *Graf Öderland*. While Kuhn discusses the interrogation form in Blaubart as an extension of the self-interrogations in Frisch's *Tagebuch 1966–1971*, Kaiser alerts the reader to parallels between Blaubart and the ending of Frisch's novel *Homo Faber*, and Kaiser reads what he calls the brilliant depiction of Blaubart's friend Neuenburger as a reference to Frisch's friendship with Dürrenmatt. Reich-Ranicki and Schuhmacher outline affinities between Blaubart and Frisch's plays *Biografie: Ein Spiel* and

Triptychon. Sibylle Cramer discusses correlations between Blaubart's victim Rosalinde Zogg and Stiller's wife Julika and mentions that in the radio-play version of *Stiller* Anatol Wadel confesses five imagined murders and is explicitly referred to as Blaubart.

Blaubart was received well by most literary critics. In his review, Joachim Kaiser warns against being lured by the work's deceptive simplicity and misjudging it as an easy read. Kaiser states that even after repeated readings of Frisch's late prose works, including *Montauk* and *Der Mensch erscheint im Holozän*, he continues to be in awe of their durability and plasticity. Reich-Ranicki, on the other hand, calls the narrative "eher originell als interessant" (inventive rather than interesting). According to Reich-Ranicki, Frisch was not a philosopher, and therefore Schaad and the other characters in Blaubart exhibit a startlingly simple way of thinking, which causes stagnation both in the trial and in the text. He posits that a speechless protagonist makes for a tiresome literary manifestation of speechlessness. Baumgart concurs that he was at first disappointed, but says that he then gradually noticed that the book was still on his mind as an unresolved project. Schaad and his world had been reduced to circumstantial evidence, to inner voices of interrogation and of conscience in a religious nexus. Schuhmacher focuses on a recurrent motif and metaphor in *Blaubart*, the protagonist's passion for playing billiards. For Schuhmacher, the juxtaposition of the billiard game and the recapitulation of the trial is an apt literary device that suggests the geometry of an imaginary web, a daring way to play with calculation and coincidence. Arnold posits that *Blaubart* is a remake of Frisch's novel *Stiller* (see Sandberg's chapter on *Stiller* in this volume), a view that is echoed by Cramer, who reads *Blaubart* as a variation on Stiller's fear of repetition. Cramer posits that Schaad's dream of flying, only to land in front of the tribunal of conscience, constitutes an imitation of Stiller's description of his state of mind after his botched suicide attempt, a state of timelessness. Admiring Blaubart for reducing the entire life of a man to being a potential killer, Martin Walser calls *Blaubart* "ein Meisterstück." For Günter Kunert, Frisch's narrative offers the story of a mysterious guilt. He argues that *Blaubart* is an instant classic whose interpretations will constantly change over time.

Praising the novel for having perfected the "Giacometti effect" of enhanced associative echoes triggered by a style that is stripped bare of ornamentation (as in Swiss sculptor Alberto Giacometti's sculptures), one of the first American reviews of *Blaubart* in English translation compares it to Beckett's works and points out correlations between the geometrical configuration of *Blaubart*'s inner workings and the game of billiards.[4]

In a later conversation with Max Frisch about Polish director Krzysztof Zanussi's film version of *Blaubart* (1983), the poet and essayist Günter Kunert offers the nexus of feelings of guilt and loss of identity at the end of the bourgeois age as a possible explanation of the fragility of human relationships. In his review of *Blaubart*, Kunert understands Schaad's guilt primarily as an emotional deficiency and inability to sustain a marriage. Kunert insists that Schaad's internal trial remains open.[5]

How is one to read *Blaubart* ten, twenty, or thirty years after its first publication? Andrea Köhler, for example, interprets the text from a woman's point of view.[6] After all, eleven of the fifteen book reviews listed above are written by men. Following Cramer's discussion of the topos of the keys, Köhler suggests a thematic link between *Blaubart* and Frisch's novel *Stiller*, published thirty years before it. She adds that twenty years before *Blaubart*, Frisch's novel *Mein Name sei Gantenbein* had included a sketch of a case of a murdered prostitute that shares strong affinities with Blaubart's predicament, including the pronounced sense of guilt in the accused. She dismisses *Blaubart* as a mere repetition of narrative patterns already used in Frisch's earlier prose works. According to Köhler, the story examines a man's life, but Schaad only seemingly accuses himself, and the text cunningly presents Schaad as being subjected to a maze of accusations, acquittals, and veiled assignments of guilt. Köhler proceeds to accuse Frisch's whole work of indirectly expressing a bias against women. Blaubart, Köhler declares, is incapable of disentangling himself from the accusation that falls back on him, and remains his own prisoner.

Blaubart starts with a forgotten tie—the word "Krawatte" is used seven times on the first page of the narrative—and ends in pain ("Schmerzen"). The text presents a defendant who denies the crime at the beginning, rightly so, as the reader learns on the final page. Nevertheless, the protagonist offers a confession after his acquittal. The book begins and ends with voices in this alleged perpetrator's head, a perpetrator with a need to narrate (*B*, 8). What follows are once again voices in Schaad's head: having returned to his home in Ratzwil and having unsuccessfully tried to take his own life by causing a car accident, Schaad finds himself in a hospital with his eyes closed after successful surgery (*B*, 167, 172). Finally, the voices in his head disappear.

In the course of the story, the narrator time and again tries to silence his inner voices: while playing billiards in the evening, feeding swans, hiking, in the sauna, and in his medical practice, where patients rarely come to see their internist anymore after the trial. More and more Schaad's whole life takes on the form of an interrogation, even his memories and dreams. He becomes an alcoholic and contemplates suicide. Nothing helps. Having sold his practice three months after his acquittal, he now hears the witnesses' voices on the street in Zurich, on a trip to Japan, at home in his bathroom, and at the sailing club.

At first the interrogating voices share information about the trial, until the narrator incrementally also subjects his present life after his acquittal to an ongoing interrogation (*B*, 36–37, 83). Schaad's son and his six ex-wives now take the witness stand. What is more painful for Schaad than their statements, which show Schaad that there is no such thing as a shared memory, are his own memories, among them his childhood memories, which the other participants in his trial are unable to witness. Toward the end Schaad encounters his deceased parents and his murdered wife, scenes that anticipate the narrator's final metaphorical commentary.

The intertextual nature of Frisch's entire oeuvre, often manifested in small details, can be seen here. For example, a phrase originally eliminated from the first edition of Frisch's *Tagebuch 1966–1971* but later reintegrated into the version of that work as printed in the *Werkausgabe*: "— ich erkläre meinen Austritt," which could refer both to discontinuing membership in the "Vereinigung Freitod" (Suicide Club) and to ending one's life,[7] is echoed towards the end of *Blaubart*: "Man erwartet meinen Austritt, glaube ich" (*B*, 153; I believe they are expecting me to resign; *BAT*, 118), a statement that at first sight concretely refers to giving up his membership in the sailing club but that also can be read as Schaad's perception of his fellow citizens expecting him to take his own life.

Materials in the Max Frisch Archive document the long writing process that resulted in *Blaubart*.[8] The narrative's first version is titled "SCHAAD." The manuscript consists of one hundred numbered pages in a red binder and is dated September 1981. It is contained in one of two boxes filled with several fragmentary early versions of *Blaubart*. Only a few pages are dated. They provide clues for reconstructing the textual genesis of Frisch's narrative. Among these materials is an early note from January 12, 1980: "Nach Nacht mit starken Träumen [. . .] keine Geschichte [. . .] traumhaft: Vertauschung von Personen, Widersprüche usw., Diskontinuität. [. . .] so kann es nicht gewesen sein!" (After a night with intense dreams [. . .] no story [. . .] dreamlike: mistaken identities, contradictions, etc., discontinuity. [. . .] it cannot have happened like this!).

This entry was written during the weekend before the aforementioned murder trial in Zurich in which Frisch took a strong interest in the context of his plan for a new literary work. Copies of the six-page indictment from August 27, 1979 and a fifteen-page copy of the trial schedule made on December 13, 1979 and covering nineteen days, from Monday, January 14 through Thursday, February 7, 1980, can also be found in the Max Frisch Archive. During the weekend of January 26 and 27, 1980, Frisch composed extensive notes, amounting to eleven pages, with the heading "NOTIZEN ZU PROZESS GEGEN H. KELLER," about his experiences during his approximately thirty-three hours as a spectator at the examination of witnesses between January 17 and January 25. On January 27, Frisch wrote: "Was mich im ganzen Verfahren stört: Es wird immer wieder mit moralischem Druck gearbeitet, ohne dass man weiß, welche Moral verbindlich sein soll." (What irritates me about the whole trial: time and again they operate with moral pressure, but one doesn't know what form of morality is supposed to be binding.)

Among the materials deposited in the Max Frisch Archive, there is a seven-page draft of *Blaubart* beginning with the title "ANFANG" (beginning), a handwritten note or title dated June 14, 1980 that says "PRAXIS," and Frisch's poetological warning to himself about the plot structure being reminiscent of his novel *Stiller*: "ACHTUNG: — es stillert" (be careful: it is "stillering"). Both in *Stiller* and in *Blaubart*, Frisch uses the realm of jurisprudence as a setting in which he explores the degree to which human identities can be experienced as arbitrary and exchangeable. As Frisch comments in the note just quoted above, "Freispruch mangels Beweis [. . .] seine Patienten haben den Arzt wechseln müssen, und das braucht noch keineswegs zu heissen, dass sie von seiner Unschuld nicht überzeugt sind" (Acquittal due to lack of evidence [. . .] his patients had to change to another doctor, and that doesn't in any way have to mean that they are not convinced of his innocence).

On the left margin of the page there is a handwritten note: "Nein, Okt. 80." The first one and a half pages are crossed out. Shortly before, in September 1980, during his stay in New York, Frisch had dismissed his earlier work on the narrative. This is documented on a single page: "KRITIK / NY, 22.9.80." In these notes, Frisch insists that his previous drafts have missed the point. The narrative's topic should not be fidelity, adultery, or openness, but rather the lack of a reliably defined biography: "Kein gemeinsames Gedächtnis. [. . .] Schaad zum Schluss ohne Biographie: Wenn er nicht den Mord begangen hat, ist alles vage. Daher sein falsches Geständnis." (No shared memory. [. . .] Schaad in the end without a biography: If he did not commit the murder, everything remains vague. Therefore his fabricated confession.)

Frisch was particularly interested in the process of establishing the truth, as a letter that he wrote to the judge who presided over the Keller trial, Dr. Otto Friedli, on August 19, 1981 confirms. In this letter, Frisch asked Friedli for a copy of the written verdict because he wanted to study its exact wording. At the end of this letter, Frisch mentions that attending the trial for three weeks was an intense experience ("eine starke Erfahrung") for him.

In a notebook with the title "Schwarzes Ringbuch / Februar 1980 / Notizen zu 'Blaubart'" (Black ring binder / February 1980 / Notes for "Blaubart"), there are eighteen handwritten notes by Frisch about the continuation of the trial after January 27, 1980. Six pages summarize the final speech of the prosecution from February 4, 1980, and twelve pages refer to the final speech of the defense from February 5. Commenting on the absence of a clear separation between moral and legal matters, Frisch is skeptical about the witness statements and calls them questionable and often hypothetical.

At the beginning of this black binder, whose cover sheet contains only Frisch's new address, "M. Frisch / Stockerstrasse 39, 8002 Zürich," there is a forty-three-page "BUCH Protokoll" (BOOK notes) about "Felix Schaad [. . .] Bürger von Zürich [. . .] Freispruch mangels Beweis—Wie lebt einer damit?" (Felix Schaad [. . .] Citizen of Zurich [. . .] acquittal for lack of evidence—How does one live with that?) The following eighteen pages are empty, followed by one page of appointment entries from the spring of 1981, one week before Richard Dindo's film, *Max Frisch, Journal I–III*, a filmic reading of the narrative *Montauk* with references to Frisch's *Tagebücher*, premiered in Zurich. The next two pages are empty again, followed by a handwritten two-page text about the right to feel the pain of loss and about self-pity. This very personal entry from Spring 1981, halfway hidden in a notebook that seemingly only contains entries from February 1980, reveals a correlation with the final words in the *Blaubart* narrative: "Sie haben Schmerzen" (*B*, 172; You are in pain: *BAT*, 134).

Immediately following the reflection on *Blaubart* from spring 1982, "Was habe ich geschrieben? Eine Fratze" (What have I written? A grimace) that was quoted at the beginning of this essay, a passage in *Entwürfe zu einem dritten Tagebuch* depicts an encounter between Frisch and his ex-wife Marianne in Berzona, interwoven with reflections on death and solitude (*GW* 6:742–47).

Frisch's two late prose works *Montauk* and *Blaubart* can both be read as partially autobiographical self-examinations. For Frisch the aesthetic self-discipline that had already been implicit in writing *Montauk* and also sustained the composition process of *Blaubart* went hand in hand with a process of finding out more about his life as a man who was "schreibend unter Kunstzwang" (writing under the pressure of producing art; *GW* 6:633). He considered the English title of Philip Roth's book *My Life as a Man* more fitting for such a project. By referring to a legendary figure, the title *Blaubart* discourages the reader from an autobiographical reading of the text. Or, as Frisch points out at the beginning of "Notizen," notebook entries that were published in a special August 1967 issue of the journal *du* on Switzerland: "Literatur — sie ist doch nur eine Fälscherin. Sie lässt nur gelten, was nachvollziehbar ist für einen Dritten. Leben ist aber auf weite Strecken und in entscheidenden Bedingungen privat, nicht exemplarisch." (Literature is nothing but a forger. It only takes into account that which a third person can comprehend. But life is mostly and in its decisive conditions private and not exemplary. [652]). In this publication, the design of the fragmentary notes is reminiscent of an obituary, announcing death as an absolutely private realm that defies literature: "Schluss mit Literatur."

But Felix Schaad is no Bluebeard. The title relates to his nickname, "Ritter Blaubart" (*B*, 119). If one wants to trace a literary tradition of

Frisch's Everyman version, it would rather have to be the medieval mystery play *Elckerlic*, as Elsbeth Pulver convincingly shows in her aforementioned review. This is corroborated by the protagonist's name: Felix Schaad, whose first and last name constitute an existential contradiction that can be paraphrased as "the happy man who becomes a casualty," or the "verunglückte Glückliche" (the happy man who suffered an accident). Or to end with a sentence that I imagine to have read at some point in Frisch's works: "Es ist *schade* um die Menschen."

—*Translated by Olaf Berwald*

Notes

[1] Max Frisch, *Entwürfe zu einem dritten Tagebuch*, ed. Peter von Matt (Berlin: Suhrkamp, 2010), 58. Quoted passages from *Blaubart* are taken from Max Frisch, *Blaubart: Eine Erzählung* (Frankfurt am Main: Suhrkamp, 1982, reprinted 1993). Subsequent references will be by the abbreviation *B* and page number in parentheses. English translations of quoted passages are taken from *Bluebeard: A Tale*, trans. Geoffrey Skelton (San Diego/New York/London: Harcourt Brace Jovanovich, 1983). Subsequent references to this translation are by the abbreviation *BAT* and page number in parentheses.

[2] Franz Josef Görtz, "'Blaubart'. Unser neuer Vorabdruck: Max Frischs Erzählung," in *Frankfurter Allgemeine Zeitung*, February 20, 1982. *Blaubart* appeared in the *Frankfurter Allgemeine Zeitung* from February 22 to March 17, 1982. See *GW* 7:533.

[3] Obermüller, "Die Wahrheit und nichts als die Wahrheit," *Die Weltwoche*, March 24, 1982; Kuhn, "Die Wahrheitsfindung und die andere Schuld," *Der Tages-Anzeiger*, March 23, 1982; Kaiser, "Vom Schuldgefühl des Mannes," *Süddeutsche Zeitung*, April 1, 1982; Zelger-Vogt, "Vor Gericht," *Neue Zürcher Zeitung*, April 2, 1982; Reich-Ranicki, "Max Frischs ungedeckter Scheck," *Frankfurter Allgemeine Zeitung*, April 3, 1982; Wapnewski, "Leben mit Mord," *Stern*, April 7, 1982; Klaus Schuhmacher, "Nur Billard kann dem Angeklagten noch helfen: Ein strenges Verhör durch die Fantasie," *Stuttgarter Zeitung*, April 10, 1982; Luft, "Mit einem Freispruch zu leben ist schwer: Darstellung einer kunstvoll nachgewiesenen Nichtigkeit," *Die Welt*, April 17, 1982; Baumgart, "Kahlschlag," *Der Spiegel*, April 19, 1982; Mayer, "Ritter Blaubart und Andorra," *Die Zeit*, April 23, 1982; Arnold, "Im Zweifel gegen den Autor, "*Deutsches Allgemeines Sonntagsblatt*, June 13, 1982; Cramer, "Mein Name sei Blaubart," *Frankfurter Rundschau*, June 26, 1982; Pulver, "Ein moderner Jedermann. Das Verhör als Erzählform," *Aargauer Tagblatt*, July 3, 1982; Walser, "Der Mensch erscheint im Kriminalroman," *Bücherpick* 1/1982; Kunert, "Die Schuld eines Nichttäters," *Lesezeichen*, April 1982.

[4] See Gody Suter, "Max Frisch und die literarische Kritik in den USA. Roter Teppich für *Blaubart*," *Die Weltwoche*, July 6, 1983. Suter refers to Sven Birkert's review of the English version of *Blaubart*, "A Swiss Master," *The New Republic* 189, no. 2, July 11, 1983, 32.

[5] Günter Kunert, "Wir leben in einer Zeit, in der die Verhörform überhandnimmt," in *Max Frisch: Blaubart; Ein Buch zum Film von Krzysztof Zanussi*, ed. Michael Schmid-Ospach and Hartwig Schmidt (Frankfurt am Main: Suhrkamp, 1985), 137 54.

[6] "Sechs Gattinnen im Keller," in *Basler Zeitung*, July 10, 1991, nine years after the book was first published.

[7] Frisch, *Tagebuch 1966–1971*, *GW* 6:403–4.

[8] The author thanks Walter Obschlager and Margit Unser for their friendly support during his research visits at the Frisch Archive in May 2005 and May 2009.

14: Max Frisch's Essays and Speeches

Régine Battiston

LITERARY SCHOLARS AND CRITICS have not discussed Max Frisch's essays and speeches in a comprehensive manner yet, even though they constitute a considerable part of his prose texts and develop thematic threads found throughout the fabric of his work. The recipient of numerous literary prizes, Frisch used the genre of award acceptance speeches to reflect on creative tensions between aesthetic curiosity and ethical responsibility. His essays and speeches can be read as one continuous text throughout which Frisch juxtaposes the conflicting but mutually enriching voices of the writer as an artist whose projects are playfully open-ended and a concerned global citizen who discusses world affairs. While Frisch's essays inhabit a border zone between artistic exploration and political engagement, he disliked the notion of *littérature engagée*.

It is impossible to discuss the full range of Frisch's essayistic work and his speeches in this chapter. The following discussions focus on Frisch's central thematic clusters: the ethics and poetics of writing and theater, global and Swiss politics, and existential questions of death and hope.

On Literature and Political Activism

Beginning in the 1930s, Frisch's essays explore the relationship of epistemic desire and the art of the narrative, as well as an anthropological condition that he calls, in the title of an essay published in 1960, "Unsere Gier nach Geschichten" (Our Greed for Stories).[1] For Frisch, literature embodies at once a continuous, open-ended aesthetic experiment and a medium for undogmatic political engagement. In May 1945 Frisch engaged in an intense polemical exchange with Ernst Bieri, editor-in-chief of the influential *Neue Zürcher Zeitung*. Their discussion addressed National Socialism, refugees, the continued relevance of guilt, as well as literature and theater. Frisch was moved to respond to an article by Bieri that attacked his play *Nun singen sie wieder*.[2] In general, Frisch argues against a petrified understanding of literature and maintains his allegiance to modernism, defending contemporary literature's new ideas and forms.

Frisch's famous polemical intervention against Emil Staiger, an influential Swiss professor of German literature, was triggered by Staiger's Zurich acceptance speech for the Literature Prize of the City of Zurich given on December 7, 1966.[3] In his lecture, Staiger accuses contemporary literature of being subservient to social or political ideas and of having turned into a "*littérature engagée*" that according to Staiger has lost its soul as well as the truth and beauty of poetic language. Resolutely rejecting what he condemns as nihilism, Staiger calls for a return to the values of classical aesthetic traditions ("zurück zu Mozart"). A wide range of responses was circulating in newspapers, and Frisch's open letter, published in *Die Weltwoche* on December 24, 1966, is considered the culmination of the debate. Frisch's letter constitutes a milestone in his development as a writer and politically engaged citizen who increasingly insists on literature as a medium that nourishes social and political awareness. In this Swiss "Querelle des Anciens et des Modernes" between Frisch and Staiger, Frisch demands that postwar literature be read in an unflinching manner, as a form of art unafraid of showing the ruined physical and mental postwar landscape after near-complete destruction. The audience had enthusiastically approved Staiger's speech, which led Frisch to state that his country was ossified in its conservatism. In his open letter, Frisch addresses Staiger with the intimate "Du" form and mentions his friendship with Staiger. The tone of the text however is marked by biting irony. He accuses Staiger of having conveniently avoided naming the targets of his attack and of having prepared an execution squad aiming at a new generation of writers. In Frisch's view, Staiger adheres to the Nazi regime's lethal logic of cultural exclusion. Frisch sarcastically congratulates Staiger for having the courage to call for a return to Nazi rhetoric: "endlich kann man wieder von Entarteter Literatur sprechen,"[4] referring to the well-known Nazi condemnation of modernist art as "degenerate."

On Theater

In his Schiller Award acceptance speech delivered in 1965,[5] Frisch encapsulates his admiration for theater in his famous statement: "Ich verstand nicht, warum Menschen, die genug Taschengeld haben, nicht jeden Abend ins Theater gehen" (I did not comprehend why people who could afford it did not go to the theater every night; *GW* 10:362). Frisch had been writing about theater since 1931. In his essay from 1948 entitled "Theater ohne Illusion," Frisch outlines his understanding of that concept.[6] This essay's sober tone and social criticism uses elements of Frisch's mentor Brecht's approach to theater. Frisch's strong interest in stage design is manifest in his 1964 essay about the stage designer Teo Otto (1904–68), who was responsible for the stage designs of Brecht's, Frisch's, and Dürrenmatt's productions at the Schauspielhaus Zurich.[7]

On November 15, 1964, Frisch gave a speech at the Schauspielhaus Zurich in memory of his friend Kurt Hirschfeld.[8] Hirschfeld (1902–64), dramatic advisor of the Schauspielhaus Zurich beginning in 1946 and later its director, produced Frisch's *Andorra* and Brecht's *Puntila*. When Peter Löffler and Klaus Völker were fired from their positions at the Schauspielhaus in 1969 after having been accused of misusing the theater for the purpose of social criticism, Frisch delivered a speech defending them. Löffler served as director of the Schauspielhaus for only one year, during which he hired the director Peter Stein, the dramatic advisor Völker, and the actors Bruno Ganz, Jutta Lampe, and Edith Clever. The Schauspielhaus's progressive repertoire was rejected as revolutionary by its conservative audience members. Its artistically accomplished and innovative productions triggered both criticism and enthusiastic support. In Frisch's view, depriving theater of its freedom to experiment constitutes a grave political problem.

Frisch's lifelong interest in the problematic relationship between author and theater is manifest in "Der Autor und das Theater," a speech he delivered at the Frankfurt Paulskirche in 1964.[9] In order to show that in his view, following Friedrich Schiller, theater is a moral and political institution that plays an indispensable public role, Frisch offers a thought experiment that hypothetically posits that all theaters in Germany have been closed. He also examines the relationship between culture and the state, and between theater and the world, and asks whether theater can help to shape society. Referring to Brecht, Frisch maintains that theater is at once an indicator of society and a pedagogical instrument to change it (*GW* 5:341). He raises questions about the playwright's purpose and usefulness, although he does not provide any fixed answers to these questions. In closing, Frisch emphasizes that theater emerges from ludic desire and should invite the public to become part of the play. Frisch then proceeds to ask whether actors can be held responsible for the society that they entertain (*GW* 5:352).

On Politics

From the 1950s on, not only Frisch's plays and prose works became more political, but his whole approach to life did also. A central question for Frisch is whether writing can be an ethical weapon. According to Frisch, the future of mankind is at stake, especially given the dangers of the nuclear arms race. Frisch also explores the concept of resignation, but he insists that for the sake of rationality we are not allowed to give up hope. With his essays and speeches, Frisch sought to foster concrete change; they can be read as an attempt to practice enlightenment without any theoretically driven programmatic ideology. He considers art and literature expressions of the unspeakable: open-ended aesthetic laboratories rather than mere instruments of communication. In his perceptive obituary for Frisch, "Wortwahrheit—Nachruf auf Max Frisch," his close friend the painter and sculptor Gottfried Honegger highlights the careful and sensual, synaesthetic approach to every single word practiced by Frisch: "alles Sehen wandelte sich bei ihm in Wörter. Alles Hören wurde zum Wort. Seine Wörter haben Gerüche. Sie sind fassbar—tastbar" (everything visible turned into words for him. Anything audible turns into words. His words have scents. They can be touched, tasted).[10] Honegger's homage to the literary artist Frisch recognizes his aesthetic achievements.[11]

In 1958, Frisch received the most prestigious literary award in Germany, the Georg Büchner Prize. Discussing the early nineteenth-century German writer and political activist Georg Büchner as well as Lenin, both of whom had sought exile in the same street in Zurich one hundred years apart, Frisch's acceptance speech revolves around the term "Emigranten."[12] In this speech, Frisch also briefly discusses other prominent authors who were exiles in Switzerland, including Stefan George, Rainer Maria Rilke, Thomas Mann, Hermann Hesse, Frank Wedekind, and Bertolt Brecht. Juxtaposing Büchner's values with mid-twentieth-century capitalism, Frisch discusses the terms "Heimat" and "Sprache," and he calls irony a form of contemporary exile (*GW* 4:240). In this context, Frisch coins the richly contradictory term "combative resignation," a productive kind of skepticism that he presents as a fruitful common ground shared by twentieth-century artists and their chosen predecessors: "Es ist eine Resignation, aber eine kombattante Resignation, was uns verbindet" (What unites us is a kind of resignation, but a resignation that is combative; *GW* 4:242). According to Frisch, politics and art are always intertwined, and our need for art is based on its ability to transgress boundaries and borders.

Criticism of Switzerland

Frisch often directed his critical and polemical energy toward Switzerland. Over the years, his criticism of his home country became increasingly polemical. Frisch discussed immigration in an essay and a speech from 1965 and 1966, titled "Überfremdung 1" and "Überfremdung 2."[13] The first part of this essay contains Frisch's famous dictum that criticizes the hypocrisy of inviting guest workers in order to support the economy while at the same time refusing to welcome them as fellow human beings: "Ein Herrenvolk sieht sich in Gefahr: man hat Arbeitskräfte gerufen, und es kommen Menschen." (A master race is panicking: they have called for a workforce, and human beings are arriving. [*GW* 5:374]) Frisch explores connotations of the words "Gast" and "fremd," as Switzerland was shifting from calling immigrant workers "Gastarbeiter" to "Fremdarbeiter." In the second part of the essay, written in 1966, he examines the term

"Überfremdung" and exposes its racist connotations. Discussing Switzerland's geopolitical position and its alleged neutrality, Frisch engages in a twofold thought experiment. He imagines what might happen if the Swiss "Fremdenpolizei" (immigration police; literally, aliens' police) were dissolved and the country were completely open to immigration. He also imagines the opposite scenario, Swiss borders being completely sealed off. Frisch outlines Swiss fear and hatred of foreigners, and he insists that international intellectuals and artists who offer new kinds of thinking are needed in Switzerland. According to Frisch, guest workers can provide a petrified country with fresh energy. In closing, Frisch points out that his own ancestors had been immigrants.

Embracing his role as a public intellectual, as portrayed in Mathias von Gunten's recent film, *Max Frisch Citoyen* (2008), Frisch wrote an open letter to the Swiss Federal Council on March 2, 1974, deploring the Swiss administration's failure to protest human rights abuses in Chile under the Pinochet regime.[14] In this polemical letter, Frisch raises doubts about the integrity of the Swiss ambassador to Chile, whom Frisch calls "the acting administrator of our national conscience" (*GW* 12:519). Frisch accuses the Swiss Federal Council of manipulating the Swiss public and of looking the other way with regard to what he views as Chile's fascist junta (*GW* 12:521). Frisch even draws parallels between the Swiss government's complicity with the Pinochet regime and the forced closing of Jewish customers' bank accounts in Switzerland in 1938. He never received any response from the Swiss Federal Council.

Frisch's essayistic struggle for a more open-minded Switzerland is condensed in his Schiller Prize acceptance speech delivered in 1974. Its title is a probing question, "Die Schweiz als Heimat?" (Switzerland as Homeland?).[15] In this speech, Frisch examines a wide range of associations triggered by the term "Heimat." He highlights the need for a home country and discusses what Switzerland means to him. He points out that many regions of Switzerland have become subject to gentrification and the pressures of the real-estate market and the tourism industry. For Frisch, the question of whether Switzerland is his home is inextricably linked to the broader question of what constitutes identity (*GW* 12:515). Frisch states that traditional Swiss concepts such as federalism, neutrality, and independence have become illusory catchwords. He alludes to hypocrisy driven by economic considerations and the desire for profit. In his concluding remarks, the dark side of the Swiss past is made explicit, for example the practice of turning refugees away from the Swiss border and delivering them back to the Germans during the Second World War. Another noteworthy text that exemplifies Frisch's fight against the Swiss establishment is his satirical essay from 1979, "Als Gulliver die Schweiz besuchte," which offers a parody of a guided tour through a kitsch- and cliché-filled Switzerland for tourists.[16] This stands in stark contrast to

Frisch's view at the beginning of his career as a writer, when, inspired by the Swiss writers Meinrad Inglin (1893–1971) and Albin Zollinger (1895–1941), he described Swiss mountains with unfettered admiration and unmediated by any sense of irony, for example in his essay "Freunde und Fremde" (Friends and Strangers) from 1932.[17]

Frisch's essays from the late 1960s at once documented and contributed to the Swiss student protest movement in 1968. In his essay "Jemand hat sich geirrt" (Someone Made a Mistake; *GW* 6, 473–75), Frisch discusses the attitude of the Swiss media and examines frequently used words, such as "Recht," and "Genossen," clearly distancing himself from the Soviet Union (*GW* 6:474).

In September 1968, along with fellow writers Peter Bichsel, Friedrich Dürrenmatt, Günter Grass, and Kurt Marti, Frisch took to the stage at the Theater Basel to speak out against the Soviet occupation of Prague and the violent end of the Prague Spring. In his speech,[18] Frisch coined the ironic term "Kremltum" to criticize the lack of free thought in the Soviet Union (*GW* 6:480). According to Frisch, literature is indispensable because it helps us to remain self-critical (*GW* 6:482). In Frisch's view, both the Eastern and the Western blocs suffered from intellectual stagnation as a side effect of the Cold War (*GW* 6:483). Frisch warns that dogmatism on both sides precludes cooperation. He expresses his hope for a future fusion of socialism and democracy, a mode of thinking that today continues to appear utopian.

In his writings about the student uprisings in 1968 and on the Cold War, Frisch explores despair and powerlessness on both sides of the Iron Curtain. Commenting on freedom rather than merely praising it, Frisch recommends making use of it. In an attempt to provoke his fellow citizens to think for themselves in a self-critical way, Frisch speaks out against hypocrisy. He asserts that Switzerland was living in fear of new ideas or innovations and had become a country of timid imitators of the past.

On Peace, Death, and Hope

Frisch was the first person officially invited by Israel to deliver a speech in the German language. His Jerusalem Award acceptance speech in 1965 focused on the need for peace.[19] In 1976, Frisch received the Peace Award of the German Book Trade. In his acceptance speech, he voices skepticism about the prospect of new beginnings in the name of peace.[20] Frisch points at the cynicism practiced by the superpowers, including that shown by the United States' use of nuclear weapons against Japan. Frisch states that the idea of peace is a utopian thought that would involve more than a temporary truce (*GW* 7:8).

In the course of this argument, Frisch discusses the meaning of the state, the lack of individual autonomy and solidarity, and the absence of political imagination. He aims his criticism at right-wing populism, insisting on democracy's need for tolerance. He also attacks consumerism and examines the fragility of democracy that in his view is threatened by a replacement of politics by business practices (*GW* 7:9–10). In this speech as well as in his later speeches, Frisch uses the word resignation with increasing frequency. Fear, he maintains, is used by political and business leaders as a means to gain power. In many of his speeches given throughout his late years, including "Der Aufruf zur Hoffnung ist heute ein Aufruf zum Widerstand" (Today the call for hope is a call for resistance), which he delivered in Solothurn on the occasion of his seventy-fifth birthday celebration in May 1986, Frisch insists on the need for utopian thought: "Ohne Utopie wären wir Lebewesen ohne Transzendenz." (Without utopian thought, we would be organisms void of transcendence.[21] Frisch voices his misgivings regarding the political left and laments the omnipresence of cynicism in static societies that are designed to be immune against change. He also predicts that environmental issues will gain importance. (*Der Aufruf zur Hoffnung*, 15) Frisch suggests that the idea of peace takes on different shapes and is contingent on the specific historical situation. At the end of this speech, he appeals to the audience by calling the belief in peace and the survival of mankind revolutionary: "Der Glaube an eine Möglichkeit des Friedens (und also des Überlebens der Menschen) ist ein revolutionärer Glaube" (*Der Aufruf zur Hoffnung*, 18).

In addition to giving high-profile speeches on art and politics, Frisch also delivered talks for smaller audiences and various organizations, including a keynote address to medical doctors, "Rede an junge Ärztinnen und Ärzte," in 1984 that focused on approaches to death and dying (*GW* 7:82–92). Since the late 1960s, Frisch had carefully examined the theme of aging, as is well documented in his *Tagebuch 1966–1971*. Tentatively referring to literature and mythology as a way to become more familiar with the ungraspable, Frisch laconically states that there is no real help with regard to death and asks what can be done in the face of our mortality. Medically assisted suicide emerged as a topic beginning in the 1970s. In this speech, Frisch argues for the human right to die with dignity. Insisting on the primary importance of the patient's wishes, Frisch also mentions the right to choose one's own death, a topic that he had explored in his literary outline of a suicide club in *Tagebuch 1966–1971* (*GW* 6:90–92, 94–95).

Frisch's speeches culminated in his speech in Solothurn in May 1986. In this speech, Frisch contemplates the meaning of hope, a concept that previously formed an integrative element in his works, and whose abandonment he now announces. He quotes several Enlightenment thinkers, including Diderot, Voltaire, Rousseau, Kant, and Lichtenberg. The speech, with its radically progressive political orientation, has the feeling of a swan song, but one marked by disappointment and sarcasm. Several literary references in the speech accentuate Frisch's criticism of Western consumer societies such as the United States, as well as emerging symptoms of what today is called globalization. In the final sentence of the speech, Frisch echoes Voltaire when he remarks that friendship remains the only indisputably meaningful aspect of life.[22]

Conclusion

Frisch's essays and speeches constitute an integral part of his work. They often condense his thought, bearing the imprint of his nuanced sense of irony and utopianism. His Socratic method of asking questions is accentuated in his speeches. While his early non-fiction was for the most part apolitical, an accelerated turn to social awareness began in the 1940s and became prevalent in the postwar era. Frisch vehemently criticized the separation of culture and politics. Consistently until the last phase of his writing career, he maintained an anti-ideological position that was highly critical of both Western and Soviet-style hypocrisy and oppression. Through his writing, he participated in resistance against all forms of totalitarianism. Much of Frisch's social criticism was in response to conditions in his home country of Switzerland.

Frisch's essays reveal that his political activism was at times interwoven with the experience of failure and despair. In the 1980s, a hitherto sustained and intensive period of social and political criticism alternated with melancholic phases, and resignation went hand in hand with acrimonious radicalism. Frisch's active role as an empathetic global citizen is awaiting renewed public attention.

—*Translated by Olaf Berwald*

Notes

[1] "Unsere Gier nach Geschichten" (1960), in Gesammelte Werke in zeitlicher Folge (*GW*)4, ed. Hans Mayer and Walter Schmitz, 2nd ed. (Frankfurt am Main: Suhrkamp, 1986), 262–64. See also "Der unbelesene Bücherfreund. Ein Plädoyer" (1935), in *GW* 1:80–83.

[2] Bieri's article, "Verdammen oder Verzeihen," appeared in the *Neue Zürcher Zeitung* on May 23, 1945. Frisch's response, "Verdammen oder verzeihen? Ein Brief an Bi, den Verfasser des Leitartikels in der NZZ vom 23.5.1945," can be found in *GW* 2:292.

[3] See "Endlich darf man es wieder sagen. Eine Antwort an Emil Staiger," *GW* 5:455 58.

[4] Frisch, "Endlich darf man es wieder sagen," *GW* 5:462.

[5] Frisch's "Schillerpreis-Rede" speech is printed in *GW* 5:362–69.

[6] Frisch, "Theater ohne Illusion," *GW* 2:332–36.

[7] Frisch, "Teo Otto," *GW* 5:335–38.

[8] Frisch, "Rede zum Tod von Kurt Hirschfeld," *GW* 5:355–59.

[9] Frisch, "Der Autor und das Theater. Rede auf der Frankfurter Dramaturgentagung 1964," *GW* 5:339–54.

[10] Gottfried Honegger, "Wortwahrheit—Nachruf auf Max Frisch," in *Widerstand aus Verantwortung* (Zurich: Limmat, 1991), 53–56; here 53.

[11] Questions of language and style occupied Frisch throughout his career; see Max Frisch, *Gespräche im Alter*, whose DVD edition is scheduled to appear shortly at Suhrkamp as *Max Frisch—Journal I–III.* From 1934 on, Frisch also reflected on the status of Swiss German. On the theme of language in Frisch's work, see also Régine Battiston, "Les interrogations fondamentales de Max Frisch," in *Lectures de l'identité narrative: Max Frisch, Ingeborg Bachmann, Marlen Haushofer, W. G. Sebald* (Paris: Éditions Orizons, 2009), 81–94.

[12] Frisch, "Emigranten. Rede zur Verleihung des Georg-Büchner-Preises 1958," *GW* 4:229–43.

[13] Frisch, "Überfremdung 1," *GW* 5:374–76; "Überfremdung 2," *GW* 5:377–99. The first essay was used as the foreword to the oral history volume, *Siamo italiani: Gespräche mit italienischen Gastarbeitern*, recorded and edited by Alexander J. Seiler, who also produced a film on the topic. The resonance of "Überfremdung 1" is shown by the fact that on September 1, 1966, Frisch was invited to speak on the topic of immigration at a Swiss border patrol police convention in Lucerne. "Überfremdung 2" gives the text of Frisch's speech and was first published in the Swiss newspaper *Die Weltwoche* on September 9, 1966.

[14] Frisch, "Offener Brief an den Schweizerischen Bundesrat," *GW* 6:519–21.

[15] Frisch, "Die Schweiz als Heimat?," *GW* 6:509–18.

[16] Frisch, "Als Gulliver die Schweiz besuchte," *GW* 7:53.

[17] Frisch, "Freunde und Fremde," *GW* 1:27–31.

[18] Frisch, "Rede nach der Besetzung der Tschechoslowakei," *GW* 6:479–83.

[19] Frisch, "Jerusalempreis-Rede," *GW* 5:360–61.

[20] Frisch, "Wir hoffen. Rede zur Verleihung des Friedenspreises des deutschen Buchhandels 1976," *GW* 7:7–19.

[21] Frisch, *Der Aufruf zur Hoffnung ist heute ein Aufruf zum Widerstand* (Sankt Gallen: Erker, 1991), 12.

[22] Frisch, *Der Aufruf zur Hoffnung*, 21.

Frisch's Major Works

(With publication information on English translations when available.)

Prose

Jürg Reinhart: Eine sommerliche Schicksalsfahrt (1934; Jürg Reinhart: A Fateful Trip in Summer).

Antwort aus der Stille: Eine Erzählung (1937; *An Answer from the Silence: A Story from the Mountains*, trans. Mike Mitchell. Calcutta/London/New York: Seagull, 2011).

J'adore ce qui me brûle oder Die Schwierigen (1943; I Love that which Burns Me, or, The Difficult Ones).

Tagebuch 1946–1949 (1950; *Sketchbook 1946–1949*, trans. Geoffrey Skelton. New York, London: Harcourt Brace Jovanovich, 1977).

Stiller (1954; *I'm Not Stiller*, trans. Michael Bullock. London/New York: Abelard-Schuman, 1958).

Homo faber: Ein Bericht (1957; *Homo Faber: A Report*, trans. Michael Bullock. New York: Harcourt Brace Jovanovich, 1959).

Mein Name sei Gantenbein (1964; *A Wilderness of Mirrors*, trans. Michael Bullock. London: Methuen; New York: Random House, 1965).

Tagebuch 1966–1971 (1972; *Sketchbook 1966–1971*, trans. Geoffrey Skelton. New York: Harcourt Brace Jovanovich, 1974).

Montauk: Eine Erzählung (1975; *Montauk*, trans. Geoffrey Skelton. New York/London: Harcourt Brace Jovanovich, 1976).

Der Mensch erscheint im Holozän (1979; *Man in the Holocene: A Story*, trans. Geoffrey Skelton. New York/London: Harcourt Brace Jovanovich, 1980; reprinted Champaign, IL/London: Dalkey Archive Press, 2007).

Blaubart: Eine Erzählung (1982; *Bluebeard: A Tale*, trans. Geoffrey Skelton. San Diego/New York/London: Harcourt Brace Jovanovich, 1983).

Theater

Nun singen sie wieder: Versuch eines Requiems (1945; Now They Are Singing Again: Attempt at a Requiem).

Die Chinesische Mauer, eine Farce (1946; The Chinese Wall, A Farce).

Als der Krieg zu Ende war (1948; When the War Was Over).

Graf Öderland: Ein Spiel in zehn Bildern (1951, final version 1961; *Count Oederland: A Crime Story in Twelve Scenes*, trans. Michael Bullock [translation of 1961 version]. In *Three Plays: The Fire Raisers; Count Oederland; Andorra*. London: Methuen, 1962, 89–164).

Don Juan oder Die Liebe zur Geometrie (1953, final version 1962; *Don Juan, or The Love of Geometry*, trans. Michael Bullock. In *Four Plays: The Great Wall of China; Don Juan, or The Love of Geometry; Philipp Hotz's Fury; Biography: A Game*. London: Methuen, 1969, 85–160).

Biedermann und die Brandstifter: Ein Lehrstück ohne Lehre (1958; *The Fire Raisers: A Morality without a Moral with an Afterpiece*, trans. Michael Bullock. London: Methuen, 1962).

Andorra: Stück in zwölf Bildern (1961; *Andorra: A Play in Twelve Scenes*, trans. Michael Bullock. New York: Hill and Wang, 1962).

Biografie: Ein Spiel (1967; *Biography: A Game*, trans. Birgit Schreyer Duarte. London/New York/Calcutta: Seagull, 2010).

Triptychon: Drei szenische Bilder (1978; *Triptych: Three Scenic Panels*, trans. Geoffrey Skelton. New York/London: Harcourt Brace Jovanovich, 1981).

Select Bibliography

Arnold, Heinz Ludwig. *Was bin ich? Über Max Frisch.* Göttingen: Wallstein, 2002.

Butler, Michael. *The Plays of Max Frisch.* London: Macmillan, 1985.

de Vin, Daniel. *Max Frischs Tagebücher: Studie über "Blätter aus dem Brotsack" (1940), "Tagebuch 1946–1949" (1950) und "Tagebuch 1966–1971" (1972) im Rahmen des bisherigen Gesamtwerks (1932–1975).* Cologne: Böhlau, 1977.

Gockel, Heinz. *Max Frisch: Drama und Dramaturgie.* Munich: R. Oldenbourg, 1989.

———. *Max Frisch: Gantenbein; Das offen-artistische Erzählen.* Bonn: Bouvier, 1976.

Heinrich-Korpys, Meike. *Tagebuch und Fiktionalität: Signalstrukturen des literarischen Tagebuchs am Beispiel der Tagebücher von Max Frisch.* St. Ingbert: Röhrig, 2003.

Koepke, Wulf. *Understanding Max Frisch.* Columbia: University of South Carolina Press, 1991.

Letawe, Céline. *Max Frisch–Uwe Johnson: Eine literarische Wechselbeziehung.* St. Ingbert: Röhrig, 2009.

Müller-Salget, Klaus. *Max Frisch.* Stuttgart: Reclam, 1996.

Petersen, Jürgen H. *Max Frisch.* Stuttgart: Metzler, 2002.

Probst, Gerhard, and Jay F. Bodine, eds. *Perspectives on Max Frisch.* Lexington: University Press of Kentucky, 1982.

Schmitz, Walter. *Max Frisch.* Frankfurt am Main: Suhrkamp, 1987.

———. *Max Frisch: Das Spätwerk (1962–1982); Eine Einführung.* Tübingen: Francke, 1985.

Steinmetz, Horst. *Max Frisch: Tagebuch, Drama, Roman.* Göttingen: Vandenhoeck & Ruprecht, 1973.

Contributors

RÉGINE BATTISTON is Professor of German at Université de Haute-Alsace, France. She is the author of *Lectures de l'identité narrative: Max Frisch, Ingeborg Bachmann, Marlen Haushofer, W. G. Sebald* (Éditions Orizons, 2009), the editor of *Max Frisch Philosophe?*, special issue of *Germanica* 48 (2011), and co-editor of *Max Frisch: Sein Werk im Kontext der europäischen Literatur seiner Zeit* (with Margit Unser; Königshausen & Neumann, 2012), and, *"Ich liebte Frankreich wie eine zweite Heimat: Neue Studien zu Stefan Zweig* (with Klemens Renoldner; Königshausen & Neumann, 2011).

KLAUS VAN DEN BERG is Associate Professor of Theatre at the University of Tennessee at Knoxville. He has published numerous articles on visual culture and the dramaturgy of space, and is also the resident dramaturge for the Clarence Brown Theatre, where his productions have included *The Seagull, Arcadia, The Oedipus/Caligula Project, The Brecht File, Nora*, and *Buried Child.* His adaptation of Friedrich Schiller's play *Die Räuber* (The Robbers), was produced at the Asolo Conservatory in Sarasota in 2012.

OLAF BERWALD is Professor of German and Chair of the Department of Foreign Languages at Kennesaw State University. He is the author of *An Introduction to the Works of Peter Weiss* (Camden House, 2003), and *Philipp Melanchthons Sicht der Rhetorik* (Harrassowitz, 1994), and co-editor of *Globalization and Its Apparitions: Intercultural Engagements and Disengagements Seen from the South and the North / La globalización y sus espejismos: Encuentros y desencuentros interculturales vistos desde el Sur y el Norte* with Michael Handelsman; Editorial El Conejo, 2009), and *Der untote Gott: Religion und Ästhetik in der deutschen und österreichischen Literatur des 20. Jahrhunderts* (with Gregor Thuswaldner; Böhlau, 2007).

AMANDA CHARITINA BOYD is Associate Professor of German Studies at the University of North Dakota. Her research focuses on early twentieth-century modernism and fairy-tale studies.

CÉLINE LETAWE is Professor of German and Translation Studies at the University of Liège, Belgium. She is the author of *Max Frisch – Uwe Johnson: Eine literarische Wechselbeziehung* (Röhrig, 2009). Her research focuses on twentieth-century literature and translation studies.

WALTER OBSCHLAGER is the former director of the Max Frisch Archive at ETH Zurich. He is the editor of Max Frisch, *"Im übrigen bin ich immer völlig allein": Briefwechsel mit der Mutter 1933* (Suhrkamp, 2000), Max Frisch, *"Schweiz als Heimat?" Versuche über 50 Jahre* (Suhrkamp, 1990), and co-editor of *jetzt: max frisch* (Suhrkamp, 2001).

JOHN D. PIZER is Professor of German and Comparative Literature and Chair of the Department of Foreign Languages and Literatures at Louisiana State University. He is the author of *Imagining the Age of Goethe in German Literature, 1970-2010* (Camden House, 2011), *The Idea of World Literature: History and Pedagogical Practice* (Louisiana State University Press, 2006), *Ego-Alter Ego: Double and/as Other in the Age of German Poetic Realism* (University of North Carolina Press, 1998), *Toward a Theory of Radical Origin: Essays on Modern German Thought* (University of Nebraska Press, 1995), and *Historical Perspective in German Genre Theory: Its Development from Gottsched to Hegel* (Heinz Verlag, 1985).

BEATRICE SANDBERG is Professor of German at the University of Bergen. She is the co-author of *Franz Kafka* (with Ronald Speirs; Palgrave Macmillan, 1997), editor of *Familienbilder als Zeitbilder* (Frank & Timme, 2010), and co-editor of *Franz Kafka: Narration, Rhetoric, and Reading* (with Jacob Lothe and Ronald Speirs; Ohio State University Press, 2011), *Entwicklungen, Kontexte, Grenzgänge: Autobiographisches Schreiben in der deutschsprachigen Gegenwartsliteratur 3* (with Michael Grote; Iudicium, 2009), and *Grenzen der Identität und Fiktionalität: Autobiographisches Schreiben in der deutschsprachigen Gegenwartsliteratur 1 (with Ulrich Breuer; Iudicium, 2006).*

CAROLINE SCHAUMANN is Associate Professor of German Studies at Emory University. She is the author of *Memory Matters: Generational Responses to Germany's Nazi Past in Recent Women's Literature* (de Gruyter, 2008), and co-editor of *Heights of Reflection: Mountains in the German Imagination from the Middle Ages to the Twenty-First Century* (with Sean Ireton; Camden House, 2012).

FRANK SCHAUMANN worked as a producer for German public television. From 2000–2009, he taught dramaturgy at the Filmhochschule Babelsberg. His publications include *Gestalt und Funktion des Mythos in Ferdinand Raimunds Bühnenwerken* (Bergland, 1970), as well as numerous screenplays.

WALTER SCHMITZ is Professor of German and Director of the Central European Studies Center at Technische Universität Dresden, Germany. His monographs include *Die Münchner Moderne* (Reclam, 1990), and

Max Frisch (Suhrkamp, 1987), and two more monographs on Max Frisch published in 1985, and he is the editor or co-editor of a wide range of critical editions of German authors, including Bettina von Arnim, Ludwig Tieck, Friedrich Rückert, Theodor Däubler, Georg Britting, Reinhold Schneider, and Max Frisch. He has also co-edited several interdisciplinary volumes, including *Deutsch-deutsches Literaturexil: Schriftstellerinnen und Schriftsteller aus der DDR in der Bundesrepublik* (Thelem, 2009).

MARGIT UNSER is Director of the Max Frisch Archive at ETH Zurich. She is the editor of several Max Frisch anthologies: *Man will geliebt sein*, *Leben, ja*, *Weiß ich es denn selbst, wer ich bin?*, and *Sind Sie sich selber ein Freund?* (all Suhrkamp, 2011), and co-editor of *Max Frisch: Sein Werk im Kontext der europäischen Literatur seiner Zeit* (with Régine Battiston; Königshausen & Neumann, 2012).

DANIEL DE VIN is Professor emeritus at the University of Brussels, Belgium. He is the author of *Max Frischs Tagebücher* (Böhlau, 1977), and editor of *Max Frisch: Citoyen und Poet* (Wallstein, 2011), and Max Frisch, *Schwarzes Quadrat: Zwei Poetikvorlesungen* (Suhrkamp, 2008).

RUTH VOGEL-KLEIN is Professor of German at École Normale Supérieure, Paris, France. She is the editor of *Die ersten Stimmen: Deutschsprachige Texte zur Shoah 1945-1963* (Königshausen & Neumann, 2010), and has published widely on late twentieth-century literature, including H. G. Adler, W. G. Sebald, and Ruth Klüger.

PAUL A. YOUNGMAN is Associate Professor of German Studies at Washington and Lee University. Professor Youngman is a digital humanist whose research centers on technology in the German culture. He is the author of *We Are the Machine: The Computer, the Internet, and Information in Contemporary German Literature* (Camden House, 2009), and *Black Devil and Iron Angel: The Railway in Nineteenth-Century German Realism* (Catholic University Press, 2005).

Index